Christopher Vecsey is Professor of Religion
and Native American Studies at Colgate
University. His work includes *Imagine
Ourselves Richly: Mythic Narratives of North
American Indians* (1988).

On the Padres' Trail

AMERICAN INDIAN CATHOLICS

CHRISTOPHER VECSEY

VOLUME I

On the Padres' Trail

On the Padres' Trail

CHRISTOPHER VECSEY

UNIVERSITY OF NOTRE DAME PRESS

NOTRE DAME, INDIANA

Copyright 1996 by
University of Notre Dame Press
Notre Dame, Indiana 46556

Manufactured in the United States of America

Library of Congress Cataloging-in-Publication Data

Vecsey, Christopher,
    On the Padres' trail / Christopher Vecsey.
        p.   cm.—(American Indian Catholics ; v. 1)
    Includes bibliographical references and index.
    ISBN 0-268-03702-7 (alk. paper)
    1. Indians of North America—Religion.   2. Indians of
North America—Missions.   3. Catholic Church—Missions—
North America—History.   4. America—Discovery and
exploration—Religious aspects—Catholic Church.   I. Title.
II. Series.
    E98.R3V44 1996
    282'.7'08997—dc20   96-9754
                                                         CIP

The paper used in this publication meets the minimum requirements of the
American National Standard for Information Sciences—Permanence of Paper
for Printed Library Material, ANSI Z39.481984.

Book design by Will Powers
Set in Galliard CC
by Stanton Publication Services, Inc.

For my parents,
May Spencer Vecsey and George S. Vecsey

A Navajo pictorial weaving, c. 1915, depicts a priest
flanked by traditional deities.

CONTENTS

III

Indian Catholicism in California

IV

Detractors and Defenders

MAPS

PREFACE

Until 1492 there were no Christians in the Americas. Native Americans oriented themselves toward the divine, the cosmos, the beings of both the visible and the unseen world (including their fellow human beings) in ways that fit their local environments. Drawing upon the conceptual resources available to them they responded with attitudes and behaviors that can be called "religious." These various religious complexes, based upon traditions thousands of years deep, informed personal ethics; joined communities in common ritual, work, and kinship; fostered faith and spirituality; and instilled whole cultures with values born of hopes and fears.

There were religious people in the Americas, but no Christians; there was religiousness, but no Christianity; religious culture, but no Christendom. When Europeans encountered Native Americans in the Caribbean islands and upon the American continents, a process began through which the indigenous peoples and their descendants entered into contact with Christians and the institutions of Christianity. Over the past five centuries these Native Americans—American Indians, as they were misnamed and are now most commonly known—have felt the influences of Christianity, and millions of them have come to identify themselves as Christians.

The form of Christianity first encountered by Native Americans was Roman Catholicism. Protestantism was yet to come, and Eastern Orthodoxy was not a force in the New World at the time of first contact. Roman Catholicism has had a greater impact on American Indians than any other Christian denomination for half a millennium, and it is the goal of this multivolume study to analyze the effects of this Catholic tradition on Native Americans from first meeting to the present day. In particular, it is my aim to provide a history of the American Indians who have become Catholics or at least have participated in salient features of the Catholic tradition.

Although I shall treat various phenomena representative of traditional American Indian religions, this is not the focus of my study, per se; however, since Indians were practicing their aboriginal religions when first approached by Christians, one must have some knowledge of Indian traditions in order to understand the ways in which Indians have combined or alternated their traditional religious beliefs and practices with those of Christianity. Many works over the last five hundred years have been written about native religions of North American Indians (for example, numerous titles listed in Hultkrantz 1983 and 1990), and particularly in the last century by anthropologists and other social scientists. There are numerous studies regarding the history of religious change among American Indians—the acculturative, transformative, syncretistic, nativistic, and revitalizationist movements—especially concerning those stirrings that have led to "new religions" like those of the Ghost Dance and the Native American Church (see Turner 1973 and Turner 1978). A number of these religious movements have appropriated aspects of Christianity, and in some one may see Catholicism taking an oblique shape; it is not my intent, however, to chronicle those influences, however fascinating. My interest is in Indians who have identified themselves, or have been identified by Church authorities, as Catholics. I wish to understand how American Indian Catholics have adopted Catholic belief, faith, piety, and behavior, and how they have adapted those features to their Indian practices.

Scholarly studies of Christian missions and missionaries, both Protestant and Catholic, often focus on the non-Indian carriers of the Christian traditions, their motives and accomplishments and errors. In these studies (see, e.g., Bowden 1981; Grant 1985; Prucha 1977: 209–214, 245–246; Ronda and Axtell 1978; Shea 1855) the Indians appear as the recipients of evangelization (often passive or impenetrable, sometimes receptive or resistant, but still largely inscrutable). The writings portray the initial contacts, the hardships, the first baptisms, the spiritual colonization of the early stages and the resulting factionalism and disorientation. Though I draw upon many of these works, my primary interest is the Indians themselves. I am concerned, naturally, with the process of missionization, and much of the narrative that follows examines that process in detail. Those details are important to an understanding of Indian Catholics, since the means by which they came to be Catholics explains to some extent the ways in which they act and think as Catholics and thus define who they are.

I am building upon a large literature, from mere sketches of converts to voluminous histories and ethnographies of the several hundred tribes of Indians in North America—mostly north of Mexico and south of Canada, but not excluding those nations. From these sources one can glean the Catholic trends, although these are usually not their main foci. Rarely do these attempts follow systematically or comprehensively the families or communities which have come to identify themselves as Catholic. It is my intent to make such a comprehensive study.

My fields of study over a quarter century have been American Indian traditional religions and religious history, missions to American Indians, American Indian history, and American Catholicism. I bring a background in the literature of Catholicism in America: its history, culture, theology, ritual life, ethnic expressions, parish structure, and in general the ways in which Catholics have adapted to America and become Americans in the process. Indians are not merely another ethnic Catholic group in the United States, like Poles or Italians or Irish; nevertheless, there is some comparison (as well as contrast) to make. One must understand the post-Tridentine Church in its Spanish, French, and later Irish and German manifestations, as well as in its Americanisms, in order to understand adequately the type of Christianity that Indians have met when they have encountered Catholicism. It is necessary to understand the plenary councils in the United States, the hierarchical structures, and the changes wrought by the Second Vatican Council, in order to see Indian Catholicism in its institutional Catholic context (see Dolan 1985; Ellis and Trisco 1982; Hennessey 1981).

Most important, however, is to understand Catholic American Indian peoples in the twentieth century, especially in the present day. I have conducted primary research at archives across the United States, particularly at the repositories of Catholic dioceses, but also at the Bureau of Catholic Indian Missions housed at Marquette University. In addition I have learned of Indian Catholic faith and identity by entering Indian communities from Maine to California, from Washington to Louisiana, attending conferences of Catholic Indians, participating in Catholic Indian liturgies, and interviewing Indian Catholics firsthand. Such research informs a great deal of this book and those to follow.

There are four parts of this volume. In the first I trace the expansion of Catholicism in New Spain, from the invasion of the Caribbean and the establishment of Christendom in the New World, through the spiritual conquest and accommodation of Nahuatl and Mayan Mexico, along the routes the missionaries took, known collectively as the Padres' Trail, to the northern periphery of the Hispanic empire, primarily among the Yaqui and the O'odham peoples. Although I briefly address Mexican Indian Catholicism of the twentieth century, my interest is in setting forth the process of evangelization of the colonial era, particularly in the sixteenth and seventeenth centuries. Regarding the Yaquis and the O'odham (Pimas and Papagos), however, most of whom live today in the United States, I carry the story of their Catholicism to the 1990s. Indeed, the bulk of my analysis regarding these Indian Catholics concerns the last hundred years in southern Arizona. As with the other Catholic Indian people I am studying, my aim is to delineate the features of their Catholicism in the present day.

Part II examines the history of Catholic faith and institutions among the Pueblo peoples of New Mexico and its contiguous states. I pay less attention to the founding of the Spanish regime among the Pueblos, the Pueblo revolt of 1680 and the subsequent reconquest, than I do to Pueblo relations with the Roman Catholic Church over the past century, since the formation of the Archdiocese of Santa Fe. I observe all of the extant Pueblo communities; however, I use two pueblos, Santo Domingo and Isleta, as case studies in the problematic of Pueblo Catholicism in the twentieth century. Finally, I refer to other Catholic Indians in the Southwest: Navajos, Apaches, and others, particularly within the Diocese of Gallup. In the first two parts I hope to portray the heritage of Spanish Catholicism among Native Americans. I cannot claim to treat every Indian community with equal depth; my hope is to discuss the main lines of Catholic development throughout the region.

In the third part I investigate at close range the history and effects of Catholic missions among the Indians of California, from the eighteenth century to the present day. In this part of the book I attempt to take stock of the Catholic heritage among Indians of the southwestern United States. The copious documentation of the Franciscan missions and the archives of the Diocese of San Diego, in addition to other sources, makes such scrutiny possible. The intense and continuing debate regarding the conduct of the missioners in California and their impact upon Indian peoples makes an evaluative probing necessary. Consequently, Part III contains ample descriptions of California mission life, in addition to an extensive survey of Mission Indian Catholicism in the twentieth century. The Luiseño Indians of southern California are the focus of my investigation regarding California Indian Catholicism and its present-day tensions.

Finally, in Part IV I inspect the history of judgments made about Catholic missionizing in California (and by extension, throughout New Spain), closing the volume with contemporary perspectives regarding the padres who first brought Catholicism to the Indians' ancestors. In the next volumes I shall develop this issue further.

Before 1492 there were no Christians in the New World. Today, among the millions of the descendants of those Native Americans (over forty million in the western hemisphere, two million of these in the United States), the majority are Christians. In the United States a quarter million are regarded as Catholics by virtue of their baptism. This book takes a long look at the southwestern Indians who comprise almost half of those numbers, many of whom harbor lasting resentments against the Catholic Church and the Spanish heritage of evangelization, five hundred years after the Columbian encounter.

While the National Conference of Catholic Bishops issued a pastoral reflection on the quincentennial and Native American people— "1992: A Time for Reconciling and Recommitting Ourselves as a People"—Catholic Indian organizations strongly criticized the Church's evangelical effort over half a millennium. The bishops admit that "As Church, we often have been unconscious and insensitive to the mistreatment of our Native American brothers and sisters and have at times reflected the racism of the dominant culture of which we have been a part" (*Tekakwitha Conference Newsletter* March/April 1992: 26), and they offer apologies to contemporary Indians for past mistreatment. Without eschewing Church claims that Jesus Christ embodies the unique revelation of God in human history, the bishops state that "the coming of religious faith in this land began not 500 years ago, but centuries before in the prayers, chants, dance and other sacred celebrations of Native people" (ibid., 26). In California, where for the last decade and more Church and Indian circles have debated the merits of Franciscan missions to the Indians in the eighteenth and nineteenth centuries, an Indian Catholic speaker at a devotional conference declared, "The European Missionaries brought with them the Gospel message and the news about Jesus. All too often though the Missionaries themselves didn't understand what the message was. . . . They were not missionaries of the Gospel but missionaries of European culture." He concludes, "This is the challenge for the Institutional Church. Examine your conscience, look upon whom you have been and compare it to the Gospel message" (ibid., 1–2).

While acknowledging that the history of Indian-White contact has been disastrous for the Native Americans, the Roman Catholic pontiff, Pope John Paul II, chose to proclaim evangelization as the saving event of the Columbian encounter. In the Dominican Republic on the twelfth of October, 1992, he stated, "To say America is to say Maria." He thanked God for "the abundant fruits of the seeds planted over the last 500 years by such intrepid missionaries." As one observer has put it, this suggests that "the very boat that brought Columbus, the Santa Maria, was a symbol of liberating faith rather than a harbinger of brutal conquest" (French, October 12, 1992). Many Indians protested the pope's quincentenary speech and the devastation their ancestors underwent; they also raised questions to him about contemporary domination of Indian people throughout the Americas. "The Pope smiled and moved on" (French, October 14, 1992).

Is the Catholic faith the consolation for those 500 years, as the pope avows? For Indians who have resisted Christianity the answer is surely no; however, for Catholic Indians the answer is filled with ambivalence. There are some Indian Catholics for whom discovery, conquest, and conversion comprise ancient history and are no longer troubling. There are other Catholic Indians who love Jesus and who participate in Church practice and faith but are angered about the ways in which their ancestors became Christians. This book and the succeeding volumes are about the problematic of Indian Catholicism as much as they are about its history and its contemporary expressions of faith.

ACKNOWLEDGMENTS

I proffer my thanks to Sister Louise LaCoste, c.s.j., Archivist, Diocese of San Diego; Dr. R. Bruce Harley, Archivist, Diocese of San Diego; Mark G. Thiel, Archivist, Marquette University Memorial Library, Department of Special Collections; Marina Ochoa, Archivist, Archdiocese of Santa Fe; and to the people who have shared their time and insight with me: Alfretta Antone; George Arviso; Milonny Arviso; Verna Ann Arviso; Janet Brown; Amelia S. Calac; Rev. Camillus Cavagnaro, o.f.m.; D. C. Cole; Rupert Costo; Rev. James Cribbin; Sister Gloria Davis; Chris Devers; Rev. James M. Dixon, s.j.; Joan Dixon; Lee Dixon; Lorena Dixon; Sister Patricia Dixon; Patty Duro; King Freeman; Richard Frost; Rev. P. Michael Galvan; Rev. Gilbert Hemauer, o.f.m. Cap.; Lorraine Hyde; Villiana Calac Hyde; Rev. William Lawson; Msgr. Paul A. Lenz; Florence Loftin; Mark Macarro; Peanuts Magee; Edna Mamake; Sister Lorraine Masters, o.l.v.m.; Rev. Daniel P. McLaughlin, s.t.; Rev. John Mittelstadt, o.f.m.; Rev. Ralph Monteiro, s.a.; Rev. David A. Myers, s.j.; Rev. James F. O'Brien, s.j.; Rev. Paul Ojibway, s.a.; Alfonso Ortiz; Rev. Ralph Partida; Most Rev. Donald E. Pelotte, s.s.s.; José Romero; Dolores Rousseau; Joseph Savilla; Peggy Savilla; Alex Seowtewa; Adele Seowtewa; Arlen Sheyka; W. Ines Stonehouse; Mark Thiel; Georgiana O. Viveros; and Catherine Walsh. Colgate University has provided generous grants of money to help defray research costs through the Division of Humanities and the Faculty Research Council. Colgate's Case Library staff has been very helpful to my study. I appreciate the support. Finally, I thank Marion Jantzen, Wanda Kelly, Ellen Myers, and Carol Smith for so ably typing portions of the manuscript, and Julia Meyerson for creating the maps.

※ I ※

*Spanish Catholicism
among Native Americans*

INTRODUCTION

In the late fifteenth century a matrix of factors gave birth to the European exploration and eventual conquest and colonizing of the Americas. The growth of self-consciously powerful, competitive nation states provided impetus for the incursions into the New World. Governments seeking favorable systems of trade in which to accumulate materials, markets, and colonies—and through them mercantile wealth—sponsored expeditions to realms hitherto unencountered by Europeans. The Renaissance spirit of adventure combined with technological advances in shipbuilding, firearms, engineering, and metallurgy to produce a capacity for invading new lands and exploiting new resources. Gold and glory, and plenty of both, became powerfully motivating goals.

Religious goals were every bit as compelling to Europeans of the fifteenth and sixteenth centuries as the quest for fame and fortune, and particularly to the various Europeans who came to the Americas under the Spanish banner. The heritage of struggle against Islam in Spain, capped by the victory at Granada in 1492, provided Christians with a militant edge to their encounters with non-Christian peoples. The Reformation of the sixteenth century only exacerbated religious competitiveness and inspired efforts at spiritual expansion on the part of Catholic standard-bearers. Not all Spanish explorers set forth with God in mind, and many of those explorers (both materialist and devout) came from lands other than the Spanish kingdoms. Italian, French, Flemish, and other European ethnicities were well represented on the ships and in the missions of Spain. Nevertheless, the most proudly flown flag of Spanish conquest was that of Christendom.

Christopher Columbus, himself a member of the Third Order of St. Francis and a visionary Christian, wrote that the primary purpose of his historic journey of 1492 was "to see the said princes and peoples and lands . . . and the manner in which may be undertaken their conversion to our Holy Faith" (in Sale 1990: 11). Although on his maiden voyage he took along no missionaries, he sailed under the banner of the Virgin Mary in his flagship, *Santa Maria*, and he brought with him to the New World a late medieval Spanish Catholic spirituality to native peoples who knew nothing of that faith. Columbus referred to himself and his men as "Christians," rather than as Spaniards or Europeans or Whites, and it was as Christians that they "discovered" the lands occupied by the Indians of the Americas.

In October 1492 Columbus wrote of his first encounter with the Caribbean Tainos: "They should be good servants and of quick intelligence, since I see that they very soon say all that is said to them, and I believe that they would easily be made Christians, for it appeared to me that they had no creed" (Columbus 1960: 24). Not only did he view the Indians as empty of religiousness, ready to be made into Christians, but he also assumed it the right of the Christians to attempt such a transformation. For Columbus, and for the Christendom of his day, the world's population was divided into those who were Christians and those who were not, and the world's geography was divided into those lands inhabited and ruled by Christians and those lands not.

The Christian authorities of Europe treated Columbus' encounter as a "discovery"—Pope Alexander VI in his papal bulls of 1493, *Inter caetera*, referred to lands and peoples "discovered" by Columbus—and when these authorities spoke of "discovery" they meant something theologically and legally explicit: that "the entire globe was the property of God and, as such, distributable by the Pope as His delegate on earth" (Green and Dickason 1989: 4). In the 1493 bulls the pope divided the newly "discovered" territories between Spanish and Portuguese sovereigns, in order for them "'to bring under your sway the said mainlands and islands with their residents and inhabitants and to bring them to the Catholic faith'" (ibid., 5). The pope conferred to those Christian sovereigns full apostolic power and jurisdiction over the non-Christian lands just "discovered." The underlying premises for such a unilateral action were these: that God rules the physical and temporal world; that He delegates His authority to the papacy; that the pope passes on that authority to rightful Christian sovereigns. The ruling Christians of Columbus' time believed that lands ruled by Christian sovereigns were Christian lands; lands occupied by non-Christians were non-Christian lands. Non-Christian sovereigns and their peoples, according to these premises, had the right to occupy, use, and rule their lands until they were "discovered" by representatives of Christendom, the visible kingdom of God on earth.

"Discovery" was an act of which seemingly only Christian sovereigns were capable. "The discoverers" possessed the right to establish Christian rule over the non-Christians and their lands—the "heathen" or "pagan" peoples and territories or "the discovered"—and "the discovered" were expected to yield their sovereignty to the Christians. In 1493 the papacy attempted to found the geographical and political contexts for the "discovery," and it is within these contexts that the Indians of the Americas came into contact with Catholics, their faith, and their institutions.

On his second journey in 1493 Columbus brought with him five *religiosos* (Sale 1990: 128), including Father Juan Perez, who said the first mass in the New World at a place he called Port Conception on the island of Hispaniola, or Haiti, on December 8, 1493, the Feast of the Immaculate Conception. By giving the islands Christian names; by marking the days according to the Christian calendar; and by celebrating the central ritual of Catholicism, the sacrifice of the mass, the Spanish under Columbus' command inaugurated the process of christianizing the New World and its native peoples, subordinating them to Christian rule.

When Columbus returned to Spain from his second voyage in 1496, he noted that "not one Indian had as yet been converted to the Catholic faith" (ibid., 166), although by that time at least six Tainos had been burned at the stake by Columbus' brother Bartolomé for having desecrated Christian icons. (The natives buried the images in their fields and urinated on them, hoping to fertilize their crops.) If we are to look for the first Caribbean converts to Catholicism—the first to call themselves Christians, the first to receive baptism, the first to receive the Eucharist, or to recite the Creed—their stories are lost in the annihilation of the Indian islanders' population. Of the estimated eight million Caribbean inhabitants on Hispaniola in 1492, there were only twenty-eight thousand in 1518, and by the middle of the sixteenth century they were almost all gone. Catholicism did not take root among the Tainos and Arawaks of the Caribbean because these people were destroyed by the Columbian encounter and indeed by Columbus' policies of enslavement, his Franciscan spirituality notwithstanding. The "discovery" led directly to the enslavement called *encomienda*, and Catholic sovereigns ruled with such violence and with such devastating effect in the islands that few natives were left to form a Catholic congregation. Hence, we must look to the mainland to find the beginnings of American Indian Catholicism.

Before the Spanish introduced Catholicism to the mainland, they solidified for themselves their right of "discovery" and established the legal procedures by which "the discoverers" were to introduce themselves to the Indians. In 1513 a Spanish jurist, Palacios Rubios, penned "the Requirement" (in Parry and Keith 1984, 1: 289–290), a document to be read aloud (in Spanish) by each "discoverer" as he encountered the natives in their lands. The Requirement recounted biblical history and the papal succession from St. Peter, "Lord and Superior of all the men in the world" (289), to "One of these Pontiffs, who . . . made donation of these isles and Tierra-firme" to the Spanish sovereigns: "So their Highnesses are kings and lords of these islands and land of Tierra-firme by virtue of this donation" (289).

The Requirement then came to the crux of the matter:

> we ask and require . . . that you consider what we have said to you, and that you take the time that shall be necessary to understand and deliberate upon it, and that you acknowledge the Church as the Ruler and Superior of the whole world, and the high priest called Pope, and in his name the King and Queen . . . as superiors and lords and kings, . . . and that you consent and give place that these religious fathers should declare and preach to you the aforesaid.
>
> If you do so, you will do well, . . . and we . . . shall receive you in all love and charity, and shall leave you and your wives, and your children, and your lands, free without servitude. (289–290)

The Requirement promised that conversion was to be voluntary, following religious instruction; however, should the Indians prevent the preaching of the Christian faith,

> with the help of God, we shall powerfully enter into your country, and shall make war against you in all ways and manners that we can, and shall subject you to the yoke and obedience of the Church and of their Highnesses; we shall take you and your wives and your children, and shall make slaves of them, and as such shall sell and dispose of them as their Highnesses may command; and we shall take away your goods, and shall do you all the mischief and damage that we can, as to vassals who do not obey, and refuse to receive their lord and resist and contradict him; and we protest that the deaths and losses which shall accrue from this are your fault. . . . (290)

The Spaniards employed this document for the first time on the shores of Panama in 1514, and many times afterward. It is said (in Thomas 1993: 72) that two Indian chiefs in Colombia once remarked that "the Pope must have been drunk" to have bestowed to the Spanish kings so much land belonging to others. European theologians and lawyers debated the wisdom (theoretical and practical) of the Requirement. Still, Cortés had it read to the Mayans and Aztecs in the course of his conquest of Mexico, and it stayed in use throughout the sixteenth century, thereby setting the tone for the spread of Christianity in the Americas.

In 1492 an estimated seventy-five to one hundred million Native Americans populated the Americas, including twenty-five million in Mexico and perhaps twelve million in what is now the United States and Canada. The populations shrank drastically during the sixteenth century (in Mexico only one million remained by 1600), but over the succeeding centuries the numbers increased, especially if one includes the *mestizo* (mixed race) figures. Today there are well over forty million Indians in South and North America, including more than ten million in Mexico alone (13 percent of Mexico's population). Most of these Indians and mestizos have been baptized as Catholics, and Catholic forms of piety constitute a substantial portion of contemporary Indian religiousness throughout Latin America (despite recent Protestant inroads). The pervasive Catholic influence derives directly from the evangelizing zeal of Hernan Cortés and his fellow conquistadors, who were determined to spread their faith to the American indigenes.

The Spanish Catholicism transplanted to the New World was not atypical of late medieval Christianity as a whole. Its central beliefs and rituals were those codified during the Catholic Reformation at the Council of Trent in the sixteenth century and grounded in more than a millennium of theological, liturgical, and ecclesiastical developments, with roots in the life and teachings of Jesus Christ. The general image among the Spanish Catholic populace of that time was of a single, all-powerful God who gives eternal rewards or punishment to humans, depending on their service or offense to Him. This one God consists of a trinity of persons—Father, Son, and Holy Spirit—each fully God and fully effective in the divine activities of creation, salvation, and judgment. Human sinfulness, epitomized by Adam and Eve's proud disobedience to God's command, is atoned for by the sacrificial suffering, blood, and death of Jesus in order to redeem humans from their alienation from God on earth, and even an eternity of alienation in hell or limbo. Most Catholics of the period believed membership in the Holy Church created by Christ was necessary for salvation. The Catholic Church was the visible means by which God provided the grace necessary for humans to overcome their sinfulness and perhaps to attain heaven. Baptism was the sacramental initiation into the Church; penance was available for the forgiveness of individual sins; and the Eucharist provided direct rapport between humans and God.

The Church's liturgical calendar designated seasons (Advent, Christmas, Lent, Easter, Pentecost) marking the salvific events of Jesus' life and individual days celebrating the Christian saints, whose lives served as models of heroic virtue and whose powers could be tapped in order to intercede to God and to aid particular enterprises, such as warfare. Mary, the mother of Jesus, was the greatest of the saints, as intercessor and helper. Rites of passage—baptism, matrimony, extreme unction before death—marked a person's life as sacred. Creeds and other prayers reminded Catholics daily of the doctrinal content of the Church's faith. Sacramentals, such as the praying of the rosary or the Stations of the Cross, helped persons to meditate upon God and practice sanctioned modes of devotionalism.

The Church itself was sacramental—an outward institution created by Christ to give grace to humans—and its hierarchical and geographical organization (its bishops, priests, dioceses, parishes, religious orders, and sodalities, all under the authority of the pope and his congregations) claimed authority to teach doctrines and morals; to nurture the faithful and punish wrongdoers; to validate and censure political rulers. Church authorities held rightful power deriving from God Himself; to exercise that power, they said, was to insure order in this world and salvation in the next. In a world in which the devil was a "theological fact" (Marzal 1993: 151), an embodiment of evil who fought mightily against Jesus, the authority of the Church was considered a bulwark in a cosmic struggle.

Spanish Catholicism's long association with Islam fostered an embattled worldview, a mentality of crusade in which Santiago (St. James)—the hellhound of the Moors, said to have spurred on the Spanish Christians against Moslems at the legendary battle of Clavijo in 844—served as a rallying cry in encounters with enemies. In the late fifteenth century the Spanish Church formulated an aggressive method of rooting out enemies (those who would not assent to Catholic doctrine and submit to Catholic authority) in the Spanish Inquisition under Tomas de Torquemada. The Inquisition was a medieval means of enforcing doctrinal, liturgical, and ecclesiastical uniformity, a way of "preventing defection from the church" (Braden 1930: 7). In 1478 in Spain it became a means explicitly of attacking Jews and Moors, including those who claimed to be Christians. Thus 1492 marked not only the discoveries of Columbus and the defeat of the Moors at Granada, but also the brutal expulsion of millions of Jews from Spain. The Protestant Reformation that began as Cortés was launching his offensive in Mexico only increased the militancy of Spanish Catholic spirituality, as each soul to be gained in the New World might replace one lost to the Protestant realms of Europe.

In the conquest and evangelization of the Americas, the Spanish Church was a partner to the Crown. The papal bulls of Alexander VI gave Spain "complete control over the church with regard to its evangelization mission in America," making Catholic Spain a "missionary state" (Marzal 1993: 141) in which the civil and the religious were intertwined, if not a single thread. Indians encountered Christianity as an integral part of conquest, hence the persisting ambivalence on the part of Indians toward the Church. A scholar writes that "the unified church and political authority undoubtedly made the conversion efforts of the Spanish missionaries seem like one more instrument of oppression, thus reducing its credibility to Indian subjects" (ibid.). Half a millennium after the first contacts between Christians and Indians, Church authorities were placed in the position of apologizing for and defending the early course of christianization.

When Pope John Paul II visited Latin America for the Columbian Quincentenary, Indians protested the genocide experienced by their ancestors. The pope tried to emphasize evangelization apart from its imperial contexts. In Brazil the pope apologized for the "weakness and defects" of some missionaries, to Indian leaders who argued that the quincentennial should not be celebrated. At the same time he defended the "shining and eternal example" of the Catholic missionary orders (in Cowell, October 17, 1991). In Mexico, the pope spoke in a Christian church built on the ruins of a Mayan temple, hoping to embrace symbolically the indigenous peoples throughout the Americas who feel ambivalence toward Catholicism. In his view, the Church has always been the "protector of their cultural values . . . against the abuses of unscrupulous colonizers" (in Cowell, August 12, 1993), criticisms notwithstanding.

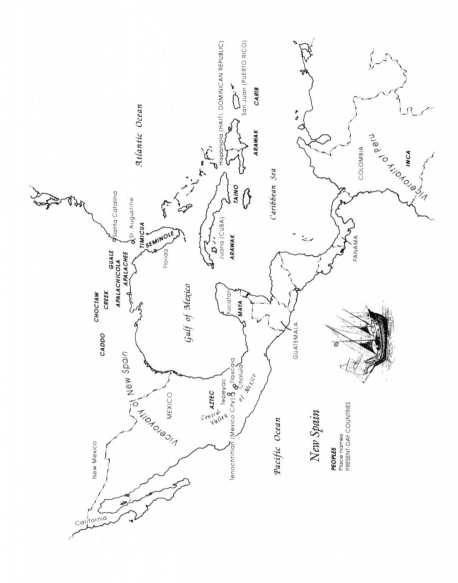

New Spain

PEOPLES
Place names
PRESENT-DAY COUNTRIES

Pacific Ocean

Viceroyalty of New Spain

New Mexico

California

MEXICO

Central Valley

Tenochtitlan (Mexico City)
Tepeyac
Tlaxcala
Cholula
AZTEC
of Mexico

Gulf of Mexico

CADDO
CHOCTAW
CREEK
GUALE
APALACHICOLA
APALACHEE

Santa Catalina
St. Augustine
TIMICUA
SEMINOLE
Florida

Yucatan
MAYA

GUATEMALA

Atlantic Ocean

Hispaniola (HAITI, DOMINICAN REPUBLIC)
San Juan (PUERTO RICO)
CARIB
ARAWAK

TAINO
ARAWAK
Juana (CUBA)

Caribbean Sea

PANAMA

COLOMBIA

Viceroyalty of Peru
INCA

HERNAN CORTÉS' CONQUEST OF MEXICO

Although other Spaniards reached the American mainland before him, it was the campaign of Hernan Cortés beginning in 1519 that accomplished the conquest of Mexico and hence the establishment of the Viceroyalty of New Spain. Cortés held "deep Christian convictions" (Ricard 1966: 15), despite his greed and debauchery. He was devoted to Mary and he conducted his conquest of the Aztecs as a kind of religious crusade, with "himself as God's appointed agent to free the natives of Mexico from the power of the devil" (Braden 1930: 77). Beneath the banner of Mary and the cross of Christ he destroyed idols and altars of the Mayans and Aztecs. Along with his yearning for riches and acclaim, Cortés sought conversion of the Indians and prosecuted his war to that end. Two priests accompanied his troops on their march — a secular priest and a member of the order of the Holy Trinity — and they cautioned Cortés against forced baptisms. He and his spiritual advisors were horrified by what they perceived to be the rank immorality of the Mexican Indians in the form of human sacrifices and licentiousness, and according to the spirit of the Requirement, Cortés had no doubt concerning his authority to evangelize forcefully.

After his defeat of the Mayan Indians in 1519, Cortés was presented with twenty women, including one named La Malinche, as symbols of tribute. The conqueror introduced them to Mary, the Cross, the rudiments of Catholic creed, an altar, and a mass said by one of the chaplains. Shortly after, "these were the first to be baptized as Christians in New Spain, and they were at once distributed among the chief officers" (ibid., 85) in order to cement the alliance between the Mayans and the Spaniards. La Malinche took the baptismal name of Marina and became Cortés' famed mistress and translator. Because she spoke both Mayan and the Aztecs' Nahuatl and became proficient in Spanish, Doña Marina played a pivotal role in the conquest of Mexico. She made Christian concepts intelligible to other converts and military demands cogent to Aztec rulers; she protected her master from plots against him and his men; and she bore him a child and served as an example of Christian devotion long after Cortés gave her to another soldier. All this has made her an enduring, ambiguous figure in Mexican history and folklore. Whatever her initial will may have been in the matter, as the first Catholic convert she has been honored as heroine and vilified as traitor against her Indian compatriots. The ambivalence that Mexican Indians have felt for her over the centuries signifies their complicated Christian identity.

As Cortés journeyed west toward Tenochtitlan, the Mexican capital, he marshaled the help of the Indians of Tlaxcala, and it was there that the first male natives received baptism in Mexico. In the Franciscan church in Tlaxcala there is a baptismal font said to have been used for this sacrament. The inscription on the font states, "At this font, the four senators of the ancient republic of Tlaxcala received the Christian faith. The rite took place in the year 1520, Juan Diaz, chaplain of the army of conquest, being minister. Captain Hernan Cortés and his distinguished officers acted as sponsors . . ." (in ibid., 103).

The conquest of Montezuma's Mexico, accomplished in 1521 with the surrender of the last Aztec ruler, Cuauhtemoc, and solidified over the next decade, took place as a kind of holy war in which Cortés attempted the eradication of traditional Aztec religion and the "superposition" (Montgomery, Smith, and Brew 1949: 265–272) of Christianity. In the capital of Tenochtitlan, Cortés called Montezuma's gods "devils," and he offered to build a Catholic church right at the temple of Huitzilopochtli, the Aztec deity of war and recipient of many sacrifices. Montezuma resisted the insult of Spaniards' replacing his gods with the Cross and Virgin. Instead Cortés built a small chapel so that the Aztecs could see the Spanish at mass, singing the *Ave Maria*. At Cholula the Spaniards placed a shrine to the Virgin on top of the great pyramid, and everywhere they preached Christian doctrines and critiques of Aztec religion. In time Cortés seized Montezuma and the Spanish began the destruction of Aztec religious monuments, constructing a chapel atop the temple of the war god. Some reports suggest, probably mistakenly (Thomas 1993: 404), that Montezuma may have received baptism before his death preceding the fall of Tenochtitlan. In any event, Cortés capped his victory by issuing the Requirement to the native populace and by calling for mendicant missionaries to enter Mexico and begin a program of religious instruction and christianization under his command.

The Aztecs were anything but devoid of aboriginal religiousness. Indeed, along with the Mayans and the Incas of South America (see Gossen 1993: 25–115), they possessed such visibly formidable religious systems that the Spanish felt the need to combat their structures frontally. The Spanish found "a very religious people" in the Aztecs and other Indians of Mexico. Religion was "a major preoccupation of the people," a "controlling factor" (Braden 1930: 20, 21) in their lives. Priesthoods, temples, liturgical calendars, large-scale ceremonials, and royal sanctions all made Aztec religion a public force of immense proportions. The Aztecs had a rich mythology, innumerable codices recording sacred information, and an ethic of sacrifice, austerity, and household devotion—all in plain view of the conquerors. The Indians were daily and ultimately concerned about their relations to the divine beings who were their sources of life. The gods had created human beings through divine sacrifice in primordial times. It was the task of humans to imitate this sacrifice in order to make themselves worthy of continued existence in this world and in the heavenly realms. Doing penance was a way of life for the Aztecs, expressed most prominently in their human sacrifices that so horrified the Spaniards. In order to know the will of the gods, in which was contained the destinies of individual persons and of the cosmos as a whole, the Aztecs and their neighbors consulted their books, their calendars, and their diviners. So that they might prosper and persist, they observed ritual offerings in their homes and in the public temples. Priests conducted state-sponsored sacrifices on behalf of everyone, and the Aztecs believed that proper behavior of all persons was necessary for the future.

The Spanish were struck immediately by similarities between their Catholicism and the Aztec religion. When the Aztecs presented their newborn children to the temple, the Christians thought of baptism. Rituals of communion evoking the body of Huitzilopochtli reminded them of the Euchrarist. The Aztecs seemed to confess their sins and concern themselves with realms of heaven and hell. They respected a priestly hierarchy; they memorialized their dead; they celebrated holy days of feast and fast. Their salvific god-man, Quetzalcoatl, seemed almost an image of Jesus himself. Since all religious complexes possess some similarity of form and function, to remark on these may seem "far-fetched and almost fanciful" (ibid., 74). Nevertheless, the Spanish Christians attempted to explain the similarities by reference to their own worldview.

Some even suggested that St. Thomas must have traveled in apostolic times to this distant land and established Christian sacraments that over the centuries were obscured and perverted without guidance from Christian teaching authority. Others thought that the Devil must have inspired the Aztecs to imitate Christian phenomena in order to mock the true faith. Indeed, the Spanish found the parallels horrifying and offensive, a blasphemy against God and Church. They argued that for all the apparent similarities, the two religious systems were diametrically opposed to one another. Not only were they distinctly different structures with separate loyalties, orientations, scriptures, cosmologies, temples, and priesthoods, but in the view of the Christians the Aztecs' faith was motivated by fear of malevolent gods who cared nothing for human persons, a far cry from the loving and beloved God embodied in the person of Jesus Christ. The Christians observed how the Mexican Indians incorporated the deities of neighbors and foes in their own theological program. Both conquerors and conquered in traditional Mexican practice adopted devotions to their enemies' gods. In various parts of the cosmos the Indians found deities worthy of worship. This plethora of religious cult stood in contrast to the dogmatic monotheism of the Christians, who, in theory at least, had no trouble distinguishing between the reverence owed saints and the adoration reserved for the one God.

In their moral code the Aztecs forbade theft, adultery, and murder; however, they did not think of humans as innately sinful and in need of the spiritual cleansing of baptism as did Christians. The Aztecs felt that a person's primary obligation in life was to provide the gods with blood and hearts of fighting, dying, and sacrificing human beings; however, this life of sacrifice had no ethical motive, according to the Christians; it was fanatical service to bloodthirsty powers, rather than atonement for sin. In personal and public conduct the Spaniards found the Indians inordinately immoral, practicing human sacrifice, cannibalism, homosexual sodomy, and inducing hallucination through drugs as a matter of course. So divergent from the Christian view of "natural law" was their sexuality that the Spanish doubted the very rationality of the Indians—at least until Pope Paul II declared in his 1537 bull *Sublimus deus* that the natives of the Americas were to be regarded "as true men . . . capable of understanding the Catholic faith" (in Green and Dickason 1989: 18). In sum, "the overall perspective of pre-Columbian aberrant behavior, as judged by Old World standards, justified the charges of irrationality brought against the American Indian on legal, religious, and biological grounds" (Guerra 1971: 263).

Moreover, the Spaniards regarded Indian immorality not as an exception to the aboriginal religious system, but as a direct consequence of it. In Christian eyes the Aztecs were engaged as a people in thoroughgoing deviltry. "Incapable of comprehending that they were faced with different cultures, the Spaniards identified the gods of the aboriginal religions with the devil of their own religion. . . . Aboriginal gods equal the Christian devil: this was the theme that dominated the work of evanglization in the New World" (*Nativism and Syncretism* 1960: 41). Hence, despite the "demoniacal parodies" (Ricard 1966: 33) the Mexican Indian religion made of Christianity, indeed *because* of them, the Spanish missioners in Mexico attempted to keep the two systems separate in the process of christianization. The Spanish Christians condemned the Indians' religiousness—a condemnation that persisted as a leitmotif in the history of Christian-Indian contact—and they tried to introduce Christianity as something totally new, rather than constructing Christian belief and practice upon the foundation of native faith.

When Cortés preached Christian cosmology and faith to Montezuma, the Aztec king rejoindered with accounts of the Mexican divinities. His faith and that of his people were not easily or immediately to be supplanted by Christianity. At the same time, the Aztecs "were not particularly averse to the worship of the God of the Spaniards, the Cross, the Virgin Mary, or their other holy objects. They would gladly have incorporated them bodily into their system. It was the exclusive claims of Christianity that aroused opposition" (Braden 1930: 163). The Aztec empire engaged in widespread syncretism, with various ethnic elements in the overall complex. They were accustomed to accommodating religious ideas and rites, the very gods themselves, of the conquered and conquerors. It is said that "the Aztecs did not regard their religion as a perfect and immutable system, revealed once and for all as Christianity is supposed to have been. Aztec religion was revealed by the gods, but the gods could change their minds and, above all, they were not omnipotent" (Madsen 1957: 118).

In the conquest, Aztec accommodationism collided with the Christian will to extirpate all forms of aboriginal worship. The Spanish victors—both military and religious—"demolished Aztec temples, smashed idols, defamed native gods, displaced Aztec priests, and closed Aztec religious schools. . . . Spanish conquerors destroyed the core of Aztec culture by prohibiting war, human sacrifice, and worship of the pagan gods" (ibid., 133), in the attempt to impose Christianity on Native Americans as an imperial right.

MIƧƧIONARIEƧ IN MEXICO

When Emperor Charles V called for mendicant orders to instruct and baptize the Indians conquered by Cortés in 1521, the first to answer were three Flemish Franciscan friars—Juan de Tecto, Juan de Aora and Brother Pedro de Gante—all of whom reached Tlaxcala in 1523. The following year Cortés greeted the next crew, the now legendary Twelve Franciscans, in the capital, kneeling publicly before them in a display of submissive devotion for the edification of the Indians looking on. These were the first of thousands of clerics who came to New Spain. Over eight thousand Franciscans served throughout the Spanish Empire into the early nineteenth century, over half of the clergy in the Spanish New World during that time; the Jesuits arrived in 1572 and numbered over three thousand during the same centuries; Dominicans, beginning in 1526, and Augustinians in 1533 also joined the enterprise of converting the Native Americans. In addition there were secular clergy and Carmelite priests. The clergy were the visible agents of Catholic institutional authority, and it was their task to attempt the spiritual conquest of the Indians, not only in the vicinity of Mexico City, but throughout the empire. In 1527 Mexico became a Catholic diocese, with Fray Juan de Zumarraga, a Franciscan, as the first bishop. Other bishoprics were to follow as the expansion of New World Catholicism took place.

Pope Leo X authorized Franciscan monks to evangelize the New World, "to preach, baptize, confess, absolve, marry, and administer the sacraments of the eucharist and extreme unction" (Braden 1930: 132). Subsequent popes widened the friars' ecclesiastical powers, and they carried the major burden of bringing Catholicism to the Indians and the Indians to Catholicism. The Franciscans and the other clergy also served the colonial powers, as they "attempted to use religion to reenforce relations of power to ensure social stability and to indoctrinate the colonized into a passive acceptance of their status in the colonial social order" (Jackson 1991: ix). But above all, their goal was to make Christ ever present in the lives of the Indians, as the pagan gods had been before the conquest. The missionaries hoped that everywhere Indians turned—in their amusements and work, in their morals and speculations—the Church would provide the frame of reference, the orientation, through its priests, churches, processions, academies, catechisms, sacraments, and sacramentals. They also hoped that in turning toward Christianity and converting to its forms of religiousness, the Indians would turn away from and leave behind their aboriginal forms. The missionaries aimed for a "total renewal" (Ricard 1966: 284; cf. 291) of Indian life according to the Christian model.

From the start the Spanish clerics began systematically to destroy pagan temples and idols throughout Mexico. Cortés thought that some relics ought to be preserved, and secular authorities feared that widespread iconoclasm would foster Indian rebellion. Nevertheless, the missioners strove to instill fear in the natives by attacking their sacred objects, and so the priests themselves led the attacks. When churches were built atop ancient pyramids, e.g., at Cholula, the aim was not to build Christianity on a foundation of paganism, but rather to replace the one with the other, with the aim of burying paganism. The priests built church structures, administered sacraments, instructed neophytes, and solidified their authority within the society of New Spain; they also attacked Aztec religion frontally.

According to the notions of the Christian right of conquest, the Spaniards had control of Mexico, and their rule was Christian; hence, it was deemed correct that the priests baptize as many infants and youths as possible as the first step toward conversion. As the priests suppressed public paganism, they also encouraged Indian parents to bring them their children for the Christian ritual of initiation. At all hours the Indians came. On some days Pedro de Gante baptized as many as ten thousand. One famous evangelist, Motolinía (Fray Toribio de Benavente), claimed over three hundred thousand native baptisms by his hands. Bishop Zumarraga wrote in 1531 that the Franciscans had already baptized one and a half million Indians only a decade after Cortés' victory. Another Franciscan declared in 1536 that over four million Mexican Indians had received the sacrament under the dictates of the Requirement. Most of these baptisms occurred prior to religious instruction, and whatever efficacy was delivered through the sacramental grace, no one could suggest that these Indians yet understood Christian doctrines or possessed intelligent Christian faith. More likely, the Aztecs were pledging ritual allegiance to the conquering powers, something people in their area of the New World had always done. They were probably accepting *"into their religion"*

(Klor de Alva 1993: 178, emphasis his) the Christian supernatural evoked in the ritual of baptism.

Having baptized millions, the Franciscans either insinuated themselves into Indian towns or established villages of evangelization where the populations could be concentrated to increase the efficiency of instruction. With a few notable exceptions, the Indians of Mexico lived in small communities rather than cities, and the priests needed to cluster them in order to reach their numbers on a regular basis. In general, "the Spaniards organized their American colonies as kingdoms, each with two republics in it: a 'republic of Spaniards' in the cities and a 'republic of Indians' in the countryside, where every effort was made to resettle them in townlike population units called *reducciones*" (Marzal 1993: 140).

The Franciscan missionary method was a strategy well conceived, consciously planned, taught in their seminaries, and refined over time. It consisted of a period of *entrada*, in which the friars "sought to dazzle natives with showy vestments, music, painting, statuary of sacred images, and ceremonies" (Weber 1992: 107). The priests gave gifts to the Indians in displays of generosity, establishing reciprocal relationships. After winning confidence, the friars sought to place themselves at the center of Indian social life, persuading the natives to build them a friary and church. From these parish centers (*cabeceras*) the missionaries set up *visitas* around the periphery of their territory, which in time might become missions with their own resident priests. Within each village the Franciscans attempted to win the loyalty of native leaders and make the children "their own" (ibid., 108), thus undermining the social order by being both authorities and sources of goods.

The Franciscans tried to conduct their missions peaceably so as not to arouse the question of scandal, and they tried to shield the Indians from the worst abuses of encomienda, while at the same time working with the civil authorities of New Spain. Franciscan missionaries such as Motolinía, Bernardino de Sahagún, and Gerónimo de Mendieta added their voices to those of other sixteenth-century Catholic theologians, Fray Antonio de Montesinos, Bartolomé de Las Casas, and Francisco de Vitoria, among others, in forwarding the notion of Indian humanity to their Spanish contemporaries. Las Casas was the most famous defender of the Indians. Due to his persistent efforts in the Americas and in Spain, encomienda came to be replaced by the system of reducciones, and knowledge of Spanish cruelties against Indians gained worldwide currency. His message struck chords among the mendicant orders working directly with Indian populations throughout New Spain.

The mendicant missionaires may have idealized poverty, but they had a "sizable state apparatus" (ibid., 111) at their disposal: Catholic patronage, military support, Crown subsidies, and supplies of wealth. Forced conversions were bad theology and bad policy—even the Requirement did not promote it—but soldiers were present to protect the padres at all times and places, not only in central Mexico but extending into the hinterlands. Some friars may have displayed ascetic virtues—wearing only coarse robes, sleeping on rough boards, going without wine or meat in sympathy with the Indians they served—but the missions themselves often accumulated sizeable fortunes through stock-raising and agriculture. The churches built by the missionized Indians were usually impressive and sometimes even magnificent structures, reflecting the grandeur of the Church and symbolizing the power of the priests who controlled them.

In the missions the mendicants ruled, and they seized control of the Indians' lives while establishing evangelization villages. Technically the Indians of Mexico were not forced to become Christians, not even by the Requirement. Yet Christian authorities were given the right to destroy temples and superimpose Christian structures. Indian children had to attend instruction and the Indians could not prevent missionary activity from taking place. Once baptized, the Indians lost their freedom of movement, and friars enforced their rules with whips and stockades, assigning punishments to be carried out by soldiers and native helpers appointed by the missionaries. On occasion the friars applied the lash themselves. At least one friar had himself scourged in public and then threw himself on coals to show the Indians how much the fires of hell would hurt them, making an object lesson of himself. Even before the conquest of Mexico the bishops of the Indies possessed the authority of the Inquisition, which until 1575 (when Indians were officially exempted from its punishments) was employed against Indian and Spaniard alike. In 1539 Bishop Zumarraga condemned to death by burning an educated Indian named Don Carlos Chichimectocotl, accused of conspiring against Catholic priests and Christianity. In the same year royal and ecclesiastical edicts forbade local priests from using rods and irons against the Indians "to teach them the

Christian doctrine" (in Ricard 1966: 96), but the friars saw physical punishment as a tool toward conversion, and they used it.

The Franciscans focused instruction upon the youths—especially the sons of the native aristocracy—as a means of building a future Church, but also of influencing the adults. If one could make the youths zealous, they would convert other youngsters, act as interpreters, and campaign in their own households against pagan practices. Some of these youths, including girls, became active evangelists. Some even initiated violence against native religious practitioners; for example, a group of children stoned a native priest to death, proclaiming that "He was not a man but a devil, and God and St. Mary helped us give him the punishment he deserved" (in Braden 1930: 167). One of the first "martyrs of faith in Mexico" (ibid., 168) was Niño Cristobal, a boy whose father kicked and beat him to death because the boy destroyed pagan idols at the instigation of Church authorities. Such was the militant nature of catechetical instruction in sixteenth-century Mexico.

The Mexican Church administered baptism immediately to the Indians without concern for lengthy instruction. A synod of 1535 tried to slow the process, insisting upon instruction, at least in rudimentary form, before christening. The publication of the papal bull *Sublimus deus* in 1537 underscored the necessity of instructing rational, ensouled Indians in Christian doctrine. At the least Indians were required to believe in one God, creator of heaven and earth and of man (soul and body); original sin; the divinity of Jesus Christ; heaven and hell; good and bad angels; and subjection of humans to the pope and the temporal authorities. Neophytes were to declare themselves against traditional Indian religion, and they were to memorize the essential prayers and catechetical lists of Catholicism: the sign of the cross, the Apostles' Creed, the Lord's Prayer, the *Ave Maria*, *Salve Regina*, the ten Commandments of God and five of the Church, seven sacraments, the seven deadly sins, eight beatitudes, the cardinal works of mercy (corporal and spiritual), and the like.

Some instructors led the Indians through their lessons with arguments against traditional religious beliefs, such as reverence for the sun, moon, and stars. These celestial objects obey the will of God, declared the priests, and He is the Prime Mover, the Creator, the Author of laws and the Rewarder and Punisher. This led to the discussion of heaven and hell, and the immortality of the soul. Missionaries often

used paintings to illustrate the horrors of hell, the protection by angels, and the temptations by devils (see Ricard 1966: 106–107). The
catechisms in New Spain offered little that differed from those in
Spain, except to counteract what the clerics perceived as a natural tendency toward idolatry, the worship of worldly objects, among the natives. For advanced students the Spanish missioners established
schools in order to train Indian teachers. Sahagún was on the faculty at
Santa Cruz; he and his confreres needed to guide their students carefully through their lessons, because there was always a danger that Indians would discover in the Old Testament justifications for human
sacrifice, polygamy, and other forbidden practices. Catechism consisted of circumscribing, as well as advancing, religious knowledge.

Sahagún's instructional sermons (*Pláticas*) contain a graphic depiction of the missionary message to the Mexican Indians in the sixteenth
century, one worth citing at some length. He quotes his fellow missionaries in their speeches to the Mexican nobles:

> Do not believe that we are gods. Fear not, we are men as you are. We
> are only messengers sent to you by a great lord called the Holy Father,
> who is the spiritual head of the world, and who is filled with pain and
> sadness by the state of your souls. These are the souls he has charged us
> to search out and save. We desire nothing better, and for that reason we
> bring you the book of the Holy Scriptures, which contains the words of
> the only true God, Lord of heaven and earth, whom you have never
> known. This is why we have come. (In Ricard 1966: 86)

Sahagún was famous in his own day—and infamous as an alleged liberal among the most conservative Spanish circles of Church and
Crown—for his careful ethnological recording of Aztec religious traditions. In the present day his works are considered authoritative in their
understanding of Aztec cosmology and ritualism. Nevertheless, Sahagún clearly differentiated between Aztec and Christian beliefs and
modes of devotion, and he attempted to prevent syncretism between
the two:

> You have a god, you say, whose worship has been taught to you by your
> ancestors and your kings. Not so! You have a multitude of gods, each
> with his function. And you yourselves recognize that they deceive you;
> you insult them when you are unhappy, . . . And what they demand of
> you in sacrifice is your blood, your heart. Their images are loathsome.
> On the other hand . . . the true and universal God, Our Lord, Creator
> and Dispenser of being and life, as we have been telling you in our ser-
> mons, has a character different from that of your gods. He does not de-

ceive; He lies not; He hates no one, despises no one; there is nothing evil in Him. He regards all wickedness with the greatest horror, forbids it and interdicts it, for He is perfectly good. He is the deep well of all good things; He is the essence of love, compassion, and mercy. And he showed His infinite mercy when he made Himself Man here on earth, like us; humble and poor, like us. He died for us and spilled His precious blood to redeem us and free us from the power of evil spirits. This true God is called Jesus Christ, true God and true Man, Dispenser of being and life, Redeemer and Savior of the world. Being God, He has no beginning; He is eternal. He created heaven and earth and hell. He created us, all the men in the world, and He also created the devils whom you hold to be gods and whom you call gods. This true God is everywhere; He sees all, knows all; He is altogether admirable. As Man, He is in His royal palace, and here below, on earth, He has His Kingdom, which He began with the beginning of the world. He would have you enter it now, and for this you should consider yourself blessed. (In ibid., 86–87)

Sahagún stated that no one is capable of entering the heavenly kingdom without becoming a subject of God's kingdom on earth, the Catholic Church, and receiving its sacraments.

Of course baptism initiated Indians to the life of the Church and opened the way for other sacraments: penance, Holy Eucharist, confirmation, matrimony, extreme unction, and on the rarest of occasions, holy orders. In addition, Mexican neophytes took part in Catholic ritualism and pageantry apart from the core sacraments.

In 1526 the Franciscans initiated confessions among the Indians, who took to them with enthusiasm and pious regularity. On Sundays the padres gathered the new Christians to review their catechetical instruction and prepare for individual confessions. They learned of repentance, acknowledgment of sins, and restitution as the three necessary steps leading to the remission of sins. They examined their consciences with the help of sin lists—which developed into *confesionarios*, full-fledged guides to the sacrament of penance, employing pictures as well as words—and confessed their sins regularly, especially during Lent, before marriage, and when ill. "Sometimes," it is said (Braden 1930: 233), "they made their confessions in writing, which . . . had been done in their confession to the pagan goddess." Perhaps drawing upon their native traditions, the Indians performed the penances required of them with fervor. In particular they were reported to have sought scourging for their sins (see Ricard 1966: 116–122), as corporal punishment made sense to them as Indians as well as Christians.

The *confesionarios* prepared by the padres took a special interest in Indians' sexuality, directing the priests to ask the Indians if they engaged in sodomy, homosexuality, bestiality, and incest (see Guerra 1971: 236–239), and if so, to confess these acts as sins to be forgiven. Fundamentally, the confesionarios' purpose was explicitly to remind the natives that, "whoever you are, . . . in order for you to gain eternal life, it is necessary that you know and remember that you are a sinner in the eyes of our Lord" (in Klor de Alva 1993: 192). To a large extent, these guides presented the indigenous Indian culture as particularly sinful, adding the burden of Indianness to that of humanness as a source of alienation from God (see Burkhart 1989: 18–19). Even if the Indians did not initially accept the Christian notion of innate human sinfulness, they often became convinced that they themselves—as Indians—were in personal need of confession and forgiveness.

The Spanish were certain that the Mexican Indians were in dire need of baptism and penance, the sacraments designed to remove the stain of innate sinfulness and actual sins; there was less certainty that Indians should be granted the grace of Holy Eucharist. In the sixteenth century many churchmen feared that Indians were too new as Christians, too imbued with native paganism, to deserve such intimate contact with God. Despite the papal bull of Paul III, Indians were often denied communion, even when they asked for it. Other Church representatives argued that communion is a remedy as well as a reward; it grants grace necessary to all sinners. Why should a priest deny such grace to a baptized Christian who confessed sins and seemed sincere in the practice of the faith? When Indians were granted communion, reception of the sacrament took place infrequently, perhaps only once a year during Eastertide, in keeping with European practice of the time.

Confirmation was not much administered in Mexico in the sixteenth century; neither was extreme unction, the sacrament for the sick and dying. Priests paid such sacramental calls only in the cases of chiefs, whose social status was deemed worthy of such attention. On the other hand, in 1526 the priests began to introduce Christian marriage, the sacrament of matrimony, among the natives. Church rules stipulated that couples to be married should be baptized; their banns should be announced; and there should be certainty that they were not relatives, nor minors, nor slaves, nor already married. In order to receive the sacrament of matrimony the partners should exercise their free will and not be coerced.

The greatest difficulty in instituting Christian matrimony among Mexican Indians was the matter of plural marriage, especially among those men of high standing. Polygamy was not only acceptable to the Indians but a necessary aspect of their economic and social systems. Officers of the Church could not condone plural marriage, but they had to exercise patience in eradicating it. The Church discovered that it could not insist that men give up all but one of their wives because their responsibilities to their spouses were too great; hence, the hope was that over time the younger generations of men would take no more than one spouse.

In the sixteenth century the Church did not permit any full-blooded Mexican Indians to become priests, regarding the natives as perpetual neophytes incapable of the sanctification necessary for holy orders. Indian men were allowed to serve as stewards, brothers, porters, exorcists, readers, acolytes, teachers, and interpreters, but even chiefs were not granted the elevation of sacerdotal office. By the turn of the seventeenth century there were some mestizos who took holy orders, and in the seventeenth century several Indians became secular clergy and members of the mendicant orders. Throughout the colonial period the numbers were few; holy orders remained a sacrament denied to almost all Mexican Indians.

Though the Spanish Catholic Church denied the priesthood to Mexican Indians, they were encouraged to engage actively in a variety of ritual activities in hope of fascinating them with the aesthetic, performative aspects of Christianity. In the teaching of the catechism, friars of New Spain used singing and pictorial representations to get across their lessons. Fray Pedro de Gante attracted the resisting Aztec adults to Church services by emphasizing dances and dramas. He also composed a whole catechism in pictures. Sahagún, Gerónimo de Mendieta, and other Franciscans employed such pictorial catechisms, and everywhere singing enhanced the memorization of lessons. To some extent these techniques constituted a deliberate accommodation to native culture and sensibility; on the other hand, every attempt was made to replace pagan songs with Christian music and lyrics, pagan ritualism with dramas illustrating triumphal Christian themes, and a pagan calendar with the Christian liturgical rounds. The missionaries discovered that the Indians responded to processions, plays, and pageants, and these were seen as suitable expressions of Christianity in the churches, the mission yards, and in the cemeteries. The friars also taught the Indians how to play numerous musical instruments, and they organized notable church choirs. Pedro de Gante introduced confraternities among the Indian Christians, and these bodies were given charge of the processional and dramatic activities on holy days, and especially during Holy Week.

The Spaniards employed the Passion Play as a means of exciting American Indian interest in Catholic ideas: the contest between good and evil, Christ and anti-Christ; the redemption of humanity by Jesus' sacrifice on the Cross; and the temporal contest between infidels and the universal Church. Moreover, the missioners reenacted the "Moors and Christians" dance drama in order to celebrate the 1492 Spanish conquest in Granada, but also by extension, the Spanish conquest of the Aztecs themselves. *Los Moros y Cristianós*, performed in Mexico as early as 1538, contained mock battles to celebrate Santiago's leadership of the Christian forces; Pilate was usually the leader of the Moors. The Christians always triumphed for all the Indians to see.

The Spaniards also introduced *Los Matachines*, a dance that memorialized the supposed conversion of Montezuma to Catholicism through the agency of La Malinche and the Blessed Virgin Mary. In sixteenth-century Europe the *matachin* was a grotesquerie performed with mask and sword, whose name (*mat*, death; *chin*, Chinese) signified an aggressive burlesque of foreigners. In New Spain the evangelizers used dancers of this name to symbolize spiritual victory over the natives; however, the Indians made their own meanings of the ceremony and created indigenous troupes that performed Los Matachines for their local purposes.

The missionaries knew how much the Indians of Mexico were accustomed to dance and sing in their traditional religions, but could these aesthetic desires be fulfilled in Christian worship without encouraging the persistence of pagan gestures and words? Just as Christian churches were superimposed on ancient temples, Christian dances and pageants had to replace pagan ones. There was the additional danger that the Indians would come to think of the pageants—rather than the mass and the other sacraments—as the core rituals of Christianity. Hence, the ceremonial displays had to be limited, and every attempt had to be made to assure clerical control over Catholic ritual life.

The Spaniards had defeated the Aztecs, and energetic missionaries now entered the evangelical field. There they found similarities between their own Christianity and the religions of the Native Ameri-

cans, and they also found seeming willingness on the part of the Indians to adopt Christian ritual and catechetical forms. With the financial
and military support of the Spanish government, the early missioners
had high hopes for a conversion of New Spain. Hence, they baptized
millions during the first decade, and although the natives may not
have understood the import of the sacramental initiation, nor the
meanings of Christian theology, there was an apparent spirit of submission and self-sacrifice that impressed the friars.

At the same time some factors hindered conversions, not the least
of which was the violent mistreatment of Indians at the hands of the
Spanish conquerors. The fact that the Spaniards referred to themselves
as Christians for many generations thereafter, reserving the nomenclature of mestizo or "Indian" for those natives who converted to Christianity, gave Christianity a racial tinge in the minds of the Indians.
Considering the gross immorality and cruelty of the Spanish (i.e., the
Christians), Indians "came to abhor not only the name Christian but
also the name of Christ himself" (Braden 1930: 213). As a result, many
Indians resisted conversion, even while going through the motions of
baptism and instruction.

THE EFFECTS

In the 1530s the Spanish missionaries were hopeful that Indian religiousness in Mexico would lend itself to christianization; however, by the 1550s the Spanish derided the natives as feeble-minded, because they had not taken to Christian theology as it had been hoped. Paternalism became more entrenched as Indians were more regarded as incapable of Christian life on their own. They were said to be inconstant, prone to evil, weak, and incapable of the priesthood. For these Indians Christianity was perhaps a veneer over their pagan core, or so the friars said. The early euphoria led to disappointment by the second half of the sixteenth century, and the Indians' image did not recover among the Spanish missionaries. Sahagún and his fellows began to report that there was "a level of native ignorance, indifference, and resistance to the teachings of the Church that suggested few if any adults were true believers" (Klor de Alva 1993: 174). There was talk in Spanish circles that perhaps the friars had accommodated themselves too much to Indian culture—Sahagún's ethnological writings were suspect in this regard—and the call came to repress "widespread idolatry" (Cervantes 1994: 16) that, according to the friars, bordered on diabolism. In 1562 the discovery of covert Indian cultic activity at one of the missionary centers in the Yucatan brought down an inquisition that killed 158 Indians and crippled many others. Fray Diego de Landa, the Franciscan in charge of the interrogations, justified his actions as appropriate measures against devil worship. By the early 1570s the Crown was ready to close down the missions and turn the Indians over to the secular clergy in central Mexico in order to combat native spirituality. In 1573 the Royal Orders for New Discoveries recommended that the religious orders serve in a pacification of new lands and peoples on the rim of New Spain, pushing out the frontiers to what is now Florida, New Mexico, California, and elsewhere. What they had accomplished so far among the Aztecs, Mayans, and other groups in the initial conquest areas was considered problematic.

Part of the problem was the missioners themselves. They argued amongst themselves, and many refused to learn or were incapable of learning, Indian languages in order to conduct meaningful instruction. Although some priests were protectors of Indians against Spanish cruelty, many others earned infamy as abusers of their charges. One bishop wrote in 1561 that the priestly orders in Mexico "have inflicted and are now inflicting many mistreatments upon the Indians, with great haughtiness and cruelty, for when the Indians do not obey them, they insult and strike them, tear out their hair, have them stripped and cruelly flogged, and then throw them into prison in chains and cruel irons, a thing most pitiable to hear about and much more pitiable to see" (in Ricard 1966: 244). Clerical scandals of greed, lust, and violence did little to win the Indians of Mexico to the Catholic faith. It is said that "the Christianity of the sixteenth century in Spain had little moral content. The clergy were, many of them, corrupt and licentious. It is not probable that the life of the people generally was any better, and more than likely it was worse" (Braden 1930: 253) under Spanish rule than it had been under the Aztecs.

The missionaries of the sixteenth century did introduce many new items of material culture to the Indians: horses, asses, pigs, dogs, sheep, wheat, barley, rice, grapes, olives, sugar cane, date palms, figs, pomegranates, apples, pears, plums, peaches, apricots, quinces, mulberries, oranges, lemons, limes, bananas, and other agricultural bounty. They introduced tailoring, sewing, embroidery, weaving, carpentry, and other aspects of mission occupation and architecture. They established schools and taught Latin, Spanish, reading, writing, math, and Christian doctrine. They taught Indians how to play European instruments: flutes, organs, flageolets, alpine horns, guitars, cornets, bassoons, trombones, and kettledrums, and they instructed them in Christian hymnody (see Van Well 1942: 16–18). Thus, they helped fill the Indians' world with new associations and occupations. But what effect did they have on the natives' religious lives?

Naturally the Indians at first interpreted Christianity through their own worldviews. Here were strange conquerors whose demands had to be met to some degree and whose ways had to be accommodated. Some might avoid the Christian priests for a time, but not indefinitely. A visible Catholicism took shape: churches were built as temples were destroyed; ceremonies, sodalities, tithes, catechisms, and ecclesiastical institutions were all set up alongside *encomienda*. The traditional priesthoods and their sacrificial systems were outlawed. The Indians were required to embrace the Christian forms, at least in public. However, at least the adults of the first generation persisted in honoring their own deities and living according to their own values while appearing to accept Christian teachings. They put their idols at the foot of crosses, the friars reported, "so that while they appeared to adore the cross, they were really adoring the demon" (in Braden 1930: 251).

Over time the range of Indian responses to missionizing included all of the following (see Klor de Alva 1982: 351–352; McDowell 1987: 319; and Weber 1992: 115–121): Some adopted a Christian worldview, identifying elements of Christianity as equivalent or complementary to analogous elements of the aboriginal religions. This adoption of Christian elements might result in a complete conversion to Christianity, in which Christian doctrines were believed and understood, and in which participation in Christian rituals and associations replaced those of the pagan traditions. For most Indians of this sort, however, conversion did not rule out the observance of indigenous customs, at least those considered inoffensive to Christian authorities. For other Indians the process of conversion remained incomplete. They were impressed with the claims of Christianity but did not understand them adequately, or understood them according to indigenous premise. These incomplete converts participated in Christian rituals but without giving up fully their aboriginal ceremonialism. Some of these Indians separated and compartmentalized their native and Christian religious forms, participating in one, then the other, according to need and situation, and using the two systems of explanation alternatingly. In some of these cases the Christian attack on native religiousness weakened the authority of the traditional system without providing a convincing case for Christianity; for these people anomie resulted as they tried to live their lives between a disfigured past and an unsatisfying present. Some Indians went through the motions of conversion but were indifferent to Christian theology and participated in Christian rituals only casually. Still others resisted Christianity more fully, either refusing baptism or acquiescing in the most minimal forms while continuing to engage actively in paganism, and in some instances working toward rebellion against their conquerors. Among all those who received Christian baptism there was the chance of apostasy, turning back toward native belief and cult, or abandoning religiousness altogether. Having compared the traditional religions and Christianity, many Christian converts engaged in nativism, openly and even violently, proclaiming the superiority of their aboriginal gods and rituals. Finally, many Mexican Indians came, consciously and unconsciously, to join together the elements of the aboriginal and Christian traditions into a syncretistic pattern of religious life (see *Nativism and Syncretism* 1960: 192–196), the controlling efforts of missionaries notwithstanding.

The intermixture of Aztec and Christian elements occurred through various processes and produced various alloys. Catholic priests used Aztec pictographs to teach the Indians Christian theology. Indians filled churches with images of saints who delivered miracles, as the gods had done in the olden days. Aztecs took a Christian name at baptism, but also the name of the Aztec god upon whose day they were born. When a Catholic feast took place, it was also fitted to the Aztec calendar, and Aztec gods were worshipped through the Christian calendar. Catholic saints and Aztec gods were fused in conception and iconography, e.g., St. Anne (the mother of the Virgin Mary), whom the Indians associated with the Goddess Toci (the grandmother of the Aztec gods). On Christian holy days, such as All Saints, the Indians offered sacrifices of wild animals, continuing ancient Aztec practices, and the Day of the Dead, celebrated throughout Mexico, combined precontact rituals and Spanish Catholicism, as the folk commemorated their ancestors, both Indian and European, in a religiousness not strictly pagan and not strictly Catholic, but a fresh evolving combination of the two traditions.

In the realm of ethics the Christian missionaries condemned the Aztec emphasis on sacrifice and ritual observance. The Indians felt that a person's primary obligation in life was to provide the gods with blood and hearts by fighting, dying, and sacrificing human beings. The Indians tried to avoid sickness, drought, pests, poverty, sterility, bad luck—basically anything that got in the way of their individual and communal happiness—by sacrificing to the gods ritually. The friars attempted to teach a thoroughgoing ethics based upon the Ten Commandments and expostulated in catechetical formulas. The priests taught the seven virtues (faith, hope, love, justice, prudence, courage, and temperance), the seven sins (false pride, avarice, lust, gluttony, envy, vengeful anger, and despair); and they encouraged the natives to engage in acts of mercy, such as feeding the hungry. Above all, they attempted to get Indians to think of themselves as inherently sinful, in dire need of moral regeneration through the Church and its sacraments in order to gain eternal salvation with God in heaven. After baptism the Indians were supposed to recognize their sinfulness through

examinations of conscience; confess their sins to priests; engage in
penitential acts; and above all, to feel contrition for one's behavior, indeed one's very being. In order to receive priestly absolution and
God's forgiveness, the Indians were to experience their personal culpa-
bility before God and to seek His mercy (see Madsen 1957: 130–131;
Klor de Alva 1993: 183–194). In becoming Christians, the Indians of
Mexico engaged in the rituals of christening and confession, and they
accepted the sacrificial nature of penitential acts; however, it is not
clear that they accepted the notion of original sin and human sinfulness. They fitted some of their behavior to Christian teachings, but not
necessarily with a concomitant change of heart, as they persisted in
sacrificial rites.

Louise M. Burkhart (1989) argues that the Christian missionaries
among the Nahuatl speakers of Mexico in the sixteenth century, in
their attempt to translate Christian moral terms into Indian languages,
made it possible for the natives to appropriate Christianity as "their
own" (44), in ways that the mendicants could not realize immediately.
In spite of systematic catechisms, in spite of Bishop Zumarraga's warnings against metaphorical translation and instruction, in spite of the
friars' intense distaste for Aztec spirituality, the process of employing
Nahuatl words to convey Christian ethics meant that Nahuatl meanings persisted.

Burkhart shows that the preachers' instructional terminology for
"sin" (Latin, *peccatum*; Spanish *pecado*)—the Nahuatl word *tlatlacolli*—
carried not only the Christian notion of immorality, but also traditional Aztec notions of damage, spoil, or harm. It could mean a
weaver tangling threads, a warrior erring in battle, a singer failing to
harmonize, a mouse gnawing garments, or hail harming crops. A person could damage someone's heart by offending them; slaves were
damaged by their servitude. Sexual excesses, intoxications, and theft
could also be depicted as tlatlacolli; so could a dislocated bone, a
woman in the later stages of pregnancy, a rotten egg, or spoiled maize.
In short, the Nahuatl term connoted the effects of action, rather than
the intentionality implied in the Christian notion of sin. Hence, a slippery conflation occurred between concepts of immorality and acciden-
tal damage.

The aim of the Christian teaching was to make Indians (indeed, all
humans) aware of their innate and voluntary sinfulness, their transgressions of divine law, so that the sinners would feel contrition and

seek God's forgiveness. The Nahuatl speakers were concerned about the effects of damage—their traditional sacrifices and ritual compulsions attempted to avoid or undo those effects in this world—but they did not accept the Christian notion of human ontological depravity before God. By focusing upon sin, the padres hoped to convert them to a Christian moral view; however, by using the Nahuatl term tlatlacolli the Indians persisted in their traditional concerns without adopting Christian concepts of guilt. The Nahuas cared about the cosmic struggle between order and chaos. Order contained chaos; chaos was part of the universal order. Things died and decayed, and their rotting fed and fertilized the future. The Indians believed in promoting order but also allowing for chaos, while all the time attempting to protect oneself against the damage wrought by chaos. Christianity possessed a different axis between moral absolutes of good and evil. Nahuas made ritual sacrifices against chaos, payments to restore order at critical moments, but they did not believe in evil as Christians did. By translating Christian moral terminology into Nahuatl, the friars were forced to use terms that connoted the axis of order and disorder rather than that of good and evil. The thrust of the Christian message was lost in the translation, according to Burkhart's reconstruction of the sixteenth-century dialogue.

In the same way, she demonstrates, the missionaries validated the existence of aboriginal deities by calling them devils; baptism and confession reinforced traditional concepts of pollution and purification; the centrality of sacrifice as a model of human activity persisted through the Christian focus upon Jesus on the Cross. Consequently, the Indians of Mexico "were able to become just Christian enough to get by in the colonial social and political setting without compromising their basic ideological and moral orientation" (ibid., 184).

Unable to take apart basic Indian convictions, the Spanish tried to alter behavior. The missionaries knew how much the Indians of Mexico engaged in dances as part of their religious expression. As a result the padres attempted to fashion Christian dances that would fulfil traditional aesthetic desires, while expressing Christian doctrines. Pre-contact tunes, dance steps, costumes, and musical instruments became part of these "native dances" (Braden 1930: 286), although in many cases the Indians adapted European instruments and steps, such as the violin and the quadrille, as part of their sacred ritual paraphernalia, sometimes outside of church, sometimes within. The Christian authorities attempted to replace Indian dances with Christian choreography, as the Christian calendar was superimposed upon the Aztec one; however, remnants of traditional calendars, gestures, and meanings persisted.

The most famous of the introduced pageants were *Los Moros y Cristianós*, the mock combats between Christians and the Moors, staged as a celebration of Santiago in his legendary role at the battle of Clavijo. In conquering the Aztecs the Spaniards called upon Santiago, considering their conquest of the pagans a continuation of their victory over the Moors. Celebrating his feast day (July 25) was a means by which Christians reminded the Indians of their subordination to Christian rule. At the same time, the Indians became fond of the conquering saint and soon came to regard him as their defender and protector of their animal flocks. They made him their own, as they made Christianity their own.

The priests worried that in introducing these pageants the Indians would come to regard them—rather than the mass—as the essential liturgy of Christianity. The missionaries attempted to limit the frequency of these dances; however, Indians persisted in performing them, especially in the absence of priests, and in staging them on their own they usurped the ritual authority of the Catholic Church and created their own syncretistic ritual life. In such a manner "the clergy was defeated little by little" (Ricard 1966: 187).

Even in the celebrations of Christ's passion, death, and resurrection during Easter week—ritual acts common throughout Spain and containing the core of Christian belief concerning the role of Jesus in salvation—Indian communities shaped the activities to fit their local ritualism and to express indigenous ideas and values. Indians translated and transformed these Passion Plays, sometimes combining them with hunting and farming themes, sometimes identifying Jesus with their traditional heroes, and often identifying Judas and the enemies of Jesus with the conquering Spaniards (the Spanish portrayed Judas as a Moor). Such a process of ritual syncretism began in the sixteenth century and continued through the centuries, as Indians came to identify themselves as Christians without ceasing to identify themselves as Indians under Christian siege (see Nash 1968; Crumrine 1970).

The most prominent feature of syncretic Mexican Catholicism by the close of the sixteenth century was the devotionalism surrounding Our Lady of Guadalupe, a cult grounded in Spanish Catholicism, promulgated (but also opposed) by missionaries, and elaborated through Indian worshippers. In succeeding centuries the devotion to Our Lady of Guadalupe became a matter of Mexican identity and national religion.

One of the ways that pre-Columbian religion persisted among Mexican Indians was the proliferation of many virgins, each one supposedly Mary the Mother of Jesus, each carrying out the powers and symbolism of ancient deities: Our Lady of the Mists, Our Lady of the Rains, etc. In such a way local and Earth goddesses combined with the Virgin Mary as sources of earthly and spiritual redemption. The virginal cults, like those devoted to patron saints, joined Christian and Indian elements in a creative syncretism. The Virgin Mary was a central icon of the conquest, universally known to the Spanish and famous among the Indians, too. Associated with the flower world, she became a beloved intercessor (to Nature, to God) for the Indians, as the missionaries encouraged Marian devotions throughout the Christian calendar.

As in everything, the missionaries attempted to direct Indian devotions toward the True God and away from traditional deities. At the same time, they wanted to employ patterns of traditional worship, if those patterns could lead efficaciously to Christian worship. It was not clear to all the padres that Marian devotions led Indians from paganism and toward orthodox Christianity; hence, Church authorities were torn between encouraging the Christian devotion to Our Lady and discouraging the cult of the virgin because it seemed a continuation of pagan cults. In regard to Our Lady of Guadalupe it is still not clear to what degree the cult was a means of weaning the Indians from their paganism toward Christianity and to what degree it was a means of the Indians' continuing their traditional worship in the guise of Christianity (see Ricard 1966: 187–193).

Legend has it that in 1531 a poor Nahua neophyte named Juan Diego (Cuauhtlatohuac, or "Speaking Eagle," as he is known today among Nahuatl speakers) was on his way to Christian instruction when he heard singing on the hilltop Tepeyac near Mexico City. There he saw a noblewoman who spoke to him in Nahuatl, identifying herself as the Virgin Mary, mother of the True God. She sent the man to the bishop of Mexico—said to be the newly arrived Franciscan Juan de Zumarraga—to report her appearance.

The bishop, it says, did not take him seriously and told him to come back another day. Juan Diego returned to the hilltop and the Virgin ordered him to return to the bishop, who now questioned him carefully and told him to bring a sign from Mary. But Juan Diego's uncle was sick, and he had to go to get a priest to hear his last confession. On his way, the noblewoman appeared again and told him his uncle was cured. For a sign, she told him to gather flowers on the hilltop where she had first appeared. He gathered roses (in December, at a spot where no flowers grew!) and placed them in his *tilma*, a long peasant cloak. When he opened his cloak for the bishop to see, there was the image of Mary on it: the Perpetual Virgin as pictured in *Revelation* 12: 1, with the moon beneath her feet and rays of sunlight surrounding her body. The bishop, according to the legend, repented his skepticism, the uncle was found in good health, and so a shrine was established on the hilltop. Over the years the shrine became a church, then a great pilgrimage basilica, as miracles blessed the spot from that day.

There is no doubt about the central role of Our Lady of Guadalupe in Mexican religious life. In 1976 a new basilica was completed at Guadalupe, replacing the 300-year-old pilgrimage church; annually over six million visitors come to the church. In 1990 Juan Diego was beatified by Pope John Paul II on a pastoral visit to Mexico. It was only in the eighteenth century, however, that the Virgin was made patroness of Mexico; only in 1754 did Pope Benedict XIV officially recognize the feast day (December 12) of Our Lady of Guadalupe as part of the Church calendar in Mexico. In 1810 the creole parish priest, Miguel Hidalgo, identified Our Lady of Guadalupe with the cause of Mexican independence from Spain, making her a mantle of patriotism in Mexico. A century later in 1910, Emiliano Zapata, of Nahuatl descent, again used her image as a banner in creating the modern nation of Mexico. In his revolution the Virgin became emblem of the poor in a class struggle against the wealthy. Hence, only over time did she come to represent Mexico as she does today.

Today proponents of liberation theology appropriate her legendary appearance to Juan Diego as a signal of social reversal; she honored the humble man just as Jesus favors the poor in their struggles (San Bernardino 1990). Mexican nationalists look to her as a symbol of their statehood with its roots in Spanish and Indian cultures (Carrasco 1990: 138). American Indian Catholics refer to her as a "pregnant Native woman, pregnant with the Native Faith communities of the

Americas, pregnant with us" (*Tekakwitha Conference Newsletter*, September 1990: 1). It should not surprise us, therefore, that in the early years of her cult in Mexico she also served the diverse (and even contradictory) needs of various peoples in the complex interplay between Christianity and Mexican Indian religious traditions.

For the Spaniards of the sixteenth century, Our Lady of Guadalupe was already a familiar focus of cult, dating back centuries to the Iberian Guadalupe, where her shrine was already popular. The Spanish conquerors promoted her cult, and thus she served as a tool for the spiritual conquest of Mexico, a part of "religion in the formation and maintenance of colonial rule" (Taylor 1987: 10). For the Spanish, Mary was intercessor to a feared God and a sacrificed Jesus. She was associated with fertility and land; she brought rain; she defeated enemies. It was this Mary that the Mexican Indians adopted in the observances to Our Lady of Guadalupe.

On the other hand, it is often stated that her cult appeared at a site long associated with devotion to the pre-Columbian goddess Tonantzin, "Our Mother," who was said to be a fertility deity (Riding 1976: 10). According to this view, the Aztec Indians a decade after their military conquest sought continuity with their past patterns of worship by appealing to Our Lady in a place inhabited by the ancient goddess at Tepeyac. Thus, "the cult of Guadalupe, while strongly Catholic in meaning, also expresses an Indian sense of sacred space and worship of a goddess and her cults" (Carrasco 1990: 137). According to this view, the padres promoted the devotion to Our Lady of Guadalupe, but the Indians shaped it to their own syncretic purposes.

Recent studies (Burkhart 1993; Poole 1996) have historicized the legend of Juan Diego and the iconography of Our Lady of Guadalupe, indicating their medieval Spanish origins. Only in the seventeenth century was there a published version of the apparition legend, possibly grafted onto a cult that began in the 1550s at Tepeyac. Church officials preached in favor of—and against—the rites to the virgin at Tepeyac, and in 1576 Fray Sahagún was the first to write that the site of the Guadalupe cult had previously been an Aztec temple to the mother of the gods. He was disturbed with the suspicion that the Indians were really worshipping their aboriginal goddess in the guise of Marian devotion. At the same time other priests promoted the cult because it brought together various Indian groups into a single worship, focused in the national capital.

Was Tepeyac a spot for aboriginal goddess worship? Louise M. Burkhart suggests not. She states that "Tonantzin" was a reverential title used by the earliest Franciscans for Mary herself; there was no such Aztec deity by that name. "Thus," she writes (209), "the link between Our Lady of Guadalupe and any pre-Columbian goddess is, at best, tenuous. Tonantzin is Mary; Mary is Tonantzin." She argues that there is no evidence that an Aztec shrine existed underneath the church where Mary is now revered, and she emphasizes the role of Catholic missionaries in creating the Guadalupe cult—whatever traditional Indian patterns it may have drawn upon. There is no evidence of a historical Juan Diego; nor is there any evidence from diocesan records of an apparition in 1531. Such is the stuff of legends which have shaped the faith of Mexican Catholics, including Indians.

Over the centuries Indian Catholics in Mexico have looked to Our Lady of Guadalupe as their deliverer, and to Juan Diego as their representative before the appearance of the Holy. They have even regarded Mary as a symbol of liberation from the Spanish. At the same time the clergy have encouraged the mariolatry in order to bind Indians, mestizos, and Spaniards to the same Catholic faith. She has become a "protean image of motherhood, nourishment, health, salvation, and national identity" (Taylor 1987: 9). In the faith of Mexicans, "she is Indian and Spaniard. She is an Earth Mother and a Holy Mother. She is a comforter and a revolutionary" (Carrasco 1990: 138). She represents a syncretism begun in the sixteenth century and still in process.

Twentieth-century scholars have debated (e.g., Braden 1930, Carrasco 1990, Klor de Alva 1982 and 1993, Madsen 1957, Ricard 1966) the question of Mexican Indian religious identity, some arguing that the natives gradually became Christians (while maintaining some vestiges of aboriginal religiousness), others claiming a superficial Christian veneer over an essentially pre-Columbian core. Surely both patterns have taken place. For some Indians, "a Christian meaning was substituted for the pagan meaning" (Ricard 1966: 280), despite the survival of numerous pre-Christian gestures. For other Indians, particularly in the first century of contact, Christian monotheism and ethics were set aside as Christian structures were "'Nahuatized' by the Indians, who considered themselves genuine Christians even as they worshipped many spiritual beings, disregarded the significance of the teachings on salvation, and continued to make this-wordly ends the legitimate object of their religious devotion" (Klor de Alva 1993: 174).

A third pattern has also taken shape in Mexico in the meeting of Aztec and Christian traditions, especially with an enormous population of mestizos surviving and thriving: "due to the mutual interpenetration of the two types of religion which met in the conquest, the resultant religion is to a degree different from either of the original cults" (Braden 1930: 308). David Carrasco (1990) notes that in present-day Mexico there are widespread folk traditions that combine stories of Jesus with precontact mythic motifs as the people of Mexico have shaped their own religious narrative theology. Thus, the Christian and the Aztec are joined into something new. The "many colonial churchyard crosses that still stand in Mexico" (126) reflect pre-Columbian *and* Christian traditions, in combination: "these crosses are neither European nor Indian, but Mexican—a fluid syncretic image of new power, decoration, and combined meanings" (127).

It is not our task here to trace the complex history of Catholicism among all offspring of Mexican Indians from the sixteenth to the twentieth century. Rather, we are trying to gain an understanding of the main currents of Christian incursion in New Spain, particularly in the first century of conquest. We see that the patterns of missionizing throughout North America (indeed, throughout the hemisphere) were set into motion in New Spain: ideas of discovery, evangelization as a goal, Church and State paradoxes, syncretism, etc. The orthodox teachings of the earliest catechisms of the sixteenth century remain in force right up to the present day, at least until the 1960s. The whole period of five hundred years is of a single piece because of the singleness of Catholicism as an institution over the period.

We also see that by the end of the sixteenth century Franciscan theorists such as Gerónimo de Mendieta were already looking back on what they regarded as the Golden Age of the Indian Church in Mexico—the several decades following the arrival of the Twelve Franciscans—a time in which the padres hoped for the establishment of a millennial kingdom among the Indian Christians. Indeed, historians have concurred that the millennial expectations of the earliest missioners led to disappointments and recriminations against the Indians, who did not become perfect Christians, and who seemed to persist in pagan religious expressions. For Mendieta the New World had been "a laboratory in which the Christianity of the Old World could be perfected" (Phelan 1970: 77); however, by the seventeenth century the zeal of the Franciscans and other missionaries in New Spain started to wane in regard to Indian conversions. Secular clergy replaced the evangelicals and parish routine replaced missions. There was greater interest in the establishment of a Hispanic Church among Spaniards, mestizos, and Blacks, and mendicants were no longer trying to learn the Nahuatl language. The arrival of the Jesuits in 1572 led in time to reinvigorated frontier missions, and certain Franciscans continued to push to the periphery of New Spain to convert newly encountered Indian nations, but in the Central Valley of Mexico and in the Yucatan, the first decades of zealous missionizing gave way to the more subtle processes of adaptation in which Nahuatl and Mayan speakers were left to practice "their own version of Christianity" (Burkhart 1989: 18).

Ethnological reports in the twentieth century suggest that the patterns of syncretism that took place in the sixteenth century have continued into the present day. At least in Mexican Indian villages, sacrificial and penitential complexes, beliefs about pollution, and traditional notions of cosmic orientation have persisted. One study suggests the term "Christo-Paganism" (Madsen 1957: 111) to describe the folk Christianity that pervades the lives of Mexican Indians, like those of a certain contemporary village located in the southern part of the Valley of Mexico within the geographic realm of the Aztecs at the time of the Spanish conquest.

The people of this village—ancestors of Indians conquered by the Aztecs in the early fifteenth century and then conquered by the Christians in the sixteenth—acknowledge the Christian God as creator, but they retain the Aztec notion of multiple creations and destructions of the world. In their myths Guadalupe, the mother of God, protects the humans from His wrath at human sinfulness, preventing certain disasters in this world but allowing others. There is still Aztec fatalism and the notion of a final battle between God and the Devil, who struggle over the soul and destiny of every person. The Indians are constantly on the lookout for omens of their destiny; at the same time, they pray to saints and nature spirits to bring rain and fertility. San Francisco, the town patron, is the most beloved for his generosity, but he also disciplines offenders, particularly those who break their vows. In these Indians' cosmology there are three Christs, said to be brothers, each of whom has special powerful domains. A fourth Christ, associated with a cave to which the people make pilgrimage, is thought of as the crucified Jesus.

In the village ritual obligations are primary over ethical concerns. It is necessary to feed the dead, honor the saints, and prepare for Christ's birth. If one does not carry out ritual duties, supernatural beings will be angry and punish the whole community or the individual. Hence, the Aztec worldview is perpetuated, only now directed toward Christian saints, Christs, and other holy personages. They do not love the Christian God, nor do they think that He loves them. Proper behavior is considered in ritualistic, rather than ethical terms.

There is no resident Catholic priest. The local community appoints a prayermaker who leads rosaries and other prayers; a bellringer marks dawn, midday, and evening; church councils direct work on Church lands; and *mayordomos* are elected for the village fiesta on October 4th each year. The eight hundred Indians attend mass perhaps twice a month, when clerics visit from elsewhere, but the church is the focus for ritual activity throughout the year, including a blessing of seeds on February 2 (Candelaria), the fiesta for San Francisco on October 4, the celebration of the dead on November 1 and 2, and nine religious dramas in December reenacting the advent of Jesus. These Christian occasions have been fused with pagan supernaturalism to create a religion partially Christian, partially Indian.

Urban Indians of Mexico have surely been initiated more thoroughly in Christian forms and meanings than the rural inhabitants, and those who have been uprooted from their traditional villages have persisted less in aboriginal religious patterns. Mestizos have integrated the spiritual heritages of their combined ethnicity. As tens of thousands of these peoples have entered the United States in recent decades, they have brought with them at least vestiges of Indian spirituality within the folds of their Catholic identity.

The same is true of the more than one hundred thousand Mayans—mostly from Guatemala—who have entered the United States since 1980, settling in at least eight different dioceses along the rim of the Gulf of Mexico and the Pacific Ocean. Eighty percent of these Indians are Catholic, constituting perhaps the largest contingent of "Native American Catholics" (Thiel, May 17, 1994) in the United States. Like the Nahuatl speakers, the Mayans have intertwined their native and Christian religiousness over the centuries, making Christianity local to themselves in their struggles against the conquering Spanish (see Bricker 1981). One finds among the Mayans "survivals" (Oakes 1951) of Mayan ritualism, calendric observance, values, and worldviews, even though ostensibly they are Catholics. For them the mass is often an invocation of spirits, and the Cross represents as much their ancestry as it does Christ. As Donald E. Thompson has written (*Nativism and Syncretism* 1960: 5, 31):

> All the Maya of Middle America . . . are nominally Roman Catholic. Yet they retain much of their own paganism, and from the fusion of the two religions have arisen new rites and concepts which are neither the one nor the other. . . . Despite the crosses, saints, and seemingly Catholic prayers, the Maya clearly are not a converted people. . . . The Maya have never been fired by a conviction that their old religion was wrong and Catholicism right; they have compromised.

The same might be said of Indians throughout the whole of Latin America. Spanish Catholicism pervaded the Indian populations that survived the initial holocaust and to a large degree intermixed with the intruders from Europe and Africa. Catholicism prevails throughout Latin America and its Indian communities; however, those communities have persistently combined Christian and pre-Christian religious forms. They have interpreted and reinterpreted Christian messages in terms of aboriginal beliefs; and they have often construed Christian belief and practice in light of the Indians' experience of conquest and oppression at the hands of the Spanish, including the missionaries themselves. Indian Christianity throughout Latin America, therefore, is a distinct creation, with its own context, history, and hue (see Swanson 1988: 165–166).

THE NORTHERN FRONTIER OF NEW SPAIN

As the Viceroyalty of New Spain solidified its rule over the remnants of the Aztec empire (and in South America the Viceroyalty of Peru did the same for the Inca dominions), Spanish expeditions pushed northward to expand imperial holdings. From the Caribbean islands explorers such as Ponce de León and Hernando de Soto entered the American Southeast. Francisco Vázquez de Coronado, lured by reports from earlier adventurers, pushed northward into the American Southwest and Southern Plains. The Spanish thus encountered Indian people in what is today the United States, and from these encounters the earliest missions grew.

Catholic priests sailed with Ponce de León in 1521 on his second voyage to Florida; Dominicans based in Cuba returned in 1526 to attempt missionary work among Florida Indians. We read of Fray Luis Cancer de Barbastro, O.P., who in 1549 tried to bring the word of God to Florida's coastal Indians but was abandoned by his native translator and killed (Gannon 1965: 9–14). There were several other such failed attempts in the sixteenth century. After the creation of a church at St. Augustine, Florida, in 1565, spiritual expeditions entered the Florida interior, and Jesuits from the newly founded Society of Jesus traveled north along the Atlantic coast, where Indians killed the priests, brothers, and novices attempting to convert them. When other Jesuits brought supplies to the outpost in spring 1571, they found the indigenes "vested in cassocks and religious robes" (in Gradie 1988: 151). Further south the Jesuits made little headway; their meager resources, their inexperience, and the illnesses of the tidal swamps, as well as the Indian resistance to all the Spanish (conquistadors having attempted to enslave the natives), combined to rout the Jesuits, who gave up on Florida and took up residence instead in Mexico.

Franciscans replaced the Jesuits in Florida in 1573, and in 1595 they began to set up more than thirty mission stations, funded by the Crown and housing a reported twenty-six thousand neophytes by the middle of the seventeenth century. Diocesan priests also worked among the Indians during this "golden age" of Florida missions, 1595–1675. The missions stretched north of St. Augustine along the coast to Santa Catalina among the Guale Indians and inland among the Timicua, Choctaw, Creek, Apalachee, and Apalachicola peoples in the Florida panhandle and southwestern Georgia.

Despite this vigorous activity, relatively little is known of the Franciscan missions of Florida because the friars left few written records; the Indians encountered by these missions were either decimated as a people (as in the case of the Timicuans), or they ceased to carry any recognizable Catholic identity beyond the early eighteenth century. The evangelical goals and procedures of the Franciscans differed little from those in Mexico, as evidenced by Fray Francisco Pareja's 1613 *confesionario*, a booklet written in Timicua and Spanish (Milanich and Sturtevant 1972), and by the firsthand report in 1675 of the bishop of Santiago de Cuba, Gabriel Diaz Vara Calderón, based on his visit to Florida in the summer of 1674.

The confesionario guided the priests to root out the ceremonies, omens, and religious beliefs of the Timicua Indians. The confessor was to ask them: Do you believe that lighting a separate fire will cure illness? Do you avoid the fire when a woman has given birth? Do you believe that a bluejay can portend an important event? Do you go to the herbalist and pray to the Devil? Do you offer maize to the Devil at the door of your house? Do you refrain from eating the first fruits of acorns and other fruits? Do you avoid eating maize in a field struck by lightning? Regarding these and other customs, the confesionario advised the Indians be told:

> In none of these things should you believe nor trust that with the prayers of the Devil you will get the prey; instead pray the things of God, and He being served, with His will you will hunt them, having left the prayer of the Devil you can hunt and trust yourself to God. . . . When you are in such distress, you will say the holy name of Jesus so that he will help you. (Ibid., 27)

The missionary's aim was to turn the Indians from their aboriginal orientation (guided by dreams, auguries, taboos, and the like) toward the Christian God. In the missionary worldview the supernaturals in whom the Indians entrusted their lives were devils, pictured in the confesionario woodcuts (77–80) carrying off a naked native or trying to keep a neophyte from making her confession. These images were used as a vivid reminder of the evil of devilish spirits, in order to hasten the acceptance of Christianity and to prevent backsliding.

The confesionario reaffirms the ethical thrust of Christianity, as each of the Ten Commandments proscribes certain behavior. It is a sin to cause an abortion in yourself, by drinking some drink or squeezing the belly to choke the fetus. It is a sin to abort pregnancy. It is homicide and prevents the child from going to heaven (instead it will go to limbo). It is a sin to steal, to lie in games, or to defeat someone by stealth. It is a sin to bewitch someone, either to cause illness or create love charms. It is a sin to desire another's goods, or to take too much tribute from vassals, or to use a slave as a concubine, or to encourage superstitions.

As with other confesionarios, the 1613 text from Florida pays especial attention to sins of sexuality: Do you delight in past sins and tell others of them? Have you fondled, kissed, embraced, or held hands with evil intent? Have you shown some part of your body to arouse lust in others? Have you done lewd things with yourself or another person? Have you desired someone carnally? Have you procured? Have you refused sex with your spouse? Have you had sexual intercourse before marriage? Have you had relations with a married woman, a young lady, a relative, in-laws, two sisters, a mother and daughter, a mother-in-law, a godmother? "Have you had intercourse with someone contrary to the ordinary manner" (38), including homosexuality, pederasty, and anal intercourse? In the Indians' sexual activity, in their daily morals, as well as in their spiritual orientation, the missionary work evidenced by the confesionario attempted to alter native Florida culture.

To what effect? It would appear that by 1675 the dozens of clerics and their assistants had established some degree of religious control over thousands of Florida Indians, with the help of civil and military authority. Bishop Calderón wrote to Queen Mariana of Spain of the many conversions:

> As to their religion, they are not idolators, and they embrace with devotion the mysteries of our holy Faith. They attend Mass with regularity at eleven o'clock on the Holy Days they observe, namely, Sunday, and the feasts of Christmas, the Circumcision, Epiphany, the Purification of Our Lady, and the feast days of Saint Peter, Saint Paul, and All Saints' Day, and before entering the church each one brings to the house of the priest a log of wood as a contribution. They do not talk in the church, and the women are separated from the men, the women on the Epistle side [of the altar], the men on the Gospel side.
>
> They are very devoted to the Virgin, and on Saturdays they attend [church] when her Mass is sung. On Sundays they attend the Rosary

and the *Salve* in the afternoon. They celebrate with rejoicing and devotion the Birth of Our Lord, all attending the midnight Mass with
offerings of loaves, eggs, and other food. They subject themselves to
extraordinary penances during Holy Week, and during the twenty-four
hours of Holy Thursday and Friday . . . they attend standing, praying
the rosary in complete silence—twenty-four men, twenty-four women,
and twenty-four children—with hourly changes. The children, both
male and female, go to church on workdays, [and] to a religious school
where they are taught by a teacher . . . whom the priests have for this
service; as they also have someone deputized to report to them on all
parishioners who live in evil. (In Gannon 1965: 66)

The Florida missions continued through the seventeenth century;
however, in 1701 the English destroyed them by repeated attack, and
by 1706 the chain of Franciscan missions had collapsed, never to be
substantially revived. In 1763 England took jurisdiction of Florida, but
even when Spain regained title between 1783 and 1819, missionaries did
not reenter the area. The English ended the Spanish missions in
Florida; however, there is evidence that the Indian neophytes used the
War of Spanish Succession, 1701–1706, to revolt against the Franciscans and repudiate their faith. These Indians were said to declare
against baptism, while striking themselves on the forehead: "Go away
water! I am no Christian!" (in Weber 1992: 144). Some hundred Christian Indians attempted a revival of mission life in 1718, but the effort
was short-lived. Whatever Indian Christianity survived in Florida, it
was subsumed under the cultural congruence created by the Seminole
people, offspring of several Indian ethnicities. Among them Catholicism did not persist as a living faith.

With the failure of their Florida missions, the Jesuits entered Mexico City. By the end of the sixteenth century they had joined the Franciscans as the preeminent missionaries along the northern border of
New Spain. Between 1591 and 1654 Jesuit missions pushed north and
west, to the Mayos, the Yaquis, the Opatas, Tarahumaras, and Pimas,
registering four hundred thousand baptisms among these Indians
during this period (see Dunne 1944: 1–12), while the Franciscans concentrated their attention among the various Pueblo peoples in the
area now constituting New Mexico. Under Jesuit spiritual guidance
Christianity entered Durango, Chihuahua, Sonora, Baja California,
and Arizona, following the spread of the Spanish military and economic frontier.

It was during this period that the Jesuits in South America were creating the famous *reducciones* of Paraguay, beginning in 1607. These theocratic communities of Indians under the rule and protection of the Jesuits were attempts to initiate a mode of frontier colonization that would replace the *encomienda* enslavement of Indians and yet still support Spanish colonial aims. From the middle of the sixteenth century, with the reforms brought about by Bartolomé de Las Casas and encoded in the New Laws of Spain, the mission pueblo came to the fore as the prime method of Spanish colonization. Each "reduction," or resettlement of Indians into a town unit, was an attempt at the kingdom of God on earth. Each was based on the principle that "baptism was only a first step toward eternal salvation and that native peoples needed to be nurtured in order for their religious beliefs to mature" (Reff 1991: 250). Hence the Jesuits protected their Indians from Spanish soldiers, miners, and civil officials—even arming the neophytes to fight slave traders, conquistadors, and foreign enemies (France and England)—and the priests worked with local Indian leadership to form societies grounded in Christian values. At the same time the clerics received payment from the Spanish Royal Treasury, working for State as well as Church.

Like the reducciones of Paraguay, the Jesuit missions of northwestern New Spain were aimed at transforming the Indians. The Jesuits stamped out native dances and other religious customs; they altered Indian sex habits; they insisted that Indians learn Spanish; they ruled over them with Counter-Reformation severity. Each mission pueblo gathered baptized Indians into a village in which the Jesuits trained youths in Christian doctrine and practice, and in which European agricultural and mechanical innovations transformed Indian economic life. In the missions the Indians tended cattle and other livestock; planted grains, orchards, and gardens; engaged in trades such as leatherworking, blacksmithery, and carpentry; and lived according to the rhythms of the Christian calendar, all under Jesuit control. Far from the centers of Spanish colonial culture, the Indians of the mission pueblos were not integrated into Spanish society; rather, the goal of the Jesuits was to isolate them in order to promote Christian perfection. This system served as the model for Jesuit missions throughout New Spain until 1767, when the Spanish Crown expelled them, reportedly for amassing too much power and wealth.

The institution of the mission pueblo was a tool of conquest and conversion, and as such it persisted beyond Jesuit use in New Spain.

Franciscans set up their own reductions in California and Florida; Jesuits attempted similar reductions in New France in the seventeenth century and in the American West in the nineteenth. Oblates set up Christian villages in western Canada in the late nineteenth century based on the Paraguay model of the seventeenth, and many Catholic boarding schools for Indians into the late twentieth century have followed the reduction model, for good and evil. In all its manifestations the reduction offered the missionaries the promise of effective cultural and religious transformation, with authority firmly resting in the hands of the priests. Such autocratic rule led to dictatorial cruelty and economic aggrandizement on more than a few occasions, and the mission pueblos of northwestern New Spain aroused resentment among many Indians, some of whom revolted against their Jesuit overseers. The Tarahumaras killed the first Jesuit to live among them, Juan Fonte, at a time (1616) when he thought them well christianized. They revolted again in 1623, 1648, 1652, 1690, and yet again in 1696, each uprising led by baptized Indian apostates (see Spicer 1972: 25–35). In the first hundred years of Spanish missions in the American Southwest, from the 1590s to the 1690s, Indians killed about twenty-five Jesuits and fifty Franciscans performing their evangelizing tasks.

Nonetheless, the Jesuit mission pueblos were also attractive to many Indians, for the protection they offered from conquistadors, for the spiritual power they promised against the contagious diseases already annihilating Indian populations, for the economic security of systematic agriculture and animal husbandry, and for the good news of the Christian faith. As with the Aztec Indians, the indigenes further north received Christian ideas and practices with native sensibilities and concepts, and in the chapters that follow we shall observe the interpenetration of Christian and aboriginal forms of religiousness.

During the height of Spanish missions in the American Southwest (north of Durango), from 1600 to 1767, an estimated two hundred thousand Indians received Catholic baptism (Spicer 1972: 502). After the Jesuit expulsion in 1767, through the Mexican separation from Spain in 1821, to the Treaty of Guadalupe-Hidalgo in 1848 at the close of the Mexican-American War, missionizing slowed almost to a halt on the northern frontier. In the late nineteenth century Anglo Protestants entered the Southwest mission field. Only around 1900 did Catholic missionaries once again devote themselves to evangelizing Southwest Indians.

During the initial century of missionary expansion the Jesuits (and to some degree the Franciscans) extended themselves to Indians who were not firmly under Spanish control, both in the American Southeast and Southwest. According to the historian Edward H. Spicer (1972: 502–506), there were not enough priests to evangelize effectively; therefore, Indians could be baptized, but then they and their children did not grow up in a thoroughly Catholic culture, despite the efforts of the reducciones. They received the gospel, christening, and other sacraments, but for many rigorous indoctrination and daily supervision were missing. This led to conversions that may have been incomplete or superficial. Syncretism took place among the Indian Christian populations, unchecked by the clerical authorities spread too thin along the frontier.

When the Jesuits were expelled, they were replaced on occasion by Franciscans; however, by the late eighteenth century the Franciscan Order had lost much of its missionizing zeal and could not even continue with its own missions. As a result, the various Indian populations of northern Mexico and the American Southwest were left to develop their own forms of Catholic religiousness without sacerdotal supervision. Mayos, Opatas, Tarahumaras, Yaquis, and to some degree the Pueblo Indians took over their own church activities and organization, filling the void left by the priests. They created their own tribal Catholicism in which the presence of an ordained priest to say mass ceased to be a necessity among these "most strongly Catholicized tribes" (ibid., 505).

Spicer suggests that three Catholic Southwest Indian groups developed different adaptations of Catholicism between 1600 and 1900. The Yaquis, he says (506ff.), fused their traditional religion with Spanish Jesuit Catholicism; the northern Pimas and Papagos adopted the forms of Sonoran folk Catholicism without giving up aboriginal religious patterns; the Eastern Pueblos of the Rio Grande compartmentalized their tribal and Catholic practices, holding them dear but separate from each other. In the sections that follow it will be our task to examine the religious forms and identity of these three sets of people—the Yaquis, the Pimas and Papagos, and the various Puebloans—in order to observe their practice of Catholicism up to the present day.

Despite Protestant inroads among all these people over the past century and more, in 1960 "a considerable majority of all the Indians in the region spoke of themselves as Catholics" (503). At the same time, however,

> the majority of those Indians calling themselves Catholic were not actually accepted as such by the Catholic Church. The Yaquis, the Mayos, the Tarahumaras, and the Eastern Pueblos were regarded by the Church as something less than Catholic. The fact was that they had developed variations of belief and practice which were not acceptable to the organized church . . . they deviated from Roman Catholic orthodoxy. (503)

YAQUI HISTORY

As the Spanish traveled northward from Mexico City in the sixteenth century, they encountered dozens of different indigenous peoples, speakers of various Uto-Aztecan languages such as Tarahumara, Tepehuan, Mayo, Pima, Opata, and Yaqui. In northwestern New Spain these peoples numbered over a half million, each with particular religious forms and sociopolitical organization.

The first contact between the Spanish and the Yaquis took place in 1533, and the Indians held their ground against the Spanish soldiery led by Diego de Guzman. The Rio Yaqui thus became the northern frontier of New Spain for many years, and the thirty thousand or so Yaquis remained outside the sphere of Spanish influence into the seventeenth century, although Spaniards raided on occasion for Yaqui slaves, and several Spanish travelers passed peacefully through Yaqui territory—a fertile floodplain supporting farming, gathering, and hunting.

For fifteen years after their arrival in Mexico, the Jesuits remained in urban areas; however, in 1587 the Crown granted the Society of Jesus the right to missionize the northwestern frontier of New Spain, and the first Jesuits began to journey along the trail west of the Sierra Madre through Guadalajara (while the Franciscans employed the northward route east of the mountains through Durango and Chihuahua), and there they started their first Indian missions, beginning in 1591. Each native people has had its own history with Catholic missions; it is the aim of this chapter to recount the Yaqui experience with Catholicism from the early seventeenth century to the present day.

In 1610 a Spanish army tried to defeat the Yaquis in battle, but the seven thousand Yaqui warriors defeated the invading troops. Several years later the Jesuits set up missions among the Yaquis' neighbors, the Mayos, and the Yaquis took an interest in the enterprise. The Yaquis sent observers to the Jesuit missions among the Mayos, seeing what the Jesuits brought with them: agriculture on a large scale and a new religious orientation. We do not know explicitly what in the Jesuit endeavor appealed to them, but in 1617 Yaqui leaders invited two Jesuits to live among them. When Fathers Andres Perez de Ribas and Tomas Basilio entered the Yaqui lands, they came to an undefeated people on

ARIZONA

Phoenix
○ Guadalupe

Tucson
○ Pascua Pueblo

O'ODHAM

NEW MEXICO

TEXAS

Rio Grande

SERI

GUAYMA

OPATA

Rio Yaqui

Chihuahua ○

TARAHUMARA

YAQUI
"Eight
Pueblos"

Sierra Madre

MAYO

Gulf of California

TEPEHUAN

Durango ○

Gulf of Mexico

BAJA CALIFORNIA

Pacific Ocean

Guadalajara ○

The Yaquis and Their Neighbors,
17th–20th Centuries

PEOPLES
○ Cities and towns
● Indian communities

Yaqui territory

the people's own terms, as guests of the Yaqui leaders and under their protection. They arrived without any military escort, greeted by the inhabitants of numerous *rancherias* (agricultural villages) who waved cane crosses to greet them. The Jesuits delivered sermons on Christian doctrine and christened the children immediately, waiting to baptize the adults until they could teach them something of Christianity at a later time. In one of the rancherias some Yaquis attempted to murder the priests, but Yaqui authorities warned and defended them, and the clerics escaped harm.

Within six months the Jesuits baptized five thousand children and three thousand adults, despite the resistance of some Yaqui medicine men and religious leaders. Within six years almost all of the thirty thousand Yaquis were initiated into Christian life through baptism, without overt Jesuit coercion; indeed, the Yaquis seemed eager to adopt Jesuit religious forms into their lives. Father Perez called the Yaquis "the most barbarous people" (in Spicer 1980: 13)—he and his fellow Jesuits sought to stamp out pagan customs and beliefs, drunken orgies, scalp dances, and polygamy—but his depiction of them illustrated their hospitality and friendliness to the Jesuit cause. The Indians built Christian churches, learned Christian catechism, and engaged in Christian rituals with vigor. On their part, the Jesuits learned Yaqui language and translated Catholic prayers into the vernacular.

Along the Rio Yaqui, from the Gulf of California into the foothills of the Sierra Madre, the Jesuits formed eight main Yaqui villages, each with a central church. The phrase "Eight Pueblos" became synonymous with the Yaqui nation under Jesuit authority (Hu-DeHart 1981: 33). There were not many Jesuits in the Yaqui mission field—for a century there were never more than six Jesuits among the Yaquis at any one time among a population that held steady at thirty thousand. Hence, the Jesuits did not constitute an apparent threat to the Yaquis, and Yaqui leaders supervised the quick and orderly baptism of the Yaqui thousands. Some Yaquis feared that the Jesuits meant to poison them or to usurp their prerogatives; however, the native leaders protected the priests for well over a century. The Jesuits became benign autocrats who attracted and held Indian loyalty to their mission pueblos by producing (through Indian labor) vast quantities of food. The Jesuits said that they converted the Indians "through the mouth" (in ibid., 24) in this manner.

The Jesuits taught the Yaquis about God the Creator and the immortal soul that needs to be prepared for the kingdom of heaven. They taught how many other peoples had already become Christians and benefitted from Church teachings and rituals. They taught about the holy law of God, which was enforced by the Church. They initiated the rite of baptism and the ritual duties between godparent and god-child. They introduced the visual and musical artistry of their Church: pictures, wood carvings of saints and the Holy Family, tapestries, and bas-reliefs showing Jesus and the Virgin at the Day of Judgment and scenes of heaven and hell. Father Perez and other padres trained choirs and orchestras, introducing organs, bassoons, sackbuts, oboes, flutes, and recorders as musical instruments associated with sacred liturgy. The Yaquis learned Christian ideas and engaged in Christian activities as taught by the Jesuits in a system differing little from the reducciones of Paraguay.

At the same time the Jesuits introduced corporal punishment to the Yaquis in order to make the Indians "tractable, loyal, and obedient servants" (ibid., 36). The priests introduced whipping posts and stocks along with knowledge of the Last Judgment. Without military support the Jesuits were able to gain authority and appointed their own pueblo officials—*gobernadors, alcaldes, fiscals de iglesia*, and *temastians* (governors, council members, church officers, and catechists, respectively), as well as others—who reported to the priests, ruled over their country-men, cared for the church properties, and taught the creeds and prayers. The Jesuits did not intend for the Yaquis to be assimilated into Spanish society; indeed they organized their missions so as to protect the Yaquis from Spanish contact—which did not take place until the eighteenth century when silver mines were established around the Yaqui area. The Jesuits created a theocratic nation in which the Yaquis performed labor under Jesuit command, and the priests opposed all attempts on the part of New Spain's civil and military order to secularize the Yaqui pueblos. In the 1700s the priests tried to prevent the Yaquis from working in the Spanish mines, and there were charges that the Indian pueblo labor was making the padres rich. In their defense the Jesuits noted that the wealth accrued by the pueblos was the communal property of the Yaquis, merely administered by the clerics in charge. Functioning within the political administration of New Spain, the Jesuits managed to maintain virtual dictatorship over the Yaquis for a century and a half.

For all their control over catechism, liturgy, and economy, for all their efforts to alter Yaqui culture according to Christian standards, the Jesuits could not oversee the minute details of Yaqui contact with Christianity. Outnumbered by the Yaquis at a rate of at least four thousand to one (Spicer 1980: 21–22), the Jesuits could not prevent Yaquis from interpreting Christianity according to Yaqui concepts. Like the other Indians of Mexico, the Yaquis fused their traditional religious culture with that of the Jesuits in ways that are difficult to know, since in the process of amalgamation the aboriginal religion (unknown to modern researchers due to a dearth of seventeenth-century documentation) became thoroughly absorbed in the emerging religious complex. It is that nascent religious matrix—part aboriginal, part Catholic, preeminently Yaqui—that has persisted and flourished to the present day.

One can see, for example, that the Jesuits, like the other missionary orders of New Spain, introduced three religious dramas to the Indians. First, the Conquest of the Moors was celebrated as a ritual battle on the final day of patron saints' fiestas. The Yaquis created two sodalities, the Moors and the Christians, to engage in this ritual, and over time these organizations took on functions unconnected to the ritual drama as it was originally introduced by the Jesuits. Second, the pageant of Malinche marked the first conversion by Cortés' padres on the Mexican mainland; in the drama the Indians enacted the wrestling of Malinche's soul from the Devil's control. Over time the Yaqui Matachin Society performed this dance as a native ritual, as part of its ceremonial functions. And third, the Jesuits introduced the ritual drama of Christ's Passion every Easter season and organized a confraternity to perform the ceremonies. Beginning in 1618 under Jesuit leadership, as many as twenty-five hundred Yaquis enacted the capture, execution, and resurrection of Jesus every spring. The Passion became the most important of the three dramas, and over time the Yaquis took charge of the events, which by the twentieth century became the "major orientation in Yaqui religious ceremony" (Spicer 1980: 70).

How did the Yaquis shape their adaptation of Catholicism? For the first century and a half the Yaquis prospered economically and their population held steady. They permitted the Jesuits to direct their culture change with only one period of revolt against the priests' rule, and even during that period of insurrection, 1740–1742, the Yaquis did not turn away from Catholic tradition. The Yaquis seem not to have developed any substantial millennial movements or nativist prophetism;

rather, they adapted to their emerging Catholic faith gradually. The Jesuits directed the religious evolution, but the Yaquis conducted the activity themselves.

The Yaqui revolt of 1740 was against particular Jesuits and the indigenous leadership under their control—the Yaqui revolutionaries called the mestizo and Opata assistants "coyotes" (Hu-DeHart 1981: 962–963). The Jesuits had tried to prevent Yaquis from earning wages in Spanish mines; the priests had not allowed the local election of Indian officials, as required by Spanish laws; the "coyotes" were often autocratic and cruel in their administration of justice; profits from agricultural produce went to the Jesuits, who distributed the moneys among their various Yaqui churches; the padres refused to recognize Yaqui resentment against the priests. Under some instigation by the Spanish provincial governor, a Yaqui militia captain and *gobernador* of a Yaqui pueblo, Juan Ignacio Usacamea (El Muni), attacked the Jesuit hegemony, but within two years the Spanish soldiers quelled the uprising. El Muni's minions had particular grievances, but they were not seeking an end to Jesuit presence or a liberation from Catholic influence, despite their revolutionary battle cry: "There is no God; there is no king; there are no priests; death to the priest!" (in Donohue 1969: 89). Rather, they sought rights as Spanish subjects, and they persisted in their Catholic identity.

When in 1767 the monarch Charles III expelled the Jesuits from all of New Spain, the Yaquis accepted the expulsion calmly. Throughout the period of Jesuit direction, the Yaquis seemed to be "one docile collective" (ibid., 4); under the secular priests who replaced the missionaries but whose presence was far less felt, the Yaquis continued to develop their local Catholicism while working for pay in Spanish mines and prospering amidst their animal stocks and farms. In the waning decades of New Spain and in the first years of Mexican independence, the Yaquis gained "increasing autonomy over their religious life. . . . The 19th century saw a steadily increasing isolation of Yaquis from evangelization and administrative contacts with representatives of the Catholic [C]hurch" (Spicer 1980: 113). Left relatively free to determine their spiritual direction, the Yaquis continued to embrace Catholic forms, making Catholicism truly their own, without pressure, resentment, or alienation. A Jesuit who has lived and worked among the Yaquis in Arizona says today that when the Jesuits were expelled in 1767 "it was the best thing that ever happened to the Yaquis"

(Myers, April 12, 1993), because the Indians then possessed the freedom to shape Yaqui Catholicism.

In the nineteenth century the Mexicans tried to take over Yaqui lands, and there developed pervasive enmity between the two peoples. The Yaquis regarded themselves not only as rulers of their own lands—inheriting their nationhood from the Jesuit organization of the Eight Pueblos—but also as representatives of true Christianity. In Yaqui eyes the Mexicans were lax Catholics, and the masks the Yaquis wore in their Easter ceremonials, representing the enemies of Jesus, often took the visages of Mexican soldiery (Spicer 1980: 157). Inspired by a vision of the Virgin of Guadalupe, the Yaqui Juan Bandera tried to lead an Indian revolution from Mexico, joining in a common cause the Opatas, Lower Pimas, Mayos, and Yaquis. He was defeated in 1832, but the Yaqui villages—organized as the Jesuits had arranged them two centuries before—continued as fighting units for decades to come (Spicer 1988: 4–5), protecting their homeland and spiritual identity.

In Mexican eyes the Yaquis were pagans and rebels whose political and religious agencies deserved suppression. In 1887 the Mexican government was finally able to enforce military rule over the Yaqui country. Refusing to accept defeat, Yaquis retreated into the mountains; however, over the next two decades the federal forces transported fifteen thousand Yaquis to the distant Yucatan, where they were sold as plantation workers and servants. Only three thousand were able to remain in their territory, and an additional four thousand escaped to the United States, some to California and most to southern Arizona, where some Yaquis had been dwelling since at least the early eighteenth century.

In their diaspora to the United States the Yaquis developed a mythology and ritualism that reaffirmed their title to the Eight Pueblo Yaqui homeland. Between 1887 and 1906 the majority of Yaquis living in the United States, near the cities of Tucson and Phoenix, "carried the scenario in their heads" (Schechner 1993: 95) of their Easter ceremonials, but they did not perform the rituals, fearing religious persecution. As their asylum became more secure, however, they began to express their religious identity in public, first with an Easter ceremonial near Phoenix in 1906 and then in 1909 near Tucson. During their generation in exile the Yaquis had not lost their religiousness; now they felt free to express it openly. In the United States the Easter ritualism became a coalescence of that spirituality, the "essence of their identity" (Myers, April 12, 1993), that which "makes the Yaqui Yaqui" (Schechner 1993: 97).

When Anglos witnessed the Yaqui Easter ceremonials in the early twentieth century, they regarded them as "pagan or barbaric" (in Spicer 1980: 250), and a slew of Protestant missionaries—Presbyterians, Jehovah's Witnesses, Baptists, Methodists, and members of the Assemblies of God—tried in vain to evangelize the Indians. At the same time, the Chamber of Commerce in Tucson and Phoenix advertised the Yaqui ritualism because it brought tourists to their towns. The Yaquis were so grateful for their freedom in the United States to revive their religious ceremonialism suppressed in Mexico in the late nineteenth century that they did not turn away the visitors who came to watch, even though they would have preferred to hold their rituals away from the eyes of outsiders, as they had for so many years after the expulsion of the Jesuits.

From the 1920s Catholic priests and other representatives of mainstream Catholicism in the United States tried to turn the Yaquis to Church authority and orthodoxy. Some tried friendship, participating in the Yaqui rites; others built chapels near the Yaqui villages, hoping that the Indians would attend that chapel rather than their own churches. The Catholic Daughters of America conducted doctrinal classes starting in 1929. Often Catholic clerics were intolerant of the Yaqui particularities of Catholic belief and worship.

On the part of the hierarchical Church, there were many problems with the Yaquis:

> Not only were the specific rituals not the prescribed ones nor carried out by persons properly qualified, but the administration of the rites included no recognition of the Catholic [C]hurch as an organization. The authority of parish priests and bishops, or any other officials in the Catholic hierarchy, were not recognized by Yaquis in their planning, organizing, and carrying out of the calendrical ceremonies which they observed. To the Catholic officials they were 'folk' or popular customs, without the sanction of the Catholic [C]hurch. The Yaquis could be indulged in carrying them on, but they had no significance with regard to being good Catholics. (Ibid., 251)

On their part, the Yaquis respected the priests and went to them for baptism and other devotional rites, but without eschewing their own Yaqui organization and ritual.

CONTEMPORARY YAQUI RELIGION

Today close to eleven thousand Yaquis live in southern Arizona in eight distinct communities and other locales, some on lands protected by United States reservation status. Guadalupe, just south of Phoenix, is "the largest Yaqui community in the world" (Myers, April 12, 1993), with a population exceeding two thousand. Several other small patches of Yaquis live in the Phoenix area. Two small Yaqui communities exist between Phoenix and Tucson, and around Tucson are three main Yaqui villages, including Pascua Pueblo. Guadalupe and Pascua Pueblo are on federally funded land. The Yaquis possess their own local chapels, and all the communities are in communication with one another.

The Roman Catholic Church maintains relations with the Yaquis of southern Arizona through the diocesan ministries of Phoenix and Tucson. Catholic priests and deacons baptize Yaqui infants, and on occasion the Yaquis receive the Eucharist and other sacraments. For the past twenty years Rev. David A. Myers, S.J., has conducted a ministry among the Yaquis at Guadalupe, although this practicing lawyer states that "the Yaquis minister to me" (Myers, April 12, 1993) rather than the other way around. He says that the Yaquis wanted him to live among them—the first Jesuit to know the Yaquis well since 1767—and so he rents a house from a Yaqui religious leader, and he dances as a member of the Matachin Society, an organization deriving from Los Matachines dances introduced by the Spaniards in the sixteenth century but adapted by the Yaquis for their own usage. He also baptizes dozens of Yaquis each year, conducts funerals, attends to their crises and social rites of passage, and provides continuity with a Church that is more focussed upon Mexican Americans than Yaqui Indians. True to the Jesuit tradition, Father Myers "runs his own show" (Dixon, August 7, 1992) without overt supervision from the diocesan offices in Phoenix.

Apart from their contact with the Church, the Yaquis in their several villages possess a ceremonial organization all their own, constituting an independent Yaqui Catholic Church. Under the supervision of their own leaders, the Yaquis conduct calendrical rituals throughout the liturgical year, as well as blessings and rites of passage. They exhibit a devotionalism that addresses the Christian God and Christian saints, as well as personages and spirits of Nature, and during the Easter season the Yaquis perform elaborate ceremonial acts that join together and express the full contours of their contemporary religiousness.

Each of the Yaqui villages possesses authoritative structures concerning its members, including councils, civil officials, police, elders, and heads of households. Prominent among the leadership are church personnel, heads of festivals, and ceremonial officials, all of whom are responsible for the religious life of the community (see Spicer 1980: 188). Yaquis engage the services of Roman Catholic priests for sacraments, and the clerics sometimes attend Yaqui ceremonies and participate in their processions in churchyards and households. Nevertheless, the Yaquis maintain their own distinct form of Catholic worship, under their own jurisdiction.

If one seeks to find religious authority in a Yaqui village, one has to look in various places, depending on situation and season. The manifestations of religious control—the altar groups, the Easter season officials, the members of the Matachin Society, the *pascola* and deer dancers—uphold the values of the community as a whole; however, each has its own discrete season, its own particular service to the spiritual and human realms.

Yaquis become members of the religious organization by virtue of gift or vow. The supernatural powers provide individuals with a gift (*tekia*) while in their mother's womb; as a result of this blessing, certain persons are suited for particular religious tasks. During the crises of life, especially at times of sickness, Yaquis make a vow (*manda*)— most often to Jesus or Mary—to join a ceremonial society and provide ritual services as a payment for cures and other ameliorations. Parents make these vows on behalf of their children, who are then obligated to carry out ceremonial duties throughout their adulthood. At confirmations the youths obtain ritual godparents and are bound to perform work for the supernatural, under their godparents' guidance. Those bestowed with an inborn gift also enter ritual service through the mechanism of confirmation. Failure to fulfill the promises of gift or vow will result in punishment from the spiritual realm, e.g., through sickness or death. In this manner the community passes down its religious duties from one generation to the next.

In the seventeenth century the Jesuits inducted the Yaquis into service of the local church. These church officers have persisted to the present day, in the absence of Roman Catholic clerical control. The *maestro* is a lay priest or lay reader with duties corresponding somewhat to the activities of an ordained Catholic priest, but the maestro is not ordained, nor are his activities recognized by Church hierarchy as official Catholic functions. Each Yaqui church has several maestros, who lead Catholic ceremonies, using a missal and breviary, as well as handwritten books in which they have transcribed the prayers, hymns, and other services of the Yaqui religious tradition. Each maestro passes down his knowledge to an apprentice, and upon his death (all maestros are male) each maestro's handwritten books are given over to the next maestro. Maestros must have knowledge of the Catholic liturgical calendar. They must be able to carry out elaborate rituals. They must know sufficient Latin and Spanish in order to lead standard prayers — the *Ave Maria*, the *Pater Noster*, the *Credo*, the Sign of the Cross, the Litany of the Blessed Virgin, the *Salve*, the *Confiteor*, and others. They sing Gregorian chants (in Latin) and *alabanzas* (Spanish and Latin songs of praise taught by the Spanish missioners). They also deliver sermons on a variety of ritual occasions: funerals, fiestas for the saints, confirmations, weekly prayer services and the like. For these services the maestros receive gifts and food and some money, provided sometimes eagerly, sometimes grudgingly, by the Yaqui congregation.

The maestros have their assistants, called *temastim*, who serve as sacristans in charge of candles, crosses, and male holy figures in the Yaqui church. Altar women look after the statues of the Virgin Mary, the female *santos*, the altar cloths and flowers. Female *cantors* help sing the alabanzas written in the maestros' notebooks. Virginal girls carry flags during processions, blessing the grounds and guarding against evil, while training to become altar women and singers upon marriage. Males and females thus join in performing the rituals of Yaqui Catholicism throughout the year.

From the beginning of Lent on Ash Wednesday to the Day of the Finding of the True Cross, the *kohtumbre* come to the fore as religious leaders. These officials, who oversee the most prominent and integrating of the Yaqui ceremonials during Lent and Easter, represent the Yaqui community as "complete Christians" (ibid., 311), and they include the providers of fiestas, the *caballeros* (horsemen), and the *fariseos* (Pharisees). Among the latter are the ritual representatives of Christ's enemies (Pilate, the Jews, the soldiers of Rome) and the masked *chapayekas* (Painter 1986: 192).

Outside the Lenten-Easter season, the kohtumbre appear only at death ceremonies and other rare occasions; however, in their liturgical realm they are everywhere to be seen. They are responsible for all money donated and dispersed during the season. The caballeros patrol the village to prevent violations or improper behavior (e.g., arguments, or displays of sexuality or wealth), and to encourage the Yaquis to attend the ceremonies.

The fariseos are ritual actors who,

> represent the people who persecuted and executed Christ. Their ritual function in the Easter Ceremony is the enactment of the pursuit, capture, and crucifixion of Jesus. This dramatization is earnestly considered to be for the eventual glory of Christ, as the fariseos are overwhelmed and ritually killed by the church group and others mobilized against them at the Gloria on Holy Saturday morning. The fariseos themselves are apprehensive lest their role of enemies of Jesus be misunderstood by spectators, when actually their hearts and actions are dedicated to Him, a dedication which is real and personal, not only philosophical. (Ibid., 191)

Jesus is considered the head of the fariseos, all of whom vow to serve Him for at least three years, more often for life. He appears to them in dreams, calling them to service, and they cannot refuse. We read, for instance, of Rosalio Moisés, who became ill in 1923 in the midst of his concern about his lack of active faith. He asked Jesus for forgiveness (he had not contributed to the fariseos during the previous Lent) and a long life, vowing to wear a fariseo mask if he were cured. Then in a dream he journeyed to heaven, where Jesus greeted him as a fariseo and led him to witness vivid scenes: condemned people, hot like frogs in the desert; a place of streams and flowers; a church baptism. Then Jesus cured him by taking out his heart and having a bird fly it around a lake three times. Moisés came out of this vision experience a cured and converted man, and the next year he became a fariseo who served Jesus ritually for over two decades (see Moisés, Kelley, and Holden 1977: 82–93).

The chapayekas are the fariesos who wear masks. They serve as the preeminent enemies of Jesus, capturing Him on Holy Thursday and deriding the maestros and others of the altar group, against whom they are ritually opposed. Like the other fariseos, the chapayekas devote themselves to the service of Jesus, performing arduous tasks, undergoing taboos, and wearing their masks as part of a "rigorous penance" (Painter 1986: 209). The chapayeka mask is sometimes regarded as evil, and it is destroyed on Glory (Holy) Saturday to mark the victorious Christ; however, it is also a sacred blessing, a flower that is said to come from the blood of Christ like other flowers and which provides heavenly glory to the Yaquis and to all creation. Each chapayeka wears around his neck a rosary given by his godparents upon confirmation into the society. He holds the cross of the rosary in his mouth under his mask and repeats prayers during his performance, saying the name of Jesus repeatedly and keeping Him firmly in mind. The cross also keeps the chapayeka from saying anything the Devil might want him to utter. As one chapayeka notes, "The mask is evil, but the man inside is not, and so he holds the cross in his mouth" (in ibid., 224).

The caballeros and fariseos have Spanish nomenclature, and they probably derive from ritual organizations introduced by the Jesuits, although chapayeka masks resemble types used by other Indians of the American Southwest and northern Mexico. The Matachin Society is a church organization that owes its origin to the dance celebrating the conversion of Malinche, Cortés' interpreter and mistress, and the conquest of Montezuma. Members of Matachin have the Virgin Mary as their patroness, and all newly dedicated members of the troupe are referred to as "Malinche." The master dancer takes the title of the monarch Montezuma, and throughout the non-Lenten season they dance quadrilles (some referred to as "battles") to violins, guitars, and drums of Spanish origin. Nevertheless, nothing apparent in their dancing makes explicit reference to the conversion to Christianity or the defeat of the Aztecs.

Men and boys under vow to the Virgin make up the Matachin Society, and although they are technically not a church group, their dance is always a blessing, always religious. On Glory Saturday they oppose the fariseos ritually, and although they have no ceremonial authority beyond their own dancing, they perform as guests at all sorts of fiestas, funerals, vespers, and processions, not only among the Yaquis, but also for neighboring O'odham (Pagagos), e.g., at the church of San Xavier del Bac to mark its patron saint's day. For all its Christian devotionalism, the Matachin Society is probably related to aboriginal Yaqui dancing societies; hence, the matachinis express traditional Yaqui social values, displayed in choreography.

The *pascola* dancers and their accompanying deer dancer are perhaps the most ancient Indian form of Yaqui ceremonialism, although it is said (Spicer 1940: 176) that the pascolas are remnants of the Moors society that performed a ceremonial battle with the caballeros on San Juan's feast day—the dramatization of the Christian-Moor battle so popular throughout New Spain. They perform in public plazas and private households, in processions with matachinis, and in Easter ceremonials, at death anniversaries, children's funerals (but never at the funerals of adults), saints' day fiestas, and weddings. They also perform for Whites and O'odham in southern Arizona. They do not require a deer dancer, but when a deer dancer performs, it is always in the presence of the pascolas.

The pascola is the "old man" of Yaqui ritual, carrying ancient meanings in their costumes and dance steps. They are associated with the world of wild animals and their spirits. They have a strong sense of duty to the Yaqui community, and more than any other Yaqui dancers, they perform for humans rather than for the spiritual world, sometimes receiving their fellows' applause. Concurrently, they are dedicated to Jesus, even when they comment upon Church rituals in a mocking manner, and in general they are christianized, despite their bawdy good humor. Pascolas are given their gift before birth—by the spirit world and ultimately by God—and before adolescence they receive frightening dreams that challenge them to carry out the ceremonial duty with which they were born. Thus they become pascolas, and they perform their individualized dance steps according to their personal gifts.

The deer dancer is most firmly associated with the world of the wild, and particularly animals of the hunt. Although the Yaquis hardly ever hunt deer in the present day, they still recall the aboriginal rite performed on the eve of deer hunts. The deer dancer recalls the power of the animals to cause and cure sickness, and thus they bring to mind the aboriginal worldview of the Yaquis. The songs associated with the deer dancer have archaic forms peculiar to them. Yet, for all their pagan content, the deer dancers help defeat the fariseos on Glory Saturday, and they remind Yaquis of their vows to Mary and Jesus.

A Yaqui sacristan says that the pascolas and deer dancers are related to Jesus' nativity. Jesus was born among animals, so the pascolas perform animal dances. They don't wear shirts because Jesus was barechested on the Cross. Perhaps the animals celebrated by the pascolas represent those saved by Noah's ark, and the hunted deer signifies the crucified Christ. As a result, the Catholic Yaquis say that the pascolas are part of "our religion" (in ibid., 198), Yaqui Catholicism.

Yaqui religious leaders are responsible for a full calendar of ceremonies. On Sunday mornings outside of the Lenten-Easter season, the maestro and his male and female assistants perform *misa*, a prayer service consisting of those elements of a Roman Catholic Mass not requiring a priest. Vespers take place in the church before major feasts, with the altar group in church and the matachinis in the plaza. The Yaquis mark the feasts of the Finding of the True Cross (May 2), the Nativity of St. John the Baptist (June 23), the movable feasts of Holy Trinity and Corpus Christi, the feasts of Saint Anthony of Padua (June 12), Our Lady of Mt. Carmel (July 15), St. Ignatius of Loyola (July 30), the Assumption (August 14), St. Francis of Assisi (October 3), Conception of the Blessed Virgin (December 7), Our Lady of Guadalupe (December 11), and others. In each case the Yaquis celebrate the *eve* of the feast day, as indicated by these dates (Painter 1986: 311–313). The Yaquis also observe Christmas vigil, the Month of May for Mary, an extended feast for San Xavier (December 2–4), and All Souls Day and All Saints Day (November 1–2).

Noncalendrical ceremonies include baptisms, confirmations, weddings, funerals, and memorials for the dead, performed by the maestros and their assistants, but also attended by matachinis, pascolas, and deer dancers. In the Yaqui households throughout the year, the maestros and cantors intone alabanzas such as the following to mark the dawning day:

> *Praise Christians*
> *Through God conceived*
> *And the light of the heavens*
> *With a Hail Mary*
> *On a fresh morning*
> *The Virgin pure was walking*
> *Then it was not late in the morning*
> *In the hours when she was walking*
> *Let us sing the dawn*
> *Here comes the day*
> *Let us give thanks*
> *Hail Mary*
> *Praised and extolled*

> *Be the sacrament divine*
> *He who with God coexists*
> *Of the souls' sustenance*
> *And the pure conception*
> *Of the Queen of Heavens.* (In ibid., 339–340)

followed by:

> *Into Thy hands I commend*
> *My spirit*
> *May it be blessed in all things*
> *With sweet song*
> *Keep on raising up*
> *The Holy Christ*
> *Holy, Holy, Holy*
> *Holy God, Holy strength*
> *Holy God, Holy immortality*
> *Have mercy on us.* (340)

At other times the Yaquis pray their rosaries. The Yaquis are intently absorbed in their ritual observances, with some kind of ceremony taking place half of the days of the year, in addition to private household observances.

The Catholic liturgical calendar is the major framework for Yaqui rituals, with the primary division marking the Lenten-Easter season (from Ash Wednesday to the Finding of the Holy Cross) from the rest of the year. These calendrical ceremonies are supplemented by the many rites of passage and private observances, and these too have apparent Catholic symbolic content. The Yaqui communities each have a church with an altar, a plaza, and several prominent crosses around the churchyard, which are used for public rituals. In addition, households have their own patio cross; indeed, the crosses introduced by the Jesuits centuries ago, along with church, plaza, and altar, are today ubiquitous among the Yaquis. Yaquis carry crosses in processions; they mark graves and boundaries with them; and the Indians perform the Stations of the Cross throughout Lent. The Yaquis keep up their churches and decorate their altars (in the church, in the plaza, and in households) with images of the saints, crosses, and colored cloth (to mark the liturgical seasons). Yaquis worship at the altars, kneeling in front of them, kissing the ground before them, crossing themselves, and kissing the altar images. Ceremonial societies lead processions each Friday during Lent and to mark the periodic fiestas, marching from altar to altar, bearing crosses, and other symbols of sanctity in gestures of penitence or festivity, depending upon circumstance.

At all their ceremonies the Yaquis emphasize social solidarity and the continuity of religious tradition. They touch hands; they eat and drink in common; they march and dance, pray and sing in unison. The maestros and the heads of the ritual societies deliver sermons that thank the people for their ceremonial work, their gifts and vows, and they extol public morality, particularly those dues of kinship and ceremonial relationship. They invoke the presence and protectorship of the ancestors, not only at funeral novenas—memorials for the dead and All Souls-All Saints Day services—but in sermons and fiestas throughout the year. In all their ceremonialism the Yaquis are intent upon themselves as a people, as well as their imitation of Christ and devotion to the divine.

The Yaquis do not attempt to make systematic or dogmatic the beliefs associated with their ceremonialism. They do not teach their young through catechisms; they do not insist upon orthodox interpretation of the world or their own place and behavior in it. They pass down biblical stories of Creation, the Flood, the Tower of Babel, and the Passion of Christ. They have books of devotion about Catholic saints. Their rituals and sermons, prayers, hymns, images, and the like express their religiousness, but their religious leaders do not attempt to codify it for one and all.

Most Yaquis know an oral tradition about a talking tree that foretold the history of the Yaquis to an old woman in ancient times. The tree prophesied not only the present shape of the world and many modern inventions, but also the coming of the Jesuits to the Yaqui people: "a god would come and show the people how to baptize themselves. When they were shown the secret of baptism, then everyone should be baptized because it was a good thing" (in Spicer 1940: 240). Some of the ancient people did not wish to receive this baptism; those who did and made it part of their own ritual knowledge became the Yaqui people. Some of the versions of this legend suggest that Yaquis were given autonomy over baptism; others emphasize the enriching influence of Spanish culture on the Yaquis (Moisés, Kelley, and Holden 1977: xxiv–xxv). Still others use the narrative as a means of explaining the difference between the present world and the mythic past.

One variant (Painter 1986: 6–9) depicts a primordial people, the *surem*, who inhabited the ancient, revered, enchanted, and powerful earth, *yoania*. They were immortals who wanted nothing to do with the innovation of baptism. When they rejected it, they went underground, remaining immortal and continuing to provide the power and inspiration for pascola and deer dances. The surem, then, represent the aboriginal Yaqui world of spirit, still alive and still functioning within contemporary Yaqui worldview and ceremony. The beings who accepted baptism and became Yaquis also became mortal through the Christian innovation and now depend upon communication with yoania (through visions and dreams) for life-giving power, to defend against deadly forces.

The Yaquis today have a concept of *huya aniya*, the wild brushland, desert, or woods. It represents not only the ancient spiritual earth, yoania, "the source of all things—the food and the tools of everyday reality, as well as the special powers of dance and song. It was the source of all, and men were merely an element within it, before the coming of the Jesuits" (Spicer 1980: 65), but also the present source of spiritual power. The Jesuits instituted towns, churches, and many aspects of Yaqui culture; however, the huya aniya persists as a force, surrounding Yaqui village life. Contemporary Yaquis still call upon the spiritual power of Nature—the deer, horned toads, water snakes, and others—to promote their community. Each species has its own language and power, which can be obtained through the motions of the pascolas and deer dancers. These powers can even influence Christianity, and they represent a specifically Yaqui source of life. Other Mexicans have their matachinis, their fariseos, their santos, but only the Yaquis have huya aniya from which to draw sustenance (Spicer 1988: 28–29).

The Yaquis believe in many sources of danger and protection in the world. They depend upon amulets to protect them, cigarettes to aid their spiritual requests, and seers to warn against the future. They fear the disease-causing evil of witches and the ill will of ghosts; they turn to native doctors to suck out disease and counteract sorcery. Many of these beliefs are pre-Christian; others are combined with Christian usage, e.g., when holy water protects against disease, or when witches are said to work in concert with the Devil. When a Yaqui infant dies after baptism, the Yaquis give the next child a Yaqui name to "preserve the generation" (in Painter 1986: 67), as one Yaqui says. In general, the

Yaquis recognize the power of both aboriginal and Christian super-nature and turn to both in times of crisis.

The Yaquis do not tend to have personal relations with God, *Dios*. Their relations with the divine are directed toward the Virgin and Jesus and certain saints, as well as angels and the dead. Mary is perhaps more prominent in daily life than Jesus. The matachinis are devoted to her, whereas the fariseos belong to her son, and the ceremonial season of the matachinis, (from Easter to Ash Wednesday) is longer than that of the fariseos (from Ash Wednesday to the Finding of the True Cross). The interrelations between Mary and Jesus are intimate and complex. As one Yaqui myth states:

> Mary always had flowers about her. Jesus was born because Mary smelled a flower; this is the way that she remained a virgin. In the time when the Jews were going to crucify Jesus, they wanted a carpenter to make a cross on which to crucify him. They found Joseph and told him to make the cross. Joseph was a good carpenter, but when he went to look at the wood which he had for making the cross, it was all too short, and there was no way in which he could cut it to make a cross big enough. While he was standing there puzzling over it, his son Jesus came and talked to him. Jesus told him that he was God and that, if Joseph went out into the hills, he would find a tree which he could cut down and make a cross out of it. Jesus then went away. Joseph stood for a long time in doubt. He didn't know whether or not to believe that Jesus was God or not. Finally he went out into the hills and found a tree and cut it down. The tree which he cut down was really Mary, because Mary had turned herself into a tree. Jesus and God had planned this out long before and had told Mary to turn herself into a tree. So, when Jesus was crucified, he was crucified on a cross made of his mother, Mary. She holds him embraced in her outstretched arms. (In Spicer 1940: 254)

The flowers associated with Mary (as well as with yoania) in Yaqui ritual are also viewed as Jesus' blood, which has curative and protective powers.

Jesus, El Señor, is God on earth to the Yaquis. He is symbolized most prominently by the many crosses in Yaqui life, and his spirit of penitence is to be imitated throughout Lent, and especially during Holy Week. As a constant source of well being, however, the Yaquis turn more often to His mother Mary than to Him.

They also turn to many *santos*—the holy figures of the saints, Mary, and Jesus—that inhabit their churches and households. The Yaquis keep these images in safe areas and bring them out for processions and the familial fiestas that mark the entire calendar. St. Francis Xavier, St. Joseph, St. Lazarus, the Virgin of Guadalupe, St. Ignatius Loyola— their images are everywhere, and their powers are invoked for the common weal, according to Yaqui beliefs.

The Yaquis also hope for protection by angel-guardians, the unnamed spirits of the dead who live on in the spirit world, and who care about the living. The Yaquis meditate upon these spirits, pray to them, and try to make them happy. The Indians refer to their virginal children as "little angels" and think that when an unmarried person dies, he or she becomes an angel-guardian.

Even more important in Yaqui cult is devotion to the named spirits of the Yaqui dead. The Yaquis keep their names recorded in their books of the dead; they honor them with funerals, death novenas, death anniversaries, October novenas, and the services at All Souls Day. Almost every other ceremony also makes reference to the dead, whose spirits stay about the households where they once lived, especially during October. While there is some fear of ghosts, there is great effort to communicate with the spirits of known Yaquis in order to promote solidarity and continuity of the tribe.

WAEHMA

No feature of contemporary Yaqui life is more visible a symbol of solidarity, continuity, and religiousness than the ceremonial cycle that occurs in virtually every Yaqui community during the Lenten-Easter season. The Spanish word for the Forty Days of Lent is *cuarsema*, which the Yaquis have modified in their own language to *Waehma*, applying the term to the several dozen ritual events performed from Ash Wednesday to Easter Sunday under the direction of the *kohtumbre*, the ceremonial officials. Culminating in the dramatic activities of Holy Week, Waehma is a single but complex pageant with unifying themes and passionate community involvement. It is an annual renewal of Yaqui community and religion,

> an intricate and structured set of rituals which define and annually reaffirm the nature of the relationships between people and supernaturals. This body of rituals defines the significance of important symbols, the realms of meaning of crosses and of flowers, of the Catholic prayers, of sacred song and of ritual dance. The Waehma expresses in long-continued, focused ritual actions the ultimate meaning of all the activity diffused through the many ceremonies of a year. It is the culmination of the ceremonial year and the concentrated expression of the central Yaqui religious values. (Spicer 1980: 71)

In the Yaqui villages around Tucson (Painter 1986; Spicer 1940 and 1980), in Guadalupe village (Guadalupe, April 3–11, 1993; Myers, April 12, 1993; Senne 1986; *Yaqui Lent and Easter Ceremonies* 1992), and in Mexico as well as in Arizona (Barker 1957), the Waehma is the Yaquis' central religious and cultural symbol.

The Easter ceremonialism of the Yaquis derives from medieval Roman Catholicism carried by the Jesuits to New Spain. Throughout the Middle Ages European Christians carried out dramatic Holy Week ritualism focussing upon Christ's passion, death, and resurrection, symbolizing human salvation through the sacramental Church. The Yaquis have adapted this ritualism to themselves, impersonating the dramatis personae of the Easter events: Jesus, Mary, and the enemies of Christ. If much of the Catholic world has ceased to enact the dramas of Christ's Passion, the Yaquis have persisted. The Easter ceremonial,

is not only a tribute to and glorification of Jesus; it is a pragmatic way
to salvation. . . . In sermons one hears that "in the very beginning" Jesus
desired to come to earth as a human being; and that He gave to Himself His sufferings, to serve as an example for the people to follow by reenacting the events of His life, as penance and for a blessing. (Painter
1986: 353)

In an extended dramatic form the Waehma reenacts "the Passion of
Christ, but also the struggle of His Church to convert and redeem His
enemies" (Barker 1957: 257) for the benefit of the living and the dead.

On Ash Wednesday each year the maestros and sacristans place upon
the forehead of each congregant the ashes made from the palms of the
previous year's Palm Sunday. The altar group dresses the church for
the Lenten season with crucifixes, *santos*, purple cloth, and books of the
dead, and the kohtumbre prepare for the ceremonials to come. For the
next forty days the Stations (or Way) of the Cross outside the church
are the central site for ritual, as the kohtumbre establish their headquarters in the plaza not far from the great central cross. On First Friday the
kohtumbre dedicate the Stations of the Cross, and the altar group sets
up a "gate" before the church altar. The ceremonies now begin.

The church bell calls the Yaquis to the church, where they venerate
before the great cross and the altar. The maestro leads the faithful
around the Stations, accompanied by altar women and girl flag bear-
ers, in imitation of Jesus' miraculous journeys throughout the Holy
Land. They recite the Act of Contrition and sing the *Stabat Mater* ("At
the cross her station keeping Stood the mournful Mother weeping
While her Son was hanging," in Painter 1986: 369). As they process
around the Way, the first enemies of Christ make their appearance, including a chapayeka representing Judas who enters the church and
crawls under the altar, searching confusedly for clues of Jesus' presence
so he can betray Him. Setting the pattern for the next six Fridays, the
chapayeka goes out among the devotees, shivering and staggering as
they mention the names of Mary and Jesus in their alabanzas.

Each Friday the number of chapayekas increases, and they become
emboldened in their insolence. They make threatening gestures toward the church; they sharpen their swords and scrape their daggers,
calling attention to their weaponry as foot soldiers of Pilate and be-
trayers of Jesus. They demonstrate that they are "intent on capturing
Jesus and killing Him" (Senne 1986: 6). They even come to disrupt the
Stations of the Cross by making noise and mocking the processions.

Each chapayeka wears a mask of his own manufacture, representing dangerous evils—Mexican soldiers were featured in the early twentieth century; hoboes were pictured during the Depression, and Japanese during the Second World War. The maskers are grotesque and ominous, as they stalk Jesus, disrupt the maestros, and try to catch frightened children about town. By the beginning of Holy Week there are several dozen chapayekas amassed in ritual opposition to Christ and Church.

On Palm Sunday all the ceremonies of the village honor Jesus. The congregation sings hymns as they bear a statue of Jesus in procession to the church area, and ceremonial members confirm their vows. The maestros distribute palms. The matachinis dance for the first time in Lent, making their presence felt in defense of Mary. The pascolas and deer dancer also make their first appearance and perform for the faithful. On the same day, however, enemies of Christ take over the town, intimidating and spying on people, and for the next several days they appear unchecked.

The fariseos arrive at the church on Wednesday of Holy Week, carrying "a veritable forest" (ibid., 11) of boughs which represent the wooded country where Jesus wandered, hiding from His enemies. In the evening the sacristan lights fifteen candles in church, setting into motion the medieval ritual of *Tenebrae*: the darkening of the "Light of the world" (in Painter 1986: 424), that is, Jesus, whose betrayal and death are foreseen. The church officials extinguish the candles, one by one, and as they do, the chapayekas enter the church, scouting out Jesus, crawling behind the Tenebrae candelabrum, signalling that they have seen signs of Him in the dense woods. They make menacing gestures and howl like wild animals, as the last lights are put out and the congregation leaves the darkened church. While the maestros and cantors intone the *Miserere*, the chapayekas and fariseos begin to flagellate each other, the superiors whipping their subordinates. Now a general rite of penitence takes place, as members of the congregation reenter and whip each other for forgiveness and blessing. Parents or godparents whip their charges gently; friends whip each other. If someone has hurt another during the year, he or she receives strokes for reconciliation. In this manner the Yaquis imitate the humility of Jesus and attempt to achieve atonement with one another, washing away their sins. The candles are now relit, indicating Jesus' expected revivification on Easter Sunday.

On Holy Thursday the Yaqui village experiences the pursuit and capture of Jesus, hence the seeming victory of His enemies. The church bells are silent, replaced by wooden clappers, as the chapayekas take over the plaza, construct a bower representing the Garden of Gethsemane, and assert their mastery over Christ. One of them represents the Nazarene, an old man said to be a manifestation of Jesus. The chapayekas lead him around the Stations of the Cross, touching him with their daggers and swords. Yet at each Station they submit to his mild whippings, showing their tractability, until he finally shows his fatigue and is led back to the church.

In the evening the church group places an image of Jesus under the Gethsemane bower, and the enemies of Jesus capture it and bring it into the church, under their control. During the capture the maestros and cantoras sing an alabanza:

> *Weep sinners*
> *With much sorrow*
> *For the passion and death*
> *Of our Lord.* (In ibid., 446)

Later, when Mary is searching for Jesus around the Way of the Cross, the singers chant another alabanza:

> *Now went out the Blessed Virgin*
> *The Holy Thursday midnight*
> *Looking for the Nazarene.* (448)

All during the night the kohtumbre inhabit the church, reciting the rosary in devotion to Jesus and Mary.

On Good Friday the enemies of Jesus make a public display of the crucifixion in the plaza, tapping hammers against the main cross and parading the figure of Jesus around the Stations. Then the kohtumbre bring a bier filled with flowers into the church, and the faithful arrive in their plainest clothing to mourn for Him. They make monetary offerings to the casket, while the maestros and cantors chant:

> *Christ on the Cross crucified*
> *May it be through telling of that misfortune*
> *That I value in death*
> *The blood that is spilled.* (459)

The kohtumbre take down the crosses of the Way, and the caballeros declare themselves "for Jesus" (460) by turning their weapons point down. The chapayekas celebrate their victory while the Yaqui faithful mourn their slain Christ throughout the afternoon and evening.

During the night the chapayekas continue their jubilation, while the church group keeps vigil over the bier and visitors come to venerate. About midnight, however, while the enemies of Jesus are processing around the plaza in victory, the altar women remove the mourning cloths from the Virgin, changing the altar colors from purple to red. The kohtumbre encounter the chapayekas on procession and a mock battle commences. In the confusion the sacristan removes the figure of Christ from the bier, unbeknownst to the chapayeka guard, replacing it with a toy or a stuffed animal so the enemies will not know He is missing. Only in the morning do they come to realize that He is gone. Their victory has been overturned.

Before dawn the church officials ring a bell to signal the resurrection of Jesus. The chapayekas take to blaming each other for this turn of events, focussing their scorn on Judas, a straw-stuffed figure dressed like themselves. In the morning they march him around the plaza. At the same time the children called "little angels" stand before the church, and the matachinis arrive with their streaming red headdresses called "flowers." Pascolas and deer dancers help, too, as they strew the soldiers of Rome with flowers, defeating and transforming them. The flowers are the key weapons against Christ's enemies. They are the flowers of Mary, akin to the innocent and faithful little angels themselves; the flowers are even said by the Yaquis to be the "grace of God" (Spicer 1980: 88). They state that "when blood fell from Christ's wound to the ground, flowers grew on the spot. The flower then indicated grace from heaven, and that is why . . . the Judases cannot stand up against flowers" (ibid.).

Having been defeated by the flowers of Jesus and Mary, the chapayekas take off their masks. They set a pyre in which they burn the effigy of Judas and then their masks—all but two that are set aside for death ceremonies during the year—to the great rejoicing of the multitudes. Glory Saturday has arrived to celebratory dancing and singing. This is the holiest day of the year for the Yaquis, as the singers chant the *Gloria*, the matachinis begin their fiesta in honor of Mary, and pascolas and deer dancer join the festivities, expressing the Yaqui faith. No demonstration of Yaqui spirituality is greater, however, than that of the transformed fariseos and chapayekas covered by flowers. The Yaquis say of them that they change their minds at the last, and go in to God. The[y] get rid of their sins, because they represent those that did not believe, but this is what they had to do in their parts. When they shed their masks, they get rid of all the sins that they have represented and come to the church as they are. The fariseos have felt closer than the rest to Jesus—they have felt closer than at any time during the year. (In Painter 1986: 485)

Some Yaquis comment that the fariseos have been rebaptized by their performance, and now they emerge from the church "like heroes of the town" (Senne 1986: 13).

For the rest of Glory Saturday, and on Easter Sunday, too, the matachinis hold their fiesta, with a celebratory maypole dance and *alleliuis* led by the pascolas. Then at midmorning on Easter the head maestro gathers the faithful for a farewell sermon (see Painter, Savala, and Alvarez 1955), at which he summarizes what has taken place, what vows have been initiated and completed. He reminds the Yaqui community of its duties toward the divine, not only this year but in all years to come. At this farewell circle the Yaquis promise to perform their Lenten and Easter ceremonies the following year, in keeping with Yaqui Catholic tradition.

The Easter season does not end, however, until May 3, the Day of the Finding of the True Cross. On this day the Yaquis dress a cross in a skirt, and it is referred to as "Our Mother Most Holy Cross" (Painter 1986: 504–510), the Virgin Mary. The maestro leads vespers and the kohtumbre retire from their duties until the next year. "And so the Yaqui Easter season ends with the Holy Cross fiesta," one scholar writes (ibid., 510):

> It is a time of exacting ritual labor in the fulfillment of individual vows, of consecrated community ceremonies in memory of Jesus. It is a time of continuity with the past in remembrance of the . . . ancient ones, revered ancestors, who, at the command of Jesus, fulfilled the same obligations in the same way in the historical eight pueblos in the homeland on the Yaqui River in Mexico. It is a time of re-assertion of Yaqui discipline, Yaqui moral and religious codes, and of Yaqui mythology, now passed on once again to the young and renewed in the minds of the old.
>
> It is a time of re-affirmation of Christian doctrine, when Jesus and Mary seem very close to the people. It is a time when, through the sermons and prayers of the maestros, [Yaquis, in their own words,] are united with "Christian people everywhere throughout the four corners of the world."

Through the Lenten and Easter rituals the Yaquis reaffirm themselves as Yaquis and as Catholics. One writer says that "the core subtext of Waehma—its overt text being the Passion—is working through how to be simultaneously Yaqui and Catholic. Since the seventeenth century that has been the major problem of Yaqui history" (Schechner 1993: 98). To what extent do the Yaquis participate in Catholic tradition? It is clear that in the seventeenth century the Yaquis adopted many forms of Catholic belief and worship under Jesuit direction. It is also clear that "Yaqui Catholicism has, for complex historical reasons, diverged from the parent church—which has itself changed over the centuries since the Jesuits were first received by the Yaquis" (Painter 1986: 108). The Yaquis possessed enough freedom under the Jesuits to accomplish a "creative syncretism" (Senne 1986: 8) between Yaqui and Catholic forms; after 1767 the local Yaqui maestros and other religious leaders guided the development of Yaqui religiousness with autonomy, in continuity with Catholic tradition but creating a Yaqui Catholicism all their own.

Yaquis attend Roman Catholic services and receive its sacraments; however, the bulk of their religious practice takes place in the Yaqui church, the Yaqui plaza, and the Yaqui household. They maintain contact with Mexican Catholics, O'odham Catholics, and even Anglo Catholics. They also are aware of Protestant forms of Christianity, although they rarely identify themselves with these traditions. They are Yaqui Catholics, but what does this phrase mean?

Roman Catholic personnel have sometimes found Yaqui Catholicism lacking in normative content and catechetical knowledge. A Catholic priest in around 1940 said of the Yaquis near Tucson: "I don't imagine they are very far removed from the primitive tribal level. I should like to do some work out there. I understand there has not been much success. It must indicate a very low level of humanity among them" (in Spicer 1988: 90). Another cleric in the same decade commented upon the Yaqui Easter ceremonies: "What primitive actions! This is hardly bearable. It is wholly sacrilegious [sic]" (in ibid.). In 1970 a Franciscan wrote from Phoenix that, "The Yaqui are tied to traditional religious and social habits which inhibit material progress, and there is a serious lack of leadership among them" (*Our Negro and Indian Missions* 1970: 25). In more recent years, Father Daniel McLaughlin, S.T., pastor of Indian ministry in Tucson, has spoken about the dangers of "cultural Catholicism" among the Yaquis. He states that "while the tribe is nearly one hundred percent Catholic, the knowledge of their faith is often weak" (in "Easter in the Desert: Signs of Hope," Summer 1992: 7).

For some Roman Catholic clerics, the Yaqui Catholic faith is only nominal. Furthermore, there are some Yaquis, McLaughlin asserts, who "want to go back to their traditional religion. . . . They think they don't need Christianity" (McLaughlin, July 8, 1992). The head of the Indian ministry in Phoenix, Rev. James M. Dixon, S.J. (Dixon, August 7, 1992), has praise for the spirituality of the Yaquis at Guadalupe. He recognizes the continuity between Jesuit teaching and Matachin Society protocol; in effect, their rituals serve to "dance the rosary," he says. What the Yaquis do in their ritual life, he notes, is "clearly spiritual," but it is "heavily adapted Catholicism, . . . so focussed on saints, pageants, dances, etc. . . . that the Eucharist goes begging. . . . They are Catholics," he avows, "but not mainstream." In times of crisis—for instance, when they are sick in the Indian Hospital in Phoenix—they request the Eucharist ("what it means to them, I don't know," says Father Dixon), but in general, they keep their distance from the hierarchical Church. Instead they focus on their santos. This is, he remarks, a valid part of Catholic faith, a community of saints; it is an admirable "entrance into Catholicism." At the same time, it is not the fullness of Catholic tradition, and in their religious practice the Yaquis participate in but a portion of the whole. Another Catholic representative says of Yaquis in Tucson that their "devotional practices to Ignatius would make a Jesuit blush" (Thiel, July 9, 1991), with choreography and processions honoring the founder of the Society of Jesus.

Rev. David A. Myers, S.J., with a score of years among the Guadalupe Yaquis, finds the Indians not only *not* lacking in Christian faith, but exemplary of it: "What I have discovered is a marvelously integrated, theologically sound, and consummately Christo-centric religious practice which forms the vital basis of community identity and morality. My stance is to encourage by following their leadership" (Marquette. JINNAM. March 15, 1988). Myers criticizes both Catholic clerics and anthropologists who have assumed that Yaqui Catholic practice falls short of a norm. As a Matachin Society member himself, Myers attests to the Catholic purpose and symbolism of the society's rituals, and he finds in the ceremonies of Holy Week an "intensely personal identification with Jesus Christ." If Christianity is a thorough religious devotion to Christ and an identification with His sufferings, then Yaquis are supremely Catholic, according to the Jesuit: "They are actually suffering for Christ" (Myers, April 12, 1993).

By and large the scholarly consensus (e.g., Barker 1957, 1958; Painter 1986; Spicer 1954, 1972, 1980, 1988) is that the Yaquis "have accepted and integrated into their own culture the central figures of Roman Catholic doctrine and ritual" (Barker 1957: 139). Whereas other Indians of the Southwest, like the Pueblos, have kept Catholicism relatively compartmentalized from native practice, the Yaquis have fused Yaqui and Catholic traditions into a coherent whole. Muriel Thayer Painter writes (1986: 71):

> The total religion as practiced currently is a combination of Catholic doctrine and liturgy, medieval liturgical drama introduced by the Jesuits, and some strong elements of pre-Spanish beliefs and behavior, which still have validity in varying degrees for most. Some of the native concepts have been integrated into the Catholic way; some have been reinterpreted; some remain untouched. All are intertwined, and it is difficult and often impossible to separate them. Most of the people see no inconsistencies in their expression of religion. Many think that the Yaquis have always been Catholic and that Catholicism was present before Christ.

The Yaquis testify to their complete identity as Catholics—albeit as Yaqui Catholics—by claiming Catholicism to be their aboriginal form of religiousness, predating the Jesuits, predating Christ Himself.

The Yaquis have adopted the many forms of Catholic symbolism: the cross, the altar, bells, *santos*, palm leaves, ashes, scapulars, and rosaries. They genuflect as a gesture of devotion; they make the sign of the Cross, twice or three times in succession. Their liturgical calendar is Roman Catholic, reliving the birth, passion, death, and resurrection of Jesus Christ yearly. The Yaquis believe in the Triune God, to whom they devote their lives. They revere the Virgin Mary, mother of Jesus Christ, and they refer to the Church as Our Holy Mother, a personification of Mary's identity. They believe in heaven, purgatory, and hell (although ultimately, they avow, everyone goes to heaven). They believe that life is a cosmic drama in which a person takes a stand either for good or for evil, and their religiousness plays itself out in morality, in having a "good heart" (Painter 1986: 97–99). Their religious life is an attempt to orient themselves to a God whom they assert to be the Christian God.

Concurrently the Yaquis hold beliefs which do not derive from Christianity, but which represent their pre-Christian concepts. They speak of the ancients who continue to be channels for spiritual powers. The Yaquis have not ceased worshipping the spirits of the forest world: the deer, the all-important flowers, the ancient beings. Christian concepts predominate today, but the *huya aniya* holds its power in the Yaqui mind. In Edward H. Spicer's words:

> The huya aniya is not subordinated to the Christian domain, and yet it is true that by the 20th century Christian values were in some degree dominant. Yaquis had by that time become powerfully affected by the Christian orientation of the many ceremonials which nevertheless depended for their efficacy on the existence of the huya aniya and its kind of power. Every ceremony devoted to a Christian supernatural required participation by ceremonialists whose power was associated with the huya aniya and the Christian world of the towns is achieved through an active process of frequent bringing together of ritual expressions of the two kinds of power. (Spicer 1980: 70)

Spicer calls this adaptation "oppositional integration . . . continuing interaction of two opposing conceptions of the universe within a common framework of religious expression" (ibid.).

Through this integration the Yaquis have engendered the "growth of a new religion . . . not known before to either Jesuits or Yaquis . . . an amalgam of North American and European traits" (ibid., 59). The Yaquis have taken ideas, symbols, gestures, organizations, and values common to both Catholic and Yaqui traditions and from these created a unified complex of religiousness. Flowers were important to the aboriginal Yaquis and also to the Jesuits. Today flowers are Yaqui Catholic symbols of universal blessing. The Yaquis have grafted the dual ceremonial organization patterns of the American Southwest onto the Catholic liturgical calendar in the making of their ritual year. Their ritual dancing by matachinis and pascolas reenact Catholic and Yaqui mythological events. Their ceremonial patterns emphasize repetitions of three and four—three supposedly for the Trinity, four for the Four Directions of the natural cosmos. In their legends God or Mary christianizes the pascolas, making them servants of Christianity rather than of the yoania or the Devil (Painter 1986: 258–261). In their music the Yaquis alternate European violin and harp with native drum and flute. In such a manner the Yaquis combine Christian and Yaqui elements into a distinctive religion.

The Yaquis call that religion "Catholic" (Spicer 1980: 59). They say that their actions today are the Yaqui response to Jesus' suffering on behalf of humankind; they are attempting to gain grace from heaven through their religious activity. They identify themselves as Catholic. At the same time they possess elements—beliefs and practices—that some other Catholics may call "serious errors or non-essential superstitions" (ibid., 60). Even more important, each Yaqui village is "an autonomous ceremonial unit" (Spicer 1954: 78), an independent church made up of family members who do not subscribe to an explicit catechism or creed. Each village community engages in a religious life that emphasizes the community itself as a ceremonial unit, an agent of blessing, a focus of concern. There is thus a tribal element to Yaqui Catholicism in which Jesus and Mary are culture heroes, imagined in local terms, serving local purposes. Yaqui religiousness is Catholic, but an independent, distinctive set of syncretized forms.

Outside the Yaqui communities of southern Arizona, individual Yaquis have evolved their own patterns of Catholic worship. Father Peter Navarra, a Yaqui descendant born and reared in San Diego, has been teaching Indian parishioners a Yaqui deer dance in order to "represent the death and resurrection of Jesus Christ" (Dale 1990: 15). In a ritual the deer "lies on the ground before the hunter, a symbol of one who gave his life that others might live." On their feet the hunter and deer dancers wear cocoons filled with seeds as symbols of new life. The hunter wears a belt of deer hooves, representing the deer who have died so the Yaquis may live. Father Navarra and his congregants dance this pageant on Palm Sunday and again on Holy Saturday, when the deer dances by himself at the *Gloria* during mass to celebrate Christ's resurrection: "The deer is no longer dead at the hunter's feet. He is risen." Navarra states that the Jesuit missionaries among the Yaquis "decided to compare the deer to the story of the passion of Christ, who himself was sacrificed. . . . The . . . hunter, called the Pascola, personified sinners and the deer represented Christ" (ibid.), the unblemished lamb of God, the sacrificial victim. Navarra notes that the syncretism inherent in his Catholic deer dance continues the practice of Mexican Catholicism. In his view the first missioners encouraged such syncretism, and over the centuries the Indians of Mexico, including the Yaquis, have continued to practice a faith that combines Indian and Catholic imagery. Says Navarra, "It is a Mexican Indian custom, to take ownership of all rituals." The Yaquis have appropriated Catholic ceremonial life: "Besides being Christian, Roman Catholic, it is theirs." (in ibid.).

JEƩUIT MIƩƩIONƩ AMONG THE O'ODHAM

In the seventeenth century the Jesuits led the spiritual advance into northwestern New Spain, baptizing as many as one hundred thousand Indians on the whole west coast by the end of the 1620s. Despite periodic rebellions, Indians like the Opatas adopted Christian identity and often aided the missionaries in their evangelical thrust northward. The Jesuits established each mission area with a central station (cabecera) and several outstations (visitas), the whole constituting a reduction or *doctrina*, where Indians received sacraments and instruction and gathered under Jesuit dominion. It was expected that in time each mission would become a parish, and its inhabitants would become taxpaying citizens under civil jurisdiction. In the short run, however, each mission was guided by Jesuit patriarchal guardianship and was exempt from total Spanish rule. The goal of the Jesuits was Indian conversion: "total acceptance of Christian dogma and Greco-Roman culture" (Polzer 1976: 40).

In order to accomplish this goal the priests attracted the various Indians of northwest New Spain with gifts, foods, and the promise of eternal life brought about by baptism. The padres explained the gospel in Indian languages and encouraged Indian leaders to send their children to mission domicile and catechesis. The priests tried to eradicate the influence of aboriginal medicine men and to foster monogamous marriages. They filled the Indian year with liturgical celebration; they built churches, engaged in productive, joyful activity such as singing and dancing. They indoctrinated the natives in the practice and ethos of sacramental confessions. They appointed Indian assistants to validate clerical authority, and in general the Jesuits aimed at "close, personal contact" (ibid., 45) with the Indians in order to convert them to Christian morals and loyalties on the rim of Christendom.

The Jesuits sought control over Indian lives, but within the limits of Christian charity (not always achieved). Thus in 1662 a rule for the Society of Jesus in northwestern New Spain ordered:

> Let all the missionary Fathers take care to show the Indians all love and charity in their dealings; they ought to avoid as much as possible all forms of strictness and harshness. . . . In those regions where flogging

has been introduced as a punishment for being absent from the doctrina, or for some similar offense, it will be done only with notable moderation lest the Indians lose their love for their pastors. (In ibid., 68)

About twenty years later a Father Visitor ruled that "no Father in any
case will bind up or shear the hair of any native, man or woman, girl or
boy. If by chance one of them deserves punishment by whipping, it
will not exceed eight lashes" (89).

In this fashion the Jesuits inaugurated their missions in Sonora,
among the Indians known to themselves as O'odham but termed
Pimas (the river O'odham) and Papagos (desert O'odham) by the
Spanish. The Lower Pimas received the priests with hospitality, as did
their neighbors the Opatas; however, the Upper Pimas "were so hostile to Christianity" through most of the seventeenth century that the
missionaries and civil authorities were "unable to penetrate their
lands" (Bannon 1955: 88). Scattered Spaniards lived among them, but
it was not until 1687 that the intrepid Italian Jesuit Eusebio Francisco
Kino succeeded in entering the Upper Pima territory in the northern
Sonoran desert, introducing the natives there to Christianity.

The O'odham were Sonoran gatherers and farmers who numbered
between ten thousand and thirty thousand in the 1680s and lived in autonomous villages. Their public ritual life emphasized the acquisition
of spiritual powers for the benefit of the group and its individuals.
They collected saguaro cactus fruit, making it into a wine, which they
drank in orgiastic delight in order to bring about summer rain and
concomitant fertility. Their men underwent an arduous pilgrimage to
the Gulf of California for salt and blessings. Their war campaigns
sought the scalps of enemies, which they "adopted" as powerful, dangerous members of their households. Their songs—for hunting success, for cures—evoked the forces of nature and supernature in the
hope of protecting and nurturing one's own. The O'odham marked
the cycles of the year and of individual development with ceremonials
that solidified community awareness and emphasized continuity
among human, natural, and divine spheres.

Before Father Kino came to the O'odham he spent two years in Baja
California on an evangelical expedition. The Indians there responded
well to his "smiles" and "gewgaws" (Bolton 1960: 140). They liked the
image he carried of his spiritual patron, Our Lady of Guadalupe, and
under his prodding they made the sign of the cross "with extraordinary

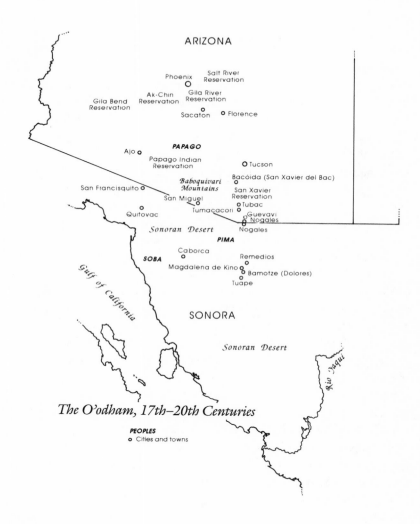

ARIZONA

Phoenix ○ Salt River
            Reservation

        Ak-Chin   Gila River
Gila Bend   Reservation   Reservation
Reservation
            Sacaton ○   ○ Florence

PAPAGO

Ajo ○

        Papago Indian
        Reservation   ○ Tucson

                        Bacóida (San Xavier del Bac)
        Baboquivari   ○
        Mountains   San Xavier
San Francisquito ○   Reservation
        San Miguel   ○ Tubac
              Tumacácori ○
Quitovac ○   Guevavi
        ○   ○ Nogales
                        Nogales
    Sonoran Desert

                PIMA
            Caborca
SOBA   ○   Remedios
        Magdalena de Kino ○ ○
                    ○ Bamotze (Dolores)
                    Tuape ○

    SONORA

            Sonoran Desert

The O'odham, 17th–20th Centuries

PEOPLES
○ Cities and towns

docility and friendliness" (Burrus 1954: 31). But they were terrified by the Christ on the large crucifix which Kino placed in his chapel. They wanted to know who he was and who put him to death and whether he was "a cruel enemy of the Spaniards" (in ibid., 53). Kino tried to convince them that Jesus was their friend; that he had gone to heaven; and that the Spanish and other Christians would one day join Him there. One of the Indians replied to Kino and his companions "that we should go right away" (ibid.). Father Matias Goñi christened a sick child—the first baptism on the California peninsula—but the child died, causing the Indians to wail and turn against the Jesuit. It is said that Father Goñi "acquired among the natives the reputation of being an unskilled medicine man, so much so that on the following day they would not let him approach their sick" (61).

Father Kino lasted two years in Baja California, 1683–1685, but drought prevented the Spanish from farming there, so they abandoned the mission, against the priest's protests. His next assignment was among the Indians of the west coast—Seris and Guaymas, who were being seized by Spanish miners for involuntary paid service (*repartimiento*). Kino wrote at the time that these Indians "are terrorized and caused to flee from conversion to the Holy Gospel, and to refuse to accept the gentle rule of our Holy Faith" (in Bolton 1960: 234). He petitioned the Guadalajara authorities to exempt Indian converts from such labor for five years; in 1686 the civil government responded to him that if he could convert Indians, they would be exempt from repartimiento for twenty years rather than five. Under that incentive, Kino turned to the O'odham to baptize them and defend them against exploitation.

Father Kino arrived in Pimeria Alta in 1687, where he hoped to find the Pimas pining for "fathers and holy baptism" (in ibid., 249). In the Indian village of Bamotze a fellow priest baptized a dying headman, and Father Kino named the village after Nuestra Señora de los Dolores. In his first months at Dolores, he baptized more than sixty Pimas, including Chief Coxi—the captain general of the Pimas of that region—and his wife. A large bell arrived from Mexico, and the Indians loved its peal. He took a hundred Pimas from Dolores to Tuape, further south, where the Spanish staged a procession of the Blessed Sacrament with forty recently baptized Indian children from Dolores adorned with the jewelry of Spanish ladies from a nearby mining town. The Pimas built for Kino a mission church, and they began to settle the area around Dolores, while the priest made his rounds to the neighboring visitas. Within a year there were three hundred baptisms; six months later the figure had doubled.

At the same time Kino encountered resistance from Remedios, his outstation immediately to the north of Dolores. The Indians there resented the padres' usurpation of Indian authority and the punishments meted out to indigenes—the father even had one Indian hanged. The O'odham said that they were laboring so hard for the missions that they could not work their own farms. In addition, the Spaniards' cattle were drying up the watering holes in Pimeria Alta. Finally, the Remedios natives accused the priests of killing Indians with sacramental oils. Kino's great inducement to the Indians was that he could protect them from slavery for twenty years if they received baptism; however, the reluctant Indians feared that this was a false promise, as native peoples southeast of Dolores were already under attack by Spanish soldiers. Kino pointed out that these besieged Indians to the southeast were unbaptized and thus unprotected. This served to bolster Kino's promises, and the threat of enslavement moved even reluctant Indians to gather around Kino's mission.

The padre brought with him a theology of Christian triumphalism familiar throughout New Spain. For instance, among the Sobas at Caborca in 1694 the priest taught:

> There was but one God. He created the heavens, light, the land, birds, animals, the fish of the sea, the water, trees, plants, and fruits for the use and sustenance of the man Adam. He made Adam from the earth and gave him a soul. His wife, named Eve, He made of Adam's own rib. He promised them the reward of glory if they would serve Him, love Him, and obey all His precepts, and the everlasting fire of Hell if they should offend Him and break His commandments. Kino told his listeners how all humankind, descended from Adam and Eve, fell under God's displeasure through original sin. But with infinite mercy and pity, in His good time, He sent His Son to save mankind from the blazing fire of Hell. He explained to them the Flood, from which only eight persons were saved, all the rest perishing in the waters. He told them of Christ's birth, suffering, death, resurrection and ascent to Heaven, whence at the end of the world He would come to awaken everybody, to judge them with His upright justice, reward good Christians with eternal glory, and condemn bad people *and heathen* to the eternal fires of Hell. Kino taught them how to make the sign of the Cross, say Our Father, the Ave María, the Credo, and the commandments, and he explained the saving grace of the sacraments. (Ibid., 275–276)

Kino's soldier-companion, Juan Matheo Manje, told the same Indians that baptized Indians "rendered vassalage to our King and natural Lord." Manje also spoke of God and His holy law "and how He rewards good people and Christians with glory, and bad people with the blazing and eternal fires of Hell, to which He condemns the miserable souls who do not love, serve, and reverence Him—and they were horrified at the burning" (in ibid., 273–274).

These and other Indians of Pimeria Alta did not resist the process of reduction; indeed, many embraced it initially. "There were inducements—simple curiosity, glass beads or tobacco, a particularly persuasive Padre, livestock and new crops and a full stomach, security from former enemies, the impressive ceremonialism, or the lance of a Spanish soldier at one's back" (Kessell 1970: 6). Nevertheless, resentments built up from the start, and it was not long before the O'odham rebelled against the intruders. In 1695 Pimas, outraged by the authoritarian regime of the Opata Indians who served the priests as assistants, attacked the new mission of Caborca, killing the Jesuit Francisco Xavier Saeta and foreign, christianized Indians on his staff. This was a "rebellion against Spanish authority and against Christianity" (Burrus 1971: 258), and it took punitive military expeditions to pacify the natives, but not before they had destroyed several missions through the spring and summer of 1695. After negotiating a settlement with the Indian rebels, Kino needed to defend his missionary efforts against those Spanish who regarded his work as fruitless. The Jesuit argued that many of the O'odham remained "constant and fervent" (ibid., 157) in their Christian faith. He declared that mission Dolores and its visitas were productive, well stocked, and conscientiously governed institutions securely under his command. He denied charges that he was baptizing the Indians without adequate instruction, and he convinced his superiors that his missionary efforts among the O'odham should continue.

Over the next several years Kino solidified and expanded his reductions in Pimeria Alta, exhorting the O'odham against "the enemies of the province" (in Bolton 1960: 356), such as the Apaches. He celebrated the Christian Indians' victories against their foes and organized them to request more priests to live among the northernmost Pimas. In the late 1690s he traversed Papago country, finding there over forty peaceful, agricultural villages. In each place he brought the gospel and the sacrament of baptism. By the end of the century he had established several mission posts among them, including a promising place in a valley oasis eight miles south of San Cosme del Tucsón. Bacóida was its name, the Place near the Spring, and it was heavily farmed, with maize, beans, calabashes, melons, and cotton in large quantities. Kino brought livestock to Bacóida in 1697 and visited again in 1699. Over a thousand Indians dwelled there—Papagos to the west, Pimas to the south and east—prospering with mission livestock. In 1700 Kino laid the foundation for a visita church to be known as San Xavier del Bac.

Kino supported the expansion of his missionary empire through the sale of produce from reductions to the Spanish mines and towns of the region. He convinced both Church and State that his evangelical enterprise made good spiritual and economic sense—as Indian souls were pacified under Spanish rule—and he defended his fellow Jesuits against those who charged them with profiteering and those who attempted to secularize the endeavor. By 1706, when Kino had built the church of Magdelena he had under his charge nine active missions and fifteen other reductions under development, including San Xavier del Bac. As procurator of Pimeria Alta, Father Kino could count over thirty-five hundred baptized O'odham to his credit. In 1711, when he died while visiting Magdelena, the figure was closer to four thousand, although but few of them had been taught fine points of Catholic doctrine, and one might say that his missions had given the natives only a taste of Catholicism (e.g., Joseph, Spicer, and Chesky 1949: 18; Fontana 1989: 55–57). After twenty-four years of missionary work among O'odham, Kino had just begun their process of christianization.

Kino's death did not spell the demise of the O'odham missions, but it did interrupt its momentum, and the subsequent decades were ones of indecision, setback, and revolt, until the Jesuit expulsion in 1767. The Jesuits in Pimeria Alta, led in 1711 by Agustin de Campos, wished to expand their activities, establishing resident priests among the Papagos and reaching out to the Hopis further north. Spanish miners, colonists, and the military wanted to secularize the missions and remove all legal protection of Indian lands. For twenty years neither expansion nor dissolution took place, with Campos baptizing over one thousand Pimas, mostly children and the infirm. But the priests' numbers lessened, and not until 1732 did a new contingent of Jesuits arrive, with the approval of the bishop of Durango, to restore the vitality of the mission enterprise. Between 1711 and 1731 Jesuits had been accused of various scandalous activities: living in too much luxury, having too

close attachments to women, working the Indians too hard or punishing them too much (see Polzer 1976: 98–101). At the same time, the
baptized O'odham were not compelled to learn Christian doctrine
or to leave behind their aboriginal religious practices. In 1732 a more
zealous contingent of Jesuits arrived in such missions as Los Santos
Angeles de Guevavi (in what is today southernmost Arizona). The
O'odham, "grown used to Christianity on their terms were in for a
change" (Kessell 1970: 43).

Guevavi was one of the most northernly Jesuit missions in Sonora,
far from administrative centers. Founded in 1691, it drew reluctant
Pima converts in its first decades, accruing one thousand or more by
the 1730s: "To the Indians the village became a concentration camp—
no matter how benevolent its purpose" (ibid., xii), and the Indians resisted the priests' authority over the years. Father Kino had described
the Pimas there as docile, hardworking indigenes ready for salvation;
however, it is noted that "Kino was a propagandist, . . . deliberately
misrepresenting the Pimas" (ibid., 50) to win civil and ecclesiastical
support for his project. When the Austrian Jesuit, Johann Baptist
Grazhoffer arrived at Guevavi in 1732, he found the Pimas engaged in
drunkenness and orgies (associated with their annual ceremony of
drinking cactus wine to bring about rain and fertility), practicing
polygamy, and resisting clerical rule. Kino had come initially with
promises and presents; the Indians had accepted baptism, whatever its
meaning might have been for them. Over the years,

> The visits of Kino and Campos had led them to believe that Christianity
> involved little more than a few symbolic gestures, in turn for which
> they always received steel knives or bright ribbon. Now, as Father
> Grazhoffer's Opata or Yaqui assistants moved among them telling them
> what to do, the natives of Guevavi resented it. (Ibid., 51)

Within a year they poisoned Grazhoffer. His successor lasted no longer,
possibly poisoned also.

It took the construction of two presidios and the influx of Spanish
cattlemen and colonists to make Jesuit rule effective at Guevavi. By the
1740s the padres were in charge, with military support and with native
governors, fiscals, and captains enforcing clerical rule and administer-
ing corporal punishment. A thousand Pimas received baptism between
1732 and 1744, but "it took the prodding of soldiers and Christian
Indians to provide converts" (ibid., 92), and abundance of food was

required to lure them to Christian services. Elders were giving up their orgies, a priest reported in 1744, and they were accepting Christian marriages; they were trying to overthrow their medicine men and were obedient to the padres, and the children were learning their catechism; however, their numbers at Guevavi were dwindling, and only twenty-three families lived at the mission. Out in the rancherias the Indians were still unchristianized.

The report said that to the north, at remote San Xavier del Bac, over two thousand Indians had received baptism since 1732, but with four hundred families living at the mission, it was "just one great heathen ranchería" (ibid., 82). The O'odham there did not know how to pray the *Pater Noster* or *Ave Maria* nor make the sign of the cross. Some fled baptism, and almost all resisted Christian monogamy. What little is known about the Jesuit missions in Pimeria Alta in the 1740s indicates that what little hold the priests had on the loyalties of the Indians was accomplished through a combination of authoritarianism and looking the other way.

In 1751, led by Luis Oacpicagigua—formerly a military agent of the Spanish who had brought in many a convert to the reductions—the Pimas asserted their desire to be rid of the Jesuit missions. In its first day in November the Pima revolt caused the deaths of twenty-five Spanish colonists, two priests, and several native mayordomos. Within a week all the Jesuit missions were in turmoil, with a hundred Spanish deaths; Indian converts deserted the reductions, taking with them mission livestock and implements. Without neophytes, missions like Guevavi closed up, and the priests took their vestments and other church paraphernalia southward to safety. Pimas ransacked Guevavi and completely destroyed San Xavier del Bac and other stations before the outbreak came to a close in January 1752.

The Pimas accused the Jesuits, like Father Joseph Garrucho at Guevavi, of abuses, from the "wanton whipping of loyal Pimas to the kidnapping of native children" (ibid., 108), charges that the Jesuits denied, or justified as proper expressions of priestly authority. "Like school children, some firmness . . . is necessary for the Indian" (in Ewing 1941: 146), one priest said. In the view of the padres, the Pimas had been encouraged by the Yaqui revolt of 1740 and the Seri uprising in 1750 to expel the Spanish colonial system; in particular they accused the Pima leader of seeking power for himself. The Jesuit response to the Pima revolt was to call upon greater military support for the

O'odham missions in the years to come. The Pimas agreed to reenter the reductions, and the Jesuits agreed to remove several of the priests accused of brutality (Father Garrucho among them). Luis Oacpicagigua urged his fellow Pimas to welcome back the padres in 1753, but it took military force to impose clerical dominion once again. Through the rest of the 1750s the O'odham persisted in their resistance to the missions, even routing the returning Jesuits, for example at San Xavier del Bac in 1756, where the priests attempted to put an end to traditional rituals such as the cactus wine celebration and its drunkenness. Some Indians preferred to sack and abandon the missions, living as "apostates" (Fontana 1989: 62), free of Jesuit rule, rather than submit once again to Catholic authority.

Between 1756 and 1763 Rev. Ignaz Pfefferkorn, S.J., worked in the O'odham missions of Sonora, primarily at Guevavi, during a time when the Indians were peaceful but "had again lapsed into their former savage existence" (Pfefferkorn 1989: 261). Reduced in numbers by disease and infertility, harried by Apaches, but unwilling to settle as a group amidst the military protection and control in the reductions, most of the O'odham lived in desert poverty. The priests fed them when "the poor people, driven by hunger come to the neighboring missions to seek food. . . . This humane treatment makes such an impression on them that each time some voluntarily remain with the Christians and seek baptism. I myself often had the good fortune to make such a joyful catch" (ibid., 30), wrote the priest. He further told how on occasion an old Papago would come into the mission, seeking a deathbed baptism, so to be "received in heaven" (281). The mission Indians of Sonora honored the feast days of their local saints with processions of the Blessed Sacrament, high mass, and bullfights. They took their catechism, observed Sundays and other holy days. They grew maize, wheat, beans, peas, pepper, and sugar cane in the reductions and raised livestock for sale to Spanish miners. Yet the missions of Pfefferkorn's time were poor in spirit and material. The Indians, he said, seemed to agree with instruction, but showed no real interest in it. They went to confession once a year but had to be dragged by the hair to perform this Easter duty. Displaying little repentance, failing to examine their conscience as proper Christians, they seemed to the clerics ineligible to receive the Lord's Supper. The O'odham appeared devoid of Christian knowledge and faith, and out of the priests' sight they continued in their drinking debaucheries during the cactus fruit season. In the mission fields they resisted the hard work expected of them, and the mission produce was meager, according to Pfefferkorn's observations of the time.

The Jesuit who replaced Pfefferkorn at Guevavi, Custodio Ximeno, S.J., reported in 1766 that fifty-eight Indians remained, forty of them confessing, the others in rudimentary stages of catechesis. There were close to a hundred Christian Indian villages in Sonora in that year, with as many as thirty Jesuits in their midst; however, almost all of those pueblos were among the Opatas, Lower Pimas, and other Indians of the southern region. Only eight desultory missions were extant among the Upper Pimas and Papagos, with loyal Christian Indians there numbering only in the hundreds. Never had there been more than five thousand O'odham living in the missions at any one time, but over the decades the Pimas had died and deserted, to be replaced by Papagos. Now these, too, were drastically reduced in number.

Fifteen Franciscans took over these O'odham missions in 1768, finding them in a "sad state" (Van Well 1942: 58). The new friars attempted to upgrade the reductions, making them more respectable doctrinally and insisting that the Indians support them financially. They rebuilt San Xavier del Bac and tried to save Guevavi and its visitas; however, the Indians often "went over the hill" (Matson 1977: 19), and the missions struggled to persist. Between 1768 and 1824 (the newly created Mexican government deported the Franciscans from Pimeria Alta at the later date), the Order of St. Francis devoted itself to the O'odham, continuing the task begun by the Jesuits, but with what immediate success is difficult to judge.

Like the Jesuits, the Franciscans faced threats to the mission enterprise raised by soldiers, colonists, miners, and bureaucrats, all of whom desired to secularize the Indian reductions and turn them into self-supporting parishes with lands available for sale and usurpation. Even more than the Jesuits, the Franciscans suffered from attack by Apaches, who stole mission livestock, burned buildings, broke statues, and mocked the priests. Epidemics spread through the O'odham populations as contact with Spaniards increased, and the Indians feared to enter the missions for terror of epidemics as well as Apache marauders. The Franciscans were daunted by the task before them, but they persevered. In 1768, when Fray Francisco Garces arrived at San Xavier del Bac, he wrote: "I am very content. There are plenty of Indians. I like them and they like me." On the other hand, he found that "these people do not know the submission they owe their king, for even when they do venerate their priests and are subject, they are little short of heathens" (in Kessell 1976: 43–44).

The Franciscan regime differed little from that of the Jesuits. A 1772 document depicts the routine at the Tumacacori visita:

> Every day at sunrise the bells are rung announcing Mass. An old Indian commonly called the *mador* and two fiscales go through the whole village obliging the children and all the unmarried persons to gather at the church to attend the Holy Sacrifice of the Mass in devotion and silence. When this is over, all recite with the Father missionary in Spanish

the prayers and catechism. In the evening at sunset this exercise is repeated before the door of the church. It is concluded with the praying
of the Rosary and the singing of the *Salve* or the *Alabado*.

On Sundays and feast days the mador and fiscales are ordered to see
that all—men, women, and children—are obliged to attend Mass, with
their meager clothing washed and everyone bathed and hair combed.
On these days Mass is sung, accompanied by harps, violins, and with
four or six male and female Indian singers.

During the holy season of Lent, everyone is obliged to attend Mass
daily and recite the prayers in Spanish. The Father explains to them the
necessity, circumstances, and method of making a good confession, and
every Sunday afternoon they are given a clear and substantial explanation of the Four Last Things [Death, Judgment, Heaven, and Hell].

During Holy Week at the mission cabeceras the ceremonies of those
holy days are conducted, with a replica of Christ's tomb, processions,
sermons, and explanations of those supreme mysteries. After Easter
the lists or census of the villages are examined to find out how many
have fulfilled their Easter duty [penance and holy communion]. (Ibid.,
69–70, *sic*)

The Franciscans learned that the O'odham were fond of joining pagan
and Christian ceremonialism under the Jesuits, so on feast days the
friars tried to ban their native dances while allowing for innocuous
amusements and games. The priests emphasized changes in behavior
among two thousand or so neophytes: wearing pants, having houses
with doors, addressing each other with Christian salutations, and they
employed christianized Indians from further south—including Yaquis
and Opatas—to serve as role models and godparents for the Papagos
and Pimas. As in other missions of New Spain, the padres appointed
officials from the local Indian population who served under priestly
command. The missions solidified as institutions, and in 1779 the papacy created the Diocese of Sonora. Three years later the Province of
Sonora formed an all-O'odham regiment to fight the Apaches. On the
northern periphery of Christendom and New Spain, institutions of
Church and State were enveloping the O'odham.

In 1796 the Franciscan priest at Tumacacori, Fray Mariano Bordoy,
made a census of 103 persons living at this outpost (Whiting 1954).
Only four, including the friar, were Spanish; there was one Yuman,
one Apache child, and a dozen Yaquis serving as craftsmen and Christian exemplars. The rest were either Pimas or Papagos—the former
with a century of missionary influence, the latter the converts of Franciscans. All had baptismal names, taking the identities of saints and

padres. There was some intermarriage among the Yaquis, Pimas, and Papagos, and the mission constituted a community with considerable social solidarity. But what of the Indians' religious identity and practice? Of that we have little knowledge beyond the external behavior they and other mission Indians exhibited. They prayed the rosary, but we do not know what it meant to them. They continued to engage in "native ceremonialism" (Kessell 1976: xiv), the padres reported, but we know not what forms that took.

In the same year, 1796–1797, Father Diego Miguel Bringas de Manzaneda y Encinas, O.F.M., sent a recommendation to the Spanish Crown regarding the means to make the Indians of Sonora truly loyal, taxpaying vassals of the Crown and faithful subjects of Christendom. Although his report (Matson and Fontana 1977) went unread, it indicates the Franciscan programme for Indian conversion and the ways in which it was falling short. Daniel S. Matson writes:

> That Spain's conversion effort among the northern Piman Indians generally failed is a matter of historical record. Many Pimans were outwardly Christianized in that they accepted a number of the formal aspects of the new religion, but few, if any, of the intended meanings of those forms survived. And most certainly Pimans never became loyal vassals of the Spanish crown. . . . they seem to have gone only so far as they had to go to give the appearance of change. They discovered soon that what the Spaniard wanted was Indians to have the *appearance* of being like themselves rather than to undergo genuine assimilation. (Ibid., 30, emphasis his)

To make the process more efficient, Fray Bringas recommended that the Pimans be required to farm, follow Spanish laws, work the mines, have straight streets in their villages, work for the private rather than the community good, speak Spanish, listen to preaching, and practice Catholic rituals. The friar wrote that the missions should organize the Indians' time to avoid idle moments. The Indians should labor hard, meditate, confess sins, participate in liturgies, take scourging like good Franciscans, and cease their scandalous native rituals and bathing. The only way to accomplish these goals was for the Franciscans to increase their control over the Indians in their jurisdictions. Father Bringas concluded:

> When the Indians have been removed (they are mostly neophytes) from the government of the religious, they will cease to receive any religious instruction and they will fail to become rooted in the Holy Faith.

> Because it is a common tendency of human beings to be bored with
> spiritual matters, they put them off in favor of perishable affairs. This
> infirmity is usually stronger in the Indians, and much more so even in
> recent converts whose tender status in religion makes them more vul-
> nerable to the powerful influence of the Common Enemy. . . . Now if at
> the very beginning of their conversion they are informed that the min-
> istro has no authority to get them to church at the regular time, that
> they can wander where they wish, and they can decide all their own
> actions and movements—their perdition will follow beyond any
> doubt. . . . The Indians . . . are incapable of governing themselves for
> many years after their conversion. They are always children. (Ibid., 5)

Even after a century of contact with Christianity the Franciscan testified
that the O'odham resisted thorough inculcation of Christian loyalty,
identity, faith, and values.

In 1810 the Mexican insurrection against Spain began, and in the
turmoil of the next decade the missions on the far reaches of the empire slipped into poverty. Spanish citizens, *gente de razon*, filtered into
the mission areas, until by 1820 they outnumbered the Indians in the
eight Pimeria Alta missions, 2,291 to 1,127 (Kessell 1976: 246), as epidemics reduced the number of Pima and Papago neophytes. In this
atmosphere of uncertainty and loosened control, the O'odham did
not deepen their Christian conversion. One friar wrote of the Indians
in 1817 from his vantage point of San Ignacio de Tubac, north of
Tumacacori:

> With regard to Christianity, only God looks into the heart, but from
> outward effects I am of the opinion that only those who die before the
> use of reason are safe, and they are many. The grownups are full of su-
> perstitions, and no matter how the ministers work they do not believe
> them because they have more faith in their old medicine men.
>
> Often one catches them in the gatherings they hold in the caves of
> the hills, burns the implements of their superstitions, breaks their ollas,
> preaches to them, punishes them—but one observes no change for the
> better. It is a peculiar thing that those who make the greatest false show
> of Christianity prove the most wed to their abuses. Great is their effort
> to hide these transgressions. Even when they are caught at them they
> do not want to confess their evil belief, saying only that the Spaniards
> have their way of curing and the Indians theirs, as they learned it from
> their ancestors. (In ibid., 236–237)

Finally in the 1820s the gente de razon overran the missions, as
Mexico gained its independence, and chaos reigned in Sonora. As the
Spanish Franciscans were being expelled, Apaches, epidemics, and

Americanos all descended on the O'odham missions. In other areas of Mexico secularization took place by official fiat; in Pimeria Alta the missions simply slid into decay, and no secular clergy came to replace the ousted Franciscans. The Mexican-American War, the 1848 Treaty of Guadalupe-Hidalgo, the Gadsden Purchase of 1853, cholera epidemics, and Apache raids all served to cut off northern Sonora from Mexico without integrating it to the institutions of the United States. The O'odham stayed by their mission chapels, watching over the relics and developing their own spiritual heritage.

A U.S. soldier wrote in 1848 about the remains of the missions in what is now southern Arizona:

> The churches in this valley are remarkable. At Tumacacori is a very large and fine church standing in the midst of a few common conical Indian huts, made of bushes, thatched with grass, huts of most common and primitive kind. . . . This church is now taken care of by the Indians, Pimas, most of whom are off attending a jubilee, or fair, on the other side of the mountain.
>
> No Priest has been in attendance for many years, though all its images, pictures, figures remain unmolested, and in good keeping. No Mexicans live with them at all. (In ibid., 307)

Two months later the Apaches devastated Tubac, and the Indians at Tumacacori—twenty-five or thirty of them—"took down the santos from their niches in the church, bundled up vestments and sacred vessels, and followed the retreating settlers down the road to San Xavier" (ibid., 308). In 1849 the residents of Tucson, in petitioning for a resident priest, noted that the christianized Indians of the area seemed especially in need of Catholic leadership:

> The pueblo of San Xavier del Bac, of catechized Indians, is composed of more than fifty families. Because they have no pastor to propagate the Faith they live practically as heathens. . . . This is the result of their having no shepherd of the flock of Jesus Christ. (In ibid., 310–311)

JONORA CATHOLICIJM

Without Catholic priests residing in their vicinity, the O'odham Indians of northern Sonora and (soon to be) southern Arizona—the Papagos and Pimas of the second half of the nineteenth century—developed their own forms of religious expression and organization. During the missionary period the Pimas and Papagos adopted Christian forms: "they were genuinely stimulated by Christianity and they wanted to acquire what they considered the best of it (fiestas, townish lifestyle, the material means of access to God and the Saints) without surrendering any important part of their paganism . . ." (Bahr 1988: 134). As the missions ended, these christianized peoples were relatively free of all external jurisdiction. In this context, "Church services were a form, continued side by side with the ancient ceremonies which persisted with a vitality impossible in the subjugated provinces of Mexico" (Underhill 1979: 31).

On their own for several generations, the Papagos and Pimas—but particularly the Papagos, who remained more isolated in southernmost Arizona than the Pimas, who had settled the areas closer to the growing town of Phoenix—continued to practice *O'odham himdaq*: the people's way or religion, constituted by shamanistic tradition, rain dances, harvest festivals, song oratory, and other elements of the aboriginal religion. At the same time many O'odham practiced *Santo himdaq*, saint way or religion. This was the earliest type of O'odham participation in Catholic tradition during the missionary period, and it consisted of obtaining images of the saints for healing and protective powers. These saints replaced aboriginal images which served the same life-promoting purposes. During the period after the missions' demise, the O'odham further elaborated these practices, partially in unison with other Sonoran peoples (and hence this religious expression is sometimes called Sonoran Catholicism), but also on their own, according to their own meanings and authority. So, for example, the Papagos built their own chapels to house the santos during the period 1850–1910.

Visitors to Papago country sometimes call the territory "a land of churches" (Bahr 1988: 133) around which the Indians organized their social and religious activities. Several dozen of these chapels derive from the period of O'odham "self-Christianization" (*ibid.*) before the return of the Franciscans around the turn of the twentieth century; the Papagos built them "for use in their own folk-Catholic religious observances" (Griffith 1975: 21). These Papago chapels were simple rectangles, averaging twenty-five feet in length and fifteen feet in width, made of adobe, stone, or railroad ties. Their doors faced east, a Papago convention, with an altar on the west wall, over which sacred images (like those of San Francisco) were placed for devotion. The Papagos built these chapels to house the images, and a typical altar housed well over a hundred santos. From the ceiling hung paper flowers, and the floor was clear for dancing and venerating. Surrounding these structures were a feast house, a ramada, a dance area, and a field cross, i.e., an outdoor arena for processions, feasts, and dances—the ritual activities of Papago Catholicism in the late nineteenth century. On saints' days, at baptisms, when pilgrims returned from sacred sites with new santos, there was ceremonial activity under the authority of Papago men and women. Inside the chapels the Indians held prayer services, using the santos and rosaries as meditative devices. The O'odham combined Indian and Catholic architectural forms—the ramada and the chapel, the dance ground and the field cross—to serve the syncretistic religious matrix called Sonoran Catholicism.

The Papagos and Pimas also enjoyed the services of Catholic priests whenever they could, and they identified themselves as Catholic peoples. As they traveled in Sonora in the late nineteenth century, the Papagos kept contact with Mexican Catholics and maintained their associations with the institutions of Roman Catholicism; however, in their own villages the O'odham fabricated their own Catholic dimensions, their own Catholicism, dedicated to their own well-being:

> It is *Papago* Catholicism even as Irish Catholicism is distinctly Irish and different from Mexican Catholicism. Among the Papagos a native medicine man may very well advise a patient to have a dance for his saint in order to cure a specific illness. Up until 1950, Catholic priests in the Papago country functioned as ritual specialists who performed special ceremonies and sometimes conferred with Papago lay religious leaders about distinctly Papago Catholic ceremonies. Other Papago Catholic ceremonies and organizations were completely in the hands of lay people. (Thomas 1967: 23)

O'odham commitment to Catholicism in this period derived in part from the sense of autonomy the Indians felt. On their own, they made Catholic life their own.

Papagos like Maria Chona (Underhill 1979), growing up in the desert of southern Arizona in the middle of the nineteenth century, received baptism on journeys to Mexico, and yet their daily life at home was filled with traditional O'odham religious culture, its myths, rituals, ethos, and worldviews. They fought the Apaches, sought crystals for curing, held cactus wine rituals, and searched for water much as their ancestors had. But Maria Chona and her people also turned to the powers of Catholicism when aboriginal medicines failed and crisis was upon them. When her people were dying of "falling hair sickness," a mysterious disease gotten from Whites, Maria Chona had a curing vision: "Very sick I was, half dead. Then, as I lay on the floor of my father's house, it seemed to me that two women came. One was a dead relative of mine and one was the Virgin Mary whom I had seen in the Catholic church in Tucson" (ibid., 80). The women showed her a "holy picture. . . . At each corner was a candle, but they were not candles, they were the blue stones which we think have magical powers. . . . So I learned how to cure" (ibid.). Maria Chona had been prevented by her family from following her vocation to become a native doctor; in crisis she turned to a symmetrical combination of Papago and Catholic images to gain curing power. This was typical of the religiousness elaborated by the O'odham in the late nineteenth century.

One should not get the misperception that the O'odham regarded the institutions of Catholicism as minor or distant features of their lives. To the contrary, the Indians embraced Catholic forms with vigorous attachment. Witness, for example, their devotion to the mission church of San Xavier del Bac. Eusebio Kino, S.J., founded the mission there in 1700; Francisco Garces, O.F.M., revitalized it in 1768. Between 1783 and 1797 the Franciscans and O'odham workers constructed the present structure, replacing an earlier church built in 1756. The church itself is Mexican Baroque, carrying all the markings of European culture rather than any ostensible Indian elements. Its iconography highlights the expansion of the Church, its missionary activity, its apostles, and the conquest of the New World (Ahlborn 1974: 25). The structure, its paintings and statuary, express Roman Catholic belief and worship, as exemplified by the colonial Spanish. Named for the famed Jesuit missionary to Asia, St. Francis Xavier, the church represents Franciscan spirituality in full elaboration.

Initially the church served the local Pima Indians; however, with their declining numbers, and with their revolt against the Jesuits in 1751, Papagos from further west became the chief inhabitants of Mission San Xavier. These Indians built the present church under Franciscan direction, and to the present day the O'odham regard the church as theirs, telling legends about their ancestors who constructed it. They interpret some of the iconography to suit their own meanings; for instance, they refer to a plaster sculpture of knotted cord (a Franciscan belt) as a great serpent who holds the church together. O'odham ritualists periodically cleanse the place of evil influences according to their own beliefs, and in general, "O'odham have developed a real ownership of this mission which was constructed by outsiders in order to bring about deep changes in the native culture" (Griffith 1992: 161). When the Franciscans were ordered out of Mexico, the O'odham tended after the church as it was abandoned to the Apaches and the hot desert sun. In 1849 O'odham from Tumacacori gathered up their Catholic statuary and brought it to San Xavier for safekeeping and continued their devotions in the church: "That the building was not entirely destroyed is due to the love and care of the Papagos, who did not forget the teachings of the padres" (Forrest 1929: 251). Within San Xavier del Bac, "Roman Catholicism, with its full panoply of saints, heros and heroines, ritual music, and religious art, came and stayed" (Fontana 1989: 57), with the Indians as carriers of tradition, maintaining for themselves the ecclesiastical titles of the colonial period: *fiscals*, *temastians*, and the like.

The church stands on Papago territory in the San Xavier Reservation area, and around the church the Papagos conduct an active social life, revolving around the Christian calendar: Christmas, New Year's, the feast of the Holy Cross, the Assumption, and especially the feasts of St. Francis of Assisi and St. Francis Xavier. For each of these feasts the Papagos have a planning committee that coordinates activities with the Franciscan friars, who returned to San Xavier del Bac in 1913. Father Walter Holly, O.F.M., noted in 1987 that, "Most parishes are trying to build community. Here it exists already. These people have lived together and shared for generations. We just give it a Christian focus" (in Hocker 1987: 7).

Throughout the twentieth century the Papagos have celebrated the feast of St. Francis Xavier (December 3) as their greatest religious festival. O'odham from all over southern Arizona are joined by Yaquis and other Catholics to celebrate the patron saint with procession and prayer, singing and dancing, fireworks and devotions. Each year the Indians clean and bless the church, and on the eve of the feast the Papago "feast chief" and his twelve "apostles" (*The Indian Sentinel* 21, no. 1, January 1941: 164) take down the statue of St. Francis from his niche above the altar, dress him in a new surplice, wash his face, and place him beneath a canopy, bedecked with bright flowers. The "apostles" carry him in procession around the mission plaza, as other Indians carry lighted candles and sing the *Ave Maria Stella*. Yaqui dancers serve as an honor guard. For several days the Indians pray the rosary, attend mass, and bring their own adorned statues of the saint to the church for veneration. They dance in the light of bonfires and feast under the banner of their beloved saint. In the church Indians come up the aisle on their knees to place their hands on the statue; they hold up their children to gaze into his face. At the end of each annual feast the community appoints a committee in charge of the next year's events; in this way the Papagos pass along their traditions.

The Papagos regard the church and its feast days as their own, and they seek blessings for their own people. The Franciscans respect the piety of the Indians at San Xavier del Bac, but they also rankle at the closed ranks of the Papago community. These Indians consider themselves part of the Catholic (Universal) Church, but their emphasis is upon themselves as a people. One can hear the Franciscans in their Sunday sermons to the Papagos, chiding them for "caring too much about your own community and not enough about the universal Church of Jesus Christ" (San Xavier del Bac, March 16, 1980). Like the Yaquis, the Papagos at San Xavier and elsewhere have developed their own insular Catholicism, in harmony with Roman Catholic tradition but attuned to their own autonomy and particularity.

One of the singular aspects of Sonoran Catholicism in which O'odham (and Yaquis) participate is the annual pilgrimage to the village church of Magdalena de Kino, sixty miles south of Nogales in Mexico. Every year thousands of Mexican and Indian pilgrims make their way by wagon, truck, bus, car, train, and even by foot in the time-honored fashion to celebrate the feast of San Francisco on October 4. For a week or more they inhabit the town, pay honor to a reclining statue of the saint, visit the exposed grave of Father Francisco Kino (who established Magdalena as a mission in the 1690s, and who died there in 1711), and enjoy the festival merriment. Many drink alcohol to excess and have sex with one another and with local Mexican prostitutes, perhaps carrying out the fructifying ritualism of the summer cactus wine festival in a Catholic habit. They ride the merry-go-rounds and watch the Yaquis and Mayos dance their *pascola* and deer dances. They dance to mariachi bands, attend freak shows, and market their wares; however, their overriding purpose is to venerate St. Francis so as to reaffirm their religious faith.

Papagos make other pilgrimages during the course of a year. They travel to Sonora in the summer to partake of the annual saguaro festival at a place called Quitovac. And even on their way to Magdalena, they stop at roadside crosses they have planted, and they pay respects to the natural shrines of their traditional culture: the sacred peak in the Baboquivari Mountains and other sites. Nevertheless, Magdalena is the "Sonoran Mecca for nearly all Papagos" (Fontana 1989: 103). They have been traveling there at least since the eighteenth century, and certainly during the period after the missions closed. Despite the vagaries of weather, revolutions, and international boundaries, they have continued the practice to the present day. Ask a Jesuit who accompanied them on their journeys if the Papagos still make pilgrimage to Magdalena, and he replies, "Do they!? It's the center of their spiritual lives!" (O'Brien, August 8, 1992).

The Papagos say that Father Kino himself promoted the pilgrimage around the turn of the eighteenth century in order to honor St. Francis Xavier, the Jesuit missionary to China. Some legends suggest that Kino tried to deliver a large statue of the saint to San Xavier del Bac, but it was too heavy to carry so far north—or in other legends the beasts of burden would go no further than Magdalena—and so Magdalena became the pilgrimage site. As Indians tell it, Kino died during the installation of the statue, or at least during a pilgrimage, and his burial there only enhanced the sacrality of the spot.

During the Jesuit era the Indians traveled to Magdalena to celebrate the feast of St. Francis Xavier on December 3; however, the Franciscans altered the date, possibly because the weather was inclement in December, or (more likely) in order to honor their own St. Francis: the saint of Assisi, the founder of the Order of Friars Minor, whose feast day is October 4. In the process the identities of the two Saints Francis—as well as the person of Eusebio Francisco Kino, too—

melded into a single, powerful San Francisco, and it is the composite santo whom the Papagos and other Sonoran Catholics venerate in Magdalena.

The life-size statue in the Magdalena church represents St. Francis Xavier, and yet he is sometimes dressed in brown Franciscan robes. Kino's burial site, discovered by archaeologists in 1966, is at another location in town, serving to consolidate the palpable holiness and power of San Francisco in Magdalena. A modern commentator observes (Griffith 1992: 43):

> So here in Magdalena we have a Saint Francis who partakes of characteristics of Saint Francis of Assisi, Saint Francis Xavier, and Eusebio Francisco Kino, S.J. He is the object of constant visits and a huge annual fiesta and pilgrimage. He is believed to work miracles on his own, and to exact payment of some kind from those whom he has helped. There is a feeling that he watches over a large part of the Sonoran Desert. In some ways he acts more like a local deity than a Catholic Saint, although there is no evidence that there was a powerful local deity worshiped in Magdalena before Father Kino's day.

A Franciscan friar in the 1940s asked some Papagos—as they tried to cure a sick child with mud made of Magdalena holy water—about the identity of the saint (San Francisco) whose picture they hung on the wall of their home. Their reply was, "'It's God.'" Indeed, "many older traditional O'odham seem to equate San Francisco with God" (ibid., 59), regarding him as a source of his own power, rather than an intermediary to a higher divine.

Why do the Papagos travel to Magdalena? Often they have vowed to make the difficult pilgrimage in return for San Francisco's aid or succor. Invariably they seek cures from maladies and the power to maintain good health and good luck by virtue of coming into contact with his statue. They hasten to the church as soon as they arrive in town, waiting for hours in line in order to make contact with the *santo*. In its presence they pray, cross themselves, genuflect, and meditate upon its power. When they reach the statue, they "touch it, kiss it, and even bite it" (Fontana 1989: 106), trying to lift its head, a feat considered a sign of special grace. They touch ribbons, medals, and other objects (either purchased in Magdalena or brought from their villages) to the statue in order to obtain its spirit, and they bring these empowered objects home for use in their houses. One Papago pilgrim says, "It's kind of like getting your battery recharged" (in ibid.). The rite is like a "baptism" (Kozak 1991: 39) for themselves and their religious paraphernalia.

One Franciscan who accompanied the Papagos to Magdalena in the 1950s testified that he was "almost overwhelmed" by "this huge and magnificent manifestation of devotion" (*The Indian Sentinel* 33, no. 9, November 1953: 132). Another Franciscan (Cavagnaro, August 6, 1988) stated that his Catholic faith was deepened by participating with the Papagos in their pilgrimage to the chapel of San Francisco in the 1970s and 1980s.

Just below the Arizona-Sonora border, south of the large Papago Indian Reservation, is a Papago village called San Francisquito, where pilgrims sometimes come in October instead of to Magdalena, in order to venerate another statue of St. Francis. Some Papagos say that their forebears carried the statue from Magdalena to the village to protect it from the secularists of the 1910 Mexican Revolution. Between 1934 and 1944 the revolutionists closed Magdalena as a pilgrimage church and threatened to destroy the statuary. Papagos regarded themselves as protectors of the holy object, so they secreted it to San Francisquito, which became a pilgrimage site as a result. In this village, as well as in San Xavier del Bac and Magdalena, the O'odham of today express their Sonoran Catholicism, as they have for the years stretching back almost three centuries.

REINJTITUTINC EVANGELIZATION

A century ago the O'odham were still developing their religious forms in relative isolation from external ecclesiastical institutions. The United States government—which gained jurisdiction over the Pimas and Papagos through the Treaty of Guadalupe-Hidalgo (1848) and the Gadsden Purchase (1853)—established reservations for the Indians in the late nineteenth and early twentieth centuries (San Xavier was created in 1874, the large Papago Indian Reservation in 1918, others in between). Only in 1895 did the Franciscans take responsibility once again for Pima and Papago ministry. They began their work among the Pimas near Phoenix and from there established stations among the Papagos further south. Their most celebrated padre was Reverend Bonaventure Oblasser, O.F.M., but one could name dozens of others. Several sisterhoods set up schools among the O'odham, including Sisters of Mary Immaculate and Franciscan Sisters of Christian Charity. At the same time Presbyterians and other Protestant denominations entered the mission field among the O'odham, creating sectarian disputes with the Catholic orders and factionalism within the tribes.

When the Franciscans resumed their work among the O'odham in the late nineteenth and early twentieth centuries, they regarded the Sonora Indians as "hardly Catholics at all; their faith, the priests said, was a 'religion of externals,' of whose real meaning they were unaware." Calling them "Montezumans," the priests tried to convert them into "good Catholics" (Joseph, Spicer, and Chesky 1949: 89), although it is unclear whether the Anglo Saxon clerics of the last century were more suspicious of aboriginal Indian spirituality or the forms of Catholicism passed down from the Spanish colonial era: the pageants, processions, pilgrimages, and veneration of santos. The friars set up several dozen mission stations among the Indians, constructing chapels for the proper administration of sacraments and as reminders of institutional Catholicism, in competition with the Papago folk chapels which remained under lay control. The Catholic clergy felt that they had two battles to win: one against the Presbyterians (who formed a Good Government League among the Papagos to lobby against the Catholic phalanx) and another against Sonora Indian

Catholicism with its composition of native and Hispanic Christian forms. Some Franciscans even discouraged in vain the Magdalena pilgrimages.

The friars distrusted the heterodoxy of the O'odham, but they respected their devotionalism. Tiburtius Wand, O.F.M., was impressed by the reverence exhibited by Papagos toward St. Francis in northern Mexico, in spite of the antireligious Mexican government in 1916 (*The Indian Sentinel* 1, no. 5, July 1917: 20–23). For all their clinging to old-time magic and medicine men, the Pimas were said to keep the Lord's Day faithfully and to live peaceful, chaste lives (ibid., 2, no. 10, April 1922: 444–445). The O'odham honored their dead, prayed their rosaries, respected the clerics, and invited Church personnel to dwell among them, even though they persisted in practices marked with aboriginal spirituality, e.g., preparing the deceased for the afterworld with fresh provisions (ibid., 4, no. 2, April 1924: 78–79). Catholic sisters teaching at a Papago Indian day school described Holy Week ceremonialism carried on by the Indians in which "devils" wearing long horns, horrifying masks, and the skins of animals raided Papago homes, taking anything not marked with a cross. After mass on Holy Saturday, Satan's reign ended, and children gleefully scourged the maskers with sticks, driving them into church where they were unmasked and liberated from their evil (ibid., 13, no. 2, spring 1933: 70). The missionaries tolerated this Papago performance that dated from Spanish colonial days and was similar to Yaqui Holy Week ceremonialism.

By the close of the fourth decade of the twentieth century, the Catholic missionaries were observing successes among the O'odham. One missionary organ noted (*Our Negro and Indian Missions* 1936: 28) that about half of the Pimas and Papagos of southern Arizona were "reclaimed to the Church by the recent efforts of the Franciscans," building upon the "affection for the Church" carried by these Indians from the days of the Padres Kino and Garces through the nineteenth century. *The Indian Sentinel* commented that the missionaries among the Pimas at ten locations "have studied how to assimilate the truths and practices of the Catholic Faith to the Pima in such a way that he becomes a Catholic Indian, that is, a real Catholic in thought and feeling, while remaining, as he wants to remain, an Indian" (19, no. 6, June 1939: 83). One-third of the six thousand Pimas were said to identify themselves as Catholics; over half of the six thousand Papagos were said to "call themselves Catholics. Those who have had the benefit of our missions during the past twenty-five years are really good and well-instructed Catholics. The others are more or less ignorant of Catholic beliefs and practices" (ibid., 20, no. 3, March 1940: 42). The Franciscans found that O'odham participation in the Second World War led to "a notable increase in the devotion of our Catholic people. Special services to invoke God's protection over the young men in the Army and the blessing of peace are faithfully attended. In fact, the Indians themselves gather in the evening for prayer at each of our eight mission chapels on the Pima Reservation" (*Our Negro and Indian Missions* 1943: 41).

From the missionaries' viewpoint, the years between World War II and the Second Vatican Council evidenced growing O'odham Catholic faith, built upon the Spanish heritage and augmented by modern schools and catechesis. The Papagos and Pimas exhibited their devotion to the saints: The Virgin Mary, St. Joseph, SS. Peter and Paul, St. Clare, St. Isidore, St. John the Baptist, and other local patrons, as well as the St. Francises. The Indians celebrated their feast days in their villages, journeyed to Magdalena and San Xavier del Bac, and prayed to the santos in the several dozen chapels of their own construction. They attended mass whenever Catholic priests reached their locales and marked the intervening Sundays with prayer services of their own. The rosary continued to be a popular sacramental; processions, benedictions, vespers, and other opportunities for song proved popular O'odham expressions of religiousness. Clerics were gratified by willing Indian support for church projects, providing labor for school farms and raising money for church operating expenses, and the priests perceived respect for their sacerdotal station.

The O'odham continued to mark Holy Week with "special devotion to the Passion of our Lord" (*The Indian Sentinel* 24, no. 4, April 1944: 61), raising stations of the cross made of giant saguaro cactus, performing native dances on Easter. On Good Friday the Papagos at one mission all wore crosses and came up the church aisle on their knees. Their priest remarked upon "the intense devotion of these people to the suffering Christ of Calvary" (32, no. 3, March 1952: 35). On All Souls Day the Indians held a "feast of the spirits" (24, no. 9, November 1944: 133) in their cemeteries after making confessions and attending mass. They danced throughout the night to honor their ancestors and recently deceased, placing candles on each grave and keeping vigil with their dearly departed. In this manner the O'odham kept continuity with their tribal identity; or, as a Franciscan said, "Catholic feasts have supplanted the old pagan ceremonials" (27, no. 9, November 1947: 133) of honoring the dead of the community, only now without the aboriginal element of dread of ghosts. Throughout November the Papagos in particular kept the graves clean and kept company with each other and their forebears. At Christmas time the Franciscans introduced old Spanish plays, *Las Posadas* (The Inns) and *Los Pastores* (The Shepherds), to develop adoration of Christ, making December the month of Infant Jesus as November was the month of the dead.

The Catholic priests found helpers among the Pimas and Papagos, some serving as catechists and sacristans, others as translators, school personnel, and role models for their fellows and their children. For example, the Franciscans praised Louise Pablo at San Miguel Papago mission and St. Joseph's School, where she was "leader, organizer, catechist, interpreter, teacher, school-cook" (36, no. 5, May 1956: 72). Alex Tashquinth, chief of a small Pima village, was one of the first converts when the Franciscans came to his community in the 1890s. He led a monogamous life and had many offspring who attended St. John's Indian School. When he died at an advanced age, a large solemn requiem mass marked his passing as a Native American Catholic leader (34, no. 2, February 1954: 26–27, 30). His mantle of leadership passed to Ambrose Jackson, a graduate of Sherman Institute, and to Anselm Shelde, a graduate of St. John's and an employee of Reynolds Aluminum in Phoenix. Shelde was president of PTA and the Holy Name Society, organizer of a Little League team, and father of five children whom he (and his wife, also a graduate of St. John's) raised with Catholic discipline, including spanking from infancy. For his family role he received an award from the Church as "Father of the Year" in 1958 (38, no. 5, September-October 1958: 67–68, 76). The priests and sisters planned their Catholic schools in order to inculcate Catholic loyalty, values, and identity, and to encourage marriages according to Catholic patterns, in order to foster cultural change in succeeding generations.

The missionaries did not pretend that the Papagos and Pimas were free of indigenous religious belief and practice. The O'odham continued to turn to local medicine men for healing, and they continued to fear the forces of ghosts and sorcerers and their tutelary animals such as owls and snakes. Newly arrived priests were struck by the lack of Catholic orthodoxy among the Indians and the persistence of traditional talismans and other magic charms. The Church personnel hoped that the death of each medicine man, the passing of each aboriginal custom, spelled the demise of the native religion among the non-Catholics and Catholic Indians alike. The O'odham, remarked one sister, "can thank their Church and schools for the enlightenment that is gradually showing them that these practices are so ridiculous: (26, no. 8, October 1946: 117). "Thank God," said a friar, "the younger generation no longer believes in things like this. Most of them come here to the mission to pray at God's altar. Once well instructed, they become good Catholics, faithful in attending Mass and in receiving the Sacraments" (28, no. 2, February 1948: 24). For all the progress, however, some O'odham communities still had the status of neophytes, praying the rosary, singing hymns, attending to their holy pictures, medals, and paper flowers in their chapel, but without receiving Holy Communion. "Perhaps the next time I come," wrote one Franciscan, "they will receive our Lord. He knows that they are still young in the Faith" (32, no. 2, February 1952: 21).

In the late 1940s those Papagos who weren't Presbyterians or Baptists continued to seek supernatural aid to bring rain through their cactus ceremonials, even those who went regularly to mass and married in the Church. One could make a distinction between Sonora Catholics and Roman Catholics, but the behavior of the two groups differed little, and the webs of kinship bound them together. They both observed ecclesiastical feast days during the year in order to show that they still believed in their religion (Joseph, Spicer and Chesky 1949: 82), holding processions of santos and dancing to mark the Catholic events. They focussed their attention on rites for their ancestors, on the anniversary of deaths, and especially on All Souls Day. Their homes had little altars with holy pictures, medals, candles, flowers, and other objects of special regard, and they continued to hold prayer services in their Papago chapels.

In the early 1950s many Papagos and Pimas left their villages to work in the mining towns of southern Arizona, such as Ajo and Florence, and to serve as migrant workers, picking cotton throughout the area. In these new locations Church personnel tried to reach them, helping construct chapels and leading services. Rev. Theodore Williges, O.F.M., set up an apostolate which he called Our Lady of the Highways, a trailer attached to a station wagon, by which he brought the sacraments to over sixteen hundred scattered Catholic Papagos. He and the other Franciscans worried not only that the O'odham would drift back to the "Montezuma" Catholicism still extant—the Papagos at Ajo, said one friar, "follow a sort of homemade religion, consisting of beliefs and practices which they have picked up from Mexicans across the border and combined with the old Indian beliefs and practices" (*The Indian Sentinel* 33, no. 4, April 1953: 52)—but also that evangelical Protestants would win them away from Catholic loyalty and practice. For both reasons, Father Williges said, "The Church in the person of the priest must come to them, since they themselves cannot go to the Church" (36, no. 3, March 1956: 39), laboring as they were in remote fields.

In the years preceding Vatican II a Franciscan described the Papagos as "docile, cooperative, and appreciative Catholics" (38, no. 3, May-June 1958: 46). In the decades that followed, the Papagos experienced less change than most Indian Catholics, indeed less than mainstream American Catholics. Their composite faith—engendered during Spanish colonialism, nurtured by the Indians themselves in the nineteenth century, and modified by Franciscan ministry in the twentieth—posed little sense of alienation among them, since for the most part they regarded it as their own local religiousness. As modern institutions impinged upon their isolated communities, they held to the matrix that had become their traditional religion—including their O'odham practices, their Sonora faith, and their Roman Catholicism. In the 1970s and 1980s they were less torn than most Indian Catholics between Indian and Catholic loyalties because they had forged long ago an identity embracing both. For the Pimas the growing metropolis of Phoenix had more of an impact on their culture, and over the decades they lost more of their traditional religiousness than did the Papagos further south. Over half of the Pimas joined Protestant churches. Nevertheless many Pima Catholics made the transition to the late twentieth century with less crisis than the Catholics of other Indian communities in the United States. Like the Papagos, they saw little need to reject their Catholicism, as they tended to practice it in ways that seemed at home to them, even when their commitment to Catholic ecclesia was tepid.

In 1976 Bishop Francis J. Green of Tucson wrote that 85 percent of the four thousand Papagos in his diocese were baptized Catholics, living in seventy villages scattered over three million acres of reservation land. At that time there were five Franciscans, two diocesan priests, a brother, and twenty sisters serving at five mission centers among the

Papagos, "guests amidst a 'foreign' culture—a deep and rich native American culture" (Marquette. DCRAA. 1976). In Phoenix, which became a diocese separate from Tucson in the 1960s, there were even more Indians than in Tucson in the late 1970s, thirteen thousand in all (including Catholic Yaquis and the northern tribes like the Havasupai, Apache, Yavapai, Paiute, etc., of whom hardly any were Catholics), but only half of the eleven thousand O'odham Indians were identified as Catholics. In the 1990s the figures are hardly different. The head of Indian Ministry in Tucson estimates that 80 percent of the five thousand Papagos in his diocese are "at least nominally" Catholic (McLaughlin, July 8, 1992). His counterpart in Phoenix says that there are thirteen thousand Pimas and six hundred Papagos in his diocese, 60–75 percent of whom have received Catholic baptism. He is careful to point out, however, that only eleven hundred of these are active in Catholic worship (Dixon, August 7, 1992).

In Tucson there is an urban Catholic ministry to the Papagos (as well as to the Yaquis), built upon the foundation of the St. Nicholas Indian Center, inaugurated in 1969, but firmly established as Blessed Kateri Tekakwitha parish in 1984 under the service of Trinity Missionaries. The Church tries to help the Indians with their problems of homelessness, alcohol and drug abuse, and crime, as well as with the racism and unemployment they face. With the leadership of Papagos such as Jose Ramon and Yaquis such as Juan Rivera, the Church tries to be a presence among urban Indians in Tucson. Nevertheless, the vast majority of Papagos still live in their villages in territory that has been theirs for many centuries. The fact that they have never faced massive relocation means that their spirituality (native and Catholic) is relatively intact, since they are still living in "their holy places" (McLaughlin, July 8, 1992).

Possessing the continuity they do with their Indian (as well as Catholic) past, Papago religiousness today is not much different from what it was a century ago. O'odham himdaq still exists; the Papagos continue to tell their origin stories in annual rituals. Their culture hero, I'itoi, is sometimes associated with Jesus Christ, or called "the Papago Christ" (Griffith 1992: 174), but more often he is kept separate in thought and practice, his cave receiving offerings from contemporary Papagos. They still perform cactus rituals, with drunkenness and dancing in hope for annual rain, and they still honor the scalps of their past enemies, the Apaches. On occasion they make

REINSTITUTING EVANGELIZATION

pilgrimages to the Gulf of California for salt, and shamanistic curing still takes place.

At the same time, the Papagos persist in Santo himdaq, their folk Catholicism. They fill their chapels and the altars in their homes with the images of the saints, from Magdalena and elsewhere, and they regard these santos as powerful beings in their own right, acquired when Papagos need help for themselves or their property. Sometimes they bring their *santos* to Magdalena to have them "replenished by the St. Francis who lies there" (in Griffith 1975: 22), as the Papagos say. This religious complex is closely related to Roman Catholicism; however, it lacks the focus of the latter on human sinfulness, Christ's salvific death and resurrection, and the individual's eschatology. This religion of the santos

> does not seem to be organized around a single, world-altering event— the death and resurrection of Christ—as is Roman Catholicism. Rather, it appears to be a borrowing of Catholic practices and supernatural beings that are then applied to the traditional O'odham needs for maintaining physical and spiritual health. Other vital O'odham needs— assuring that the rains arrive, for instance—are met through the philosophical system called O'odham himda[q], or Papago way. (Griffith 1992: 98)

Like O'odham himdaq, the complex of Santo himdaq emphasizes the good of the community in this world at this time and devotion to the O'odham ancestors.

Since the beginning of the twentieth century, Franciscans and other Catholic personnel have attempted to make the Papagos more orthodox in their beliefs and practices, and the result of this ministry has been the establishment of *Kaho:liga himdaq*, the Catholic way or religion. For all their involvement in the O'odham way and the way of the saints, most O'odham today identify themselves with this tradition and its sacraments: baptism, confirmation, matrimony, the sacrament for the sick and dying, and above all the mass and its Eucharist. By the 1970s this third religious complex was becoming prominent among the Papagos (Kozak 1991: 12–13), and it remains so today.

In their practice of Kaho:liga himdaq the Papagos take part in calendrical festivals (to honor their patron saints), they mark their rites of passage (birthdays, graduations) within the community, and they honor their dead at wakes, death anniversaries, and All Souls Day ceremonies. In this manner they seem to continue their other two forms of religiousness within the Catholic tradition, or what one researcher refers to as an inclusive religiousness called "God's way" (Bahr 1988: 149), whose purpose is to promote the general welfare of all O'odham.

In particular the Papagos pay attention to their dead. Since the time of first contact with the Spanish, the O'odham have been known (Bannon 1955: 20–21) to mark the graves of their relatives who died in accidents with trailside cairns, much as the Spanish marked with crosses the graves of their countrymen killed by Apaches. In the 1950s the Indians began to mark these sites—now numbering over a hundred along the highways of southern Arizona, commemorating unusual deaths, usually traffic accident victims—with crosses and votive candles (Kozak and Lopez 1991). By helping the ghosts of the deceased to find their resting place, by promoting prayers for the dearly departed who died without last rites, and by warning the living against the imminence of untimely deaths, these memorials play an important role in contemporary Papago religious expression.

In 1965 the O'odham constructed the first shrine chapel to supplement these roadside shrines. Constructed as miniature versions of the Papago chapels, these shrine chapels were ways to harness the power of the saints (especially the Virgin of Guadalupe) to protect the living and the dead. Each chapel has an area where fiestas can take place; the interior of the structure holds santos. In an age when Papagos are often on the road for seasonal employment, the roadside memorials and shrine chapels are means by which sudden, violent deaths away from home can be ameliorated through religious ritual: places where the living can focus their grieving—like the cemeteries on All Souls Day—and where the divinities can help the soul of the dead to the other world. This devotion to the dead is part of the Papago "integration of aboriginal and Christian religious tenets, with the ultimate goal of personal and social amelioration of violent, bad death" (ibid., 18).

Over the twentieth century the three forms of Papago religiousness have become more closely fused than in the past, so that today the Catholic way is the dominant matrix, but the other two ways are imbedded in it. By and large the superimposition of Catholicism over the O'odham way and the way of the saints has been the work of the Franciscans and their associates, the sisterhoods. These clerics and religious have tried to mold Papago religiousness into orthodox Catholicism, but even before the Second Vatican Council the missionaries tried to work with the Papagos as they were, without changing them too radically.

Beginning in the 1960s priests such as Camillus Cavagnaro, O.F.M., encouraged the use of Papago designs on mission chapels and commissioned nativity figures of saguaro cactus ribs, made by the Papago artists Domingo and Chepa Franco (Monthan and Monthan 1990: 58–59). The chapel of St. Catherine's Papago Mission contained choir benches covered with tanned skins of local desert animals. Papago basketry covered the monstrance and censer. Father Cavagnaro wrote that such a use of native design helped uphold the Indians' "self-respect" (*The Indian Sentinel* 40, no. 4, winter 1962: 54).

After four decades of ministry among the O'odham, Father Cavagnaro says today (Cavagnaro, August 3–6, 1988) that the Indians are devout, spiritual people, brought up within their culture to have a deep faith in God. They have a religiousness that is unpretentious and profound. They have their moral lapses, as every person does, but in the main he finds them "exemplary" Catholics and "lovable" people, "devoted" to Christ in their daily lives. If they engage in "excesses" during their saguaro cactus drunkenness, that is an expression of their conviction that there must be ritual chaos each year for the new year to be reborn. Engaging in such native expressions does not make them any less Catholic. He has found the imitation of Christ among them, in their simplicity, poverty, and communal ethic, and those values express the congruence of native and Catholic ideals. Cavagnaro, for one, does not lament the Papago genius for joining O'odham and Catholic forms of spirituality; indeed, he praises them for the religious life they have created for themselves.

Among the Pimas (and Papagos) of the Phoenix diocese, Catholic ministry has also worked without overt opposition in the most recent decades. The late Reverend James F. O'Brien, S.J., formed a Catholic Urban Indian Council in the 1970s to reach the O'odham in Phoenix parishes who were away from their reservation homes for reason of employment. He encouraged inculturation and the formation of an Indian diaconate and tried to build a ministry in the local reservations—Gila River, Salt River, Gila Bend, Ak-Chin, and others—founded upon O'odham culture with its "family gatherings or 'life celebrations'" (O'Brien 1982: 7). "It is a total aberration . . ." he wrote, "to look upon Indian Catholics as somehow strange, different, or inferior because their style of aligning themselves to the Church and celebrating their faith is not ours" (ibid.).

On the Salt River Reservation he found in 1977 "a very disorganized, disunified, and demoralized group of Catholic people with a crumbling church and . . . the majority of Catholics were uninterested in participating in any Church activities" (ibid., 12–13). He tried to revitalize Salt River Catholicism by focussing on the family life of the hundred or so kin groups. Liturgy centered on communal meals, funerals, and "Family Days" on Sundays. He developed Catholic leadership through Cursillo programs, and he gained the help of local leaders such as the "Pima holy man and Catholic layman," Joseph Giff. In the process he found his own spirituality growing as he journeyed with Indians to Magdalena, and he began to carry his own santos in solidarity with the devotionalism he discovered among the O'odham. Like the Franciscan Cavagnaro, who admitted that he "went native" among the O'odham ("It was the right thing to do, I suppose." Cavagnaro, August 6, 1988), the Jesuit O'Brien found what he called "true Catholicism" (O'Brien, August 8, 1992) in O'odham spirituality.

Rev. James M. Dixon, S.J., continues O'Brien's ministry among the Pimas and Papagos, and like his predecessor he admires much in the Indians' religious life. He tries to instill a love of the mass and the Holy Eucharist at the core of their religious lives, and he emphasizes Catholic sacraments, but he also recognizes the worth of the "Indian baptisms" (Dixon, August 7, 1992) they administer themselves as initiations to their own tribal society.

At Ak-Chin he finds a "thriving, industrious, lively community" of Papagos and Pimas, "fairly active" in Church life and eager to expand Church activities. The O'odham conduct a Christmas Eve mass; their First Fridays are "well organized." When he arrives for mass, a reader is always ready and the choir sings with "pizzazz" (ibid.).

The Salt River Pimas suffer from some "infighting and family politics"; nevertheless, they are said to be "vocal, articulate" Catholics (ibid.). Their vice-president and third-generation Catholic, Alfretta Antone, speaks openly to strangers of her Catholic faith (Salt River Reservation, January 7, 1987), and when Pope John Paul II visited Phoenix in 1987 (Phoenix, September 14, 1987) she spoke in public to him of the contemporary strength in Indian Catholicism. Even years after her presentation to the pope, she still speaks (Fargo, August 5,

1989) of the spiritual "radiation" she feels when she thinks about that great moment in her life.

At a particular Easter Vigil on Holy Saturday (Sacaton, April 10, 1993) in St. Anthony's Catholic Church on the Gila River Pima Reservation, Father Dixon presides over one hundred to one hundred fifty Pimas from five different communities. After night has fallen the celebrants light the Paschal Candle from a fire outside the church, and the congregation processes into the dark church, proclaiming Jesus Risen, the Light to the Nations. Although the priest leads the service by saying the mass, there are many active Pimas who participate in the rituals with him. They sing in English and O'odham languages, accompanied by guitarists. There are two lectors, four Eucharistic ministers, and a translator. The community is engaged in the Catholic ritual, as on this night a dozen adults and adolescents receive baptism and confirmation and three children receive the chrism of salvation. A video camera records the proceedings, as nearly all persons renew their baptismal vows by reciting the Apostles' Creed and blessing themselves with holy water. Everyone receives communion.

Like the Yaquis, the O'odham have made Catholicism their own; however, the Papago and Pima Catholics engage more readily in Roman Catholic rituals and institutions. They have produced contemporary Catholic leaders such as Sr. Lucia Antone, O.S.F., and Vivian Juan of the National Tekakwitha Conference and, for all their indigenous spiritual expression, many thousands of them seem secure in their association with the larger Church.

Even when O'odham individuals journey far from their homeland, they tend to maintain Catholic ties. Witness Lucille Sanderson who was "pushing eighty" (Sanderson, November 19, 1992) when she died on the Hoopa Valley Indian Reservation in northern California 1993. Of mixed Native American heritage (her parents met in boarding school), she was raised by her Papago grandmother on the Papago Indian Reservation in Arizona. In bringing up her own brood of seven girls and one boy, she tried to pass down what she considered the essence of her grandmother's Catholicism: "There is a stick in the road, and two paths lead out. Don't take the crooked road" (ibid.). She remembered the ministry of Father Bonaventure Oblasser in her early youth, how he and the Papago community built a church and celebrated the mass in the Indians' language. "He was a wonderful priest," she said; "he was at home with us" (ibid).

At the age of eleven she was kidnapped by U.S. government boarding school employees and taken to Fort Mohave School, where she lived for several years before graduating to Sherman Indian School. She never saw her grandmother again, and by the time she completed her schooling she had forgotten how to speak her native tongue.

With the first of three husbands, Sanderson moved to Hoopa. Married to a Protestant, living among Indians with no Catholic heritage and without priestly connections for many years, the O'odham woman continued to regard herself as a Catholic Papago. Her children attended a "Holy Roller" church until a Catholic priest arrived at Hoopa in the 1950s and built a church, now named for Kateri Tekakwitha. For several decades Lucille Sanderson and her family have occupied the same pews at weekly mass. Her extended family, she remarked, "would fill the church" (ibid.) if everyone came. But most do not. Those who have gravitated back to Papago country in Arizona have kept their Catholic identity, and Sanderson expressed pride at one granddaughter in Tucson public school who defended the Catholic doctrines of Blessed Mary's immaculate conception and virginity as mother of Jesus before her classmates. Most of her relatives living at Hoopa, however, have left the Church. Up to her death Sanderson was known to pray publicly for the continued Catholicism of her family, a "most faithful" (Monteiro, November 19, 1992) matriarch with a strong sense of her Papago grandmother's heritage. At Tekakwitha conferences Sanderson liked to mingle with Catholic Indians from around the country, and she felt comfortable with various native liturgies performed at the annual gatherings. Not speaking Papago, she found that the O'odham tended to "shy away" (Sanderson, November 19, 1992) from her. Nonetheless, she maintained solidarity with them and their Catholic faith throughout her life.

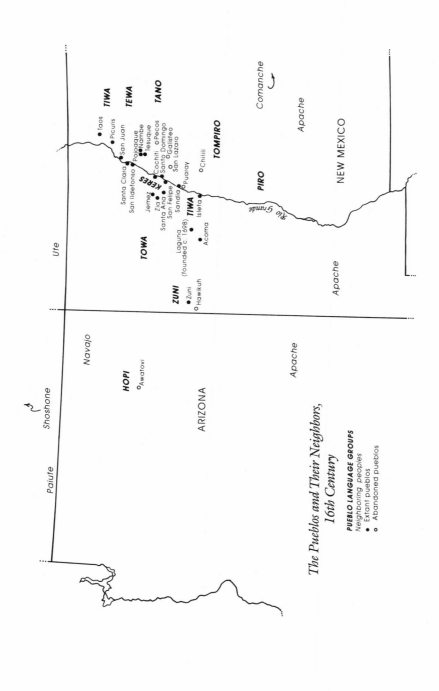

The Pueblos and Their Neighbors,
16th Century

PUEBLO LANGUAGE GROUPS
Neighboring peoples
• Extant pueblos
○ Abandoned pueblos

✳ II ✳

The Pueblos and Their Neighbors

THE SPANISH REGIME AMONG THE PUEBLOS

At the northern reaches of New Spain in the sixteenth century, in the territory that is today New Mexico (and part of Arizona), lived Indians of several language groups (Kiowa-Tanoan, Keresan, Zunian, and Uto-Aztecan) dwelling in as many as one hundred and forty agricultural pueblos with a population exceeding forty thousand. Each of these pueblos was a tightly knit society with numerous sodalities that enforced the will of the group in order to foster cooperation in distributing meager water resources and arable lands. The religious lives of these peoples expressed the overriding concern for fertilization through seasonal ceremonials and rites of initiation into the various sodalities. Priesthoods upheld cultural values, kept calendars, and passed down myths and esoteric knowledge, and elaborate masquerades maintained symbolic contact between the spiritual sources of life and the Pueblo communities.

In 1528 Álvar Núñez Cabeza de Vaca and three companions, shipwrecked off the coast of Texas, heard rumor of these farmers of the upper Rio Grande Valley, thus piquing Spanish interest in the potential wealth of these peoples. In 1539 a party of Spaniards, including Fray Marcos de Niza, came within sight of Zunian villages reputed to be seven fabulously endowed cities. Following these lures, Francisco Vázquez de Coronado led an expedition of three hundred men (including several Franciscan friars) in 1540 to the famed Seven Cities of Cibola, storming the Zuni village of Hawikuh. Disappointed with the poverty they found, Coronado's soldiers explored the pueblos of the Hopis. Looking for gold, the Spaniards terrorized Tiwa Indians, and they journeyed as far north as what is now Kansas in vain search for fortune.

For all its material motives, the Coronado expedition was dressed in Christian imagery, carrying out the symbolism of spiritual conquest established by Cortés. The Spaniards brought with them crosses large and small, rosaries, and images of Jesus and Mary as signs of Christian spiritual power, which they displayed to the Indians for their edification. One of Coronado's padres, Fray Juan de Padilla, wrote:

> In the places where we erected crosses, we taught the natives to vener-
> ate them, and they offered them their powders and feathers, some even
> the blankets they were wearing. They did it with such eagerness that
> some climbed on the backs of others in order to reach the arms of the
> crosses to put plumes and roses on them. Others brought ladders, and
> while some held them others climbed up to tie strings in order to fasten
> the roses and feathers. (In Bird 1992: 2)

What the Puebloans perceived in the Cross is unknown, but it made a
mighty impression upon their native religiousness. In 1541 or 1542 the
same Fray Padilla became the "first Christian martyr in the Southwest"
(Forrest 1929: 28), the first of several dozen Franciscans killed in the
line of duty, when he tarried among the Pueblos, trying to convert
them to Christianity.

Coronado's expedition initiated what would be three centuries of
Spanish contact with the Pueblos, during which time these Indians
would come to know intimately of Christian institutions. It was not,
however, until the end of the sixteenth century that Spanish Christian
conquest took place among the Pueblos. In 1573 the Spanish Crown issued Ordinances of Discovery, which outlawed (at least in principle)
conquest expeditions like those of Coronado in 1540. Henceforth,
peaceful missionary enterprises were to replace "conquest" on the periphery of New Spain. In 1581 the Franciscans commenced their first
mission among the Pueblos, having lost their missions in central Mexico to secularization. For the next hundred years, sometimes called the
"Franciscan Century" (Gutiérrez 1991: 46), more than two hundred
friars traveled the road from Mexico City through Durango and Chihuahua to these northern lands, hoping to establish Christian theocra-
cies, hence bringing the millennium closer as all of humankind became
christianized.

Father Agustin Rodriguez and two other padres established themselves in 1581 at a mission they called San Bartolomé at old Puaray
pueblo. As soon as their military escort left, however, the Indians killed
all three. Several parties of Franciscans tried to introduce the Christian
faith at Acoma, Zuni, and Hopi pueblos in the 1580s, but without positive results, and the Spanish concluded that evangelization was to require military conquest, Ordinances of Discovery notwithstanding.
During the 1580s the Spaniards met repeatedly with peaceful Pueblo re-
ceptions, which led to violence when the invaders demanded food and
clothing to sustain themselves. Pueblo revolts produced military force,

with violence serving as a lesson to other Indians. The Spanish required that the Indians submit to the Crown and to the friars, reading versions of the Requirement in order to establish the right of conquest. The Spanish admired the Pueblos for their industry, cleanliness, and craft, but they despised their religious ceremonies: their masked dances in the plazas and their secret meetings in underground chambers called *kivas*, which the Spanish referred to as "mosques." In 1590 Gaspar Castaño de Sosa defeated the pueblo of Pecos after a fierce battle, leading to Franciscan implantation. In 1598–99 Don Juan de Oñate enforced Spanish rule at several pueblos, laying the foundation for a permanent Christian presence among the Indians.

Oñate was commissioned to pacify the Pueblos for Franciscan benefit; like other Spanish conquerors of his era, he staged for the natives a reenactment of Cortés' famous conquest. His soldiers carried the banner of Our Lady; a Pueblo woman was chosen to act the part of Malinche in an enactment of Los Matachines; Franciscan priests and brothers played the roles of the first twelve missionaries of 1524. At other villages the Spanish enacted the pageant of *Los Moros y Cristianós* to demonstrate in dramatic form the Spanish military might, supported by Santiago. In the summer of 1598 Oñate began the task of what he called "the conversion of the souls of these Indians, the exaltation of the Holy Catholic Church, and the preaching of the Holy Gospel" (in Kessell 1979: 78–79). He gathered the chiefs of thirty-one pueblos to obtain their pledge of allegiance and to make clear the Christian foundations of his mission. Through interpreters he declared to leaders of Tiwa, Puaray, Keres, Zia, Tewa, Pecos, Picuris, and Taos Indians that the king of Spain had sent him for,

> the salvation of their souls, because they should know that their bodies had also souls, which did not die even though the bodies did. But if they were baptized and became good Christians, they would go to heaven to enjoy an eternal life of great bliss in the presence of God . . . [if not] they would go to hell to suffer cruel and everlasting torment. (In Gutiérrez 1991: 49)

In the great kiva at Pecos he proclaimed "one God, creator of the universe and judge of all men; good and evil; heaven and hell; God's servants on earth, the Roman pontiff and the Spanish king. He admonished them to obey and respect the representatives of pope and king" (Kessell 1979: 81), and he claimed that the Indian chiefs knelt before Fray Alonso Martinez and himself in submission to the rule of

Christendom. To commemorate the event the padre said a mass, attended by the Spanish and the Indians.

At Acoma Oñate read the Requirement and provided the same theological message as he did at Pecos. In his journals he noted the Indians' meek acceptance in kissing his ring and accepting the rule of king, pope, friar, and conquistador; however, when Spanish soldiers violated Acoma girls—there was immediate sexual contact between the Spanish and the Pueblos—the Acoma Indians attacked the invaders and killed thirteen of them in December 1598. Oñate consulted with the Franciscans to determine if an attack of retaliation on Acoma constituted just war—the Requirement having already been read and allegiance supposedly declared by the Indians—and when they assured him of his military prerogatives, he and his soldiers stormed the Sky City and defeated the pueblo. Fighting under the banners of the Virgin and Santiago, the Spaniards killed eight hundred Indians (some Acomans killed each other rather than surrender) and captured five hundred women and children, along with eighty men. After a trial the Indians were sentenced to slavery and butchery: everyone over age twelve was condemned to twenty years of servitude; all men over twenty-five had a foot amputated. Children under twelve were distributed to the friars as servants.

Such force made for the conquest of the Pueblos, but it served as a deterrent to conversion to Christianity, as the Indians asked the friars: "If [you] who are Christians cause so much harm and violence, why should [we] become Christians?" (in Gutiérrez 1991: 54). When Oñate quit his command over New Mexico in 1607, there were no more than six hundred baptisms of Pueblo Indians, including those children taken from Acoma. That is, few of the natives turned willingly to Christian initiation, despite (or because of) the military conquest.

A year after Oñate's resignation, and before Pedro de Peralta took over as governor in 1610, Franciscans began to report large numbers of conversions, seven to eight thousand with "others . . . clamoring for baptism" (in ibid., 55). There are no extant records of such baptisms, and so no one knows if the putative conversions were "fact or fiction" (Kessell 1979: 93); nevertheless, report of them meant that the Franciscan missions continued. In 1610 Santa Fe became the presidio and capital of New Mexico, and in 1626 the pueblo of Santo Domingo became the ecclesiastical center. In 1607 there were only three padres in New Mexico; by 1630 there were over thirty among the Pueblos, in addition to other priests at a monastery in Santa Fe. San Ildefonso, Nambe, Santo Domingo, Zia, Galisteo, San Lazaro, Sandia, Isleta, Pecos, and Chilili all had mission centers, with visitas at neighboring Indian towns. Acoma, Zuni, and Hopi gained mission stations in 1629, as the Franciscans tried to establish their spiritual regime over the western Pueblos as well as those along the Rio Grande.

In 1630 the former custodian-commissary of the New Mexico missions, Fray Alonso de Benavides, wrote a summary of Franciscan "pious tasks" (Hodge 1945: 100) among the Pueblos of that time. The padres, he reported, were gathering the Indians into schools to learn Christian prayer and song. Under the friars' direction the Indians attended mass and received communion, singing the *Salve* in their own languages. Each padre made the Indians grow grain and raise cattle, and, he wrote:

> more than twenty Indians, devoted to the service of the church, live with him in the convent. They take turns in relieving one another as porters, sextons, cooks, bell-ringers, gardeners, refectioners, and in other tasks. They perform their duties with as much circumspection and care as if they were friars. At eventide they say their prayers together, with much devotion, in front of some image. (Ibid., 101)

Each priest, Benavides wrote, distributed goods and settled disputes among the Indians, "for, since they look upon him as a father, they come to him with all their troubles" (ibid., 102). In his view, each pueblo had become a doctrina in which Christianity was taking firm foothold:

> Once the Indians have received holy baptism, they become so domestic that they live with great propriety. Hardly do they hear the bell calling to mass before they hasten to the church with all the cleanliness and neatness they can. Before mass, they pray together as a group, with all devotion, the entire Christian doctrine in their own tongue. They attend mass and hear the sermon with great reverence. They are very scrupulous not to miss, on Saturdays, the mass of our Lady, whom they venerate highly. When they come to confession they bring their sins, well studied, on a knotted string, indicating the sins by the knots; and, in all humility, they submit to the penances imposed on them. During Lent they all come with much humility to the processions, which are held on Monday, Wednesday, and Friday. On these days of meeting with the friars, they perform penances in the church. During Holy Week they flagellate themselves in most solemn processions. They take particular care in bringing their children to be baptized. When they fall sick, they at once hasten to confess, and they have great faith and

confidence in the priest merely laying his hands upon their heads. They
are very subservient to him. When the bell tolls for the Ave María and
the praying for the dead, they all come out either in their corridors or in
the fields wherever the call reaches them, and in a loud voice they pray.

They all assist in a body in the building of the churches with all good
will, as can be seen by the many we have built, all spacious and neat.
The first of their fruits they offer to the church in all reverence and good
will. Lastly, they are all very happy and recognize the blindness of idolatry from which they have emerged and the blessings they enjoy in being
the children of the church. This they often admit. (Ibid., 99–100)

Benavides' memorial was a "very roseate view" (ibid., 320, fn. 148),
when seen in the light of Pueblo mission reality of the seventeenth
century. It was what the Franciscans wished to happen under their
charge; what did occur in the doctrinas was somewhat different. The
Franciscans served as agents of occupation among the Indians, establishing Spanish rule according to patterns of encomienda (supposedly
outlawed, but continuing in fact in these northern provinces) and
repartimiento, a system of forced—but reputedly paid—village service.
The Church claimed the Indians' souls; the State claimed their allegiance; and the Spanish soldiers and colonists claimed the Indians'
labor, to such a burden that the natives had little time for their own
fields. Spaniards were so disappointed in the dearth of mineral resources in New Mexico that they determined to gain their wealth
through the toil of the Indians; the friars worked the natives less hard,
but the building and upkeep of churches was no mean occupation.

In order to make more effective the processes of evangelization and
control, the Franciscans concentrated Indian populations into fewer
and fewer pueblos, so that only a third of the pueblos remained by the
late seventeenth century. The friars devised to wean Pueblo youths
from their parents, realizing that the older generation was generally incapable of real conversion. As in Mexico in the previous century, the
padres offered gifts to woo the youths to the Church, turning them
against their elders doctrinally and providing them with wealth and
status that upturned Pueblo society. The priests tried to show the
young how "impotent their fathers and native gods were before the
padres" (Gutiérrez 1991: 76) by forcing the older men to perform
women's work and by humiliating them in public.

The clerics organized the hours of the Puebloans' days with prayers
and lessons based upon Fray Alonso de Molina's *Doctrina christana*

(1546), employed originally in Mexico, through which the Indians memorized Christian ideas about God, humanity, sinfulness, forgiveness, and the sacramental authority of the Church. Fearing that the Indians were incapable of understanding the sacraments accurately, and so to avoid heresy—especially since the priests did not understand Indian languages by and large—Franciscans emphasized dances, plays, processions, and the paraliturgical displays of incense, candles, vestments, and music, in order to compete with pagan ceremonialism. The padres tried to fill the Pueblo calendar with Christian plays that retold the stories of Christianity: the betrothal of St. Joseph and the Virgin Mary; the search for an inn before Jesus' birth; the shepherds' visit to Bethlehem, and the like. They recreated Montezuma's defeat on Christmas Day through Los Matachines and emphasized the power of Christ and the saints in producing Christian military victories. The story of Christ's life was intertwined with the narrative of Indian subjugation, and both were played out in public dramas. The moveable feast of Corpus Christi celebrated the living presence of Christ in the Eucharist, as the priests displayed the monstrance in procession, roughly at the time of the summer solstice. Between Palm Sunday and Easter the friars staged rituals dramatizing the Stations of the Cross. On Holy Thursday the padres wore girdles of thorns; there were bloody whippings and prayers for forgiveness of sins. On Good Friday the congregations carried crosses, large and small, in doleful processions. The lessons were those of penitence, self-mortification, self-flagellation.

In the seventeenth century the pueblos were *republicas* within the Viceroyalty of New Spain, semiautonomous municipalities with supposed rights of self-government. The Spanish Crown gave land grants to the Puebloans and canes of authority to the "little governors" of each pueblo, with traditional chiefs maintaining many powers associated with ceremonial life. At the same time, the Franciscans imposed themselves upon Puebloan jurisdiction, appointing fiscals to administer punishments and *temastians* to lead compulsory prayers and catechetical lessons. The Indian "officers were merely figure heads. The missionary, with the nearby presidio, was the directing and restraining force behind the pueblo governments" (Kelly 1940: 375).

The priests used their authority to suppress as much of Pueblo religion as they could, destroying whatever ceremonial aspects they found objectionable—e.g., the masks worn in many rituals—and coercing the Puebloans to participate in Catholic services. The padres burned thousands of religious objects, storming the kivas periodically and confiscating masks and statuary. The Franciscans used whipping and other forms of corporal punishment to expunge aboriginal religious-ness from Indian culture, especially those aspects of religious expression that the priests found inappropriately sensual. Pueblo ceremonialism was suffused with sexual expression, including displays of homo-sexuality and bestiality, and the padres were determined to wipe it out. When Indian villages resisted Franciscan authority, the priests flogged themselves in public to demonstrate the intensity of their displeasure; individual Indians received whippings for their intransigence, includ-ing a Hopi in the 1650s who died after being smeared with hot turpen-tine and beaten by the clerical authority for the crime of practicing his traditional religion. Another Hopi, who dressed up in clerical garb while the priest was absent from the pueblo, censing the altar and sprinkling holy water while chanting the *Salve*, was sentenced to servi-tude in a Santa Fe convent. Still unrepentant, he received 200 lashes and was paraded publicly before being sold into servitude at auction (Espinosa 1988: 25). Even this form of punishment did not cow the Hopis, many of whom resisted all missionary inroads and killed the evangelists whenever they could.

In their resistance to Franciscan theocracy, the Indians sometimes could count on civil authorities for support. Don Juan de Eulate, the governor at Santa Fe 1617–25, openly encouraged the Pueblo Indians to "continue their pagan ways" (Kessell 1979: 106), in opposition to the padres. Governor Luis de Rosas (1637–41) went so far as to urge the Indians at Taos to kill the resident friar and destroy his church (Espinosa 1988: 30). The civil and religious authorities were constantly at odds, accusing one another of abusing the Indians. Within this "evil tradition" (Scholes 1937: 19) of internecine feuding, the Indians attempted to maneuver and preserve their way of life, even as the missionaries sowed seeds of factionalism within each of the Pueblo communities.

Against their Spanish enemies the Franciscans employed the Inqui-sition, beginning in the 1620s; however "because they were considered perpetual minors in the Faith, Indians who retained their Indian iden-tity were exempt from prosecution by the Inquisition, which was not necessarily a blessing. Mission discipline, depending on the friar in charge, could be much more arbitrary and even sadistic" (Kessell 1979:

173–174). Puebloans conspiring against the missions were considered treasonous and seditious and were sentenced (by the civil authorities, but with the friars' impetus) to "the gibbet or slave block" (ibid., 197). Indians were subject to both civil and canon laws in the "dual system of jurisprudence" (Scholes 1937: 7) of New Spain, and although they were technically free of the Inquisition, they were punished severely for their practice of traditional religion.

With perhaps twenty thousand baptized Pueblo Indians by the middle of the seventeenth century and only thirty to forty Franciscans at any one time, enforcement of Catholic orthodoxy was nigh impossible, try as the padres might. Revolts at Taos in 1639, Jemez in the 1640s, Cochiti in 1650, and elsewhere, reduced the padres' power periodically. At Zuni in 1632 the Indians killed the missionary and treated his body parts as "beneficent domestic gods" (Gutiérrez 1991: 66), akin to enemies' scalps. At Pecos before midcentury the Indians learned their prayers, helped build a church, and attended Catholic rituals, but they persisted in their traditions, venerating their Corn Mothers and other spirits of nature: "They simply went underground whenever the missionary put the pressure on. He could punish idolaters at the mission whipping post, along with chronic truants, but that only made them resentful and more secretive" (Kessell 1979: 132).

The Catholic and Pueblo priesthoods were in direct competition with each other in the seventeenth century. Both headed religious systems possessing calendrical ceremonialism that expressed the themes and values of mythology. Both had ritual structures—kivas and plazas for the Pueblos, churches for the Christians—in which they held their community rituals according to strict rules of propriety. Both had religious paraphernalia—prayer sticks, fetishes, masks, yucca suds, tobacco for the Indians; crucifixes, statues, medals, holy water, incense for the Catholics—that aided them in prayer and purification. The rites of passage—name-givings and initiations into kiva sodalities, versus baptisms and confirmations—revealed two separate orders of membership, one native, the other Christian. The Puebloans prayed to their divinities and invoked their sacred presence in the kachina ceremonies; the Spaniards held to the dogma of monotheism despite a triune deity and an elaborate cult of saints. Both communities engaged in worship, elaborated through an individual's life and through the daily activities of the whole community, that aimed to align human existence according to divinely ordained patterns. Compliance with these holy powers had positive benefits, according to both priesthoods, al-though what those powers and what those patterns were differed from one to the other. For all their similarities of structure and religious-ness—both priesthoods believed firmly in theocracy in the face of enemies, witchcraft, and disorder—they constituted different religious systems that found themselves in opposition to each other (cf. Bow-den 1975: 221–222; Bowden 1981: 46–47; Spicer 1954: 679).

The Franciscans regarded Pueblo religion as devil worship. Their Christian monotheism viewed the kachina cult as polytheistic idolatry and the Indian priesthoods as infernal foes of Christendom. What the Puebloans thought is less easy to ascertain. The Franciscans claimed that the Indians saw them as supernaturals whose powers superseded native force. The Indians' magic had not impeded the Spanish ad-vance, and the palpable evidence of Spanish potency—their military might, their horses, etc.—gave the padres status among the natives as miracle workers. The friars tried to show their power over rain, thus becoming something akin to the Pueblo rain priests; the clerics also claimed to heal with images of the Virgin and with the sign of the cross. They brought with them huge herds of livestock, thus demon-strating their prowess over animals. Perhaps these strange men were witches, perhaps they were magicians; in either case, they had powers to be reckoned with.

It is suggested (see Gutiérrez 1991: 55–61, 82–88) that the Francis-cans established new loci of spiritual power among the Puebloans. The Christian tabernacles, altars, relics, reredos, statues and the like, in-cluding the ever present crosses, constituted sacred space, and the Christian calendar with its feast days suggested a new order of time that Puebloans wished to appropriate. Perhaps the kachina cult could be combined with the cult of the saints. Perhaps chapels could serve as aboveground kivas. Animal and vegetal dances might be held in coor-dination with Christian holy days. Prayer sticks and crosses might be interchangeable as signs of divine power and aid. Jesus, Mary, and Santi-ago could be war gods in the potential syncretism of Pueblo and Catholic religious systems.

At the same time, Christian and Pueblo systems held theologies and anthropologies at odds with one another: monotheism versus the in-numerable kachinas; focus on the sky-heaven as opposed to the under-world; emphasis on the afterlife versus a this-worldly concern. The Puebloans did not believe in original sin, nor in the need for atonement through the sacramental Church. Their reverence for Nature was at odds with Catholic spirituality, for all its sacramental symbolism of natural forms such as bread, water, and oil (see Bowden 1975: 223–225; Bowden 1981: 47–51; Spicer 1954: 668–669). In the seventeenth century there was little evidence that the Puebloans adopted the Christian worldview, despite the thousands of baptisms, despite the churches built and the friars supported by Indian labor. Ramon A. Gutiérrez (1991: 93) writes:

> whether the Puebloans offered feathers and corn meal to the cross as they had to their prayer-sticks, honored the Christ child on Christmas as they had the Twin War Gods during the winter solstice, or flogged themselves on Good Friday as they had called the rain gods, the meanings attached to these acts were fundamentally rooted in Pueblo concepts.

Fray Angélico Chávez, O.F.M., concurs that "their limited grasp of Spanish Catholic doctrine and external worship dovetailed nicely with a native mythology which was their very life" (Chávez 1967: 86). As for syncretism, the Franciscans wanted nothing of it and did all they could to destroy the paraphernalia, structure, and expressions of native religion. They "suppressed ruthlessly" Indian religiousness and Indian revolts; despite this "brutality" (and because of it), "Christianity was a failure" (Frost 1992) among the Puebloans of mid-seventeenth century.

In 1660 the Franciscans complained that the Pueblo Indians of New Mexico were still "undisciplined, reveling in the old pagan rites 'with costumes, masks, and the most infernal chants,' goaded by Spanish Christians" (Kessell 1979: 180). The next year the priests seized sixteen hundred kachina masks, prayer sticks, and effigies and destroyed them in a bonfire, to the outrage of the natives. At the same time as they attacked the Indians for their supposed immorality, the Franciscans were accused of engaging in sex with Pueblo women, fathering bastards, and in one case murdering a woman after raping her and burying her in a *convento* cell. At least one padre confessed to sexual immorality; most of the friars regarded themselves immune from civil investigation and refused to cooperate with trials initiated by the provincial governor, Bernardo Lopez de Mendizabal. By the 1660s "the Pueblo Indians were seething with discontent" concerning the missionaries, directing their fury at the reputed "half-breed children fathered by the Franciscans" (Gutiérrez 1991: 123–124). At Isleta they held a kachina dance in which they beat one such child lifeless; the friar stripped naked and carried a cross around the square, flagellating himself and wearing a crown of thorns, all the while wailing in order to stop the Indians' performance.

The governor also charged the Franciscans with gathering wealth from the Indians in order to build up Church property, despite vows of poverty: "the Church had accumulated large tracts of land, stocked granaries, built up immense herds, and constructed an extensive collection of buildings, while the kingdom as a whole bordered on economic disaster" (ibid., 125). These charges remained unproven, as the Franciscans employed the Inquisition to arrest their accuser. The governor died in an Inquisition prison and was exonerated of the padres' charges posthumously.

With the Indians, as well as the civil authorities, however, the missionaries were encountering determined opposition. In addition the late 1660s brought an extended drought, followed by pestilence and famine in the early 1670s, causing the deaths of many Puebloans. Navajos and Apaches attacked the Spanish colonial settlements and the pueblos in 1672, killing many Indians under Franciscan rule. When the divinities of neither the Pueblos nor the Christians came to the aid of the natives in the face of these disasters, there was talk of rebellion. In one village in 1672 the Indians murdered the friar after tying him to a cross. In other pueblos in 1673 the Indians danced forbidden native rituals, asking their deities to return and promising to forsake veneration of the Christian powers.

The Spanish regime reacted vigorously, according to the principles of colonial and spiritual conquest: "From the outset the friars set themselves the goal of stamping out every particle of native religion and substituting Catholic doctrines and practices, using force if necessary" (Bowden 1975: 222). With the support of the Spanish military the friars persisted in whipping the neophytes, coercing attendance at Church services, and destroying native religious regalia. In 1675 the governor arrested forty-seven Indians—many of them native priests and medicine men—on the charge of witchcraft directed at the friars. He hanged three and one committed suicide, before a delegation of angry, armed Puebloans negotiated for the release of the remaining forty-three. The governor said that the Indians promised they would "forsake idolatry and iniquity" (in Kessell 1979: 227) in the future.

Instead the freed religious leaders, led by a San Juan Tewa named Popé, began plans for a revolution against Spanish rule. Inspired by three gods of the underworld, Popé and his compatriots—some of whom were mulattos and mestizos—determined to rid their religious life of Christian contamination and their lands of the Spaniards. The Tewa organized virtually every pueblo into the insurrection, from Taos in the north to Hopi in the west, isolating those Indians deemed loyal to the friars and soldiers and establishing a chain of command capable of maintaining discipline through the battles to come. The Pueblos sent delegates to the Navajos and Apaches, securing their support for the duration of the revolt, and among their own people—reduced in numbers to thirty-thousand, of whom two-thirds were baptized—the organizers made clear their reasons for fighting.

A month after the Pueblo revolution of August 1680, an aged Christian Indian told the Spanish why the rebellion had taken place:

> He declared that the resentment which all the Indians have in their hearts has been so strong, from the time this kingdom was discovered, because the religious and the Spaniards took away their idols and forbade their sorceries and idolatries; that they have inherited successively from their old men the things pertaining to their ancient customs; and

that he has heard this resentment spoken of since he was of an age to understand. (In Hackett and Shelby 1942, 1: 61)

A year later another Pueblo Indian recounted the insurrectionist aim espoused by Popé, to:

> break up and burn the images of the holy Christ, the Virgin Mary and the other saints, the crosses, and everything pertaining to Christianity, and [to] burn the temples, break up the bells, and separate from the wives whom God had given them in marriage and take those whom they desired. In order to take away their baptismal names, the water, and the holy oils, they were to plunge into the rivers and wash themselves with . . . a root native to the country, washing even their clothing, with the understanding that there would thus be taken from them the character of the holy sacraments. (In ibid., 2: 247)

Popé told his people to rebuild their kivas, carve new masks, and go back to the ways of their ancestors.

In order to accomplish their nativistic aims, the Puebloans needed to drive out the men who ruled over them. In 1680 there were fewer than three thousand Spanish inhabitants of New Mexico province, including mulattos and mestizos. Against them Popé amassed eight thousand Indian warriors, located throughout the pueblos, who targeted particular enemies for death. In the first day of the revolution the Indians killed twenty-one of the thirty-three religious—eighteen missionary priests, two lay brothers, and the Santa Fe church prelate; in the whole of the revolt they put to death an additional 380 men, women, and children, before the remaining Spaniards escaped to El Paso del Norte (now Ciudad Juarez in Mexico). Hundreds of Indians died also in the battles of that 1680 summer.

In their attacks the Puebloans directed particular fury against Church property and personnel. At Sandia the Indians defecated on the mission altars and statues and threw the chalices into piles of manure. They whipped the crucifix until its paint was stripped off and hacked away the arms of a full-length figure of St. Francis. Then the natives filled the church with straw and set it afire. At Jemez the rebels took Fray Juan de Jesus to the cemetery, where they lit many candles, stripped him naked, mounted him upon a pig, and then beat and ridiculed him, whipping him until he died of the wounds. At Acoma the Indians stripped and bound together two friars and a Christian mestiza and led them around the pueblo, eventually stoning them to death and mutilating them with lances. A Spanish official, surveying the destruction of Church accoutrements, saw evidence of "the iniquity of those barbarians and the hatred which they feel for our holy faith. These are sufficient reasons," he declared, "for war being waged against them without mercy, and for declaring all those who may be captured slaves for a period of ten years . . ." (in ibid., 1: 45).

On the other hand, the Indians gathered many items of Catholic worship—vestments, crosses, and other paraphernalia—to wear and to safekeep in secret. One modern-day writer comments:

> Whether because of superstitious fear, or because of a degree of attachment to the Catholic faith on the part of some of them, it seems that the Indians had to be ordered by their leaders to destroy the material manifestations of Christianity. The fact is that much was recovered, proving that enthusiasm for the destruction of sacred images and other religious articles was not as universal as some writers imply. (Espinosa 1967: 16–17)

Not all Puebloans, not all pueblos, joined wholeheartedly in the revolution. The Towas of Pecos warned the Spanish of the rebellion and later claimed that they had been loyal to the Church and State, despite having killed one Franciscan brother and a Spanish family. Factions within the pueblo opposed one another over Popé's uprising, as they did at several other pueblos, particularly in the south among the Tiwas. The southernmost pueblos, those of the Piros and Tompiros, refused to join the rebellion, and many of them joined Tiwas and Spaniards in the retreat to El Paso, where they formed a new community, Tigua Pueblo. Over time this pueblo took on a highly Mexicanized culture and still exists to this day, with over a hundred Indian families receiving Catholic ministry at Ysleta del Sur Pueblo in Texas.

In 1681 Antonio de Otermin and his troops recaptured Isleta after a siege, and the procurator, Fray Francisco de Ayeta, entered the pueblo on horseback. The five hundred and some Indians of the village made a procession to him, as he called out, "Blessed be the most holy sacrament and the purity of our lady, the Virgin Mary, conceived without sin!" The Indians replied: "Forever!" Then Father Ayeta dismounted, and the Indians warmly embraced him (in Hackett and Shelby 1942, 1: cxxxiii). The next day there was a mass and rosary said at a portable altar in the middle of the plaza. Fray Ayeta granted forgiveness to the Indians for their participation in the revolt of the year before; he baptized children born since the revolt and encouraged husbands and wives joined in matrimony to rededicate themselves to one another.

He reminded them of their vassalhood to the Spanish Crown and received apostates back "into the bosom of the church" (ibid., 1: clxxv). Some of these, however, turned out to be spies for the rebel forces. Within a month a fifth of the Isleta population had disappeared from town, joining the Indians at other pueblos who were prepared to retake Isleta.

Otermin soon discovered that the Puebloans did not wish reconciliation with Spain or Church. One of his lieutenants told him, after attempting to retake several pueblos, that, "The unanimous opinion was that the Indians were very tenacious of their religious and economic customs, and, being apostates and rebels at heart, it was a hopeless task to try and get them to conform to Spanish and Christian ways of living." One squad leader "did not detect one trace of Christianity in any of the Indians." Another "could detect no true signs of repentance among the Indians." It was said that "it would be an impossible task to subjugate the apostates" (ibid., 1: clxxx). As a result, the Spaniards burned eight of the southern pueblos, (including Isleta) sacked three others (all villages belonging to Piro and southern Tiwa Indians hardly involved in the revolt) and took close to four hundred Christian Indians to El Paso for their protection. The Northern Tiwas, Tewas, and Towas who had fomented the insurrection, as well as the Western Pueblos from Acoma to Hopiland, were left untouched by Otermin's expedition. For the remainder of the 1680s the Pueblos lived free of Spanish control. Popé's legions destroyed the churches and the Christian images; they abandoned Christian names and bathed ritually to cleanse themselves of their Spanish associations. The Pueblos returned to their kivas and plazas to worship in the traditional manner.

Nonetheless, drought continued and Popé's reign was anything but beneficent for Puebloans, as he assumed the title of governor for the pueblos. He made servants of his opponents and executed others who wished for accommodations with Christianity or Spanish material goods. Within the pueblos and among them bickering took place, and eventually the Keres Indians fought against the Tanoans, deposing Popé and placing their own Don Luis Tupatu in the position of governor. The fragile truce between Pueblos and their Indian neighbors collapsed as Apaches resumed raids on the villages of the Rio Grande Valley, in search for horses abandoned by the Spaniards.

The Spaniards did not abandon their hope to recapture their Indian subjects, and under the banner of Mary, Our Lady of the Rosary, Virgin of the Conquest, they vowed to reinstate Christianity among the Pueblos. Diego de Vargas Zapata Lujan Ponce de León became governor of New Mexico in 1688, and in 1691, when he took possession of the El Paso government, he made his plan for reconquest. The next year, accompanied by friars, he led a military expedition into Santa Fe and the various pueblos. Vargas and the clerics pleaded with the Indians to become vassals of the Crown and obedient servants of the pope once again, and without a single casualty the Indians seemed to acquiesce. Wearing a cross, a rosary, relics, and an image of Our Lady of Guadalupe, Don Luis Tupatu genuflected before Vargas, "promising fidelity to God and King" (Gutiérrez 1991: 144). Missionaries baptized over two thousand Indians, mostly children born since the 1680 revolution. Although between 1680 and 1692 "virtually every vestige of Spanish religious worship (with the dramatic exception at Zuñi . . .) was systematically destroyed" (Espinosa 1988: xv), Vargas elicited a seeming Puebloan enthusiasm for reconciliation with the Church. When he entered Zuni in 1692, the Indian governor and his captains kissed him and took him to a room where they kept an altar with two large candles burning. For twelve years the Zunis had maintained Catholic devotions focussed upon religious articles, which Vargas took away to have reconsecrated. A priest should be sent immediately to the Zunis, he said.

But when Vargas returned to the Pueblos in 1693, only Pecos, Santa Ana, Zia, and San Felipe were willing to receive him. He arrived with a hundred soldiers, seventy families, and eighteen friars—a Spanish force of eight hundred in all, hoping for resettlement in Santa Fe—and he found it necessary to lay siege to the town before he could reclaim it. Invoking La Conquistadora (The Virgin Mary) and Santiago, Vargas defeated the resistant Indians, killing over eighty and executing another seventy for their continuing threats against Spanish soldiers, settlers, and missionaries. Another four hundred he sentenced to slavery.

By the beginning of 1694 Vargas and his legions held Santa Fe. They placed a statue of La Conquistadora in a chapel. In 1948 the Archbishop of Santa Fe, Edwin V. Byrne, wrote that this statue continues to symbolize "the spirit of deep-rooted Faith and Devotion which characterized the *Conquistadores* of this land, no matter what their individual or collective faults . . ." (in Chávez 1948: viii; cf. Grimes 1976). From Santa Fe the Franciscans began to reenter the pueblos and reestablish Catholicism among the Indians. Some padres viewed the process as one in which they had to start afresh among pagans and idolaters; others noted the extremes to which some Pueblo communities went to avoid contact with the missionaries, e.g., at San Ildefonso, where the Indians took refuge on a nearby mesa. Still others characterized their task as a rudimentary one: reinstating catechism to willing Indians (see Espinosa 1988: 91–159).

In 1695 warnings came to the priests of an impending revolt, which took place in June 1696. The Indians killed five of the friars, a score of other Spaniards, and once again they burned and desecrated the mission churches and convents, repeating the patterns of 1680. At several villages the Indian leaders remained loyal to the Spanish, but everywhere else there was rebellion. This time, however, the Spanish soldiers prevailed after six months, and an era of permanent Hispanic settlement of northern New Mexico began.

The Reconquest had taken hold, but to what effect upon Pueblo associations with Christianity? By the beginning of the eighteenth century, after many decades of Catholic hegemony, Pueblo religion was deeply affected by Christian influences. However hard the missionaries had tried to destroy native religiousness, and however hard the Indians had tried to compartmentalize the two religious traditions, there was cross-fertilization of ideas, images, organization, and practices, although the exact form of these syncretisms is hard to know with any precision. Some Puebloans might say that "when Padre Jesus came, the Corn Mothers went away" (in Gutiérrez 1991: 162); others might combine Jesus and the Twin War Gods or the lone Poseyemu. Saints and kachinas, ritual calendars, crosses, and prayer sticks combined, intertwined, and overlapped in function. Church personnel in each pueblo might serve as types of native sodalities, one sodality among many of the kiva organizations, each with its own ritual and mythological knowledge. Caciques and other native functionaries served as mediators between priest and parish. In such an atmosphere, some fusion occurred between the two religious traditions coexisting among the Puebloans.

It is sometimes said that the Franciscans reentered the pueblos with a more tolerant attitude toward traditional Pueblo religion. After the reconquest, "later generations of Pueblos grew up in an environment in which one could be nominally Catholic and still be loyal to another tradition. . . . Since 1700, the Pueblos have added an unobtrusive Christianity to traditional patterns without fundamentally altering their solid precontact core" (Bowden 1981: 57). Perhaps the Spanish accomplished the reconquest with promises of leniency, as long as the Indians kept up the churches and attended Catholic services. In addition, the eighteenth century witnessed the secularization of New Mexico. The Spanish kings cared less about missions than empires, and although the Franciscans might have wanted to end the religious practices of the Pueblo kivas, they lacked the resources to suppress them to any considerable extent.

The number of pueblos had shrunk through revolution and reconquest to twenty-five, with a population dwindling towards fifteen thousand by mid-eighteenth century. The number of Franciscans was hardly enough to assert authority over the native Christians—no more than one to each pueblo, and in some cases the padres stationed themselves at Santa Fe, venturing only on occasion to their Indian missions. The growing population of Spaniards (and mestizos)—the Spanish numbered fifteen hundred in 1696, four thousand in 1750, and almost ten thousand in 1776; by 1790 the figure was over fifteen thousand—required attention from the priests, and over time the Pueblo missions fell into relative neglect. And yet in the early part of the century the Spanish attempted to stamp out Pueblo kiva life, dances, and religious organization as they had in the previous century.

In 1707 Admiral Don Jose Chacon Medina Salazar y Villaseñor, Marques de la Peñuela, became governor of New Mexico, and he "declared war on kivas" (Kessell 1979: 310). Not all the friars agreed with his strategy; however, in 1709 soldiers toured the pueblos and demolished the kivas while condemning Indians' ceremonialism. The governor's men accused the Franciscans of laxity in regard to the Indians' religion, as rivalry between Church and State heated to fever. Peñuela charged the padres with encouraging syncretism and abetting the Puebloans as they rebuilt their kivas in 1710–1711. At Taos the Franciscan priest was accused of soliciting sex and urging the Indians to rebuild two kivas. The governor scolded the Franciscan adminstrator, Custos Juan de Tagle for allowing kivas in the pueblos, "where they commit sundry offenses against God Our Lord, performing in them superstitious dances most inconsistent with Our Holy Catholic Faith, from which have resulted diverse witchcraft and things most improper" (in ibid., 311). In 1714 Peñuela's successor, Juan Ignacio Flores Mogollon, ordered the destruction of the rebuilt kivas, as well as all rooms in the pueblos entered only from the top by ladder, where secret ceremonies might take place. Lashes and forced labor were to be punishment for rebuilding such kivas and hidden chambers. Flores followed with other "Christian reforms" (316): disarming the Pueblos, disallowing contact with hostile Indians such as Comanches and Apaches, and forbidding native dress and ornament: "These Indians still painted themselves with 'earths of different colors' and wore feathers as well as skin caps, necklaces, and earrings, as they had before their conversion. . . . If Christian natives dressed like heathens, how could anyone tell friends from foes?" (317).

The Franciscans dissuaded the governor from these prohibitions, finding feathers and face paint at mass as "innocuous" (318) as Spanish ribbons and makeup. Why risk rebellion over such trivialities, they argued; allow the natives to adopt normative Christianity gradually; tolerate their expressions of native culture. Perhaps the Franciscans were adopting the latitudinarianism of the eighteenth century; perhaps they were losing their zeal for catechesis and orthodoxy. The judgment of their contemporary churchmen was that the caliber of padres was not what it used to be. Willing to rely on soldiers for protection when they needed them; ready to dwell among fellow Hispanics in Santa Fe when they could; all too willing to engage in sex with the Indians but unprepared to speak any native language and hence unable to hear proper confessions—some of the Franciscans of the eighteenth century appeared tepid in missionary ambition. When the bishop of Durango, Benito Crespo, paid an apostolic visit to the Pueblos at the request of the governor in 1730 (the bishopric of Durango claimed jurisdiction over the Franciscans in the 1720s), he found seven of the forty padres lacking in zeal to convert. Among the Puebloans he found "signs of paganism, idolatry, apostasy, 'and the reciprocal lack of love' between missionaries and Indians" (327).

In the period following the reconquest, many Puebloans from the Rio Grande Valley sought refuge among the emergent Navajos and among the western Pueblos, particularly the Hopis, who remained unrepentant and unconquered. Factions dating from the days of Popé persisted at most if not all pueblos, disputing strategies of accommodation with Spanish rule and Catholic institutions. On occasion these factions moved to other locales, abandoning their villages and shifting their allegiances. Some pueblos swelled as others disappeared. Six Zuni villages became one. Southern Tewas created the village of Hano among the Hopis. Displaced Keres established Laguna. Tiwas, who had found refuge with the Hopis, returned to the Rio Grande and reestablished Sandia. Simultaneously, Comanches, Apaches, Utes, and other Indians surrounding the Pueblo area attacked the villages periodically and took captives; at other times they traded with the Puebloans and the Spaniards, bartering their captives for desired goods. From this flux of Indian populations, and particularly from the captives, came new breeds of people. These Genizaros, as they were called, were the detribalized offspring of various Indian groups. Franciscans and Spanish officials sometimes ransomed these brutalized Indians from their captors, baptized them, and brought them up as servants or slaves. (In 1700 Custos Juan de Zavaleta tried in vain to prevent the ransoming of such children, "even with good motive of Christianizing them and teaching them to serve the missions," in Chávez 1957: 157.) As their numbers increased, they came to live apart from Indians, in special settlements, e.g., at Abiquiu, Albuquerque, and Santa Fe, creating their own communities and becoming christianized through the sacraments and hispanicized by degree, unless the Puebloans gained them, in which event they became absorbed into the population.

Among the westernmost Pueblos, the Hopis, Catholicism never took hold again after the 1680 revolution in which five Franciscans met their death. Neither missionary *entradas* nor punitive expeditions between 1699 and 1732 could move the Hopi officials to permit the padres to stay among them. At the Hopi village of Awatovi, where the Franciscans first established a mission in 1629, some Hopis tried to reestablish their Catholicism after the reconquest; however, Hopi military societies destroyed the town in 1700–1701.

The Spaniards may have regained a position of power among other Puebloans. "But not for the Hopi! The struggle, lost by the Christian God in [Hopiland] in 1680, stayed lost" (Montgomery, Smith, and Brew 1949:18). The Hopis served as hosts for those christianized Indians who were fed up with their faith or service to the Spanish, and they influenced the Zunis to maintain their independence from Catholic clerics living among them. In 1742, however, Fray Carlos Delgado, O.F.M., journeyed to Hopiland and managed to gain the allegiance of over four hundred exiles among the Hopis, who accompanied him back through Zuni to the Rio Grande, where in 1748 they joined some Tiwas who had come from Hopiland in previous years in order to reestablish the abandoned pueblo of Sandia as a Christian Indian village. Individual Hopis also left their traditionalist pueblo at various times in the eighteenth century in order to move in among the Christian pueblos along the Rio Grande. In this way the Hopi community continued to resist Catholic inroads, whereas individual Hopis associated themselves with the Catholic Church by emigration. Only in the second half of the twentieth century have Hopi villages permitted Catholic missions once again, but even with some Hopis and Tewas from Hano attending sacraments in the 1960s, Church officials acknowledged that "the Hopis generally still mistrust us" (*The Indian*

Sentinel 40, no. 2, summer 1962: 20). Now, three hundred years after the Reconquest, Catholic missionaries are still attempting to make contact with the Hopis and win them back to the faith, but without sustained success (Hastrich, September 3, 1989).

In the second half of the eighteenth century, Spanish colonialism and its missionary efforts were expanding to new frontiers, northward along the coast of California. Junipero Serra's Franciscans initiated Mission San Diego in 1769, with another score of missions to follow over the next half century. In New Mexico, however, Franciscan evangelism had reached a standstill. The non-Indian population of New Mexico was growing—it would approach fifty thousand by the time of the Mexican-American War in the 1840s—and the Indian numbers declined gradually to about ten thousand by the same period. The padres' numbers, too, were in slow dissolution. An historian says: "The Franciscan missions of New Mexico by 1750 had long since passed through their Golden Era, and were sinking gently into a mellow decline, disturbed only by spasmodic and ineffectual bursts of energy. . . . the heathen remained unconverted, and nomad ravaged the land, and the missions vegetated" (Kelly 1941: 183). Secular authorities hurled accusations at the priests—they didn't learn the Indian languages; they made profit off Indian labor—but these administrators were far from protectors of Indian rights; they were more interested in extracting labor from their Genizaro slaves and Pueblo servants. The cruelty of the Spanish rulers made Indians resist Catholicism, since it meant association with a way of life that was to them subservient and miserable.

In 1760 the bishop of Durango, Pedro Tamaron y Romeral, conducted a supervisory tour of the Franciscan missions, and he determined many of the charges laid against the friars to be true: there were too few of them—twenty-four north of El Paso—and among these zeal was often lacking. They could expect no help from the Spanish laymen in attracting or retaining Indian Christians, so hostile were the Spaniards both to the Indians and the Franciscans. The clerics did not speak Indian languages, and the Indians' Spanish was not sufficient for them to make intelligent confessions or discuss theological ideas. Above all, the traditional religions of the Pueblos, he found, remained strongly entrenched, even among the baptized: "The Christianization of the Indians was hardly more than a superficial conformity to a few outward practices which they did not understand or have much interest in" (Adams 1954: 31).

The governor of New Mexico at that time was pressing charges against "idolatrous Indians and witch doctors" (in ibid., 80). Bishop Tamaron could find no evidence of such, although he continued to have his suspicions. In particular he suspected that the Puebloans were carrying on their native worship in their kivas, and he ordered the friars "to keep their eyes open. They argued the difficulty of depriving them of that dark and strange receptacle [the kiva]," but the bishop impressed upon them the "temptation to evil" posed by such secret chambers (in ibid., 74). Since the Franciscans did not recognize his episcopal authority, he had little hope that they would enforce his commands or improve in their enterprise.

Where were the Indians of New Mexico in 1760? About El Paso Bishop Tamaron counted 1,343 natives—Piros and others—living in five locations. As he traveled north among the pueblos, he found over 300 Tiwa Indians in Isleta (a 1749 census indicated 500 in this village); almost 200 Hopis and Tiwas at the newly inhabited pueblo of Sandia (400 counted in 1749); 424 Keres at Santo Domingo (300 in 1749); 458 Keres at San Felipe (400 in 1749); 404 Keres at Santa Ana (600 in 1749); 568 Keres at Zia (600 in 1749); 373 Towa Indians at Jemez (574 in 1749); 450 Keres at Cochiti (521 in 1749). At Galisteo he counted 255 Tanos (350 in 1749), and at Pecos 344 Towas (1,000 in 1749); the same priest served both of these pueblos. Among the Tewas the bishop located 484 at San Ildefonso (354 in 1749); 232 at Tesuque, a visita of Santa Fe (171 in 1749); 204 at Nambe and another 99 at its visita at Pojoaque (350 together in 1749); 328 at Picuris (400 in 1749); 316 at San Juan (500 in 1749); and 257 at Santa Clara (272 in 1749). The northern Tiwa pueblo of Taos had 505 (540 in 1749). The bishop enumerated Genizaros (e.g., at Abiquiu) and citizens of Spanish and mixed descent; and among the western pueblos he located 600 Keres at Laguna (528 in 1749), 1,502 Keres at Acoma (960 in 1749), and 644 Zunis (2,000 in 1749). North of El Paso, then, there were twenty-one pueblos with populations in regular contact with Christian personnel, teachings, and sacraments (see Adams 1954: 34–71; cf. Kelly 1940: 362–363), not counting the Hopis, who remained almost completely free of Catholic influence.

Bishop Tamaron was impressed by the respect and service given to the Franciscans by the inhabitants of the pueblos; he did not interpret their decorum, however, as commitment to Christianity. Nor did he vouchsafe their sincerity in their displays of deference to his priests or to himself. Several months after his visit to Pecos, where he confirmed many, a principal man of the village, a carpenter by trade named Agustin Guichi, made a mitre of parchment and a crozier of reed. Putting on a cloak, he mounted an ass, and with other Indians playing his assistants, he enacted a burlesque of the bishop's visitation. They paraded into the plaza with drums and shouts. Women knelt in two rows while the "bishop" distributed blessings. In parody he confirmed the village, giving each a sign of the cross on the forehead and a buffet on the cheek. A feast ensued, then a dance. The next day Guichi, still in his episcopal togs, pretended to say a mass, distributing tortillas as communion. On the third day the Pecos Indians danced again, completing the parody.

There are some who say (e.g., Freese 1991) that the performance of Guichi and his fellow Towas—so typical of Pueblo clowns over the centuries, who have mocked the appearance and behavior of Catholic clergy in their ritual pantomimes—constituted a form of rebellion against forced baptisms and the imposition of Christianity in their villages. But making fun of the Church has been part of Pueblo accommodation to Catholicism. At the same time, the Indians of Pecos, insofar as they imitated the gestures and dress of the bishop and his clerics, were incorporating sacerdotal behavior into their religious expression. The tone was that of mockery, but who knows the long term effect of such imitation?

Agustin Guichi had little time to learn from his actions. The day after the burlesque ended he went to his field and was killed by a bear. Before he died the Indian was said to confess his sins and receive last rites from the local padre. The Indian regarded his death as punishment from God for ridiculing the bishop, and the bishop hoped that the events in Pecos would serve as a "warning" (in Adams 1954: 53) to others. Nonetheless, at other pueblos the priests sometimes complained of chronic disrespect toward themselves and the accoutrements of the Church: stealing holy oils for their own rituals, paying no heed at mass, and engaging in obscenity in the churches.

In 1776 Fray Francisco Atanasio Dominguez, O.F.M., penned a substantial description of the Pueblos of New Mexico and the missionaries among them, and he was not impressed by the Indians' participation in the Christian tradition. They received Christian names at baptism, but they were hardpressed to remember them. Instead, they went by their Indian names—which he called "bad names" (Adams and Chávez 1956:

255)—according to their ancestral traditions. The Puebloans had a confused notion of prayer and its intents, he charged, because they did not
understand Spanish or Christian doctrine. "They are exceedingly fond
of pretty reliquaries, medals, crosses, and rosaries," he wrote, "but this
does not arise from Christian devoutness (except in a few cases) but
from love of ornament" (256). The most solemn events for the Pueblo
Indians in 1776 were their native dances: those performed in their
plazas to mark the seasons, as well as the scalp dances, in which they
brought back trophies of their enemies, such as the Comanches. The
Pueblo communities welcomed these scalps into their villages, and the
men even went into church to offer thanksgiving for so great a boon.
Fray Dominquez noted that the priests tried to stop the scalp dances
(the seasonal celebrations seemed harmless to them), but to no avail.
The secular officials of New Mexico reminded the clerics that the Indians were still neophytes, not to be expected to live completely according to Christian habits and rules. The friar commented: "Even at the
end of so many years since their reconquest, the species title or name of
neophytes is still applied to them . . . , for generally speaking they have
preserved some very indecent, and perhaps superstitious, customs"
(254). In general, then, Fray Dominquez doubted the Christian allegiance of the Pueblo Indians, who were rarely capable of receiving
communion, who did not confess their sins annually, and who did not
even pray or cross themselves during the course of a day. At death the
Indians would make their confession through an interpreter, but during their lives they demonstrated little of Christian identity: "Their
repugnance and resistance to most Christian acts is evident, for they
perform the duties pertaining to the Church under compulsion, and
there are usually many omissions" (255).

Fray Dominguez toured the pueblos, counting their numbers (for
the most part lower than those recorded in the previous decades) and
delineating the duties of the twenty-nine friars. Of these, he said, only
thirteen were performing their tasks acceptably. Eight were either too
old or too infirm; one was blind, and two were habitual drunkards.
One lived openly with a married woman, one brawled periodically and
exploited Indian labor. One he called ungovernably scandalous, another disobedient and disruptive to the Indians he was supposed to
serve. The priests conducted catechism, or had the *fiscals* perform the
task; they said mass on Sundays and holydays, baptized children, led
rosaries, and heard some confessions through interpreters. In return
for these divine services the Pueblo Indians donated a portion of their

produce to support the padres and paid them money for blessing their dead. Some of the Indians the friar found "very docile and gentle" (202), for instance at Zuni, but others had to be whipped to attend mass and to put on clothing within the chapels:

> The Indians of Picuris and Taos outdo all the rest in all the general customs. . . . They are so notably opposed to Christianity that they cannot even look at Christian things, for they are unwilling to give charity . . . or lodging to a Spaniard. If they see a Spaniard, they hide; if he is the father (this is the worst in their eyes), they are as terrified as if they were to see Lucifer himself. . . . They flee from him like the devil from the cross, and the children even cry, running as if from their cruelest enemy. (258)

Fray Dominquez recommended a fresh influx of Franciscans, and in 1778 seventeen new friars arrived among the Puebloans. Nonetheless, evangelization failed to take firm effect. Diseases and Comanche raids disrupted the populations; two pueblos—Pecos and Galisteo—were sinking into oblivion. The friars might try, for example at San Ildefonso in 1782, to stop "indecent dances of Indians" (Chávez 1957: 43), and the civil authorities might explain to them why they were required to provide goods and services to the Church. Nevertheless, the Pueblos resisted Church and State. There were rebellious plots at several of the pueblos—San Juan in 1784, San Ildefonso in 1793, Taos and Picuris well into the nineteenth century—and administrators tried to prevent the pueblos from communicating with one another by restricting travel. But the faltering number of Franciscans—sixteen of them in New Mexico in 1792—were unable to make a positive impression upon the minds of the Pueblos. In the judgment of historian John L. Kessell (1979: 355):

> Whatever the reasons, the friars had failed to impose upon the Pueblos more than a patchy veneer of Christianity. For all their zeal, they had not stamped out kivas or kachinas, neither by violent suppression nor by gentle persuasion. They had not broken the Pueblos' pagan spirit. They had not learned their languages. In fact, during the eighteenth century, they had come grudgingly to accept coexistence. They kept on baptizing and marrying, but by now they recognized that spiritual conquest had eluded them, that the ultimate salvation of the Pueblo Indians lay beyond their means.

In 1793 Viceroy Conde de Revillagigedo reported to Spain in his account of the missions of New Spain that the Pueblo Indians, after two hundred years of missions, are as ignorant of the Faith and religion as if they were just starting catechism. . . . When the Indian reaches the age of six or seven he must attend instruction morning and afternoon. But this is achieved only with difficulty, and as a result, since the beginnings of their Christian education are so feeble and cease the day of their marriage or in the first years of their youth, they forget rapidly the little they learned, abandoning themselves to their evil inclinations and customs and dying not much different than heathens.

They are heathens underneath and very given to the vain respect and superstitions of their elders. They have a natural antipathy for everything to do with our sacred religion. Few confess until the moment of death, and then the majority by means of an interpreter, and in order to get it over they do no characteristic Christian works nor do they contribute a thing in gratitude to God and king. (In ibid., 354–355)

The first half of the nineteenth century saw no change, except that New Mexico became even more remote from the centers of New Spain. As Mexico struggled to gain its independence, the few Franciscans continued their work on the periphery of the collapsing empire, vilified by the secular authorities and avoided insofar as possible by the Puebloans (who numbered about ten thousand in an 1808 census, Kessell 1980: 241). It may be an exaggeration to say that the two dozen friars serving New Mexico in 1818 were the "dregs" of the order, and that New Mexico was a "dumping ground for unruly and depraved friars" (ibid., 14), but however deserved was their disrepute, they were not making Christians out of the Pueblo Indians.

With Mexican independence in 1821 the Franciscan missions eroded to almost the disappearing point, as the new civil powers removed the Spanish padres from their posts. As few as five remained by 1830. The Mexican government did away with all legal distinctions concerning the Pueblos, regarding them as taxpayers and landed citizens with municipal governments and self-sustaining agricultural economies. The bishopric of Durango claimed spiritual charge of the Indians and even issued epistles concerning their treatment in the 1830s and 1840s (Chávez 1957: 182, 185); however, with the Franciscans gone the Indians received little, if any, attention from the Church. In effect, "the missions existed in name only" (Van Well 1942: 54) by the time the United States wrested control of the area and took legal charge with the Treaty of Guadalupe-Hidalgo in 1848.

THE VICARIATE APOSTOLIC OF NEW MEXICO

When Pope Pius IV established the Vicariate Apostolic of New Mexico in 1850 and appointed John Baptiste Lamy to its leadership, the last of the Franciscans among the Pueblos, Fray Mariano de Jesus Lopez, was two years deceased. Until his death Fray Lopez had tried to serve all the Indians between Isleta and Zuni. With his passing the Pueblos continued to pay tithes to the Church but rarely received sacraments, as a traveling cleric visited at most a few times each year. In 1851 Bishop Lamy arrived at the new diocese, which included the territories of Arizona and New Mexico (until 1868, when Arizona became a separate district). There he found (by his own count) approximately nine thousand Pueblo Indians amidst sixty-eight thousand Catholics, two thousand heretics, and thirty to forty thousand infidels—Apaches, Navajos, Hopis, and other Native Americans (Horgan 1975: 127).

Lamy's task was to assert his authority over the Catholics living within the new territory of the United States and under the jurisdiction of the newly created diocese. The emotional loyalty of these Mexican Catholics was still to the bishopric of Durango—from which New Mexico was carved—and to their Hispanic culture. The Frenchman Lamy took office with a new political regime; his allegiance was to the papacy, but also to the United States. Hence, he had difficulty winning the respect and obedience of the people, including the dozen or so priests whom he viewed as "incapable or unworthy" (in Kessell 1980: 14). His struggle with Father Antonio Jose Martinez and the Hispanic clergy of New Mexico took much of his energy, and as a result Lamy devoted little of his resources to the spiritual care of the Pueblos.

He was much more concerned with La Fraternidad Piadosa de Neustro Padre Jesus Nazareno—the Penitentes—a lay brotherhood developed in New Mexico around 1800 and possibly modeled on the lay Third Order of the Franciscans. The brotherhood was strongest around Abiquiu and Taos. The Penitentes expressed Hispanic forms of Catholic spirituality, including imitation of the Passion of Jesus through self-flagellation and the bearing of the cross; their devotionalism focussed upon purification and death. Lamy, in his Gallic Catholicism, thought them heretical, and he tried unsuccessfully to stamp out

their organization within his diocese. Some said that there were Indian influences on the Penitentes, particularly among the Genizaros
(Adams and Chávez 1956: 124–126; Ahlborn 1986: 127); however, there
was no evidence of Pueblo religiousness in the cult. An Indian from
San Ildefonso noted that the Penitentes were Catholics who possessed
penitential aspects as a special area of their cult, "the way the kiva is
with us." At the same time, he saw a key distinction between Penitente
and Pueblo spirituality: "The Indian religion is to be happy, but the
Spanish religion is to be sad. That's why they are two different people"
(in Marriott 1948: 51; see Weigle 1976: 28).

For all their differences the Hispanics and Puebloans shared certain
ritual events, most prominently *Los Matachines*, the "semireligious
dance-drama" (Champe 1983: xii) of Spanish origin. It is little understood how this ritual became embedded in New Mexico communities—Oñate had it performed for the Indians in 1598, but it was not a
prominent aspect of Franciscan evangelization among the Puebloans.
We have seen that the Yaquis developed an indigenous Matachin Society; however, its dances differ from those of the Pueblo Indians and
their Hispanic neighbors. Perhaps after the Reconquest the Spanish-
American community shared with the Indians this representation of
"Montezuma's struggle to accept Christianity" (ibid., 84). In any event,
the Hispanics served as musicians for these dances in the pueblos and
used the occasion of Los Matachines as a time for visiting Indian
friends and relatives. The Matachin dances of the Hispanics, as well as
the Penitente services, were well known to the Puebloans.

With the Penitentes as a major concern, a Hispanic clergy unwilling
to accept his authority, and a large population of disgruntled but faithful Catholics, the new bishop did not rekindle Pueblo missions in his
early years. As evidenced in the following missive to the pope in 1856,
his enemies charged him with neglecting the Pueblos and jeopardizing
their future by his refusal to recognize the Hispanic priests:

> Our Christian Towns of Indians (converts of Catholicism, as they are),
> and numbering some 18 towns, are thus also left without spiritual
> administration, harshly abandoned to their own ignorance; and I have
> no doubt that within a short time they will revert to their primitive and
> savage state of idolatry. (In Horgan 1975: 226)

Even as his diocese grew, more than doubling in Catholic population
by the time of his death in 1888, and even as the number of baptized

Pueblos doubled to eighteen thousand, his administration paid only secondary attention to the Indians, including the non-Puebloan natives whom he regarded as "almost cannibalistic" (in ibid., 335). In the face of Protestant inroads—most prominently at Laguna, commencing in the 1870s—Lamy defended his proprietary rights to the Pueblos, and he requested U.S. funds for a Catholic system of education among them. Nevertheless, the Indians were not his chief priority.

In 1874 Archbishop Lamy wrote a "Short History of the Pueblo Indians of New Mexico" (Santa Fe. Microfilm 57) in order to impress upon Brigadier General Charles Ewing in the U.S. War Department (and the newly appointed director of the Bureau of Catholic Indian Missions) the longstanding Catholicism among "our pueblo Indians." He said that "the civilization of our pueblo Indians is contemporaneous with the discovery of New Mexico by the Spaniards who brought with them the Catholic faith and within a few years converted most of the Indians." Diocesan archives, he claimed, demonstrated continuous clerical ministry "without interruption" among the nineteen extant villages, although he also acknowledged that before his arrival the Pueblos had been "abandoned . . . during almost a hundred years, cut off from the balance of the world by immense distance on every side, with great danger from the neighboring savages, and also often in the midst of scandals on the part of the Spanish or Mexicans." "I have been here 23 years, having very limited means," he wrote. "All I could do was to provide some priests for the principal pueblos, who instruct them in their religious duties, administer to them the Sacraments." Six of the larger pueblos in 1874 had resident priests, he said; the rest received clerical visitations. The Indians had "the greatest respect for their clergy and refer to them for their difficulties, etc. And abide generally by their decision." He stated that they attended church services regularly, even after the centuries of revolt, reconquest, and relative neglect. "We cannot deny that some of them have superstitions, but we hope that those abuses will disappear by degrees. Many of them are good catholics and have the strongest attachment to their faith," Lamy concluded.

Eight years later, in 1882, Lamy's archdiocesan office reminded the U.S. Congress that the Pueblo Indians were "members of the Catholic Church" (Santa Fe. Microfilm 58). Nonetheless, it was not until later in the decade that Pueblo missions were revitalized with the opening of St. Catherine's Indian School in Santa Fe, founded by Mother

Katherine Drexel in 1887 to supplement the rudimentary day schools among the various pueblos. This was the first of over sixty schools and missions financed by Drexel; in 1894 she saved the institution from an early demise by forming the Sisters of the Blessed Sacrament, whose nuns served as teachers and administrators. The goal of St. Catherine's was to make practical inroads into the Pueblo communities, whose residents were baptized and buried by the Church, but whose religious life, it was recognized, still bore the mark of their traditional religion. The Church authorities hoped to effect a change in the spiritual orientation and doctrinal knowledge of the Pueblo children. It was hoped that upon their return to their villages, they would help catholicize their families. The instructors thus described their pupils as firm in their Catholic faith against the "idolatry" of their "pagan companions" (*The Indian Sentinel* 1903–1904: 15, 17). With accruing funds, the archdiocese was able to open other such boarding schools, and their graduates showed the signs of acculturation the Church officials desired: going to confession, marrying in the Church, sending their children outside the pueblos to be educated by the Catholic religious.

When the Franciscans reentered the mission field in New Mexico around the turn of the twentieth century, they found the Pueblos "still strewing corn meal," in the words of Fray Barnabas Meyer, O.F.M. (*The Indian Sentinel* 12, no. 3, summer 1932: 118). Some of them wondered "whether the Catholic policy of tolerating paganism, while hoping and trying to unsnarl the pueblo religious dichotomy, half pagan, half Christian, would net any long-term results; or whether the Protestant approach in demanding of its converts a complete cultural rupture with pueblo life was not sounder policy" (Wilken 1955: 168). Judging from his experience at Zia, Jemez, and Santa Ana, Fray Meyer stated:

> It would be in vain to deny that the Jemez Indian is superstitious and to a certain extent idolatrous and that he has not forsaken all the customs and pagan practices of his forefathers. Yet it would be an injustice to assume that he does not wish to be a sincere Catholic. At present he leads a dual religious life; he tries to interweave his pagan ideas with the Christian religion and adheres with tenacity to his pagan-christian cult. (*The Indian Sentinel* 1911: 43)

At Cochiti another Franciscan saw great faith in the intercession of saints to deliver rain, so long as their statues were borne about in the plaza on the feast days, but "their old heathen customs, so deeply rooted in their Indian blood, are still at least to some extent, practiced in secret" (*The Indian Sentinel* 1914: 27). The Indians would not admit the extent of their native religiousness, the friar said, but he took consolation in knowing that they "die as Catholics" (ibid., 28), with last rites.

The same priest heard legends of the 1680 revolt, told by the Cochiti Indians, about refuge provided by the Indians of San Felipe to a priest the Cochitis wished to kill in the rebellion. According to the tale, the San Felipes refused to surrender him, and he wrote a prayer with his blood on a hide, telling the pueblo sacristan to read it aloud. The prayer caused rain to come to the village, and after he died in the pueblo his skull was preserved in the sacristy. The Franciscan learned that on All Souls Eve the skull was to be taken from its bindings and placed on a table in the church, where it was surrounded by hundreds of lighted candles while the mission bell tolled (ibid., 24–28). Thus was the display of Catholicism among the Pueblos in the early twentieth century. They received baptism and last rites. They honored their saints and other spiritual patrons at fiestas. They continued to pray for rain and fertility, and they were constant in communing with their ancestors as in aboriginal times, only now in coordination with the Christian calendar.

Puebloans combined aspects of Christian and native mythology by turning Jesus into a culture hero, e.g., at Laguna, where it was said that his "spattered blood" gave birth to all the "living beings . . . , horses and mules and all creatures" (Parsons 1918: 257), and by associating the santos with traditional spirits who were sources of light, rain, and reproduction, as at Zuni. In one pueblo chapel a photograph of Theodore Roosevelt received veneration as Santiago. At Tesuque the Indians danced to St. Isidore, the patron of farmers, wearing coyote tails as a sign of their "veneration" for this personage (*The Indian Sentinel* 2, no. 8, October 1921: 379). They cared for their old Catholic statues, "usually with ugly, misshapen, long-faced heads and faces, and dressed in silks and satins." When one priest got them to buy a new statue, they would not throw out the old one. When he asked them to discard the "ugly" old one, they replied, "Why not burn your mother? She old and ugly, too" (ibid.). These Pueblo Indians venerated their Catholic paraphernalia as they did their coyote tails. Both were part of the totality of their religious expression, just as were their processions and dances in honor of *Santo Niño* (Holy Infant) at Christmas. At Jemez the pueblo governor appointed a husband and wife to serve as patrons for the Christchild at Christmas. They treated him with solemnity and placed him on an altar in their home. On Christmas Eve the priest led a procession of village officials, Indians, and Mexicans from the area to the sponsors' house, where they took the statue (plus one of Our Lady) to the church for mass, after which the priest led the adoration of Jesus, and everyone knelt and kissed the statues. Then the Indians held a dance in honor of the Holy Infant (ibid. 3, no. 4, October 1923: 171). Puebloans often marked their marriages twice, once in the community with family and village religious leadership presiding, and once in church before a priest.

When Pueblo Indians made pilgrimages to the Sanctuario of the Santo Niño at Chimayo, they were known to rub themselves with the soil beneath the sanctuary, scraping it loose with a Catholic holy medal. The soil, they said, had power to heal: "This is good earth. The Indians knew about it and how to use it a long time ago. Then the padres came and learned about its power, and the Santo Niño came and told them what to do, so they built the church here" (in Marriott 1948: 37). If challenged by Church personnel regarding these beliefs, Puebloans retorted that "Faith in the earth and faith in the Santo Niño go together, and both heal the sick. Each is good, but together both are better" (in ibid., 38).

Zuni proved a particularly difficult pueblo for the twentieth-century Franciscans to reenter. Founded as a mission in 1629, with a long history of violent revolts against the Spanish Catholic regime, the village had its last regular priestly visitor in the 1840s. From the 1860s to the turn of the century, occasional contacts with clerics netted baptisms, making the sixteen hundred Zunis "Catolicos" (*The Indian Sentinel* 1909: 43), as they said, but only in name. As at Jemez, the Zunis danced to Santo Niño, a statue dating to colonial days, carrying out devotionalism with seeming Christian content. The family in charge of the icon was said to descend from colonial sacristans, and the principal dance in its honor took place just after Christmas. Nevertheless, the ceremonies sought the ancient pueblo goal of agricultural fertility, and the statue was thought of as the child of the daughter of the Sun (ibid. 27, no. 2, February 1947: 26, 32; Murphy 1986). Whatever their Christian veneer, the Zunis in 1905 were staunch traditionalists, so much so that Archbishop Peter Bourgarde forbade priests from baptizing any more Zuni infants because they would not grow up in a Christian culture.

The following year Rev. Anselm Weber, O.F.M., journeyed to Zuni, hoping to establish a mission and school in order to produce rigorous Catholic faith and practice. Finding some Zunis agreeable to the notion, he asked the Zuni council for permission to rebuild the church, then "in a state of picturesque ruin and dilapidation" (Forrest 1929: 187), and to create a Catholic presence. In 1907 the Zunis denied the request—perhaps with the guidance of the ethnologist Matilda Coxe Stevenson, who warned the Indians that the Franciscans would reintroduce the old Spanish practices of tithing, whipping Indians to coerce attendance at Sunday mass, and interfering with native ceremonies. Whatever her influence, the Zuni council stated firmly that its people "had a religion of their own and did not wish another on top of it" (*The Indian Sentinel* 1909: 44). Weber argued that denying a Catholic mission constituted an infringement upon religious freedom for those few Zunis who wished to express Christian faith, and he won the right to visit the pueblo once a month. Nevertheless, with the Zuni council upholding its right of sovereignty based upon the 1848 Treaty of Guadalupe-Hidalgo, Weber had little hope of success in converting the Zunis:

> It is my candid opinion that practically nothing can be done with these ultra-conservative, stubborn, obtuse and dense Pueblo Indians till their village government is broken up. In saying 'nothing could be done' I meant not only by way of christianizing them, but also by way of civilizing them. If the Government does not do anything in that line, the Pueblos will be still the same as they are now 'when Gabriel blows his horn.' (In Wilken 1955: 167)

The pueblo governor and his council discouraged baptisms and attendance at masses. Catholic Zunis, said Father Weber, feared "corporal sanctions, derision, whispering campaigns, forms of community ostracism against those white-loving upstarts who would break down the good old life of their forefathers" (ibid., 168).

The Zuni authorities tried to prevent any further Catholic incursion beyond the weekly visitations; however, the small Catholic faction managed to obtain a plot of land through the Indian agent (a Catholic), and in 1922 the Franciscans founded St. Anthony's Mission and School on the reservation. The construction of the mission created severe factionalism at Zuni (exacerbated by a Protestant presence), making it difficult for the Indians to agree on their officeholders and their policies. The school inculcated Zuni youths with Catholic doctrines and loyalties, and confirmations succeeded baptisms among the youths in the 1920s. Church officials reported "success and progress" at Zuni, where the "piety" of worshippers was "impressive," and where several chiefs were "good Catholics. . . . One day Zuni will again be Catholic" (*Our Negro and Indian Missions* 1928: 26). More objective observers said that of all of the Pueblo Indians the Zunis were still "affected the least by christian influence" (Forrest 1929: 184). Whatever "progress" the Franciscans made at Zuni, they had to content themselves with coexistence with an overwhelming majority of traditionalists within the pueblo.

Some Franciscans working with the Pueblos in the 1920s were keen to preserve the Indians' culture as it stood at the time. They wished that the Indians could become more normative as Catholics, but they respected their native religiousness in the Christian forms it took. At least one friar, Fridolin Schuster, O.F.M., tried to protect the Pueblo Indians against the passage of the Bursum Bill in 1922 (legislation affirming the claims of non-Indian squatters to Pueblo territory), which, he said, "will mean the extermination of the Pueblo Indians," eradicating their land titles, their self-government, and their claim to special status within the United States. Schuster said that the future of the Puebloans "concerns us as Catholics because all the Pueblo Indians are Catholic" (Santa Fe. Indian Affairs. November 13, 1922).

THE CAMPAIGN TO REGULARIZE PUEBLO CATHOLICISM:
SANTO DOMINGO

When Rudolph A. Gerken became Archbishop of Santa Fe in 1933, he expressed concern to the missionaries in his province that the Puebloans had retained too much of their traditional religiousness. He directed the missionaries to reorganize their efforts in order to produce greater results among the Indians: "It took 200 years to bring any pagan nation to . . . Christ.—We must not pass up any occasion to rid them of their pagan practices. However, we must be careful and prudent in our methods. We don't want the revolutions of the past" (Santa Fe. Jemez. October 17, 1934). He felt that the greatest progress occurred where priests and sisters resided in the pueblos, and he encouraged such inroads. At the same time, he hoped "to make use of the laity of the Catholic Indian people" to help convert their fellows and put an end to native practices. To further these ends the archbishop created a Catholic Indian Mission Federation of the Santa Fe Province with himself as president; however, the agency had little effect and was short-lived. Two years later the archbishop acknowledged that of the ten thousand Pueblo Indians in his archdiocese, many maintained a "large measure of ancient paganism" (*The Indian Sentinel* 16, no. 7, September 1936: 101). At the end of the 1930s a prominent anthropologist agreed with the archbishop's assessment: "Catholicism has by and large enriched Pueblo religion, contributing God and the saints to the pantheon, fiestas to the calendar, candles and who knows how many other details to ritual" (Parsons 1939 2, pt. 2: 1132), but traditional Pueblo religiousness was still in force, still resistant to Catholic ingress.

The Towas at Jemez held secret dances that competed with Sunday mass, and they called for the Catholic priest's resignation when he scolded them (Santa Fe. Jemez. October 19, 1933). They refused to pay for confirmation fees and resisted the authority of the archbishop. Despite their Catholic allegiance, many Indians at Cochiti refused to attend mass as a way of protesting baptismal fees; at most of the pueblos sacramental fees were still waived, to the annoyance of some priests. One father reported several dozen confirmations at the Tiwa pueblo of Taos: "but, as you know, these blessed Redskins have the privilege of enjoying everything freely, and still doing a big favor to the donor" (Santa Fe. Taos. October 11, 1935). When peyotism came into use among some youths at Taos, the same priest bemoaned "one more superstition added to the many already existing among the Indians" (ibid., October 21, 1936).

At Zuni hundreds of children attended classes at St. Anthony's Mission School, and nearly all of them attended Sunday masses, but "without any encouragement on the part of their pagan parents" (Santa Fe. Zuni. November 21, 1933). Zuni adults eschewed Catholic marriages and other sacraments. Despite attempts on the part of the Franciscans to "promote devotion to the Blessed Virgin Mary" (ibid., August 3, 1936) among the youths with gifts of rosaries and medals; despite Confraternity of Christian Doctrine classes; despite confirmations, Zuni children in the 1930s were said to "return to their pagan customs to the great detriment of their religion" (ibid., March 31, 1938). Traditional religious culture persisted, with its elaborate ceremonialism—"The constant spectacle of antique lives being lived in our own days" (*The Indian Sentinel* 17, no. 2, February 1937: 19), as one Franciscan called it—even though the native religious beliefs and practices of the two thousand Zunis were "being challenged by the Government and mission schools and the Catholic mission chapel on the fringe of the village" (ibid.).

At the Tewa pueblo of San Juan the Indians kept up their traditional ceremonialism, even inviting Archbishop Gerken to attend a buffalo dance on January 6, 1934 (Santa Fe. San Juan. January 4-5, 1934)—and he accepted the offer. The next year, however, the Puebloans removed a bridge connecting the local priest's ranch to the village, thereby preventing him from regular visits to the pueblo. Although they replaced the bridge at the archbishop's urging, the San Juan officers tried to keep the Church at a distance throughout the 1930s.

At Cochiti, when the Franciscans questioned the Keres Indians about "pagan practices" within the pueblo, "the Governor practically admitted that idolatry was practiced there. Indians that faithfully followed their Catholic Religion were persecuted and [were] molested in different ways if they refuse[d] to take part of those secret dances" (Santa Fe. Peña Blanca. September 17, 1941). The Keres at Acoma reacted to the more forceful Catholic evangelization efforts of the 1930s with stiffened resolve. Rev. Agnellus Lammert, O.F.M., reported to his archbishop in 1938 of nativism at the Sky City: "The new regime were put in by the Medicine men and they seemed determined to get back to all the old customs. My lay Catechists were very much alarmed about the situation, but they tell me that many of the people want to be real Christians and do not want to follow the Governor" (Santa Fe. Laguna. February 5, 1938).

Archbishop Gerken's strategy to regularize the Pueblos' Catholic practice met its fiercest resistance at the village of Santo Domingo, one of the largest pueblos and perhaps the most conservative. After serving as the Franciscan center from 1629, the Keres pueblo took a leading role in the revolution of 1680, and the Indians there deserted their town to avoid Otermin a year later, when he camped at Isleta and tried to regain the pueblos. He sacked the village, finding masks and other items of traditional worship. When he left the area, the Indians returned, and during the Reconquest (1692–1696) the pueblo resisted mightily, if unsuccessfully, against the reinstitution of Catholicism.

Through the eighteenth century and the first half of the nineteenth, Santo Domingo housed a padre, and the Indians kept up their church and rectory in attractive decoration. At the same time, they maintained a strict distance between their native religiousness and the prying of outsiders. The village exhibited little factionalism, since for the most part the people remained committed to their own way of life, and the pueblo organization controlled whatever urges there were on the part of individual Keres to adopt white manners. When several of the Santo Domingoans sent their children to St. Catherine's School in Santa Fe, the pueblo council put pressure on the parents to remove them. The council permitted baptisms to all members of the pueblo, and a priest was allowed to say mass several times annually; however, virtually no one at the pueblo received communion, nor any of the other sacraments—except for those students returning from St. Catherine's, who were in the habit of confessing their sins. The pueblo authorities had particular aversion to confessions, where tribal secrets might be revealed to a priest. Antonio Seonra was perhaps the first Santo Domingoan to receive last rites, before his death in 1923 (*The Indian Sentinel* 4, no. 2, April 1924: 72–73).

Their church officers, like the sacristan Juan Garcia in the 1920s, maintained control over Catholic paraphernalia, holding the keys to the church, admitting and refusing whom they willed. Catholic missionaries were bemused by the way Garcia wielded his jurisdictional authority:

Curiously enough he will sometimes refuse to let the priest have free access to the church. But the priest, having a sense of humor, does not
take the sacristan as seriously as that dignitary takes himself. The padre
usually lets him exercise his childish authority. (Rev. William Hughes in
ibid. 3, no. 3, July 1923: 132)

Despite their condescension, Church authorities could do nothing to
assert control over the church at Santo Domingo. The Indians regarded the property and its effects as their own, and they guarded their
sovereignty steadfastly. They forbade outsiders—including teachers,
U.S. government officials, and Church personnel—from viewing their
native ceremonies, and almost no white person was allowed to stay in
the pueblo overnight, except on Christmas or on the feast of Santo
Domingo on August 4. Instructors in the government school on the
reservation had their quarters placed outside the village proper, to
keep them segregated from the Puebloans, and the teachers were
locked in their residences when masked dances took place. It is reported that, "on at least one occasion a Commissioner of Indian Affairs was forbidden entrance to the pueblo during a pagan religious
rite" (ibid.). The men in charge of Santo Domingo guarded against the
telling of pueblo secrets; they arranged marriages, proscribed clothing
styles, and enforced participation in all ceremonials, holding their
tribal members to a uniform way of life in which traditional cosmology, ceremonialism, religious organization, and values persisted (see
White 1935: 7–34). They fit the occurrence of Christian holidays into
their own calendar, and in their mythology a contest between a native
deity and the Christian God ended in the defeat of the latter: "God got
tired and gave up" (ibid., 179), the story concluded. If the new archbishop of Santa Fe was going to attempt a transformation of Santo
Domingo religiousness, the Keres leaders there might have anticipated
that their own persistence would outlast the prelate's efforts, as their
native divinity outlasted God.

In November 1933 Archbishop Gerken interviewed Rev. Ulric
Kreutzen, O.F.M., who was assigned to Santo Domingo from his station at Peña Blanca. Gerken learned that of the one thousand families
in the pueblo, perhaps two hundred attended the monthly mass:

None ever go to Confession and Comm. All are baptized. All are married by the Church. Fiesta is held on Aug. 4th (St. Dominic). All marriages are on the Fiesta & Jan 6th. No Catechism taught, because the
children don't come. No sisters have ever taught Catechism; suppos-

edly not wanted. No sickcalls and no funerals. Church established there many years. (Santa Fe. Peña Blanca. November 3, 1933)

Gerken wondered how he might increase sacramental participation and catechetical knowledge among the Keres Indians. A Franciscan advisor—Rev. Barnabas Meyer, O.F.M.—suggested to him that the Church might accomplish these goals by using a "disguise, as it were, as he did in Jeme[z], with the result that all receive Sacraments well now" (ibid.). The "disguise" consisted of stationing sisters and a priest on the reservation, in order to get a foot in the door of the pueblo. Their presence might lead to greater knowledge of the Puebloans' ways, and might undermine the pueblo council's authority over its own people. The problem was, how to get permission of the council to establish Church personnel on the reservation, when tradition there prohibited outsiders from living among the people.

For a year and a half the archdiocese negotiated with Santo Domingo officials, but the pueblo council would not budge in its refusal to allow a priest and sisters to live in the village. Tensions mounted as the new visiting priest, Rev. Remigius Austing, O.F.M., tried to increase his ministrations. If he arrived to say mass at a time unacceptable to the pueblo, the church was locked, and he was told that everyone was unavailable at home. Father Austing called the situation "Trouble and more trouble" (ibid., May 6, 1935). In July 1935 Archbishop Gerken met with Santo Domingo officials at the pueblo, but in the view of the archbishop they accomplished nothing. The council refused to permit the people of the pueblo to receive the sacraments of Penance and Holy Eucharist, which Gerken regarded as their duty. He pleaded with the Santo Domingoans, but they would not budge. They did not want their children instructed in Christian doctrine, and they did not want an increase of sacramental participation. Finally, they would not allow clerics and religious to live among them.

Gerken instructed the Franciscan to say mass on Sunday, July 21, at a time when a substantial number of Indians would be present. At the end of mass—without announcing it in advance—the padre was to read a proclamation slowly and clearly, in English and Spanish; then he was to hand a copy to the governor of the pueblo. In his instructions the archbishop defined the issue concerning him, that the Indians thought that receiving baptism alone made them good Catholics. Priests baptized them even though the Indians did not make confessions or receive the Eucharist. "This is a point that really resolves itself into heresy," Gerken wrote (ibid., July 16, 1935); hence, the Church must take severe action to uphold minimal levels of sacramental participation.

The proclamation, "To THE GOVERNOR, OFFICIALS AND PEOPLE OF THE SANT[O] DOMINGO PUEBLO" (ibid.), asserted the archbishop's authority as "head of this Archdiocese . . . obligated to rule the Church and to safeguard the spiritual interests of the faithful." Gerken re-counted his meeting with pueblo officials regarding the stationing of a priest and missionary sisters on the reservation, to teach religion, visit the sick, organize sewing clubs, and to be "agents of mercy in your midst. . . . The officials of the Pueblo denied us this right to do for the Catholics what is our duty," even though the archbishop explained that such arrangements were common throughout the Catholic world, and that religious instruction was greatly needed among the Puebloans.

In Gerken's view, the Pueblo officials were interfering with the "rights" of their people to practice their Catholicism by receiving penance and holy communion. The officials argued, according to the proclamation, that "this was not necessary to be good Catholics." The archbishop felt that he was not interfering with the council's "purely civil" authority; neither should they interfere with his "spiritual" authority. The people have no duty, he wrote, to obey civil officials in matters "purely spiritual." Indeed, they must do what is necessary "to save their immortal souls so that they may hope to go to Heaven when death takes them from this world."

Since the officials refused to reconsider the archbishop's request, and since they refused to respect Church authority over the baptized Santo Domingoans, and since they were "disrespectful and disobedi-ent," the archbishop would no longer permit his priest to visit the pueblo. He would no longer baptize children, except those very sick and in danger of death; he would no longer say mass; nor would he unite Santo Domingoans in marriage—as long as the officials re-mained in office, or until those officers or their successors changed their decision. The proclamation exhorted "you good Catholics . . . sincere in your faith" to rid themselves of their officials (as "tyrants") and it offered prayers that such an effect might be accomplished.

Father Austing read the proclamation as instructed. Then he re-moved the chalice from the church, without the knowledge of the pueblo officials, and the interdict went into effect. There would be no services at Santo Domingo henceforth, including their major feast of

St. Dominic on August 4th (the interdict was timed to give the pueblo officials a chance to change their minds before that date). The civil officers of the pueblo, in Gerken's view, wanted to rule in spiritual matters, where they ought to have "no jurisdiction." In short, "they are so pagan in many ways that they refuse to accept the authority of the Church" (Santa Fe. San Juan. July 23, 1935). The archbishop was determined to teach them a lesson in ecclesiology.

The Santo Domingo governor Francisco Tenorio complained immediately of the archbishop's actions to the United Pueblos Agency, whose assistant superintendent, Lem A. Towers, attempted to serve as mediator in the conflict. Through Towers the governor said that the dispute was a "misunderstanding" (Santa Fe. Peña Blanca. July 22, 1935). The officials had no objection to a priest performing his functions "as in the past," and if the archbishop would rescind his proclamation, the Puebloans were ready to establish "the old basis" of relationship between pueblo and Church. Their only objection was to house sisters at their village. In this way the officials of the pueblo expressed loyalty to the Church, but they reiterated their refusal to allow Church personnel to live on their reservation, and they sidestepped the question of increased sacramental participation. In short, they wanted to return to the equilibrium established over centuries, in which they received baptism but maintained control over their religious lives. Archbishop Gerken, on the other hand, desired a new equation which denied religious authority to the pueblo officials and which might lead to a greater catholicizing of the Santo Domingoans. Gerken responded to Towers (ibid., July 29, 1935) that no "misunderstanding" had taken place. The officials of Santo Domingo refused to let the priests administer penance, communion, and last rites; they refused to allow Church personnel to teach Catholic children on the reservation. The archbishop reminded the U.S. officer that there were many Catholics at the pueblo who wanted to receive the sacraments, and by denying them this right, the pueblo authorities were denying them their religious freedom.

Through the aid of Lem A. Towers, Archbishop Gerken wrote a "COPY OF AGREEMENT" (ibid., August 1, 1935) that appeared at first to resolve the dispute largely in favor of the Church. Gerken agreed to provide a priest on August 4 for the pueblo's "festive Mass," at which time baptisms and marriages would take place. In exchange, the Indians were to agree that the Church was free to send priests and sisters to the pueblo "as often as they see fit," to teach Catholic doctrine; to deliver penance, Eucharist, and extreme unction to the Indians, who would be free to receive the sacraments; to say mass on Sundays and feast days; and to perform Church burials. Gerken signed the concordat but the Santo Domingo officials were "very reluctant to sign any formal agreement" (ibid., August 2, 1935) that would bind future pueblo administrations. They hoped that the archbishop would accept their verbal promise to live up to the arrangement; however, he would not. August 4 passed without the fiesta for St. Dominic.

Santo Domingo residents Augustine Aguilar, Reyes Quintana, and John Bird wrote to Gerken on August 6, 1935, expressing their dismay at the standoff:

> For hundreds of years at Santo Domingo we have taken care of the Catholic Church. Never before until this time has any church father said to us the things you have said.
> We have been Catholic Christians according to our own consciences for these hundreds of years. . . . We have not changed in any way. (Ibid., August 6, 1935)

In the view of these Indians, it was the matter of resident priests and sisters demanded by the archbishop that caused the objection in the pueblo. In their view, the prelate was "unkind" to take away baptisms because the Indians would not allow "a convent . . . in our pueblo. . . . We do not believe that a community of white Catholic[s] would be punished in such a manner." The Indians explained that they could not accept an agreement that allowed priests and sisters to enter the pueblo whenever they wanted: "all who know our life and customs know that such an agreement is impossible and that we have days and occasions when no white man or woman can come among us. We can not grant it," said the Indians, even though they regarded themselves as Catholics and wished the continuing ministrations of a priest.

Gerken replied to the Puebloans, expressing in authoritative terms his perception of the conflict: "I want you to accept the entire Religion as it was given to us by Jesus Christ, as it was taught by the Apostles and as it is brought down to us by the Church established by Jesus Christ nearly 2000 years ago" (ibid., August 8, 1935). To Gerken there were two primary issues: sovereignty and native rites. The pueblo regarded itself as sovereign over all its affairs, its land, its ceremonials, its secrets, its calendar, and its people. The Church regarded itself as sovereign over the spiritual lives of its people, including those within the pueblo, and it would brook no power that attempted to prevent the sacramental, teaching authority from reaching its people. Gerken told the Indians that they were breaking Canon Law, a code made not by men, but by God Himself. Breaking such rules had resulted in far greater punishments for Whites than the Pueblos had received thus far.

Secondly, the Church had reluctantly but pragmatically permitted the Pueblos to perform their community rites, some in public, some secret, some overlaid with Catholicism (especially those held in public), some supercharged with aboriginality (especially the private ones). The official position of the Church was that these private rites were societal and therefore civil, not religious; hence, the Church officials permitted them to continue, hoping to undermine them in the long run with education. The archdiocese was now attacking the secrecy necessary for that arrangement to continue. Archbishop Gerken was no longer willing to maintain the fiction that Puebloan rites were merely cultural. Recognizing their dimensions of native spirituality, he was determined to root them out.

The Puebloans argued that to have sisters or a priest on Pueblo land, either in a convent or whenever they pleased, was to intrude on the long-standing, tacit arrangement of allowing Indian ritualism. The new Church policy seemed to them an attack on both the sovereignty and the religious rites of the Santo Domingo Pueblo.

By delineating the issues of sovereignty and religious rites, Gerken made it clear why he could not back down from the confrontation. In the prelate's view the refusal of the pueblo officials to allow their members to receive penance meant their inability to have their sins forgiven; hence, they would not go to heaven. Such an arrangement was impossible for the Church to condone. Gerken said that up to that time the bishops had been lenient with the Pueblos because they hoped that the Indians over time would become Catholics "not only in part but in full." But the pueblo officials were not allowing this progression to take place; they were not allowing their Indian people to "save their immortal souls." It was equally clear, however, why the Santo Domingoans could not compromise. Their sovereignty, their community's ritual life, were both under frontal attack by the Church. They could not allow Gerken to destroy their cultural existence.

From 1935 to 1940 the Church performed no masses at Santo Domingo, as the interdict continued, although there were unverified rumors of a "Mass" (ibid., July 21, 1940) on the feast of St. Dominic each year. The Indians were said to place a priest's vestments on the altar and proceed through the form of a mass with no padre. In 1937 several of the Santo Domingo Catholics, including Francisco Garcia and Juan Caté, tried to arrange a settlement that would bring a visiting priest back to the pueblo, but in each case the demands of the archbishop—catechetical instruction, confession, communion, and last rites, as well as mass "as often as we request it" (June 30, 1937)—proved unacceptable to the pueblo council. Individual Keres Indians received baptism in Peña Blanca, and the archdiocese maintained friendly contacts with many of the Indians from the pueblo, but officially the sacramental connections were cut for five years.

When the mass returned on the feast of St. Dominic in 1940, Archbishop Gerken exulted, "Rejoice with us that this unpleasant situation has now been solved," and his press releases and private correspondence with the apostolic delegate in Washington D.C. made it seem that the Indians had met all the demands of the Church (July 18–20, 1940; July 23, 1940). Nevertheless, one of the Indians from Santo Domingo, John Bird, published his own version of the dispute and its resolution, asserting that the initial Church demand "for ground within the pueblo on which to establish a home for Priests and Sisters" (August 2, 1940) had created the fracas, and that demand was still denied.

Despite attempts on the part of Gerken's assistants (e.g., Fray Angélico Chávez, O.F.M.) to discredit John Bird, the Indian's review of the dispute held. The pueblo council in 1935 would not give the Church land in the pueblo. Its members "firmly objected to having the services of the Priest at our burial time. . . . The majority of the Council was opposed to the Indians going to Confession." The pueblo could not allow clerics and religious to intrude on the village during special ceremonial days. And in general,

> It was also agreed any further concessions to any white religious organizations would tend to break down the ancient Indian religious practices which are a normal part of our lives. We could see no reason to give up our religious customs in which we are happy and to take in their place that which is foreign to our natures.

Gerken denied in public that the Church ever wanted to build a home for priests and sisters on the Santo Domingo pueblo, contrary to Bird's charges. The archbishop also claimed that during the five year

hiatus he had tried to protect the pueblo council against forceful overthrow by Catholic loyalists at Santo Domingo: "I forbade them to re-
sort to any such measures" (ibid., August 3, 1940), Gerken avowed.

The Franciscans began the process of baptizing the Keres children
born during the five years—Fray Chávez christened close to a hundred
by August 18, 1940—and the Church tried to establish a regular pattern for weekly masses and periodic instruction. Nevertheless, well
into the 1940s the pueblo council continued to balk at allowing its
Indians to receive penance and Holy Eucharist. The new archbishop
of Santa Fe, Edwin V. Byrne, reminded the Santo Domingo governor
that,

> all authority comes from God. The authority then that is being dele-
> gated to you by your people comes primarily from God, the Ruler of all
> people and all individuals. Temporal rulers on this earth are subject in
> everything to the Divine Supreme Ruler. They should exercise their
> authority then in accordance and in harmony with the divine laws and
> regulations. (Santa Fe. Indian Affairs. December 30, 1943)

Nonetheless, the pueblo council kept its own way, even when individuals from the reservation went to confession and received communion
in missions and parishes beyond the reservation.

The governor and the council did want to make sure that baptisms
continued in the pueblo—these were initiatory rituals firmly grounded
in cultural life—and in the late 1940s there was even some interest in
doctrinal training and Catholic literature. When the pueblo authorities
met, however, there were many who refused to allow confessions to
take place in the reservation. A meeting of the Santo Domingo council
in 1948 affirmed the absolute authority of the visiting priest in all religious matters ("Sacristan can be barred from performing all priestly
functions"), as well as the principle of religious freedom for Puebloans
who wished to receive the Eucharist. The Sacrament of penance, however, was "the big stumbling block" (Santa Fe. Peña Blanca. June 16,
1948); council members could not countenance the sacrament taking
place on the reservation, even if village members went elsewhere to
confess their sins.

The following year the Franciscan priest, Julian Hartig, O.F.M., refused to baptize children at Santo Domingo unless the parents made
"vows against the Indian religious worship." The governor and his
councilmen protested this action to the archbishop: "By tradition, we
were taught to worship both, Indian ways and the Catholic ways."

They told the archbishop that if Father Julian's orders came from the archdiocesan offices, it might "well be the end of our union among us. . . . We remain your humble people" (ibid., March 2, 1949). They expressed their desire to continue as they had, with respect for Church hierarchy; however, they noted that in all their generations such an order had never before been given them. Archbishop Byrne responded that there is only one true Church, one True God: "the Catholic Church teaches that all other forms of religion are false" (March 15, 1949) and so insists that godparents promise their godchildren against "false worship." The prelate told the Indians that his order was in keeping with Catholic requirements the world over and was nothing new; like his predecessor he was insisting upon "non-participation in false worship."

These orders were part of the process set into motion by Archbishop Gerken in 1933, a process attempting to engage the Puebloans more thoroughly in mainstream Catholic instruction and worship, and to wean them from their native traditions. In the 1950s the visiting priest at the pueblo was "very critical of our Indian ways" (August 28, 1950) in Sunday sermons, according to Governor Tenorio and his council. Pueblo authorities tried to keep his masses on a biweekly basis; however, he made his appearance every Sunday, part of the plan, as Archbishop Byrne noted, to make the Santo Domingoans "become more and more Catholic" for their "peace and happiness" (August 29, 1950). Religious instruction became part of the weekly routine in the pueblo, and in 1954 the reservation held a First Communion ceremony for forty children, a "history making event" (May 24, 1954), according to the Franciscan in charge. Confirmations took place the following year. Nevertheless, twenty years after the 1935 interdict, a missionary among the Santo Domingoans acknowledged that "although the Indians there say they are Catholics, few were by any count model Catholics" (*The Indian Sentinel* 35, no. 9, November 1955: 139).

More and more Keres Indians from the pueblo have participated in Catholic sacramental life in succeeding decades; the community renovated its church in 1972, and if anything, the native and Christian calendars of worship have become more intimately intertwined. Yet, in the present day, one can still refer to the "longstanding, though sometimes tenuous presence of Roman Catholicism" (Lange 1979: 379) at Santo Domingo pueblo.

During the 1940s and 1950s Church spokesmen commented upon the catholicizing effects of the 1930s campaign. At Laguna and Acoma, Father Lammert built chapels and commissioned Sisters of the Blessed Sacrament to train local Indian women as catechists. Whereas he found initially among the Western Keres "a population nominally Catholic but ignorant of their religion" (*The Indian Sentinel* 16, no. 1, January 1936: 9), he was able to report a marked increase in the number of Indians attending mass and receiving the Eucharist. The Acomas and Lagunas voluntarily refurbished their churches and built new ones—"so that God would be pleased with them and give them rains for their crops and much grass for their sheep and cattle" (ibid. 20, no. 9, November 1940: 131)—and with increased church activity among them, their participation in Catholic tradition grew. Lammert wrote (*Our Negro and Indian Missions* 1942: 41) that

> While in some places there has been a tendency among the Indians to return to their old ways, because of the influence of the so-called admirers of Indian customs, it seems to me that since we are giving them holy Mass oftener and since we are giving regular instructions in the Government day schools, the Laguna and Acoma Indians are taking a greater interest in the Catholic religion and are attending Mass more regularly. Quite a few of the younger people are not only not taking an interest in the old customs, but they actually ridicule them.

During World War II the Western Keres soldiers kept contact with Catholic chaplains, and on the reservations the populace held prayer services and performed devotions to the Cross "for the safety of our boys" (*The Indian Sentinel* 23, no. 2, February 1943: 23). Upon receiving blessing from Archbishop Edwin Byrne for his gubernatorial cane, the governor of Laguna, Robert Accalla, assured the prelate that the pueblo had,

> from time immemorial, recognized, that "Temporal Rulership" comes from "God," who is the "Supreme Ruler of the Universe," and whence all pure and good inspirations are implanted in minds of Rulers of good intentions towards the exercise of good Government, which the "Canes" of Authority signify. (Santa Fe. Indian Affairs. January 23, 1946)

His people performed a procession in honor of the statue of Our Lady of Fatima in 1948, on its nationwide "Pilgrim Virgin" tour to promote world peace and convert Communist Russia (*The Indian Sentinel* 28, no. 8, October 1948: 117–119), and they began devotions to Kateri Tekakwitha, at the urging of Father Lammert.

When approached by evangelists from Protestant bodies, virtually all Puebloans—including the governmental officers of the Pueblos—put them off. In 1947 the governor of Cochiti, Joe Toujillo, forbade a Holiness Church minister to visit the pueblo (Santa Fe. Peña Blanca. December 30, 1947). The Taos governor and council resisted the proselytizing of a Baptist preacher in 1950; they "insisted that the Indian people were very satisfied with the Catholic religion and did not want to have religious discord" or "bloodshed" aroused by sectarianism on the reservation. They did not mind if Taos Indians went into town for Baptist services, but they maintained the right to keep anyone out of the pueblo who might "cause disturbance." The Santa Fe chancery praised their decision, commenting, "Taos Pueblo is considered about the best Catholic Pueblo" (Santa Fe. Indian Affairs. April 14, 1950). Five years later the archbishop could still report of Taos: "This Pueblo is almost entirely Catholic" (Santa Fe. Albuquerque Indian School. April 29, 1955); its members packed St. Jerome's Church in the pueblo, receiving the sacraments, sitting on the floor when the pews were filled, and contributing free labor to expand the edifice.

When pueblo governments blocked the religious expressions of Protestant minorities in the reservations, most prominently at Jemez in the early 1950s, the archdiocese supported their sovereignty. Archbishop Byrne informed Commissioner of Indian Affairs Glenn Emmons that the Jemez officials had the right to keep Protestant members of their community—numbering about ninety of the thousand in the pueblo—from holding services in the village and burying their dead in the pueblo cemetery. To Byrne, the Jemez Indians were Catholics possessing impressive "religious spirit and observance," who should be encouraged "to conduct their own affairs as much as possible" (Santa Fe. Indian Affairs. August 25, 1953). When several Jemez Protestants brought suit against their government, U.S. District Judge Carl A. Hatch dismissed the charges as an internal Jemez matter of governance. The archbishop concurred that the pueblos were "independent communities having certain attributes of sovereignty, one of which is the right to self-government" (ibid., July 21, 1954)—at least in cases in which the Catholic majority protected the establishment of Catholicism. (When the pueblo governments asserted their sovereignty and ruled against Catholic persons or institutions in order to defend the integrity of Pueblo culture, the archdiocese cried that the rights of individual Catholics were being trampled.)

For all the growing solidity of Pueblo Catholicism in the middle of the twentieth century, Puebloans continued to be irked by canonical and monetary stipulations of the hierarchical Church and by the policies of individual priests. At San Juan the council resented the fees for baptisms, weddings, and funerals (Santa Fe. San Juan. December 13, 1958). Nambe Indians requested dispensation from certain fasting (Santa Fe. Santa Cruz. September 26, 1957) and objected to attending services in neighboring Catholic churches when the priest would not come to them each week (Santa Fe. Nambe. September 8, 12, 1960). Governor Seferino Martinez of Taos protested the archdiocesan attempt to join the pueblo church of St. Jerome to the Hispanic congregation in nearby Guadalupe parish:

> We do not like innovations and we want to do as our forefathers did; therefore, we do not like the fact that Fr. [Albert] Chavez baptizes our babies in Guadalupe Parish instead of baptizing them in our Church in the Pueblo. . . . The feast we usually have for baptisms is spoiled in many cases by this new rule. (Santa Fe. Taos. June 15, 1955)

Governor Martinez expressed the desire of most Puebloans at midcentury to continue their associations with the Church in the manner to which they were accustomed. They wanted liturgical attention from the priests; they did not wish to be combined with Hispanic parishes; they wanted their Catholicism to be a matter of pueblo community practice, a part of their overall religiousness—which in the 1940s and 1950s continued to embrace native forms. Governor Martinez told the chancery office that he was trying to keep his people "united in the Catholic Faith" (ibid.), and he warned that Protestant defections could be stemmed only if the local priest paid attention to Taos Catholic prerogatives and traditions. At the same time, Governor Martinez was petitioning the United States for restitution of the "Sacred Area" (ibid., May 16, 1955) north of the pueblo, including Blue Lake. As governor, his job was to maintain all aspects of his people's traditional religion, which in the twentieth century included both Catholic and native forms.

In the middle of the century Catholic Indians at Jemez had their babies baptized and then held native feasts, offering prayers before a perfect ear of corn, in order to assure the children's health. Matachinis danced after mass on the Feast of the Epiphany, at which the local Franciscan blessed canes—"emblems of authority" (*The Indian Sentinel* 26, no. 2, February 1946: 27)—held by the local elected officials of the pueblo. The Indians stated that the matachin dance portrayed "the contest between the victorious Church and the devil and sin" (ibid., 28), as introduced by the Spanish centuries ago. The Jemez Towas considered the Catholic feasts their own and argued with Church personnel over the proceedings and the proceeds. When the November 12 fiesta in honor of San Diego netted monetary offerings from tourists, the pueblo council decided that the funds belonged to the pueblo rather than the parish treasury. The local Franciscan told them that the padres always took these moneys; however, "I didn't get very far with them. Sometimes we think we are making progress, but then again we are back where we started. They insisted they keep the Shrine money" (Santa Fe. Jemez. November 25, 1950). The Jemez officials maintained autonomy over their church, opening and locking it as they wished, despite the objections of the priests.

The Jemez pueblo celebrated not only its own feasts but also that of the Pecos people who took refuge in Jemez when their village became extinct in 1838. The Pecos Towas brought with them to Jemez some aboriginal ceremonial knowledge and organization, as well as their celebration of Our Lady of the Angels each August 2nd, and the Pecos remnant persisted in marking the feast with a bull dance on the eve and morning of the holy day. In the ritual the "bull" was too strong and wild to be subdued. However, after the mass and a procession of Our Lady's statue, he became "calm and tractable." The Towas related a legend of a bull long ago, subdued by a statue of the Virgin, and the missionaries possibly encouraged a reenactment in order to demonstrate the power of Christian divinity over "beasts of passion" (*The Indian Sentinel* 25, no. 7, October 1945: 102). For well over a century since emigrating to Jemez, the Pecos Towas continued to make pilgrimages to Pecos, maintaining shrines there, and at least on one occasion they carried the banner of Our Lady of the Angels in the company of the archbishop to mark the rebuilding of the church at Pecos as a public monument (Kessell 1979: 487).

In many cases native and Catholic ritualism united in common interests. San Felipe Pueblo celebrated Christmas Eve by having "naked, painted dancers file into the ancient candle-lit church to dance before the Manger" (*The Indian Sentinel* 23, no. 10, December 1943: 147). But at the same reservation Governor Jose Rey Sanchez and his councilmen argued with the priest over the food offerings they brought to the church on All Souls Day. Governor Sanchez said that for generations his people made such offerings; the priest replied that the practice and its underlying belief had no "connection with the Catholic practice. And is not according to the laws of the Catholic Church" (Santa Fe. Peña Blanca. November 16, 1947). The Indians brought the offerings anyway, and the cleric called it "all foolishness. . . . The dead, or the spirits, would not eat the stuff." He questioned the Indians' knowledge of Catholic doctrine and—according to the governor—"said insulting things of the Indian belief and religion and customs." The Indians felt "greatly insulted" and called for his transfer, telling the archbishop that the San Felipe Keres did not want to abolish their Catholicism, but to "continue as we have been before" (ibid.). The priest retorted that the Keres should worship God alone, "but you Indians have false Gods" (December 9, 1947). Archbishop Byrne admitted that his priest was "in a very difficult position" (December 23, 1947) because of the continuing duality of San Felipe religion.

At San Ildefonso, masses and native dances alternated on feast days, and when clerical schedules (e.g., the timing of the Christmas mass) got in the way of traditional liturgy, the governor and officers protested. The priests tried to "please them" by modifying their calendar to the Indian dances, but they chafed under the tension of two religious systems coexisting in an uneasy peace: "Indians are Indians, and [it] is hard to deal with them most of the time. . . . God pardon the[m], they are made that way, I guess" (Santa Fe. Santa Cruz. December 23, 1940).

Sister Mary Bernardine, O.S.F., reported in 1949 that "Two forces are contending for the soul of the Zuni Indian, the old paganism and Christianity" (*The Indian Sentinel* 29, no. 10, December 1949: 152). The Shalako ceremonies in early December, with their masked impersonations of the native gods, were public exhibitions of the old religion; at Christmas there were no corresponding Christian celebrations, except for those conducted by the teachers at St. Anthony School. Several years later the Franciscan priests and sisters "got thirty of our mission high school pupils to go carolling around the village" for three nights before Christmas. As reported by a Franciscan priest, it was brave of the youths to sing Christian hymns in public: "A majority of these people were stoutly opposed to any encroachments on their old, primitive, pagan ways. Our Catholic children know that by experience. Many of our elders cruelly make fun of them" (ibid. 35, no. 11, January 1955: 8). Each night more and more Indians followed the carollers and enjoyed the songs. Some families asked the singers to come to their houses, and at midnight mass the school gymnasium was overflowing with Zunis. On the feast of the Epiphany, over a hundred families asked the priests to bless their homes. The priest commented that "You learn patience in dealing with Indians like these" (9), and he prayed "that Mary may once again crush the head of Satan and paralyze his influence here" (ibid., 34, no. 3, March 1954: 38). In 1956 St. Anthony's Mission performed its first Catholic burial since the Franciscans returned in 1921, but by and large the Zunis remained "a pagan lot" (ibid. 36, no. 8, October 1956: 120), according to the padres. When Sister Mary Bernardine returned to Zuni after nine years' absence in 1962, the Indians told her, "I have not been good; I did not go to Sunday Mass as you taught me to do. But I will try again" (ibid. 40, no. 4, winter 1962: 57–58). She vowed to "pursue like the hounds of Heaven . . ." (58) those former students of hers who fell away from the Church. And so the interplay between Pueblo and Catholic religions continued.

In general it was understood by knowledgeable observers that Pueblo religion persisted, augmented by, intertwined with, but kept ritually separate from normative Catholicism. The Indians did not give up their old communal rituals—"These ceremonies persist to the present time among all the Pueblos and in many cases are surrounded with such secrecy that white people know little or nothing of them" (Hodge 1945: 225). Simultaneously, they identified themselves in public as Catholics, resistant to Protestant overtures: "Today these people continue their native religious practices but likewise remain loyal Catholics (by their own word) and see no real difference between their re-tailored interpretation of the Church and that of Anglo- and Spanish-American Catholics" (Hawley 1946: 407).

Within the Church hierarchy, the Pueblos posed a singular difficulty. When Pope Pius XII asked Archbishop Edwin V. Byrne of Santa Fe about the spiritual conditions of the Pueblos, the archbishop reported that "almost 100 per cent of New Mexico's 14,000 Pueblo

Indians are members of the Church and that 18 out of the 19 Indian Pueblos within the state are officially Catholic" (Santa Fe. Missions, Indian—General. [1943]). The pope was interested in the "romance" of the tribal customs, and the archbishop told him that going to the pueblos was like taking a step back in time. Byrne was impressed by the Indians' stone-faced reverence in chapel, their courteousness before clerical authority, and their pageantry. He also noted their technical proficiency in irrigating their fields and repairing their tractors, and their governmental stability. Thus he respected them for their traditionalism, their religiousness, and their elasticity in the modern world. Of course, he added, no white man knows what takes place in their kivas, and so far there were no Pueblo Catholic priests; however, in good time, he said, "God will take care of that" (ibid.). Among the Franciscans, however, the view was less sanguine. It was well understood that in the nineteenth century "practically all of these Pueblos were left unattended," and "the Indians, never quite fully Christianized, slid back into their paganism, curiously taking with them the name of Catholic and some of the external rites and devotions that appealed to their essentially religious nature" (ibid., 1946). Almost a century after the arrival of Archbishop Lamy, a half century after the return of the Franciscans, the situation had not changed considerably, according to Fray Angélico Chávez, O.F.M., in 1946. Most of the pueblos still lacked resident priests; there was little coordination of mission efforts; the traditional religion still held against Catholic efforts. Chávez called for "*zealous*" Franciscans (but not the "bull-dog type of Padre") to effect the changes in Pueblo faith by living in each village as in a parish. Should any pueblo refuse a resident priest, "let it be left without Mass and all ministrations or visits until it gives in" (ibid.). Hence, Church officials vacillated between romanticizing and pressurizing in responding to Puebloan religious persistence.

Father Regis Darpel, O.F.M., extolled the virtues of Cochiti Catholics who made All Souls offerings of corn, bread, tortillas, peppers, beans, and melons, which were stacked along the central aisle of San Buenaventura church (*The Indian Sentinel* 32, no. 9, November 1952: 144). He described with aplomb the "mixture of Christian observances and Indian survivals" (ibid. 33, no. 7, September 1953: 106) as the Cochitis celebrated their patron saint with a rain dance, vespers, confessions, and a procession with the statue of the saint. The friar noted that a torrent of rain arrived two days later. Whatever irregularity of their worship, Darpel praised the Christmas ritualism of Jemez Indians: kissing the statues of Jesus and Mary at their household shrine. "A white Catholic would have been thrilled at being in the midst of one of the still surviving groups of Indians and witnessing what devout Catholics they are" (ibid. 29, no. 10, December 1949: 148), he wrote. Catholic Indians from the northern Plains remarked upon the public devotion of the Pueblo Indians: "These Southwest Indians stand up for their Catholic religion when they make a speech. . . . I can see that though they have kept their Indian culture, they are better Catholics than we are" (Santa Fe. Indian Affairs. October 21, 1952).

The Pueblos and the Archdiocese of Santa Fe in the 1950s tried to maintain the equilibrium between Catholic and native religiousness, while resisting the "terrific onset being made by the Protestant sects to take our Indians away from us" (ibid., October 29, 1952), in the words of Archbishop Byrne. Byrne wrote to a fellow archbishop that the Pueblo Indians had expressed "how proud they are to be Catholics." Their statement to him that "they want nothing to be done to affect their Catholic faith" (April 10, 1954) might be interpreted to mean that they were satisfied with the arrangements that permitted them their traditional Pueblo worship, compartmentalized with Catholicism. Certainly the missionary organs recognized that "In the Southwest the hold of the native Indian religions is still strong and is reenforced by social bonds" (*Our Negro and Indian Missions* 1957: 25).

Anthropologists continued to remark upon the "most interesting blend of native religion and Spanish Catholicism (Lange 1952: 19) among the Pueblos. Scholars employed various models and metaphors to describe the relationship between native and Catholic forms. Edward Spicer said that "the Saint's cult and the church building were not integrated into the ceremonialism system. They were . . . employed to satisfy Pueblo interests, but they remained adjuncts rather than intricately linked elements in the whole" (Spicer 1954b: 669–670). Edward Dozier suggested that the Rio Grande Pueblo Indians "grafted on" aspects of Catholicism to their traditional system, keeping the two "distinct from" one another, and yet the Indians believed that the "purposes and objectives of both systems . . . appear to be the same" (Dozier 1958: 442): good weather, good crops, good animals, cure of disease, longevity, children, a good life. Some noted that the Pueblos compartmentalized their Catholic and native religious activities; others suggested that the process of amalgamation took place.

Florence Ellis, e.g., stated that the old Pueblo faith had to "merge" (Spicer 1954b: 679) with Catholicism, since the agricultural functions of the traditional religion were no longer as relevant as they had been before the coming of modern wage labor.

Academics observed Pueblo ritualism in the 1950s in order to see the ways in which native and Catholic forms were interconnected (see, e.g., Vogt 1955). They examined the processions and dances marking the feast days of patron saints, almost always celebrated in conjunction with corn or animal dances. On those days, mass, procession of the santos, and traditional masquerades alternated in what could be called a single ceremonialism (made up of diverse parts of native and Catholic origin). They observed the penitential activities during Lenten season performed in accordance with Catholic liturgy but in a manner derived from the Spanish forms introduced during the colonial era. They analyzed the matachin performances, derived from the ceremonies originally introduced to New Mexico by Juan de Oñate during the initial conquest. These pageants were supposed to replace the native dances but were added to them instead, becoming part of the larger whole of Pueblo ritual life. In Los Matachines the Indians impersonated Montezuma as he succumbed to the Christian entreaties of La Malinche. The Aztec monarch and his captains danced in the design of "La Cruz, the Cross, the full acceptance of Christianity" (Champe 1983: 84), while the Puebloans rejoiced.

In general, Pueblo religious ritualism in the 1950s included the following elements: (1) masked kachina ceremonies under the direction of kiva sodalities, guarded from all outsiders, even those Puebloans not members of the particular sodalities; (2) plaza ceremonials in which the whole pueblo participated, under the supervision of the native priesthoods: corn dances, tablita dances, animal dances, including the pageants celebrating saints' days; (3) individual rites of passage, defined by Pueblo tradition, but joined with Catholic sacraments such as baptism, confirmation, matrimony, and extreme unction; (4) the ritualism of Catholic derivation, including mass, saints' day celebrations, All Souls Day, Christmas, Lent, matachin dances, and other rites according to the Christian calendar, and under the leadership of officials whose positions were created by the Spanish centuries ago (see Dozier 1958: 442–444). Puebloans accommodated themselves to the Catholic rituals, claiming them to have been introduced by a mythological figure from the south, an Indian deity wearing European

clothes, who foretold the coming of the Whites and suggested cooperation, but who also advised the Pueblos to retain their aboriginal customs. This being was a combination of Poseyemu (of the Tewas) and
Montezuma (see ibid., 444–445; cf. Parmentier 1979), a native personage who pointed the way toward accommodation with Christianity
without giving up the old ways.

In their plaza ceremonies and Catholic ritualism the Pueblos permitted the presence and even participation of outsiders; however, in
their kachina ceremonialism they maintained secrecy, which they regarded as necessary because the history of Pueblo-White relations contained so many episodes of religious persecution—not only in the
seventeenth and eighteenth century under Franciscan regime, but also
in the twentieth century under U.S. Indian Bureau injunctions against
Native American ritualism (see ibid., 445–447). It was possible, then,
for Catholic priests to observe the Catholic rituals of the Pueblos,
including the corn and animal dances connected to saints' days, but
remain ignorant of the kachina ceremonies taking place in kivas, or in
secluded villages that were closed to all outsiders during certain ceremonials. By keeping themselves partially isolated from outsiders, including Catholic personnel, the Pueblo religious officials maintained a
compartmentalization and accommodation that was several hundred
years deep by the middle of the twentieth century. They could use holy
water in mass but corn meal in their native ceremony; they spoke
Spanish, Latin, or English in Catholic worship but employed their
native languages in their kachina rituals; they kept kivas and chapels
separate, their church plaza apart from their dance plaza. Their masses
contained some Pueblo ritual paraphernalia but not much, and their
kachina services were kept free of overtly Catholic forms. In continuing to make these arrangements, the Pueblos maintained an equilibrium of their own making. According to an ethnologist:

> Pueblo Indians affirm that they are good Catholics and also feel that
> they are conscientious and zealous practitioners of their own native
> Pueblo religion. This paradoxical situation apparently presents no con-
> flict to the individual Pueblo Indian. He serves each religious tradition
> separately and, to his manner of thinking, fully and adequately. (Ed-
> ward P. Dozier in Spicer 1954b: 681)

Anthropologists emphasized the tribal quality of Pueblo Catholicism, the ways in which the Indians appropriated Catholic days in the
year in order to celebrate and promote their own community, without

considering themselves part of a larger Roman Catholic Church organization. The Puebloans allowed priests in their villages, and they
appointed fiscals and sacristans who kept up the churches over the
decades. The priests said mass in the churches, and the people received
baptism and other sacraments. The community marked Christmas and
Holy Week with prayers and processions. On All Souls Day they honored their ancestral dead, and on their walls they hung pictures of
saints. And yet Jesus was not central to their religious lives; he was not
considered their savior but rather a companion to Santiago, and his
life was "a matter of indifference" (Spicer 1972: 507) to the Indians.
The celebrations of the saints' day emphasized traditional religious
organization and masquerading. On those days the Pueblo honored
itself and its kachinas as much as its saint. As for the Christian God,
He was simply another deity among others in their pantheon. There
was little cult to Him, and He was sometimes known as the "Mexican
God" (ibid.). Notions of heaven and hell remained relatively unimpor-
tant; Indians rarely received communion or went to confession. At
least in the years before the Second Vatican Council, Catholicism
seemed to observers to be an appendage to Pueblo religious culture—
an important attachment, an enrichment, but not the core of their
lives.

On the part of the Church officials, the public stance was one of relative satisfaction with the status quo. Archbishop Byrne wrote in 1961:
"Our Pueblo Indians are friendly in their relations with priests . . . and
evince interest in Catholic activities. Even though their customs seem
suspicious at times, they proclaim their Catholicism and do not wish
to associate with Protestants" (*Our Negro and Indian Missions* 1961:
26–27). A decade later, his successor, Bishop James P. Davis, wrote that
there are those who think that the Pueblo Indians are still tied to old
ways, living their religious lives according to a "mixture between old
ways and Catholicism. Others feel that for the most part they are as
good Catholics as anywhere. I think this latter is true" (ibid., 1971: 27).

Despite hopeful evaluations of Catholicism in the pueblos in the years surrounding Vatican II, not every pueblo was at peace with the Church. In 1965 one priest working among the Pueblos said that "The Indian believes in God; but he doesn't want this Catholic God to get too close" ("Investiture Controversy," July 24, 1965). Another priest, writing of the 1680 revolution but reflecting upon the tensions between Catholicism and Pueblo traditionalism in the late 1960s, made it clear that the Church still had to contend with "Native pueblo ritual and government," which "required total surrender of the person" (Chávez 1967: 86).

The most rancorous dispute between the Church and the Pueblos, at least in the twentieth century (and perhaps since the Reconquest) took place at the Southern Tiwa village of Isleta in 1965. In that year the civil authorities of the pueblo forcibly removed the resident Catholic priest, setting off a jurisdictional conflict with the Santa Fe Archdiocese that lasted for years.

Isleta's long association with Christianity dates at least to 1613 when its church was built. The walls of this edifice are still part of the present structure, arguably the oldest Catholic church walls extant in the United States today. The 1680 revolution, Otermin's attempt at recovery in 1681, and the Reconquest of 1692–1696 left Isleta a ghost town, but in 1710 Fray Juan de la Peña gathered Tiwa Indians from various places in New Mexico to found a new village situated around the church, now dedicated to St. Augustine. Through the eighteenth century and the first half of the next century, Isleta housed several Franciscans and received the visitations of others, but like the other pueblos, it was left mostly to develop its own forms of religious expression. Only after the arrival of Archbishop Lamy did the pueblo receive resident priests, several of whom were famous for their steadfastness and continuity. Father Anton Docher, for instance, served at Isleta from 1891 to 1926, constructing prominent spires on the adobe church. The priests of this era did not insist upon Catholic orthodoxy among the Pueblos, and Isletans persisted in many native practices.

When Archbishop Gerken conducted his inaugural inspection of

Isleta in 1933, he "became convinced, that the work of Religious In-
struction is entirely insufficient in the Pueblo for the Indians" (Santa
Fe. Isleta. September 11, 1933), and he instructed the pastor to secure
the local U.S. Indian School for catechetical training. Sisters taught
catechism at Isleta thereafter, and despite attempts by Baptists to lure
Isletans from the Catholic fold ("coaxing the children to . . . Sunday
School with candies," according to the governor of Isleta, Jose F.
Jojola, ibid., May 20, 1939), the pueblo earned a reputation among the
Catholic hierarchy as a "model for all our Indian Pueblos in New Mexico" (March 16, 1951). Virtually every child attended Sunday masses,
and despite occasional complaints on the part of pueblo inhabitants
regarding church personnel (a rectory cook, May 10, 1942; a new
priest, April 12, 1944), there were amicable relations between clergy
and community. Isletans received communion and confessed their sins
to the priests, often in the Tiwa language. One priest let the Indians
know "that I could understand them if they told me their sins in the
Isleta language. It sure went over big" (February 16, 1948), and the
turnout for the sacrament was immense. In the early 1950s the pueblo
sent two young men to seminary—potential vocations that did not
succeed but which indicated the community's close involvement with
Catholicism. When Father Fred Stadtmueller received appointment to
the parish of Isleta in 1955, he reported to Archbishop Byrne, "All is
well here. The people are accepting me better than I had expected. I am
very happy that Your Excellency gave me this parish" (August 3, 1955).

It was not long, however, before Father Stadtmueller ran afoul of
Isletan tradition. He objected to the Indians' practice of dancing in the
church during Advent, "to 'adore the Infant', as they put it," and he
spoke in the pulpit "against their customs and traditions." Ramon
Zuni, the Governor of Isleta, complained to the archbishop of these
tensions, and Byrne suggested to his priest that Pueblo customs "be
dealt with by using persuasion and *time*, instead of an 'ex nunc'" (December 21, 1956). Stadtmueller was rankled by the Indians' challenge to
his authority, however, and he determined to take a stand against Indian insubordination and native religiousness. "Christmas is over," he
wrote to the chancery office (December 26, 1956), "and I still have my
scalp. The dance took place in Church, but I believe the church won a
moral victory. . . . good parishioners . . . are with me." Of Governor
Zuni he remarked that the Indian had lived in wedlock blessed only by
an Indian ceremony, and that he rarely attended mass: "Still: he thinks

that he is the head of the church (like the queen of England) and I am his assistant, vice president in charge of ecclesiastical ceremonies." The pueblo governor and the priest argued over the timing and placement of rituals marking the Christian calendar, and Stadtmueller tried to dissuade the governor from holding traditional dances. When Zuni asserted his authority in the pueblo, the priest told him, "I was not a little boy that could be called on the carpet." When Stadtmueller argued that inebriated and divorced persons should not be permitted to dance in church on Christmas Eve, the governor "mumbled about his 'old customs'" (ibid.). The issues that sizzled in Santo Domingo in the 1930s—who holds sovereignty over religious matters in the pueblo and what native religious rituals should be performed—were becoming incendiary matters in Isleta under Stadtmueller's charge.

Father Stadtmueller was a stickler for rules, not only among the Isletans, but in his other parishes. He followed strict canon law regarding confirmations, marriages and divorces, and church burials. To him, Pueblo ritualism—especially those ceremonies that seemed "cruel, or detrimental to Church worship"—should have no place in the lives of baptized Catholics. Chancery personnel tried to deflect his public preaching against Pueblo religiousness "until the right attitude about the traditional Pueblo ceremonials can be discussed by a conference of the priests working in Pueblos" (ibid., March 24, 1959); however, Stadtmueller insisted upon attacking the native rites frontally. In 1959–1960 he had the church of St. Augustine remodeled—removing Father Docher's spires—and the priest had a thirty-foot slab of concrete poured in the churchyard. This was a deliberate affront to the Indians who traditionally danced there, their feet touching the sacred earth of the plaza. He called the concrete a dance platform, and the Isletans were incensed. Some of them conducted a letter campaign against the priest—now a monsignor—accusing him and his housekeeper of immorality (November 15, 1960). The monsignor retaliated by postponing confirmations at Isleta.

The Indians there followed the colonial Hispanic practice of infant confirmation. Stadtmueller was convinced "that the faith of our Indians could be greatly helped if Confirmation were for them the great Sacrament of Adolescence. It would help to combat the initiation of so many of them into the secrets of the 'kiva' when they reach the age of puberty" (October 8, 1961). The monsignor argued to his archbishop that the Isletans should undergo catechetical training before confirmation in the Catholic faith. In his view, the majority of the Puebloans were deficient in their knowledge of Catholicism; they thought that "one can practice two religions" (January 10, 1963), and they were attempting to receive the sacrament of confirmation without participating in his catechetical program. "Confirming infants here," he wrote, "would not only destroy this work, but would also make me the laughing stock of every member of the 'Indian Religion'" at Isleta. Stadtmueller said that he had suffered "indignities" for many years in the pueblo, but "take my word for it, I will not be made the laughing stock of the medicine men and their followers" (ibid.). The archdiocese did not support Stadtmueller in his campaign against infant confirmation, causing greater resentment on the part of the monsignor against the Indians of his parish.

Archbishop James P. Davis had just begun his tenure in Santa Fe in 1964, when representatives of Isleta petitioned him to resolve "the conflict and controversies of our people and Monsignor Stadtmueller" (ibid., April 9, 1964). The monsignor had become more strident in his condemnation of the "pagan savages" (July-September 1965) of Isleta, bragging to tourists at St. Augustine Church of his guns and tear gas, which he stashed in his rectory, ready for use should an Indian uprising occur against him. When the civil authorities at Isleta put up ropes to screen their ceremonial dancers from automobile traffic on the reservation, Stadtmueller cut the cords and threatened to tote a shotgun in defense of his actions. Isleta governor Juan B. Jojola asked Archbishop Davis to remove the priest for his challenge to pueblo jurisdiction, for his insults to the community, and for his allegedly immoral relations with his housekeeper (April 24, 1964).

A year passed and Davis continued to consider the request for Stadtmueller's transfer, without taking action. Further petitions came to him, recounting familiar charges, and in June 1965 the new Isleta governor, Andy Abeita, requested a meeting with the archbishop to resolve the matter. To Abeita the major issue was that of religious practice. The Isletans wanted to continue "certain Catholic religious ceremonies" (June 7, 1965), passed down by elders and the ancestors before them. These ceremonies were part of Isleta tradition, part of their Catholicism. They included processions, dances, the blessing of fields, and the sanctifying of canes of civil authority, the corpus of Hispanic Pueblo Catholicism, dating at least to the eighteenth century and beyond. And yet Father Stadtmueller informed the Indians that "our traditions were nothing, that they can be changed" (June 12, 1965), even though the Isletans learned them from the Spanish, and the Church approved or permitted them for centuries.

With copies to New Mexico governor Jack M. Campbell, Archbishop Davis, and General Superintendent Walter O. Olson of the United Pueblos Agency, Governor Abeita and his council informed Monsignor Stadtmueller in writing that he was to leave Isleta Pueblo on June 20, 1965, by 6:00 p.m. or risk eviction by the pueblo officials the following day. But on June 21 Abeita still hoped to find "some peaceful solution" (June 21, 1965) in a closed-door meeting with the archbishop, the monsignor, and the Isleta council. Previous governors of the pueblo testified to Davis of Stadtmueller's "disrespectful attitude" toward Isleta "traditional ceremonies" (June 25, 1965) and called for his dismissal. Governor Abeita and his lieutenant governor, Louis Leute, made it clear that "the admitted policy of Monsignor Fred Stadtmueller to eliminate the Native Indian Religion by any means possible" (June 26, 1965) constituted grounds for removal from the pueblo. They told the archbishop that Stadtmueller's presence was creating conflict between "Catholics and non-practicing Catholics" on the reservation, and the "safety of his life or limb" was in danger (ibid.) if he stayed on. The governor's hope was that Davis would act so that he, Abeita, would not be forced to evict the pastor; however, he was prepared to act forcefully should Davis decline.

In their meeting with Davis, the Isleta authorities were unwilling to discuss with him the specifics of their ritual activities. He wanted to know what the ceremonies meant to their religious complex; they were willing only to say that the rites constituted their religious life. The archbishop refused to replace Stadtmueller (present at the meeting, along with several Isleta supporters holding no official position in the pueblo), citing a shortage of priests as a reason. More significant, Davis regarded the matter an issue of Church and State, and he was determined to protect his priest from civil coercion or interference. This was a matter of sovereignty, and in the archbishop's view the priest had command over a parish, under the authority of the archdiocese. In the governor's view the crux of the issue was whether the Isleta people could practice their religion (a combination of native and Catholic forms) without interference or coercion from an outsider to their community, dwelling under their jurisdiction. Abeita stated: "Monsignor says that you can't practice two different religions. Then

we are not practicing Catholics, because we take part in our own ceremonies." The archbishop replied: "That is a good statement" (June 26,
1965).

Davis hoped that his support of the monsignor would end the dispute. He told Governor Abeita and the council to "pay an official visit
to Monsignor Stadtmueller in the near future for the express purpose
of promoting better relations" (ibid.). Within twenty-four hours, however, on June 27, the governor delivered the monsignor his eviction.
When the priest tried to barricade himself in the rectory, defended by
his faithful housekeeper, the governor pursued him. Amidst an argu-
ment over civil and religious jurisdiction and mutual recriminations
of "totalitarianism," Abeita handcuffed the cleric and led him to the
pueblo's edge. Stadtmueller was thereby ousted and given twelve
hours to return a final time for his belongings. The governor avowed
that the eviction was "not a move against the Catholic church, but
against Msgr. Stadtmueller personally. . . . We've taken it for nine
years," Abeita declared, "but not any more" (June 27–28, 1965).

The following Sunday, July 4, Archbishop Davis went to Isleta,
where he said mass in the 350-year-old church, and then padlocked the
doors, stating that he was not going to "put up with any 'monkey
business'" (ibid., n.d.) from the Isleta governor. The doors of the
church would stay bolted, he stated, until Stadtmueller was taken back
by the Isletans. The prelate reiterated in public the principles upon
which he was acting. Davis claimed archdiocesen ownership of the
church, although it stood on Isleta territory. He declared the Church's
right to campaign against paganism and to protect its jurisdiction
against civil authority. Finally, he reminded the Isleta officials that
Isleta Catholics were being denied their religious freedom by having
their priest removed from their parish. He also threatened a lawsuit on
these grounds against the civil government at Isleta.

The Isleta controversy made sensational copy for New Mexico
newspapers and even national magazines such as *Life*. In public and
private correspondence it became evident that Isleta contained both
citizens who favored and those who opposed the decisive actions of
their governor. Some Isletans praised Abeita for standing up to Stadtmueller; others decried his "dictatorship." Bernie C. Abeita wrote that
only half of the Isletans engaged in ancient rituals, and many of them
only for "entertainment" (ibid., n.d.). Some wept at the closing of the
church; few rejoiced, even though many were glad to see Stadtmueller

go. Archbishop Davis received missives from around the nation and even from Europe, some commending him for standing up to the Indians, others condemning him for his cultural insensitivity and decrying Stadtmueller's "evil action" (ibid., n.d.), so apparently discordant with the tolerant humanism of the Second Vatican Council.

Governor Abeita and his council attempted in vain to engage the services of a Franciscan to replace Stadtmueller; they approached the Franciscans, they said, because of the order's "awareness of the bicultural atmosphere" (ibid., July 5, 1965; cf. July 7, 1965) at Isleta. Other council members conferred with the archbishop regarding ways of maintaining sacramental contact between Isleta and the Church, through parishes in Albuquerque only thirteen miles away. Davis told Isletans whom he regarded as loyal Catholics not to take any violent action against Governor Abeita, but he encouraged petitions to friendly council members and exhorted the community to vote Abeita out in upcoming elections. Abeita communicated with the apostolic delegate in Washington, Archbishop Emilio Vagnozzi, justifying his actions and protesting his loyalty to the Church. Vagnozzi recommended reconciliation with Archbishop Davis so that the church might be reopened (July 18, 1965; July 31, 1965). In his own correspondence with Vagnozzi, Davis reaffirmed his commitment to Stadtmueller and his hope that Abeita would be defeated in year-end elections (July 27, 1965).

A year passed. Abeita was reelected. Stadtmueller remained pastor of Isleta in name, making his residence in Albuquerque. Abeita and Davis maintained contact, but neither would yield his principles. At Isleta governors were permitted only two consecutive one-year terms, so in 1967 a new governor, John D. Zuni, took office.

Immediately thereafter, the archdiocese drew up a "TEMPORARY CONCORDAT ON RELIGIOUS FREEDOM, ISLETA PUEBLO" (February 1, 1967), which placed blame for the "unfortunate prior episode" on the "headstrong efforts" of the previous Isleta administration, which, it said, "abridged rights to American citizens of Isleta descent" by preventing them to "worship their religion at St. Augustine Church with a Pastor of their choice without fear of reprisal." The concordat aimed to return Msgr. Stadtmueller (or a successor designated by Church authority), with the understanding that the Isleta government would protect him and the Catholic Isletans in their worship. If these conditions were met, the archdiocese would reopen St. Augustine's Church for sacramental use.

When Governor Zuni brought the concordat to the Isleta council, its members balked at signing it; however, they authorized Zuni to negotiate another agreement with the archbishop. The council, including former governor Andy Abeita, expressed the desire of the Isleta people for "the Catholic Church to provide . . . religious services on a regular and full-time basis" (April 6, 1967). Zuni was unable to meet immediately with Davis. In the meantime Msgr. Stadtmueller met with a "Committee on Religious Freedom" headed by Isletans Joe L. Montoya, Robert Lucero, and a handful of other laymen, which on its own authority—said to "represent . . . the great majority of the Catholic people of Isleta"—invited him to return as pastor. In effect, Stadtmueller bypassed the government of Isleta and chose to deal with a parish committee created with his help. He notified the parishioners by newsletter that he would return to say mass on July 23 (July 18, 1967).

Stadtmueller's public letter caused "quite a bit of tension" (July 20, 1967), according to Governor Zuni, who complained to the archbishop regarding the priest's unilateral actions. Davis, who supported the monsignor's strategy, replied, "I do not quite understand your complaint to the effect that you have been by-passed" (July 21, 1967), and he refused to meet with Zuni or the pueblo council. As a result, the council passed a resolution forbidding Stadtmueller's return (July 26, 1967), and he stayed away.

The Committee for Religious Freedom was stymied in its attempt to "render atonement for the shocking display of barbaric conduct" by Abeita and his "thugs" (August 24, 1967), as the committee put it, and so its members sought redress through legal agencies—the Bureau of Indian Affairs; Congress; local, state, and federal courts—only to be told that theirs was an "internal" affair beyond U.S. jurisdiction. The committee then vowed to overcome the Isleta civil authorities, perhaps in "violence, or perhaps peaceably" (ibid.), to restore Stadtmueller. Their lawyer, Edward J. Apodaca, hoped that the passage of the Indian Civil Rights Act of 1968—which extended the U.S. Bill of Rights to Indian reservations and their citizenry—would provide the leverage necessary to reopen the church on terms agreeable to the archdiocese. Archbishop Davis paid for half of the lawyer's fees, sending his check through Monsignor Stadtmueller to the committee (ibid., February 26, 1968). While Zuni attempted to communicate with Davis to negotiate an end to the impasse—"Three years without a church weigh heavily upon my people and we long to again hear the Mass and receive the sacraments in our own church" (April 27, 1968)—the archbishop, the monsignor, and the Isleta committee threatened to bring suit against the pueblo. The committee demanded the keys to the church (July 27, 1968), but the council refused to relinquish jurisdiction over the edifice.

Three years after Stadtmueller's ouster, Governor Zuni reiterated the Isleta government's view on the whole affair, naming the monsignor as the "source of the dispute." In Zuni's view (October 8, 1968), the priest offended those Isletans,

> who have tried at all times to live within the doctrines of the mother Church and at the same time, observe those Indian religious practices handed down from time immemorial as a part and parcel of our culture and belief. The Church, in its wisdom, has always recognised [sic] the dual nature of much of our belief and our people in turn are grateful for the benevolence of the Church in its recognition of our cultural heritage. Father Fred tried to upset all of this and in doing so, debased and scorned much of what lies deepest in our hearts.

At the same time the Committee on Religious Freedom, represented by Isidore Abeita, initiated a civil action suit against the pueblo government on behalf of fourteen hundred Catholics at Isleta, "deprived from worshipping said faith in their Pueblo and at their Church" (October 1, 1968). The committee accused Andy Abeita of "dictatorial control" in threatening physical violence to those Isletans wishing to worship as Catholics, and it characterized his eviction of Stadtmueller as, "savage anger, hate, lust . . . and . . . depraved desire to fully obliterate all semblance of Christian worship at said Pueblo." In the words of the suit, "the former governor publically beat upon, handcuffed, kicked, and expelled a helpless priest" and deprived Isletans of their civil rights. The present government led by John Zuni, the suit said, was little more than a "puppet" of Abeita's, jailing those opposed to its tyranny.

Abeita v. Zuni, the civil case in the U.S. District Court of New Mexico (October 25, 1968-January 15, 1969), served to uphold the Isleta civil government against the Committee on Religious Freedom and the Archdiocese of Santa Fe. Judge H. Vearle Payne's decision concluded that "the Tribe as such can not be sued without its consent since it is a sovereignty," and as for Andy Abeita, the judge stated, "I cannot find any allegation" against the former governor to justify a ruling against him. The fact that Msgr. Stadtmueller was not an official party to the suit made the charges irrelevant, since he was the only person with potentially justifiable grievances against Abeita. Judge Payne dismissed the plaintiffs' notion that there was a freedom of religion issue involved in the case. The judge said there was not, nor should it be so misconstrued:

> There seems to be no question that this is really a suit which has arisen because Monsignor Stadtmueller has been evicted from the Isleta Pueblo. There is no question among the parties that Archbishop Davis or any other Priest which he might name could go to the church in question and hold Catholic services. The testimony of the Archbishop bears this out. The parties have arrived at the stalemate because the Archbishop will not send some other Priest to the Pueblo and the Pueblo will not let the one Priest hold services. (Ibid., January 15, 1969)

In the course of Archbishop Davis' deposition (October 25, 1968), he acknowledged that it was he, rather than the pueblo authorities, who closed the church to Catholic services—although at a later date the Isleta officials padlocked the door to prevent Stadtmueller's return. Occasional services took place at St. Augustine's—some funerals, christenings, and special masses—during the hiatus, permitted as long as Stadtmueller was not the officiant; and if Davis had so desired, he could have appointed another priest and ended the fracas. On his part, however, he testified, "We don't recognize evictions of Pastors," and so he could not consider naming another priest to replace the monsignor. Rather, he assigned Stadtmueller to live in a parish at Albuquerque, making Isleta a mission ("no longer an independent Parish. We have changed the classification") with virtually no sacerdotal visitations. Despite Davis' repeated denials to the contrary, the trial made it clear that the archdiocese created the Committee on Religious Freedom in an attempt to gain through the courts the return of the evicted priest and the legal control over St. Augustine's, under the cover of a freedom of religion allegation. The Church failed in both of these aims. The trial also showed that Abeita did not kick the monsignor.

Having failed in the courts, Davis faced alternative decisions. As he mulled over his choices, he received a missive from the new governor of Santo Domingo Pueblo, Diego Rosetta, encouraging him to make peace with Isleta: "You as a spiritual leader over all Catholic people must open your heart to your flock and bring them back to their proper place of worshiping so that its members may continue practices according to the Catholic Church" (February 7, 1969). Thirty years after Santo Domingoans had outlasted Archbishop Gerken, their governor exhorted Davis to exercise the spirit of compromise in the Isleta case.

Stadtmueller offered to remove himself from the pueblo in order to resolve the issue (February 11, 1969), even though he justified his behavior as pastor in terms of the head-to-head "battle" between the Indian religion and Catholicism. The archdiocese lawyer drew up a memorandum or agreement, never consummated, in which the Isleta governor "expresses regret and apologizes for the forcible eviction" of Stadtmueller, and the monsignor "expresses regret and apologizes . . . for all derogatory remarks and criticisms at any time made by him of the tribal customs of the Pueblo of Isleta." But Davis would not back down on the question of Stadtmueller's reinstatement as pastor. The new pueblo governor, Pablo Abeita, could not convince the archbishop to change his mind, as the prelate still hoped that the anti-Stadtmueller party on the reservation might lose elections. When the governor asked Davis for a priest to say midnight mass at Christmas in 1969, the prelate replied that he had a critical shortage of priests. Why not invite Monsignor Stadtmueller to celebrate mass, he wrote, as a "manifestation of the Christmas spirit" (December 11, 1969)? The pueblo declined the recommendation.

In 1970 Alvino Lucero—a member of the Committee on Religious Freedom and an ally of the monsignor—became governor at Isleta. Davis thought that the time had come for him to assert his will in the Isleta case. He approved arrangements for Sunday and holy day masses in return for a ninety-nine-year lease on St. Augustine's Church, with the implicit right of the archdiocese to appoint whomever it wished as pastor. Even Lucero could not convince the pueblo council to accept these terms, so Davis threatened to transfer Isleta to a parish other than the one in Albuquerque. The Catholic Isletans who had traveled to Ascension parish over the five years, 1965–1970, had established collegial contacts with the Hispanics of that parish—serving mutually as godparents, e.g.—and they were loathe to be shunted to another parish. Davis hoped to employ their fear of the transfer as a means of gaining approval for a long-term lease with autonomy over St. Augustine's. His plan aroused so much opposition, with many petitions stating that the Isleta Catholics would simply cease their associations with the Church (March 30, 1970-April 1, 1970), that he canceled the proposed transfer.

Davis did not gain his lease, nor did Stadtmueller ever again enter Isleta Pueblo. The years passed, and it was not until 1974, after Archbishop Robert F. Sanchez had succeeded Davis, that rapprochement took place between the Church and Isleta Pueblo. In that year the new prelate assigned Msgr. Francis A. Reinberg as pastor at Isleta, which once again became a Catholic parish in the Archdiocese of Santa Fe. The new pastor agreed to remove the concrete slab in the churchyard, which had been the symbolic foundation of the dispute with Stadtmueller. After a decade the dispute finally came to an end, but without a conclusion to the issues that lay at the base of the quarrel.

During the ten years many Isletans became more integrated with the Catholic Church in New Mexico through their association with non-Indian members of Ascension parish in Albuquerque. Other Isletans turned to charismatic Protestant sects, and the long hiatus from catechetical training on the reservation set back the catholicization of those Isletans who chose not to journey to Albuquerque for Catholic services and instruction. As a result, in 1983 a new parish priest, Father Bernard Loughrey, noted that at Isleta "the majority of people although Baptized Catholics are poorly informed and no longer identify with the Church" (Marquette. DCRAA. August 10, 1983). Two years later, however, the same cleric reported that "people returned to the Sacraments. . . . today our parish enjoys a very good spirit" (ibid., July 3, 1985). In the present day there are some Isletans who still feel "ashamed to be a Catholic" (Savilla, August 6, 1993) as a result of the set-to created by Stadtmueller, but for many the events of the 1960s and 1970s are but distant memory or a patch of history. Father Loughrey endeared himself to the Isletans in his decade of service—he "had them eating out of his hand," according to a Church official (Lenz, November 19, 1993)—and opened up St. Augustine's to Hispanics of the area, a sign of the Isletans' increasing association with non-Indian Catholics and mainstream Catholicism in the Archdiocese of Santa Fe.

THE CONTEMPORARY SITUATION

In the 1970s, Archbishop Robert F. Sanchez created an Office of Indo-Hispano Affairs, and then an Indian Affairs Office, in order to foster "a greater awareness" (Marquette. DCRAA. 1976) of Catholic faith among the Pueblos, and he labored vigorously to integrate the Indians into the life of the Church. Sanchez argued with his fellow Hispanics in the Santa Fe Archdiocese that they must soften their triumphalism regarding the Indians, particularly at the annual Santa Fe Fiesta, which commemorated the Reconquest of 1692–1696. He wrote to the president of the Santa Fe Fiesta Council, stating that the pageant must not "celebrate a conquest of people, but rather . . . the re-entry of the Colonists into Santa Fe, and the second beginning of harmonious and peaceful living with the Indian people." We must work with "our Indian brothers and sisters" (Santa Fe. St. Francis Cathedral. September 23, 1977) at future fiestas, he added. For these efforts he received the thanks of the All Indian Pueblo Council, through its chairman, Delfin J. Lorato (ibid., September 26, 1977). And yet, for the eighteen thousand Pueblo Catholics out of the twenty-two thousand Indians in the Santa Fe Archdiocese in 1980 (Marquette. DCRAA. 1980)—not counting Laguna, Acoma, and Zuni, which were part of the Gallup Diocese—the paradox of their Catholic identity persisted. The missiologist R. Pierce Beaver concluded in 1979 that "All Pueblo Indians are baptized in infancy, but few become active Catholics" (Beaver 1979: 176).

In the modern era, several Puebloans have taken vows of Catholic religious life, including the Lagunas Sr. Mary Consolata Beecher, S.B.S., and Sr. Rosita Shiosee, S.B.S. Some Pueblo artists of the recent decades have embraced Catholicism more fully than the scholars would have it, creating an art form of *nacimientos*—scenes of Christ's nativity—that express Christian devotion through native aesthetics. Cochiti, Tesuque, and Santa Clara were the first to produce these devotional figures in the 1950s and 1960s, and in the 1970s the movement swelled, "the first widespread expression of the Christian religion to emerge among the many art forms of the southwest Indian" (Monthan and Monthan 1990: 2). With encouragement and patronage from

the Church, Pueblo artists such as Manuel Vigil of Tesuque and Helen
Cordero of Cochiti have used native styles to portray the Christchild
and his attendants of Bethlehem. Many of these artists were involved
in the charismatic movement of the Catholic Church in the 1960s; in
their artistry they have felt the spirit of faith, and they experience no
ambivalence in expressing their Christian faith through Pueblo form.
For them the two combine in ways that belie the notion of compartmentalization as a static model of religious life.

No Pueblo artist has done more to combine native and Catholic religious forms in the twentieth century than Alex Seowtewa of Zuni.
Whereas the creators of nacimientos have employed traditional sensibilities to portray biblical events, Seowtewa has used the interior walls
of Our Lady of Guadalupe Church in Zuni to paint the summer and
winter divinities, with the blessing of the Franciscans who rebuilt the
edifice in the 1960s. He began his project in 1970, and when he com-
pletes it, perhaps before the next millennium, he will have incorporated Jesus as the central figure (in traditional Zuni dress) into the
pantheon, over the altar and above the clouds in the apse, with the
fourteen extant Zuni clans all around Him.

A former student of St. Anthony's Mission School in Zuni, Alex
Seowtewa was trained from infancy in Zuni traditional learning by his
maternal grandfather, the ritual leader, Na-Seowdewa. Alex's father,
Charlie Chuyate, painted the ceiling of St. Anthony's rectory in the
1920s. He was also a tribal historian who told his son that the village
church, built in 1629 but left to ruin in the 1800s, had been adorned
with paintings of kachinas in the colonial period. According to Chuyate, several disciplinarian ogres of Zuni religion were painted on the
church nave "as a reminder to the people that they must attend mass
and lead their lives according to the teachings of the church and
Zuni traditions" (Seowtewa 1992: 12). As a youth, Alex and his fellow
Zunis climbed the abandoned church walls to view native dances in
the village.

After attending art school for two years, serving in the army during
the Korean War, and working as a bus driver and maintenance man,
Seowtewa helped to carve confessionals in the refurbished church. His
father encouraged him to reproduce the native iconography in the
nave, and after consultation with Father Niles Kraft, O.F.M., he began
to paint. When he told his spouse Adele—mother of ten and his
"first and only wife" for over forty years—that he was going to paint

the church, she asked him, "What color will it be?" (Seowtewa and
Seowtewa, February 11, 1991). She thought he was going to use rollers
and paint to do the work. She hadn't considered that he would decorate the walls with Zuni deities. When he finished the first kachina, he
asked his wife and mother-in-law to evaluate his accomplishment.
They liked it, and he determined to carry on.

And carry on he has, with the help of art grants and various contributions over the years. Seowtewa has attracted international attention,
and he often receives visitors from afar, curious about his project. The
artist keeps records of his work, for example saving all his used brushes
and tubes of paint, so that future generations will be able to document
his labors. At the same time, he looks forward to ending the task and
retiring from his vocation as "The Michelangelo of the Americas," as
one enthusiast refers to him. Says Seowtewa: "It is a labor of love. This
will be my first and last mural" (Seowtewa, October 14, 1994).

Seowtewa did not want to paint punishing kachinas in the church
because he did not want to scare the children or draw attention away
from the Catholic services. He did not wish to recreate the threatening
aspects of traditional Zuni religion, nor the coercive features of Spanish Catholicism. Therefore, he painted the blessing kachinas—those of
the winter on the north walls, those of the summer on the south, almost thirty in all. Combined with the Christian iconography of the
church—the Cross, statues of Mary and Kateri Tekakwitha, and the
like—Seowtewa describes his art as "a work of Eucharist, . . . meant
to show that Zuni and Christian spirituality have much to offer
each other" (in Walsh, December 1987: 19). He regards himself as a
builder of bridges between the two traditions, suggesting that people
today should "put the two religions on one scale and let them be bal-
anced" (in ibid.). Just as he speaks two languages, Zuni and English,
Seowtewa aims to express the values of two religious traditions, his
native Zuni faith and Christianity.

Not everyone has been happy with his cojoining of Zuni and
Catholic spirituality. One parish priest in the 1980s found the project
offensive, but he was transferred to another post. Seowtewa says of the
priests at Zuni, "They come and they go. In five or six years they will
pack their bags and move on, but I'll continue here. I am permanent at
Zuni" (Seowtewa and Seowtewa, February 11, 1991). Rio Grande
Pueblos—such as those from Santo Domingo and San Felipe—are accustomed to keeping their native religiousness secret and separate

from their Catholicism, and so they criticize him for mixing Zuni and Catholic forms openly. Some of his own people resent his art, either because they are strict Catholics (who do not want to see kachinas in church), or because they are strict traditionalists (who want the kachinas honored in the kivas only). Adele Seowtewa suggests, however, that the majority of Zuni have been made proud by his display; they feel that the church is more fully theirs, now that the kachinas are joining Jesus, Mary, and the saints in Our Lady of Guadalupe Church. She says that Zuni Catholicism has been strengthened by his art. When Seowtewa began his masterpiece, Zuni was the least catholicized of the Pueblos (except for Hopi), with only 30 percent of the Indians there baptized. Today perhaps as many as half of the Zunis are christened, although the degree of devotion varies considerably. Alex and Adele Seowtewa are engaged in Cursillo; they credit their Catholic faith with upholding their emotional lives when a son committed suicide in 1986. Alex says that Catholicism has helped him combat alcoholism by providing him with spiritual discipline and direction. Others suggest, however (e.g., Frost 1992), that the Seowtewas represent but a handful of Zuni families thoroughly committed to Catholicism. Nonetheless, the Seowtewas—ever aware of their place in Indian Catholic history—would like to have the pope come to Our Lady of Guadalupe in Zuni when the murals are completed.

Three hundred years following the Pueblo revolution of 1680 and the Reconquest of 1692–1696, it could still be said that "The Roman Catholic Church continues to play an important role in all the Pueblos, except for the Hopi and Hopi-Tewa villages, but the Catholic priests are often in residence only on feast days and special occasions and are content to let the Pueblos work out their own versions of Catholicism" (Eggan 1979: 230). Each pueblo makes its own arrangements with its own officers and its own traditions, but in all villages the native and Catholic elements continue to exist side by side—to the relative satisfaction of the Indians and Church hierarchy. Puebloans continue to be initiated through ritual into the ceremonial and organizational life of pueblo and church, growing up simultaneously in two separate organizations with overlapping interests and values. In a given year, each pueblo ritual calendar is grounded in the natural cycles of the Southwest, as well as in the "liturgical calendar of the Roman Catholic Church, where the celebrations of ecclesiastical feast days include Christian elements, but feature indigenous Pueblo rites. . . .

Although certain portions of these activities are tied to the Catholic Church, the basic underlying power is directed toward the native religion" (Roberts 1980: 109). In Pueblo theology three centuries after the Pueblo revolt, "there are many gods in the Pueblo pantheon and one of them just happens to be the Christian god" (ibid.). Pueblo Catholic devotion to Jesus, Mary, and the saints constitutes but a dimension (albeit an important part) of the whole of Pueblo worship.

At Sandia, Roman Catholicism is fully part of community identity, and the people say there is no felt conflict between native and Christian spirituality (Brandt 1979: 346–347); after all, Sandia had its beginnings among Puebloans in the eighteenth century who wished to embrace Catholic forms. At most of the other pueblos the relationship is more problematic. At Acoma there have been some Catholics—e.g., John and Mary Sarracino—who have been "special friends" of the Catholic Indian mission agencies (*Bureau of Catholic Indian Missions Newsletter* 9, no. 1, January 1990: 1), attending Tekakwitha conferences and leading marriage enrichment programs. Inhabitants of the Acoma pueblo and its neighboring villages speak of their "great devotion" (Acoma Reservation, New Mexico, January 24, 1987) to Pope John Paul II and Kateri Tekakwitha. At the same time, they recount with vehemence the tales of conquest, mutilation, and enslavement of their ancestors by the Spanish Catholics of Oñate's time. An Acoma tourguide reminds visitors that St. Stephen's Church in Acoma required the slave labor of Western Keres people for its construction, and in one insurrection the people of Acoma threw a Franciscan friar off the mesa of the Sky City to his death. An ambivalence still adheres to Acoma Catholicism.

At nearby Laguna the church altar screens still syncretize Indian and Christian cosmologies, and cornmeal offerings are made to Kateri Tekakwitha's statue. In the struggles of the past century against Protestantism at Laguna, the traditionalists and Catholics often combined forces, and the Western Keres of Laguna continue to regard native and Catholic forms as part of their religious lives. The Keresans at Zia and Cochiti celebrate the feasts of Roman Catholicism, but they do so with native dances organized by the kiva societies. Both tend to compartmentalize their Pueblo and Catholic religious forms, as do their colinguists at Santa Ana, Santo Domingo, and San Felipe, and "Zia protects itself as best it can from all non-Catholic missionizing efforts, but its devotion to Catholicism is largely external and a protection against other European religions" (Hoebel 1979: 417). Nonetheless, Keresans express satisfaction at the balance they have struck between native and Catholic practice. José Romero of Cochiti says that when the Franciscans first came to the Pueblos they considered Pueblo religion to be "paganism" and "devil-worship" (Potsdam, August 4, 1995) — but no more is this attitude expressed in the Church. Everyone realizes, Romero states, that Cochiti religious practice is directed to a Supreme Being, just like Christianity. Hence, the Puebloans engage in a ceremonialism which combines reverence for saints with traditional dancing. At the cathedral in Santa Fe, Romero adds, the Pueblo dancers perform. "It's all one religion," he notes calmly.

San Ildefonso was one of the least receptive pueblos to Christianity, and only in the nineteenth century did Catholic practices begin to merge with traditional elements, for example in the celebration of their saint's day each January 23rd, when the Tewas performed their animal dance and their Comanche dance. There have been some Tewas from San Ildefonso who have identified themselves thoroughly as Catholics, like the former governor Martin Aguilar, who has worked for over three decades at Los Alamos National Science Laboratory; however, most of the Indians have maintained strong identification with the native forms of their religiousness. As recently as 1969 the pueblo supported the rebuilding of their church. The Indians receive baptism and first communion, and some even marry in the church; however, confessions are "few and far between" (Santa Fe. St. Francis Cathedral. 1981). The overall structure of San Ildefonso ceremonial life is still overwhelmingly native.

Each January 23rd the pueblo celebrates the feast of San Ildefonso (San Ildefonso Pueblo, New Mexico, January 23, 1987, January 23, 1988) by engaging in a composite of ritual events. The Summer and Winter clans, each with its own kiva in adjoining plazas, south and north, alternate each year in staging deer-buffalo-antelope and Comanche dances. Early in the morning — after a firelight vigil the night before — the "animals" enter the village, where they are greeted by the populace, represented by drummers, hunters, and women. Later in the day, masqueraders representing their former enemies and trading partners, the Comanches, also receive ceremonial welcome and perform their dance in the plaza. The community marks this day by serving as hosts to outsiders: providing food to tourists and other foreigners to the pueblo. In this manner the Tewas incorporate outsiders to the village. The animals, the Comanches, and even the non-Indian aliens find ritual acceptance among their hosts.

In the morning, during a rest period for the animal dancers, a Catholic priest performs mass in the village church, and many of the Tewas attend, along with Hispanics and other non-Indians. Following mass the priest and his entourage stand at the church gate in front of the *campo santo*—the church plaza which constitutes a third dancing ground in the village—as the animal dancers perform before them. The priest does not bless them or greet them with marked gesture, but each group—one representing the Church, the other the indigenous religion—acknowledge one another's presence. Then the dancers re-turn to the primary events of the day in their own plaza, and the priest departs. In this way the feast of San Ildefonso is incorporated into the traditional patterns, as the Comanches and non-Indians are. The core of Tewa ritual on this day takes place in the south and north plazas belonging to the native ceremonial organization, but the Indians also recognize the existence of Catholicism in their midst. The Church is incorporated into the San Ildefonso system as a whole, but it stands at the periphery, rather than at the center.

Among the Tewas at Nambe, Pojoaque, Tesuque, Santa Clara, San Juan, as well as San Ildefonso, the ritual patterns are similar. The Indi-ans provide for the upkeep of the Catholic worship. The Christian cal-endar is fitted to the native cycles, and the people almost universally receive Catholic baptism. Nonetheless, traditional Pueblo religion re-mains a strong force in all these communities.

In the northern Tiwa villages of Picuris and Taos the situation is the same: the pattern is that of two coexisting traditions more or less at peace with one another. Between 1966 and 1970 the archdiocese strongly supported the right of Taos Pueblo to regain its "sacred" Blue Lake, even though the sacrality of the land derived from native reli-gious belief and practice (Santa Fe. Indian Affairs. 1967–1970; Taos. 1966). At Christmas the deer dancers journey from Blue Lake to St. Jerome's Church in the pueblo in a joining of two liturgical calendars and belief systems. Taos Pueblo is famous for its standoffishness, its re-fusal to speak its language in front of outsiders, its prominent role in rebellions against the Church. Nevertheless, its life cycle rituals "generally reflect Roman Catholic practice" as well as kiva organization, and in general,

> The Taos are considered and consider themselves to be Roman Catholics. . . . It is an important focus for religious belief and even the staunchest member of the kiva religion does not find participation in Catholic ritual incompatible. (Bodine 1979: 263–264)

With six kivas, a peyote movement, and Catholicism at Taos, each element functions in an atomized manner, each with its own group of adherents, each engaged in valid religious behavior. At Taos Catholicism is one religious organization among several. Yet Taos inhabitants, in speaking about St. Jerome's Church in the pueblo, say that "It is ironic that on Sundays, people come from outside the pueblo to attend Mass here. Our people mostly stay away and keep to our old religion" (Taos Pueblo, New Mexico, January 21, 1987), a pattern that holds true for many Puebloans. "Catholicism is widely observed among the tribe, at least among the elderly, who give pride of place in their kitchens, alongside photos of former war chiefs and tribal governors, to . . . pastels of the Last Supper or the Holy Family. Catholic and Tiwa imagery have mingled," says a contemporary journalist, "but themes of alliance and conflict, coexistence and subjugation are never far below the surface" (Byrne, December 11, 1994).

A very different picture emerges among the Tiwas, Piros, and Manso Indians living south of Las Cruces. Known as the Tortugas or the San Juan de Guadalupe Tribe, these multiethnic people owe their origin to missionized Indians who remained loyal to the Spanish in the 1680 Pueblo revolt. In 1888 a nucleus of Indian families from the Mission of Nuestra Señora de Guadalupe, Mexico, created a new community, and they were joined by Tiwas from Ysleta del Sur and other Indians.

Throughout the past century the Tortugas have maintained devotion to Our Lady of Guadalupe, constructing a church in her name in 1914 and celebrating a three-day ceremonial to commemorate her feast each December. The Tortugas have kept alive several indigenous rituals, which they perform annually; however, the "major ceremony of the year" (Beckett and Corbett 1994: 641; cf. *Bureau of Catholic Indian Missions Newsletter* 14, no. 2, February 1995) celebrates the Indians' Catholic faith. They pray the rosary, perform matachin dances, attend mass, and make a pilgrimage to a nearby mountain, accompanied in

1994 by Bishop Ricardo Ramirez of Las Cruces and Monsignor Paul A. Lenz of the Bureau of Catholic Indian Missions. The Indians honor the image of Nuestra Señora de Guadalupe not only on her feast day but throughout the year, demonstrating their solidarity with Indian-ized Catholicism in the Hispanic tradition of New Mexico. Even more than most Puebloans they are comfortable as Catholics.

Every June 24th the Towa people of Jemez celebrate the feast of St. John the Baptist with a rooster pull, the "gallo" (Johnson, June 24, 1995). Following mass the men named John or Juan bury a rooster up to its neck and horsemen vie for possession of it, invariably spilling its blood on the soil. "Like the holy water St. John used to baptize Jesus," the blood of the rooster is said "to baptize the earth in this driest of seasons." The Pueblo scholar Alfonso Ortiz attests to the beneficial ef-fects of the sacrifice. For the Towas, "it's all to the good because the rooster has given its life to fertilize the earth" (in ibid.). The Jemez governor, Paul Chinana, attests to the spiritual importance of both the mass and the "gallo." "We are a people who believe in the Catholic way . . . ," he declares. "We go to church and ask the Lord for his bless-ing. But we also believe in our own tradition" (in ibid.).

During Archbishop Sanchez's reign in Santa Fe the archdiocese continued its attempts to make the Pueblos feel more at home in the Church as a whole. In 1976, during his tenure, the first Pueblo Indian, Edmund Savilla from Isleta, received ordination to the Catholic priest-hood, although his ordination did not lead to others among the Pueb-los. The Indians feel that the seminaries are too far from their homes, and there is the fear that seminarians will lose cultural identity. The requirement of celibacy means that children and grandchildren will not be produced, and the spiritual chain of ancestry will be broken. Furthermore, the Puebloans suspect that seminarians will tell the se-crets of kiva ceremonialism once they join the Catholic priesthood. By becoming priests of the Catholic Church they will turn their loyalties from the native priesthoods (Santa Fe. St. Francis Cathedral. 1981). Nonetheless, Father Savilla insists that his fellow Puebloans are de-voted Catholics; when they celebrate their feast days with dances, they are not "tokenizing" Christianity ("Native American Catholics . . . ," 1986), but rather participating in it with renewed vigor.

In 1980 Church personnel cooperated with the All Pueblo Council to commemorate the anniversary of the 1680 Pueblo revolt, and a Franciscan, Father Conran Runnebaum, O.F.M., served on the Indians' Tricentennial Commission. Liturgies under the direction of the Pueblos took place at Tesuque, Santa Clara, Picuris, Santo Domingo, and elsewhere, with the blessing of the Archdiocese of Santa Fe. Father Runnebaum was interested in the "Indianization of Christianity" (Santa Fe. St. Francis Cathedral. 1981), and he saw his role in commemorating the Pueblo revolt as a means of establishing rapport between the Church and the Pueblos, still somewhat estranged from Catholicism despite centuries of participation in its traditions.

The Church attempted to accommodate itself more willingly to Pueblo ritualism during Sanchez's years in office, a policy that has caused unrest among some Puebloans and others in his archdiocese. For the last seven years of his reign, he held annual Native American liturgies in the Cathedral in Santa Fe. He apologized to the Pueblos for centuries of conquest and honored the Indian people for upholding their native traditions against persecution by Europeans and Euroamericans. Finally in 1992 Sanchez changed the annual fiesta of Our Lady of the Conquest (celebrating DeVargas' feats of 1692) to one honoring Our Lady of Peace. After three centuries the archbishop declared it "offensive" for the Hispanic Catholic community to continue its triumphalism over Indian peoples in Santa Fe. His Church is a community of Indians as well as Hispanics and others, and his job is to reconcile them to each other, he said. He invited Pueblo masqueraders to perform during mass, and his innovations in ritual syncretism made some folks uneasy. How much accommodation can there be to native religiousness in the Church? For the Indians, like Acoma Catholic Howard Paytiamo, giving up any part of his culture is "terrifying" (in Walsh, December 1987: 22) and a native ceremony in Church outside the pueblo threatens tradition. On the other hand, when Sanchez allowed a buffalo dance and eagle dance at mass in the Cathedral in Santa Fe, he was accused by non-Indians of "introducing 'paganism' to the Church" (ibid.). The prelate's response was that some people worship by singing or writing, some by dancing. For him, as for many Puebloans, native dance is a gift to God. For this stance (and despite the sexual scandal that ended his episcopacy) he continues to be "loved" by Pueblo peoples (Savilla, August 6, 1993). Sanchez not only tolerated Pueblo ceremonialism but embraced it, at least as thoroughly as Puebloans have embraced Catholicism. The head of the Bureau of Catholic Indian Missions, Msgr. Paul A. Lenz, takes a similar stand when he describes the funeral for a prominent Catholic Laguna man,

John Sarracino in December 1989. First there was a funeral mass, then four days of native funeral tradition. "I'm convinced," said Lenz of the Pueblo Catholics, "that they can live in two traditions and be faithful to both" (in Wolcott 1990: 10).

Contemporary Pueblo Catholics—there are around fifty thousand in Santa Fe Archdiocese and another fourteen thousand in the Diocese of Gallup—still engage in dual religious participation, although various Church programs of the last several decades since Vatican II— including Cursillo, the charismatic movement, the Tekakwitha Conference, and the Indian ministry of Santa Fe—have brought increasing numbers of Puebloans into contact with non-Indian Catholics, and today they are more likely than ever before to engage in Catholic liturgies with non-Pueblos, both within their territory and around the United States.

Urbanization has become a fact of Pueblo life, and many Pueblo Indians have left the area to find jobs and to follow spouses who are not of the pueblo. Thus, Dolores Rousseau, born in Santa Fe, the daughter of Tesuque and San Juan Tewas, married a Sioux from South Dakota. She moved to Salt Lake City to earn a master's degree in social work, and now she lives there. Both she and her husband take part in Catholic community services, and they have helped form a Kateri Circle. She performs a "ministry" of social work: counselling Indians in a center funded by the United Way. At church she is a lector, studying to be a Eucharistic minister, and she has taught in the Confraternity of Christian Doctrine since 1983. Rousseau still visits home, but since she is an "urban Indian," she does not participate in Pueblo rituals. She has sought the help of a Tesuque medicine man who uses Catholic and native spirituality in harmony to effect cures, but by and large her religious life is focused thoroughly on Catholic forms. Like other urban Indians, however, she finds that her offspring are firm neither in their Indian nor Christian faith. Her son is approaching thirty and is "still struggling" with his faith. He does not attend any religious services, and although he lives with her, she does not goad him toward Catholicism; rather, she "prays for him" (Rousseau, August 6, 1992).

Other Puebloans closer to home are thankful for the changes brought about over the past several decades, particularly since the Second Vatican Council. In the Archdiocese of Santa Fe in the 1990s, 90–95 percent of the Puebloans are baptized Catholic. They recall the

days when Pueblo religion—although tolerated by the local priests—
was condemned officially as paganism. Had it not been for Vatican II,
and more explicitly the reforms of Archbishop Sanchez, "we'd still be
in the dead Church" (Savilla and Savilla, August 5, 1992), they attest.

Joseph and Peggy Savilla—he of Isleta, she an Oneida Indian from
Wisconsin—served for a decade in the Indian Ministry of Santa Fe
until 1993. They recite the history of Pueblo association with Catholicism as one of domination and subterfuge. Before the Spaniards arrived, they say, the Puebloans were "richer in spirituality" than they
became after contact. The Pueblos under Franciscan control "had to
say they were Catholics" in order to survive the regime, while "the
missionaries claimed they converted them all." For the Savillas, those
Indians who resisted Oñate and his followers—those who had their
limbs amputated, or who were executed, or who were sentenced to
servitude to the padres, building churches as slaves—were "martyrs for
their native faith." After the revolution and reconquest of the late seventeenth century, the Indians determined that they "better play ball
with the Spanish, while maintaining their own spirituality underground" (ibid.). In Joseph Savilla's view, the Pueblos have maintained
two parallel religious systems over the centuries, systems whose elements seemed "so similar" that being Pueblo and Catholic seemed a
duplication of religious forms. Thus, Pueblo children were—and still
are—named by their community ("baptized in their tradition") and
baptized by the priests of Catholicism—two parallel rituals producing
the same function. Because the parallels are so close, the Indians felt,
and continue to feel, at home in the Church, say the Savillas. Over the
centuries the Pueblos have joined the Catholic tradition without eschewing their Pueblo religion; so, today, when a Pueblo child is born
and raised, he or she becomes a Catholic in the process of becoming a
Pueblo Indian. Joseph Savilla states that he is a Catholic because he is
"branded as a Catholic; this is what you have to do" as a Pueblo Indian. Catholicism for the Puebloans is "your inheritance," he says. It is
made up of "respect for the elders, . . . loyalty to great grandparents, . . . ancestral respect." The Pueblos "never forgot their ancestors, . . . no matter how far back," and because their ancestors made
Catholicism part of their religious life, the present generation partici-
pates in the same religious tradition as their forebears. Today, say the
Savillas, "Catholicism is a Pueblo traditional religion" (ibid.).

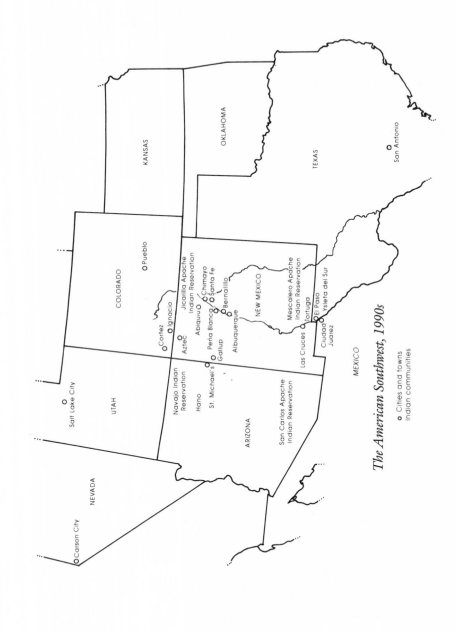

The American Southwest, 1990s

o Cities and towns
Indian communities

NEVADA

o Carson City

UTAH

Salt Lake City

ARIZONA

San Carlos Apache
Indian Reservation

Navajo Indian
Reservation

Hano

St. Michael's

COLORADO

o Pueblo

Cortez

o Ignacio

Aztec

Gallup

Peña Blanca

Jicarilla Apache
Indian Reservation

Abiquiu

Chimayo
o Santa Fe

Bernalillo

Albuquerque

NEW MEXICO

Mescalero Apache
Indian Reservation

Las Cruces

Tortuga

El Paso

Ciudad
Juarez

Ysleta del Sur

MEXICO

KANSAS

OKLAHOMA

TEXAS

San Antonio

OTHER CATHOLIC INDIAN/ IN THE /OUTHWE/T

Missionaries established many outposts of Christianity along the northern rim of New Spain in the seventeenth and eighteenth centuries. In order to counteract French penetration from Louisiana, the Franciscans set up missions in eastern Texas beginning in 1690. El Paso del Norte on the Rio Grande possessed a "flourishing mission life" (Van Well 1942: 59) as the last secure station along the road to the pueblos of New Mexico, and in the region around San Antonio in the 1700s there were reductions as well, several of which functioned energetically into the waning years of the Spanish empire (see Gómez 1991). Nevertheless, in the nineteenth century these missions "finally passed out of existence" (Van Well 1942: 74), leaving little traces of Catholicism among the surviving native peoples of Texas, except for those in the area of El Paso.

In what is now New Mexico and Arizona the Spaniards encountered Athabascan peoples still arriving and in flux in the American Southwest after centuries of migration from the north. These were the ancestors of the present-day Apache and Navajo peoples, many of whom have been touched by the Catholic tradition and who comprise sizable portions of the Catholic population of the dioceses of Gallup and Las Cruces. Finally, there are some Catholic Indians in Colorado, Nevada, and Utah, areas once within the farthest reaches of New Spain.

The Apaches resisted Catholic entreaties during the colonial period, and throughout the Province of New Mexico they were the scourge of New Spain, especially after the Pueblo Revolt of 1680 when they obtained many horses and became mobile as warriors. They obtained vague aspects of Catholicism when they captured Mexicans and Indian converts, and hundreds of Apaches received baptism when they were enslaved or adopted by the Spaniards, but only in the twentieth century did the various communities of Apaches—e.g., the Jicarillas in northern New Mexico, the Mescaleros in the southern part of the state, and the San Carlos Apaches in western Arizona—accept baptism and adopt Christian patterns of worship.

With a strong Mexican influence, the Mescaleros received services from El Paso; by the time of the Second World War a majority of the Indians were baptized and considered by Church officials to be loyal Catholics. A Franciscan in the 1950s found the Mescaleros "much confused by the white man's demoralizing entertainments. . . , a spiritually dispossessed people, very primitive in their judgment of the benefits of the Faith, and concerned mostly about material comforts" (*Our Negro and Indian Missions* 1956: 32). On the other hand there were "devout" members of St. Joseph's Mission, such as Mrs. Virginia Shantas Klinekole—a president of the Mescalero Apache Tribal Council and an alumna of the Haskell Institute in Kansas—who impressed the missionaries with her Catholic loyalty (*The Indian Sentinel* 40, no. 3, fall 1962: 45). In the 1980s the new diocese of Las Cruces, New Mexico, reached out to the Mescaleros with Cursillo, Marriage Encounter, Tekakwitha conferences and catechetical programs. At the same time, the Catholic ministry began to accept and even promote traditional Mescalero ritual elements, including the dancing of the Mountain Spirits (the Gaan dancers) and the puberty rituals of the Apache girls. Gaan dancers perform regularly in coordination with Catholic services at St. Joseph's Church, and a contingent of these ceremonialists acted out their sacred motions at the Tekakwitha Conference in 1987 when Pope John Paul II met with thousands of Indian Catholics in Phoenix. Today over 85 percent of the Mescaleros are baptized Catholics, including at least one religious, Sr. Juanita Little. For most of these the traditional religion is still a matter of enrichment, especially when adolescent girls come of age by taking on the persona of their benevolent goddess, White Shell Woman (Changing Woman).

Among the San Carlos Apaches, "the penetration of Christianity has . . . been a slow, uneven process" (ibid. 40, no. 3, fall 1962: 35), and even today only a minority of the community identify themselves as Catholics. Despite Catholic boarding schools and summer camps and a persistent missionary effort for over seven decades—and despite the exemplary Catholicism of Apaches like the late Louis Machukay and his family—the San Carlos Apaches still constitute a mission field for the Church. Even those Apaches who participate in national Catholic conferences speak vehemently of the need to keep Apache and Catholic practices apart from one another. A baptized San Carlos Catholic, a graduate of Catholic boarding school, perceives inherent conflict between Catholicism and his native religion: "They believe in hell; we don't" (Potsdam, August 4, 1995), and he suspects that the Church is intent upon destroying his traditional culture.

Among the Navajos the history of Catholicism is similar. During the Spanish colonial era the Franciscans attempted conversions in order to pacify these raiding peoples, trying to win them with gifts and threats, but with little effect. In the eighteenth century and the first half of the nineteenth, many hundreds of Navajos—whose lineage and culture by then included many Pueblo sources—took baptism when they were captured by the Spaniards. Such christenings provided "ceremonial relationships" (Brugge 1985: 125) with the Church that often protected the captives from the worst forms of enslavement and exploitation. On occasion a band of Navajos might seek asylum from their enemies (e.g., Utes) by requesting baptisms for all their members (Adams 1954: 68–69). Navajos in constant contact and intermarriage with partially christianized pueblos such as Acoma, Jemez, Zia, Cochiti, and Zuni sometimes joined in the Catholic Indian fiestas, and at least one band of Navajos maintained an interest in Catholicism for well over a century, into the latter part of the 1800s, even seeking a priest to live among them.

Archbishop Lamy did not succeed in implanting a more pervasive Catholic faith among the Navajos; only in 1898 with the financing of Mother Katherine Drexel and the spiritual guidance of Our Lady of Guadalupe did Franciscans establish a permanent mission among them at St. Michael's in Arizona.

Rev. Anselm Weber, O.F.M., became the "Apostle to the Navajo People," serving over twenty years at St. Michael's with his fellow Franciscans. They learned Navajo language, hoping to effect slow but permanent change among them. Weber and the missionary-turned-ethnologist Rev. Berard Haile, O.F.M., learned about traditional Navajo religion—its Emergence mythology, its devotion to Changing Woman and the Sun, its system of curing ceremonials and dread of witchcraft and the dead—and Weber reported that "without being idolators, the Navajos have an elaborate pagan cult" (*The Indian Sentinel* 1905–1906: 42). The Franciscans aimed for their boarding school to be a haven for Navajo children, and Weber forbade corporal punishment in its halls, stating that "an Indian School is not a Prussian soldiers' camp" (in Wilken 1955: 105, fn. 67). His hope was that the boarding school graduates would return to their home areas scattered around the large and growing Navajo reservation and spread the Catholic faith.

Weber recognized the difficulties: "Here among the American Bedouin we face practically unsurmountable obstacles" (in Wilken 1955: 190) among people too far-flung to create a cohesive Catholic culture. When boarding school graduates returned to their families, they immersed themselves in their Navajo ways. They participated in native ceremonies, and many became traditional singers, the carriers of Navajo religious culture. When missionaries sought them out they hid, refusing to assist at mass and balking at the notion of having their children baptized. The Franciscans learned that most Navajos regarded Catholic ritual as an analogue to the traditional Navajo Blessingway: a means to obtain good health, long life, and food from the Holy People. Despite baptisms, communions, and even some marriages in the Church, the Navajo people were slow to embrace Catholic values and theology during Father Weber's lifetime. Navajos appreciated Weber's successful efforts to increase their reservation land holdings; they respected him for his generosity and hospitality. Nevertheless, for the most part they did not convert to his faith. To his death in 1921 Weber was satisfied with the preliminary results: a couple thousand baptisms, a few prominent conversions like that of Navajo politician Chee Dodge, and a tradition of Franciscan neighborliness upon which to build a potential Catholic future.

When Archbishop Gerken took over the Archdiocese of Santa Fe in 1933, he was less content to tread slowly among the Navajos, five-sixths of whom were, in his words, "still living in pagan darkness and super-stition" (Santa Fe. Farmington. January 7, 1934). He coordinated the Franciscan missionary efforts among the Navajos in Arizona, New Mexico, and Utah, with ten priests among the fifty thousand Indians, twenty-five hundred of whom had received at least a Catholic baptism in their youth (another twenty-five hundred were initiated into Protes-tant traditions). In 1935 Gerken gathered all the Catholic missionaries among Indians in his archdiocese. They discussed the Navajos:

> Since these people are Nomads following their herds from one part of the Reservation to another as the Seasons change, it has ever been a most difficult problem for the Church to convert these people. Now, however, our opportunity is golden. (Santa Fe. Indian Affairs. January 17, 1936)

The United States was placing forty-five government day schools around the reservation. Gerken hoped to situate chapels at each of these, to catch the youths during their years of education. The Church lacked the funds and personnel, however, to carry out this ambitious plan, and so Catholic evangelization progressed piece by piece.

When Gallup became a separate diocese in 1940, the Navajo missions in New Mexico as well as Arizona became part of its domain. St. Michael's was still the central station, in addition to six outlying missions, one Catholic boarding school conducted by the Sisters of the Blessed Sacrament, and a Catholic day school. The Franciscans also conducted a portable chapel—a truck cabin placed on the back of a pickup with an altar facing out the back for use in the widespread Navajo lands. In some cases the Franciscans encountered Navajo families who recalled the kindness of priests a generation back, who wished to receive baptism and instruction (see Santa Fe. Crownpoint. April 3, 1939). The Indians appeared interested in Christian iconography and myth and the reception of the Eucharist; however, it was more difficult to interest them in matrimony: "The Indians are just well enough instructed to know that when married by a priest this marriage counts and there is no divorce or . . . remarriage at will" (Santa Fe. Tohatchi. February 11, 1939); hence they eschewed the rite. When there was a chance to "rectify" native marriages by sacramental blessing—even to non-Catholics—the priests tried to do so "on the spot while they are in a good mood or before they travel to some other part of the Reservation" (ibid., December 27, 1939).

Through vigorous proselytizing, the Catholics were able to claim about ten thousand Catholic baptisms among the Navajos by the middle of the twentieth century (*The Indian Sentinel* 29, no. 7, September 1949: 99–101). Protestant competition was stiff, and the Franciscans acknowledged that Navajo response to Catholic missionizing was "usually slow, very slow in coming" (ibid. 36, no. 4, April 1956: 56). Where the priests and sisters' presence was felt among the Indians, the missioners could say, "All the Navajos here have decidedly Catholic leanings. This is not to say that every one of them is a baptized or practicing Catholic . . . but they all want their children to be taught our religion" (ibid. 36, no. 3, March 1956: 35). But there were still areas of Navajoland where Catholicism was virtually invisible: "Most of the Navajos in this western part of the reservation . . . know practically nothing about the Church or priests—I might even say, about religion; certainly, nothing about the Catholic religion" (ibid. 36, no. 10, December 1956: 151). Priests and sisters traveled these areas, saying mass, distributing clothing, or dispensing medicines for the Navajos' aches and pains. Nonetheless, on the eve of the Second Vatican Council a Franciscan still spoke of his Navajo mission as a "virgin field," where the Indians were "quite satisfied with their traditional beliefs and practices" (ibid. 39, no. 2, March-April 1959: 19).

The decades following Vatican II have brought an increase in Navajo converts to Catholicism, at least judging from the number of baptisms. Between 1960 and 1980 eighteen thousand Navajos were christened (Beaver 1979: 38). Today there are approximately fifteen thousand living Navajos (out of a population exceeding two hundred and twenty thousand) who have received Catholic baptism, but far fewer participate in regular sacramental life. In 1987 the Vatican approved a mass translated into Navajo under the direction of Father Cormac Antram, O.F.M., of Our Lady of Guadalupe Church in Kayenta—the first such approved Indian-language mass since the Iroquois mass of the 1600s. Five priests and five Navajos worked on the project for over twenty years before it passed through American and Vatican liturgical committees for the final go-ahead (Sitts 1987). Bishop Donald E. Pelotte of the Diocese of Gallup praises the fervor of Navajo Catholics in his district, and he predicts a solid future for their faith based upon a century of Franciscan thoroughness (Pelotte, August 6, 1993). Stationed at St. Michael's, Father John Mittelstadt, O.F.M., says that the Sisters of the Blessed Sacrament have provided Navajo students with high academic standards and discipline along with religious training, leading—he hopes—to a future in which Navajos will lead their own Church life without the need for non-Indian priests and sisters (Mittlelstadt, January 18, 1987).

Navajo Catholics have included sisters such as Gloria Davis, S.B.S., Mary Theresa Chato, S.B.S., Mary Immaculata Charlie, O.S.F., Celestine Rivera, O.S.F., and Jeanette Kinlicheeny, S.B.S. Lorenzo Martin was a Franciscan brother who is still active in lay Catholic circles, although he has left the order. A common refrain among these Navajo Catholics (e.g., Davis, August 7, 1992) is that the Church has provided them with a means of maintaining their vibrant Navajo religious culture while embracing the faith founded by Jesus Christ. A Navajo laywoman, Martha James, states that her family came to the Church in the 1970s with the understanding that "if we become Catholics, then they would let us be ourselves always . . . if we are Catholic, we would keep our harmony with traditions and our Faith as Catholics" (in Farrell, September 3, 1989: 1). To this day she finds that Catholic priests and sisters do not force the Navajos to "burn their Sacred Bundles and Tools" as evangelical Protestants do. At the St. James Navajo Mission of St. Joseph's Parish, Aztec, New Mexico, she fulfills her identity as Navajo and Catholic: "As a Catholic, I learned that when one sings they pray twice. I've learned of our traditional Sacred Tools. As a Catholic, I've become aware of their tools. And combined we are here to help. . . . This is why I'm happy to be Catholic" (in ibid., 2).

Most Navajos—in addition to the Western Keres Puebloans of Acoma and Laguna, Zunis, Apaches, Hopis, and several other Indian peoples—live in the Diocese of Gallup. When the Franciscan Bernard Espelage took over the new bishopric in 1940, Gallup was the "Indian Capital" of the United States, almost completely a mission field among many "pagan" natives (*The Indian Sentinel* 20, no. 9, November 1940: 141–142). In the late 1970s Bishop Jerome J. Hastrich wrote from Gallup: "This diocese does not *have* Indians—it *is* Indian" (Marquette. DCRAA. 1976). He claimed over ninety churches with special Indian use, with a need to open over a score of others in order to "compete" with other Christian denominations (ibid., 1978) and to complete the conversion process for Indians he referred to as "Catholic Side People," those who received baptism but who did not "meet the minimal requirements of church attendance" to be called truly "Catholic" (ibid., 1979).

According to a Glenmary Research Center report in 1978, half the population within the diocese was Indian: rural, scattered, and by and large segregated from the Anglos and Hispanics. Twenty-three of the parishes in the district were on reservations (sixteen of those among the Navajos) amidst the poverty, unemployment and high alcoholism rates endemic among the Indian communities. These Indian parishes tended not to support their priests financially, receiving money instead from the Bureau of Catholic Indian Missions; hence, they functioned as missions. Despite energetic diocesan outreach through Cursillo, Apostolic Formation, Permanent Diaconate, Vocations Office, and an urban ministry in Gallup, only 4 percent of the Indians within the diocese were practicing Catholics, even though many unchurched Indians possessed some Catholic heritage and leanings.

In the 1980s Bishop Hastrich claimed as many as fifty thousand (and as few as twenty thousand) Catholic Indians in the Diocese of Gallup (ibid., February 16, 1981; 1983) out of an Indian population of more than two hundred thousand. A figure closer to thirty thousand seems more realistic in the present day, including the christianized Puebloans at Laguna, Acoma, and Zuni, as well as Apaches and Navajos. Hastrich found it hard enough to get the Pueblos to support their churches; the Navajos he regarded in a state of mission, requiring the funding and "responsibility of the Catholics of the entire Nation to assist them in becoming Christians" (February 27, 1982). The situation today is little different.

In Nevada there are several hundred Catholic Indians, mostly Paiutes and Shoshones; Corpus Christi Parish in Carson City has some Indians among its congregants. Well under a thousand Utes in Colorado, at Ignacio and Cortez, are part of the Diocese of Pueblo. Catholic outreach to these Indians has taken place in the twentieth century, and it has had to overcome the intense bitterness of these Indians (particularly the Utes) toward Whites in the reservation era. A pastor among the Utes at St. Ignatius Mission, Ignacio, Colorado, has said that there is some hope for future commitment to Catholicism, but among the youths there is but a vague sense that the Church might help them with their desperate lives: "They wander in a spiritual desert and drugs and alcohol are their replacements" (1976).

In Utah the diocese of Salt Lake City has conducted an Indian ministry for the past decade among the twenty-four thousand Native Americans in the state—Utes, Paiutes, Shoshones, Navajos, and various urban Indians; only five hundred of these Indians are Catholics, mostly Utes. In 1983 Sister Lorraine Masters, O.L.V.M., became the coordinator of the Office of Native American Ministry, over two centuries after two Franciscans—Fray Francisco Atansio Dominguez and Fray Silvestre Valez de Escalante—entered what is now Utah, searching for a northern route from New Mexico to California in 1776. The Utah Indians invited them to return; however, only with Sister Lorraine Masters' ministry has the Church attended to the spiritual welfare of the state's native population.

Masters organized Tekakwitha circles, attempting to incorporate pan-Indian spirituality and the Creation Theology of Matthew Fox into Catholic Indian liturgy. Today she is Director of Ethnic Ministry within the diocese, providing a Catholic presence among Catholic Indians who are a minority within a minority within a minority in a largely Mormon, non-Indian state (Masters, August 6, 1992). Aiding Masters' ministry is Dolores Rousseau, a Catholic Tewa from Santa Fe, who serves as a social worker in Salt Lake City. Rousseau says that the

Catholic Church in the state, through the person of Sr. Lorraine Masters, provides spiritual resources to the native population, many of whom experience the alienation and dislocation typical of Indian modernity. In her words, "Their reservations have nothing to offer them any more, and they are unprepared for urban life" (Rousseau, August 6, 1992). Rousseau tries to find jobs and shelter for the urban Indians she counsels. She also refers them to medicine men for healing of body and soul. For the few who are Catholics, or who take an interest in Catholicism, she recommends that they get in touch with the Church.

Yaquis enact a Palm Sunday ritual, near Tucson, Arizona, 1921.
Used by permission of Marquette University Memorial Library, Milwaukee, Wisconsin.

Tohono O'odham (Papago) Catholics carry the saints in
procession, St. Catherine Mission, Topawa, Arizona, 1953.
Used by permission of Franciscan Friars, Province of St. Barbara, Oakland, California.

A Tohono O'odham (Papago) woman leaves a memorial
in the cemetery of San Xavier del Bac Mission, Arizona,
on All Souls' Day, 1947.

Used by permission of Franciscan Friars, Province of St. Barbara, Oakland, California.

Laguna Catholics honor the "Pilgrim Virgin" statue of
Our Lady of Fatima in procession, St. Joseph Indian Mission,
Laguna, New Mexico, 1951.

Alex Seowtewa displays some of the murals he has painted of traditional deities above two stations of the cross, in Our Lady of Guadalupe Church, Zuni, New Mexico, 1995.

A sister employs a visual catechism at the
Tekakwitha Navajo Mission, Arizona, 1946.
Used by permission of Marquette University Memorial Library, Milwaukee, Wisconsin.

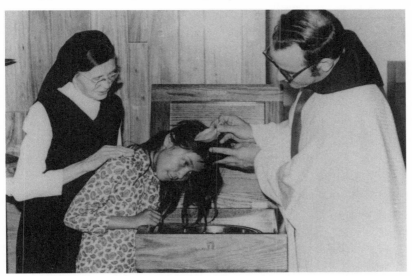

A Navajo child receives baptism, Our Lady of Fatima Mission,
Chinle, Arizona, c. 1975.
Used by permission of Franciscan Friars, Province of Our Lady of Guadalupe,
Albuquerque, New Mexico.

Luiseño and Cupeño children prepare for their first communion at San Antonio Mission, Pala, California, 1926.

Newlyweds
Raymond Machado
and Joyce Freeman
pose in the
churchyard,
San Antonio Mission,
Pala, California, 1946.

✳ III ✳

Indian Catholicism in California

THE FOUNDATIONS

In 1542 Juan Rodriguez Cabrillo, a Portuguese navigator serving Spain, landed at the Pacific coastal harbor now named San Diego (but which he called San Miguel). He encountered Indians there, most of whom ran away from him. Those few who remained informed him of men like himself who had passed inland to the east, arousing fear and armed defense of native territory. They told Cabrillo's crew that the Spanish they had encountered were killing Indians. Cabrillo's diary reports: "These people are comely and large. They go about covered with skins of animals" (in Engelhardt 1920: 4). Sixty years later another Spanish expedition that entered San Diego met armed resistance from the Indians, who withdrew to safety with their bows and arrows and then sent two old women to the invaders as emissaries. The Spanish gave them beads and biscuits. As a result of these gifts, the rest of the locals—who wore black and white paint and feathers on their heads—turned out to observe the Spaniards. It took another century and a half for representatives of Christianity to meet again with the San Diego natives and to establish the first missions of Alta (Upper) California.

In the meantime, beginning in 1595 Jesuits and Franciscans conducted missionary activity in Lower California. The Jesuits controlled the field between 1697 and 1768, influencing thousands of Indians until the suppression of The Society of Jesus (see Crosby 1994). A Jesuit who served for seventeen years among those peoples wrote in 1771 that "the results of our work among them . . . are very poor indeed" (Baegert 1979: 7). He said that baptizing them was easy because "they had no other religion with which to contradict the teachings of Christ" (ibid.), and over the seventy years of Jesuit missions in Baja California more than fourteen thousand "young Californians" were "sent to heaven." Nevertheless, he contrasted his lack of success in producing sanctified Christian life with the reputed advances of Jesuits in New France: "So much more remarkable is Catherine [Tekakwitha] . . . , whose grave with its many miracles shines brightly in Canada, and likewise the fortitude of so many others, women among them, who faced the cruel torture of fire among the inhuman Iroquois Indians" (ibid., 86).

As the Crown was evicting the Jesuits in 1768, the Spanish realized the threat of the Russians, who were extending their New World empire down the coast of western America. José de Galvez, visitor-general to New Spain, commissioned the Franciscans to establish a chain of missions in Alta California to counter the Russian advance and to substantiate Spanish claims by establishing colonies in the lands they would inhabit. Galvez defined his goals, "to establish the Catholic faith, to extend the Spanish domain, and to check the ambitious schemes of a foreign nation" (in Geary 1934: 40). His public stance was to "have it appear that the chief motive for the conquest and occupation of the new territory was religious" (Engelhardt 1912: 5); however, his goals were political and military as well as spiritual. He helped pay for Father Junipero Serra's expedition of 1769 with money from the Pious Fund, a trust established by wealthy patrons of the Jesuits (by then disbanded and their wherewithal confiscated by the State).

Don Gaspar de Portola, governor of Lower California, was military commander of the 1769 expedition; Serra was *presidente* of the missions to be founded. They arrived in San Diego in June, bringing with them baptized Indians from the south, as well as Hispanic soldiers of mixed Spanish, African, and Indian ancestry to help in what they termed their "sacred expedition" (in Castillo 1978: 100).

The Indians they encountered there were Yumans of the Hokan-Siouian family called Kumeyaay, or Ipai-Tipai, but soon to be known as Diegueños. Their linguistic relatives to the east were Quechans, Cocopas, and Mohaves. To the immediate north were Shoshoneans of the Uto-Aztecan family, including the Takic-speaking Cupan group of Indians now known as Luiseños, Cupeños, and Cahuillas; further north were the Serranos, Juaneños, and Gabrieliños. These represented the southernmost representatives of perhaps one hundred and fifty thousand to three hundred thousand native inhabitants of California from dozens of distant ethnic and language groups: Chumash, Yokuts, Salinan, Costanoan, Miwok, Pomo, Wintun, and Hoopa, (from south to north), and many others.

Governor Portola described the Yumans of San Diego in his first letter as "exceedingly numerous" and "very friendly. . . . They would treat us with such confidence and ease as though they had known us all their life" (in Engelhardt 1920: 21). One of the clerical members of the party described the Indians as "without religion, or government, [having] nothing more than diverse superstitions and a type of democracy

HOOPA

WINTUN

POMO

MIWOK

COSTANOAN

SALINAN

YOKUTS

CHUMASH

SERRANO

MOHAVE

CHEMEHUEVI

GABRIELIÑO
JUANEÑO

CAHUILLA

LUISEÑO

CUPEÑO

KUMEYAAY
(DIEGUEÑO)

QUECHAN

COCOPA

Alta California Indians, 1769

similar to that of ants" (in Phillips 1974: 291). Father Juan de Crespi, the first missionary to write a letter dated at San Diego, observed, "The gentiles all over the country are numerous and much more so farther inland" (in Engelhardt 1920: 15). These Spaniards described the Indians fishing in the sea, gathering maguey plants, painting themselves, and decorating their noses with shell. Although the men were docile and lively traders, some seemed to intend attack with their bows and arrows. The men went naked, and the women wore fiber skirts, which the padres regarded as inadequate coverings.

From the time of this encounter, the "Indians were regarded by the Spanish government as subjects of the Crown and human beings capable of receiving the sacraments of Christianity" (Castillo 1978: 100). The task of the Franciscans was to create a system of missions that could reach them all, receiving supplies from Spain and serving as a bulwark against Russia. Serra's plan was to institute farming and stock-raising communities in Indian population centers. Within three years he was to found five missions, each attracting Indians for possible conversion, and each asserting the sovereignty of Spain.

Serra chose July 16, 1769, as the founding date for the San Diego de Alcalá mission, for on that day—the Feast of the Triumph of the Holy Cross—the Spaniards, fighting under the banner of the Holy Cross, had gained a victory over Moslems. Serra hoped, wrote Father Francisco Palóu in his history of the California missions, "that under the same Standard of Christianity, we should likewise succeed in putting to flight the whole infernal army, and subject these barbarous savages to the sweet yoke of Christ" (in Engelhardt 1912: 19). July 16 was also the day of Our Lady of Mount Carmel, "through whose intercession Fr. Serra hoped to wean the savages from their beastly practices and induce them to accept the ennobling Faith of Christ" (Engelhardt 1920: 24). Hence, he planted a cross on that day, and with the help of the scurvy-stricken crew, constructed some huts which he inaugurated as Mission San Diego de Alcalá—named for a fifteenth-century Andalusian saint. Serra distributed gifts to the Indians who visited him in 1769, and they stole whatever they could, including supplies from the Spaniards too helpless from scurvy to resist. In particular they carried off cloth; they even tried to cut away ropes and sails from the ship in the harbor. They did not fear the noises of the Spaniards' guns, and the expedition was under orders at first not to shoot the Indians. The natives would eat nothing offered by the Spaniards, regarding their scurvy as a result of the Spanish diet. Not even sugar interested them; they spit it out when put in their mouths.

The Indians turned hostile to the mission within a month of its founding. On the Feast of the Assumption, August 15, they attacked Serra's camp with bows, arrows, and clubs, only to be repulsed by musket fire. A blacksmith healthy enough to wield a weapon shouted, "Long live the Faith of Jesus Christ! Death to the hostile dogs!" (in ibid., 28), while Serra and the other padres huddled in their hut, praying in vain that no one would be killed. For several days following, the Spaniards heard the Indians wailing for their dead and from their wounds; then the natives came down to the camp where the surgeon treated them, and once again the Indians were receptive.

Soon after, the Spanish built a stockade which the Indians visited. Serra possessed a painting of Blessed Virgin Mary with the child Jesus in her arms, which the Indians wanted to see. Father Palóu reported that the Indian women, forbidden to enter the stockade, thrust their breasts through the stockade poles, "thus signifying their love for the divine Infant and their desire to nourish the beautiful Child" (ibid., 29). Nevertheless, Serra could not interest the Indians in his faith, except for a teenage boy whom the priests and soldiers "petted and entertained" (ibid., 26), in the hope that he would serve as the first California convert and interpreter. They taught him Spanish, and later in the year Serra induced the boy to bring forward a child for baptism. With the infant's relatives looking on, Serra chose a corporal to serve as sponsor and prepared to pour water on the child. At that moment, however, an Indian snatched the child and ran back to the Indian town, the other Indians laughing and jeering. Serra was mortified at this rejection, although it is unclear what he hoped to accomplish in baptizing the infant of gentile parents. Nonetheless, he restrained the soldiers from seeking revenge for the insult.

It was well over a year before Serra accomplished his first baptism in San Diego. By 1773 he had counted eighty-three christenings to his credit. In that year the padres assigned baptized Indians from Baja California to teach the female Indians of Mission San Diego to spin and weave the wool from the mission sheep, thus enabling the Indians to fashion dresses more substantial than their traditional fiber aprons, which the fathers regarded as too scanty for "decent society. . . . the Fathers had no longer to worry on this score" (ibid., 47). At the same time, Indian converts at the nearby rancheria of Rincon were, according to Palóu, "kneeling down in the road, . . . these poor Indians, who till a few days before had been savages, knowing nothing about God, now as children of the Church of God were singing the *Alabado*! We rewarded them with a sack of pinole (ground corn) and some Rosary-beads" (in ibid., 49). By 1775 Serra reported 106 baptisms of adults and children at San Diego and nineteen marriages, including two involving neophytes from Baja California.

While Serra was founding Mission San Diego in 1769, Governor Portola and Father Juan Crespi journeyed north. At a place they called Los Cristianos, not far from the future site of Mission San Luis Rey, Fray Francisco Gomez baptized two little girls who were in danger of dying. The first was named Maria Magdalena, the saint for that day (July 22) in 1769, the other was Margarita. Crespi wrote: "We doubted not that both would die and so partake of the joys of paradise" (in Engelhardt 1912: 29). These were the first two baptisms of Indians in Alta California. Several days later, both Spanish and Indians were terrified by earthquakes that shook the region, and both the Christians and gentiles responded with prayer, according to their respective traditions. The Spanish recited the *Ave Maria*; what the Indians said in their own tongues was not recorded.

By December 1769, Portola and Crespi had planted a cross in Monterey Bay. When they returned the following May, they found the cross surrounded with feather-topped arrows and sticks driven in the ground. Meat and fish were attached to these sticks. Later on, the Spaniards learned from the gentiles what they had thought at their first encounter with the explorers:

> the first time they saw our men they noticed that each one wore on his breast a small, glittering cross; that when the Spaniards had gone away and left this large cross on the shore the Indians dreaded to draw near to the sacred sign, because at night they would see it surrounded by brilliant rays which would even dispel the darkness; that the cross appeared to enlarge so as to reach the skies; that in the daytime, when it stood in its natural size without the rays, they would approach it and offer meat, fishes and mussels in order to enlist its favor, lest it harm them, and that, when to their amazement, they saw that the cross did not consume these things, they would offer their plumes and arrows in token of their desire to be at peace with it and with the people who had planted it there. (Palóu, in ibid., 72)

Such was the mysterious attraction and the sacrality of the Christian symbol to the California natives in the earliest years of the mission. In

1770 at Rio de los Temblores, where the San Gabriel Mission would be founded, the natives attempted to prevent two friars from advancing into their village but fell before a canvas painting of Our Lady of Sorrows. Father Palóu said that they were "overcome by the sight of the beautiful image." They threw down their weapons, and their chiefs offered beads to the painting. Then their women and children "flocked" to see her and make offerings of seeds. Palóu claimed that Mary's image "transformed" them (in Engelhardt 1927: 4).

Missions San Carlos Borromeo de Carmelo (1770), San Antonio de Padua (1771), San Gabriel (1771), and San Luis Obispo de Tolosa (1772), which quickly followed San Diego, stretched along the Pacific coast; however, events were not entirely peaceful at the first mission. Indeed, from the initial mission to the last, Indians who had been drawn to the missions, and those who had not, attempted to put a stop to the Franciscan activity through revolts and attacks.

In 1774 Serra moved Mission San Diego several miles from the presidio because of soldiers' outrages against native women. Then in October 1775, two neophytes escaped from the mission: the chief of the Christian Indian village, Carlos, and his brother Francisco. When the sergeant of the presidio and a party of soldiers went in search of the "deserters" (in Engelhardt 1920: 60), as the chronicler Palóu called them, they discovered that the "two apostates were going from village to village, exhorting the pagans to put an end to the mission and presidio." They wanted the Indians to kill the fathers and the soldiers, "because these intended to abolish paganism by converting all to Christianity." The call to arms proved successful, partially because the Indians of a local pagan rancheria "had been reprehended for holding a pagan dance in which Christians had participated" (Geiger 1959: 61) and partially because the pattern of sexual attacks by the Spanish soldiers upon Indian women and girls had persisted. On November 4 about eight hundred warriors attacked the mission from as many as seventy rancherias, looting chests of vestments and church furnishings and setting fire to the buildings. They removed statues of the Immaculate Virgin Mary and St. Joseph—which were never recovered—and with arrows and clubs murdered Fray Luis Jayme along with two workmen who defended the grounds.

In his sorrow, Serra was reported to exult: "Thanks be to God! that land is now watered; now the conversion of the Diegueños will be effected" (in Engelhardt 1912: 170). He prevented military revenge upon the Indian villages, although his soldiers seized the leaders of the attack. After the rancherias calmed down, he rebuilt the mission the following year. Two years later, however, in 1778, the friars discovered another plot against Mission San Diego, following a year of repeated attacks on the Spaniards. The soldiers seized four chiefs and publicly executed them—the first such executions in Alta California—giving the friars time to convert the men before their deaths.

A decade later, in 1787, Governor Pedro Fages said of the Diegueños that "In the beginning they resisted conversion as they did nowhere else. But afterwards they subjected themselves with such rapidity that this was the first of the missions to count one thousand baptized converts" (in Engelhardt 1920: 121). In the first decade the mission had too few supplies to feed the Indians because of aridity and infertile soil, so the new Christians lived on their accustomed fruits of the earth and sea at a distance from the mission. After 1779 rains increased and provisions made it possible to bring in half of the baptized Indians to the mission grounds, particularly unmarried females, the sick and elderly, and those Indians with utile crafts. The friars tried to oblige all neophytes to enter the mission regularly for catechism, prayers, and reproofs for their "transgressions," for which (Fages remarked) the fathers "punish only those who relapse and who are willfully negligent" (ibid., 122). The governor averred that the Diegueños ill attended religious services. He wrote that the Diegueño tribe was "the most restless, stubborn, haughty, warlike, and hostile toward us, absolutely opposed to all rational subjection and full of the spirit of independence," and concluded that soldiers were necessary to "repress their natural and crusty pride." More recently a scholar has remarked that "of all mission tribes of the Californias, Tipais and Ipais most stubbornly and violently resisted Franciscan . . . control" (Luomala 1978: 594–595).

Despite their resistance, hundreds received baptism in the late 1700s, and in 1795 Fray Juan Mariner journeyed east to a fertile valley in order to attract Indians from outlying areas. After a generation of contact, the Mission San Diego established in 1818 a mission outpost called Asistencia Santa Ysabel, where several hundred Ipai Indians worked surrounded by their gentile relatives. The asistencia had no resident clergy, but every two weeks a priest visited, conducted instruction, and performed baptisms and other sacraments. Several Spanish soldiers maintained daily order.

Elsewhere in California, Serra continued to plant his missions. In 1776 he founded San Juan Capistrano and San Francisco de Asis (Dolores) followed the next year by Santa Clara. San Buenaventura, in 1782, was the last mission, the ninth, constructed before the death of Presidente Serra in 1784. By the 1820s there were twenty-one main missions and several asistencias along the Padres' Trail in California, all conducted by Franciscans.

San Francisco Solano

San Rafael
San Francisco de Asís
(Dolores)
San José
Santa Clara

Santa Cruz
San Juan Bautista
Monterey
San Carlos Borromeo de Carmelo
La Soledad
San Antonio de Padua
San Miguel

San Luis Obispo de Tolosa

La Purísima Concepción
Santa Barbara
San Buenaventura
Santa Ynez
San Fernando
San Gabriel
Los Angeles
San Juan Capistrano
San Luis Rey de Francia
San Antonio de Pala
Santa Ysabel
San Diego de Alcala

Alta California Missions,
1769–1848

o Missions
● **Cities**

CHURCH AND JTATE

Since there were two goals of the California missions—evangelization and the establishment of Spanish colonial claims—there was an intrinsic conflict of aims to the project from the outset. Both ecclesiastical and civil authority were in force, and it was unclear to what degree each would yield to the other. In 1772 Serra received orders to obey the civil authority; in 1773 he traveled to Mexico City to rescind the commands and gain autonomy. The viceroy, Antonio Bucareli, ruled in Serra's favor, charging that the civil government's task was to aid missions, not rule them. A 1774 decree granted the padres authority over the Indians they baptized. It explicitly stated that, "the control, education, and correction of neophytes are left exclusively to the missionaries, who act in the capacity of fathers toward their children" (in Engelhardt 1912: 133). When Felipe de Neve was appointed governor of Alta California in 1777, however, he sought to limit the fathers' practical control over the Indians. The Franciscans were able to annul his 1779 *Reglamento*—which would have allowed but one friar per mission, thereby vitiating agriculture and stock-raising, and increasing the self-rule of the Indian neophytes, advancing them toward hispanicization through contact with colonists—but the lines were already drawn in Serra's time between the priests and the civil authorities.

"Secularization" is the term for the issue over which they fought. Secularization had been a matter of dispute in Mexico as early as the conquest. Civil (and even ecclesiastical) authorities wanted the religious orders to retreat to their convents after an initial period of evangelization, allowing secular priests—those belonging to dioceses rather than orders like the Franciscans—to minister to the Indians in parishes. The question of secularization was related directly to the concepts of conquest by the Catholic nation of Spain. Conquest meant that the Indians owed work, tax, and tithe to the State and Church. As long as the Indians continued in the status of mission neophytes, they were temporarily exempted from those services, as codified by royal rules of 1607–1608. The expectation was that each mission would last for ten years; however, missionaries held to their administrative units for decades and then centuries, despite edicts and pressures from kings and bishops alike. Ferdinand VI passed a law in 1749 "ordering the transfer of all parishes and missions in the Americas from the care of the religious orders to the secular clergy" (Geary 1934: 250), but to little avail. Ferdinand's viceroy of New Spain, Revillagigedo, asserted that if the neophytes had not been segregated under the rule of the orders for so many years:

> The Indians would now be better disciplined and advanced in the spiritual as well as the temporal, and imbued with a greater spirit of subordination and obedience; in a few years the missions would have been abolished and the Indians would be enjoying freedom and the fruits of their labors, while the King would be enjoying the payment of tribute; the dominion would have been more populated and its most distant provinces developed, provinces that are very rich in fruits and mines; and finally, with the Indians instructed and accustomed to everything pertaining to their Christian, political, civil and social life, there would be no fear of the danger of their insurrection. (In Geary 1934: 28)

This statement revealed a combination of motives on the part of civil authorities to apply pressure for secularization: they could collect taxes and other duties from the Indians currently exempted in missions; Spanish settlers could colonize the Indians' lands; the Indians could attain freedom from the missionaries and make life choices as citizens. One can also find in Revillagigedo's justification the reasons that the missionaries resisted secularization: to protect the Indians and their lands from exploitation and appropriation and to maintain control over the choices available to the neophytes.

In California the Franciscans set up their missions in the most arable lands along the coast—"Gargantuan areas," according to one scrutinizer (Servín 1991: 121)—and applied all their legal power to assert control over the lands and the baptized Indians upon them. At the same time, colonists were entering California—there were over a thousand by the turn of the nineteenth century. Calling themselves *gente de razon* (people of intelligence, or reason), in contrast to the Indians, whom they regarded as brutes, these Spaniards and mixed-bloods settled originally around the four Spanish presidios at San Diego, Santa Barbara, Monterey, and San Francisco. Later immigrants from Mexico settled at San Jose and Los Angeles. Over time, some of them hungered for the lands held by the Franciscans in trust for the neophytes, a hunger that fueled the engines of secularization. Whereas it was true that "a movement to secularize the California Missions manifested itself almost on the first day of their settlement" (Geary 1934: ix), the meaning of secularization shifted from 1769 to 1834:

> The term, secularization, originally meant the substitution of secular priests for the religious order priests and the conversion of the mission into a parish. Later it also meant the raising of the Indian community to the status of a self-governing pueblo and, finally, in practice it often resulted in the confiscation of the mission property and lands by white settlers or government officials. (Ibid., 16)

Throughout the late eighteenth century the governors of California pressed for neophytes to have their own elected officials and argued that the Franciscans should minister to the gente de razon as well as the Indians. The padres resisted these pressures as far as they could, appointing alcaldes (councilmen), fiscals (church officers), and mayordomos (stewards) rather than permitting elections.

In 1549 Emperor Charles V had ordered that the Indians of New Spain were to dwell together under the government of Indian alcaldes elected by the natives. If the California governors were going to interpret this ancient rule as applicable to missions before secularization took place, the Franciscans were at least going to insist that alcaldes be subject to the priests' authority in all matters. Governor Neve tried to exempt the alcaldes from corporal punishment, but in 1780 Presidente Serra argued against such exemptions and in favor of corporal punishment in general. He said that from the Franciscans' experience in other parts of New Spain they had learned the necessity of the lash in maintaining authority and producing Christian virtue. Serra wrote:

> The punishment of the lash which the spiritual Fathers of the Indians inflict upon the Indians as upon children, seems as old as the conquest of these dominions, and so general that it does not seem that even the saints departed from this manner of correction. . . . The alcaldes themselves are children mentally and as such in charge of the Fathers. They are not less in need of education, correction and support. (In Engelhardt 1912: 342)

The padre reminded the governor that Cortés himself commanded himself to be whipped publicly by the fathers in the presence of Indians in order to convey the supreme authority of the Church. Serra reasoned that given the earthly condition of alcaldes—who had been known to provide Indian women to soldiers, who practiced adultery, who were sinners like all other Indians in the initial stages of Christian formation—they needed to feel the physical authority of the priests along with the rest: "When we came not a Christian existed here; . . . we regenerated all in Christ; and . . . we have come and we are all here for their welfare and salvation. At all events, I believe it is well known that we love them" (ibid., 343). Such love would not permit self-rule among the neophytes. As Serra's successor, Presidente Fermin Francisco de Lasuen wrote in 1796, when Governor Diego de Borica ordered annual elections for Indian alcaldes:

> elections were to be considered mere object lessons which were to prepare and instruct the natives to appreciate full citizenship in time; but as for allowing the missions to be governed by such Indians, that was out of the question until the king himself should declare that these establishments ceased to be missions and became pueblos or curacies. In that event the friars would withdraw. (In ibid., 541)

As for the missionaries' responsibilities to the Hispanic colonists, the priests supplied sacraments to the non-Indian population but kept to their missions, over which they claimed administrative autonomy. By 1790 there were eleven missions, housing over eight thousand neophytes; almost thirteen thousand Indians had received baptism since 1769, and almost ten thousand had been confirmed as Christians.

Since the sixteenth century the padres had developed techniques that drew Native Americans into their establishments: the planting of a large cross raised their curiosity; gifts (trinkets, food, clothing), endearing smiles, and gentle gestures were the "lure" (Webb 1982: 25) that kept the natives close at hand. Next the building of the mission began, and the padres "rewarded" (ibid., 26) with regular meals those locals who helped clear fields, gather materials, and construct buildings. The Pious Fund provided money for supplies and food, and so the Indians were attracted to the wherewithal in the priests' possession. Although some evidence indicates that the natives cared little for the Spaniards' victuals, Engelhardt, the Franciscan historian, remarked:

> it was through the stomach that the Indians were gained for Religion. Only after the Indians had received gifts from the missionaries and felt satisfied that Christianity would provide food and clothing much better than paganism, could the Fathers hope gradually to ennoble and supernaturalize and firmly ground the Indians half-hearted desire for Baptism. Therefore, they found themselves obligated to feed, clothe, employ, and even divert their overgrown dusky children. (Engelhardt 1920: 130)

Some authors have understood some Indian baptisms, e.g., among the Chumash, as part of an Indian strategy to make use of mission foodstuffs during years of lean resources (Sandos 1991: 68). Whether food or cloth or metal tools, the Spaniards' material goods could not but attract the gentiles at first. A recent Franciscan scholar calls the inducements "indirect, diplomatic, and ingenious" (Guest 1989: 1). The pastors cultivated good will and gifts of beads, trinkets, cloth, and ribbons, trying to win the favor of chiefs and others. They gathered what the same writer calls "the brighter Indian boys" into cadres, teaching them to sing Spanish songs conveying Christian doctrines. This method introduced basic ideas into the lads' consciousness and fostered pride in their accomplishment. The boys' parents indulged them their new songs, and hence "they were won over to Christianity all the more easily" (ibid., 2). This was not a method new to the Franciscans of Alta California but had been developed by Fray Pedro de Gante, one of the Flemish Franciscans who came to New Spain to proselytize Indians in 1523. It was through the songs that the friars began an exchange of vocabulary. The padres were able to compose catechisms of Christian doctrine and thus prepare adults for baptism, taking several months to teach them before applying the water. While the construction of mission buildings proceeded, the missionaries tried to communicate the rudiments of the Christian gospel message, although at first this was nigh impossible, since each new group of Indians spoke a different language, often unintelligible even to baptized Indians from other communities.

We can observe this process in the founding of a new mission, San Luis Rey de Francia, in 1798. The Franciscans needed a mission between San Diego and San Juan Capistrano, with many Indians rancherias lying between them. The priests had planned to situate their missions at one day's walking distance from each other (Franciscan scruples forbade themselves the luxury of riding horses under normal circumstances), and the distance between San Diego and San Juan was too great. After receiving permission from Governor Diego Borica, the padres chose a site and broke ground. Gentile Indians observed as Father Antonio Peyri, soldiers, and neophytes from other missions raised a cross, performed a high mass, and shot off firearms. Father Lasuen reported that the gentiles were so impressed by the pageantry that they brought twenty-five male and twenty-nine female children to him for baptism immediately. Others gathered around Peyri, San Luis Rey's pastor, for instruction. "Thus possession was taken of this site," said Lasuen (in Engelhardt 1921: 9).

Within six months of the ground breaking, Peyri and his assistant had baptized 210 Indians, blessed thirty-four marriages, and buried five deceased. Already over two hundred Indians were living with the fathers at the mission, with 162 head of cattle, six hundred sheep, twenty-eight horses, and ten pack mules—animals contributed from other California missions. By the end of 1800 San Luis Rey had 337 neophytes, as "the Indians applied in ever-increasing numbers for admission into the Christian fold" (ibid., 16). In the first two decades of the nineteenth century San Luis Rey grew to be the largest of all the Franciscan missions in California, with twenty-six hundred neophytes living about the grounds in 1820 under the continuing supervision of the beloved superior, Peyri. There were four rancherias within twenty-five miles of the main buildings, each with an Indian village, a chapel, granaries, and livestock; the largest of these was San Antonio de Pala, an asistencia founded in 1816, with several hundred neophytes. In time Pala became a mission in its own right, with chapels at outlying rancherias.

In the same year as San Luis Rey's founding, Fray Juan Cortés wrote a booklet (Kelsey 1979) for instructing the Indians at Santa Barbara Mission in Christian doctrine, employing the Chumash language of the natives there. The priests were supposed to read from the booklet to the Indians and to ask them the prepared questions. His catechism, to which was appended a guide to hearing the neophytes' confessions, followed the pattern of Catholic catechisms prevalent from the Council of Trent in the sixteenth century to the Second Vatican Council in the twentieth. Spanish missionaries had created such doctrinas and confesionarios in sixteenth-century Mexico, following the basic formulations of Christian doctrine codified by the Trent theologians (we have discussed such a confesionario from Florida). By observing Cortés' doctrina and confesionario one can perceive the missionary message of the friars: the ideas and values they attempted to inculcate to the California Indians.

Cortés taught what a person must "know and believe" (ibid., 93) in order to receive the sacrament of baptism: that there is only one true and eternal God, creator of all things; that this God is a Trinity of Father, Son, and Holy Spirit; that Jesus Christ, the Son, became man in the womb of the Virgin Mary and suffered and died, "in order to forgive us our sins and to take us to Heaven"; that God is just, sending to heaven and hell those who deserve reward and punishment, respectively, for their goodness and wickedness; that when humans die, the soul lives on in heaven or hell. The doctrina encouraged the Indian receiving baptism to think of God always and also of Mary, Mother of God, who can intercede to her Son to obtain forgiveness for sin.

The doctrina then instructed the Indians in the Sign of the Cross, the Act of Contrition ("I a miserable sinner," 97); the Lord's Prayer ("your will be done," 98); the Hail Mary ("Holy Mary, Mother of God, pray for us sinners," 99); and the Creed ("I believe in God . . . Jesus Christ . . . the Holy Virgin Mary . . . the Holy Spirit, the Holy Catholic church . . . the forgiveness of sins, the resurrection of the body . . . ," 99). It taught the Ten Commandments of God, which are encompassed in two: "to serve and to love God above all things and to love your neighbor as yourself" (101), and the Five Commandments of the Church: to hear mass on Sundays and holy days of obligation; to confess sins at least once a year during Lent; to receive communion at Eastertime; to fast when the Church commands; and to pay tithes and first fruits to the Church. It listed the seven sacraments—baptism, confirmation, penance, communion, extreme unction, holy orders, and matrimony—which are the means by which humans receive the grace necessary to be saved.

Cortés' catechism emphasized the powerful, just, and merciful trinitarian God and the pure Blessed Virgin Mary, in contrast to human sinfulness, which necessitated Jesus' entry into the world "to save us" (104), meaning the human soul, which never dies. The Church provided the means of that salvation for Indians (and all humans) through its central sacrament of Jesus, received in communion.

The doctrina taught that in order to be worthy to receive Jesus, the neophytes must examine their conscience, confess their sins, and be truly sorrowful for committing them, in order to obtain God's forgiveness. The confesionario provided examples of sinful behavior, querying the Indians about their participation in such acts. Cortés asked the neophytes to consider if they had missed mass on Sundays or feastdays, or acted irreverently during mass. Had they eaten meat on Friday, or disobeyed their parents? Had they mistreated a spouse (matrimony played a prominent role in the text), or wished evil of people.

Cortés' confesionario suggested to the priests that the Chumash Indians maintained native religious beliefs and practices even after baptism. Did they disrupt the truths of the padres' teachings? Did they believe in the curative powers of "the water, the acorn, . . . in dreams? in the Owl" (110)? Did they engage in shamanism or scatter seeds in honor of deities? These were questions to be asked and sins to be confessed.

The most salient concern of the confesionario, however, was focussed upon sexuality in its various manifestations. The padre asked the neophytes if they had wished, or acted upon their wish, to do "bad things for pleasure with a Woman, with Women, with a man, with men" (115). Did they engage in fornication, adultery, masturbation, bestiality, incest, or sodomy? Did they procure a woman for sin, wish to see a woman nude, or give away a wife to someone else so he could sin with her? The text asked, "Did you couple in the right way?" (116). In addition, Cortés asked the Indians if they had practiced birth control (spilling semen during intercourse) or abortion, for these, too, were sins.

Finally, the confesionario reminded the neophytes of the importance of a good confession: keeping no sins secret from the priest and feeling true contrition for one's wrongful actions and desires, with a will to sin no more:

> if you die in sin, your soul goes to Hell to suffer forever from every ill and every infirmity, much hunger, much thirst, much coldness, eternal darkness, and you will be there burning like a tile in the furnace, suffering such as I am unable to describe. But if you are good and have no sin, you will go to heaven with God for eternity, where all the good things and all the sweet things and all the beautiful things are. There, best of all, you will see God, Jesus Christ, Blessed Mary. . . . (118)

The priests hoped that by reciting such doctrinas and reflecting upon such confesionarios, the California Indians would enter the Christian worldview and lifeway.

The Franciscans expected these baptized Indians—who were capable of reciting the catechetical requirements—to remain in the missions and submit to their rules:

> It was, in fact, the essential feature of what came to be known as the Mission System. As soon . . . as the rites of baptism had been performed the Indian became an active participant in that system, subject to its rules and regulations. . . . Before baptism was administered the Indians were warned that when they had become Christians they would no longer be allowed to roam . . . whenever they felt so inclined; they must thenceforth live at the mission. If they left the . . . Indian village . . . they would be followed, brought back, and punished. (Webb 1982: 27)

Married couples with young children lived in their own homes in the neophyte villages; however, girls from age nine, single women, and widows were confined to the *monjerío* (nunnery) for their protection; boys and single men lived in barracks. The missionaries tried to control the marriage practices of the Indians. If a young man—either another Indian or one of the white soldiers, blacksmiths, carpenters, etc. who lived at the mission—wanted to marry a girl, he was supposed to approach the priest, who might then approve with the girl's permission. Despite the friars' objections, however, soldiers and other Hispanic men produced mixed offspring with Indian women, creating a hispanicized Indian culture.

In 1852 Hugo Reid, a Scotsman married to a Gabrieleño neophyte, provided a different perspective on the process of conversion, based upon oral traditions passed down by his wife and her relatives. Reid wrote that at first the Indians saw the Spaniards on horseback and thought them to be gods. The women ran to the brush and hid. The men saw the Spaniards make fire with flint and thought they must be divine. When the Indians saw the Spaniards kill birds with guns, however, they thought it impossible that gods would kill, so they must be humans like themselves—ugly ones with blue eyes. The Indians called them "reasonable beings" (Reid 1991: 131), a term they used for themselves when they finally learned to use Spanish tools of steel. The proof of the Spaniards' humanness came when they demanded Indian women with whom to fornicate.

Those women who were thus "contaminated" were "put through a long course of sweating, drinking of herbs, &c," and for many years the Indians strangled and buried any offspring of these forced sexual encounters. The Indians liked the Spaniards' tools but hated most of their foods, which they buried in the ground. The natives liked *panache*, a fudge made of brown sugar, butter, cream, and nuts, but called it the "excrement of their new neighbors." This they buried with the beans and grains. Imagine their surprise when cornstalks grew up in these middens. This was "*white* witchcraft" (ibid., 132–133, emphasis his). In time, Reid said, the Indians at San Gabriel received baptism:

> The priest having converted some few by giving them cloth and ribbons, and taught them to say *Amar á Dios*, they were baptized and co-operated in the work before them.
> Baptism as performed, and the recital of a few words not understood, can hardly be said to be a conversion; nevertheless, it was productive of great advantage to the Missionaries, because once baptized they lost "caste" with their people, and had *nolens volens* to stop with the oppressor. This, of course, was put down by the Padre as a proof of the influence of religion on their minds, and the direct interposition of the Virgin Mary! Poor devils, they were the *Paríah* of the West! Not one word of Spanish did they understand—not one word of the Indian tongue did the Priest know.—They had no more idea that they were worshipping God, than an unborn child has of Astronomy. (Ibid., 136)

Being a Catholic to the neophytes, said Reid, consisted of crossing themselves, working, receiving hard blows, and tolerating the degrading practice of having water poured on them.

Moreover, Reid asserted, since the Franciscans at San Gabriel could not baptize adults against their wills, they sent out expeditions of soldiers to bring in converts. The military whipped the gentiles and drove them back to the mission, where they were commanded to throw down their weapons before the priest. Then the infants and children to age eight were baptized. The infants were allowed to stay with their mothers, but the youths were kept separate. Consequently, the women agreed to baptism so they could be reunited with their children, and the men then agreed to baptism so they could be with their wives and families. Thus the Gabrieleños became "followers of Christ" (ibid., 138). Only later did they come to know anything intelligible of the Catholic religion.

Within the mission the priests regulated time and activity according to a system of bells. At sunrise bells called all Indians nine years or older to mass, accompanied by prayers, catechetical instruction, and the singing of the *Alabado*. Breakfast consisted of *atole* (an Aztec word signifying a mixture of corn and water, a gruel), consumed by families, single females, and males, all in their separate quarters. Then the community went to work. Agriculture was the main occupation of the California mission neophytes. They planted, weeded, harvested, and milled the corn, wheat, lentils, garbanzos, peas, etc. and tended the kitchen gardens. They herded sheep and cared for the livestock; they tended orchards and vineyards. In addition, they constructed and maintained aqueducts, dams, reservoirs—a water system for irrigation and milling. The neophytes made pottery and also bricks and tiles, from which mission buildings were fabricated, and they hauled and carpentered wood, laid adobe walls, and layered masonry. During each day (except, of course, for Sundays and holy days) they engaged in a round of trades: making shoes, saddles, hats, clothes, candles, soap, wine, and olive oil. They tanned hides and melted tallow, which were sold to English, Yankee, and other traders throughout the Franciscan period, and which provided the two primary sources of mission revenues. They also spun wool, sheared sheep, wove, and blacksmithed. Indian artists decorated the walls of churches, and Indian musicians performed in orchestras and choirs, playing instruments such as bass fiddles, contrabassos, and drums made in the mission workshops. None received wages, but all shared in the common property, which was managed wholly by the missionary. Profits purchased church embellishments, as well as tobacco, cloth, and baubles for the Indians.

While adults worked, children and those who were about to be married received special instruction. At noon the Angelus bell announced dinner, consisting of *pozole* (an Aztec term for soup or broth) with beans, lentils, and sometimes meat. After an afternoon siesta, the neophytes resumed their tasks until the early evening, when they received their second round of instruction followed by a supper of atole. In the evenings the Indians played at native games until bedtime. On Sundays there was a high mass in Latin with Indian musicians and choir followed by Christian instruction. Then each member of the community kissed the padre's hand, as each one's name was called out from a book, to see if anyone was missing. Sunday afternoon devotions consisted of rosary, Litany of Saints and the Virgin, and short prayers. Every Friday, and throughout Lent, afternoon work was curtailed for the Way of the Cross.

In 1821 a French visitor at San Luis Rey reported on the routine of the mission and the treatment the Indians received:

> Not only were they well fed and well clad, but on their feast days they were given some money. Every Saturday soap was distributed to the women. On such an occasion all the women passed in review before the missionary Father, and while two men fished from two enormous baskets for each woman the piece of soap to be given her, Fr. Antonio addressed his words to her. He knew them all. One he kindly commended, another he reproved gently. One he offered a good-natured courtesy, another a paternal admonition. All went away satisfied and charmed. (In Engelhardt 1921: 63)

Ceremonial life at the California missions was rich: blessing flags and ships, laying cornerstones, consecrating churches. The most elaborately ritualized days were the celebrations of various feasts throughout the year. Not only was each day regulated by bells, but the whole year was fashioned by the Christian calendar, punctuated continually by ritual. It was partially the pomp—the marches, the music, the displays—that initially attracted the Indians, and these same grand gestures were also part of the system designed to transform them. Mission decorations—statues and pictures of Christ, Mary, angels, saints, heaven, hell, death, judgment, purgatory, the Stations of the Cross—were meant to inspire devotional attitudes. Processions were frequent, especially on the feast of Corpus Christi. Soldiers fired their muskets and wore dress uniforms. The community carried a crucifix around the mission to the accompaniment of chants and incense. The padre carried the Sacred Host—the body of Christ—under a silken canopy.

From the first Sunday of Advent, the choir and orchestra prepared for *Las Posadas* ("The Inns"), a pageant commemorating the journey of Mary and Joseph from Nazareth to Bethlehem, and the *Pastorela* nativity play on Christmas Eve. Pastorela took place after midnight mass, with characterizations of the Archangel Gabriel, The Devil, and shepherds of Bethlehem. It marked the appearance of the angel to the shepherds to mark the birth of Christ. El Diablo tried to prevent the shepherds from journeying to Jesus, but Gabriel overcame him and the Evil One submitted. Then everyone came forward to see the *Niño Santo* in the manger. Indians gathered at the creche, an important element in Franciscan missions, since it was St. Francis of Assisi—the thirteenth-century founder of the order—who began the Christian practice of displaying the scene of Jesus' birth.

California Mission Indians celebrated particular saints' feast days—those of St. Joseph, St. Francis, St. Isidro, etc.—but the ceremonies of Holy Week were especially impressive. Solemn high mass took place on Holy Thursday; the priest washed neophytes' feet on that day. On Good Friday the body of Christ was taken from the cross (a lifelike doll with hinges was used) and placed under the altar. This took place in the hushed church, with dark velvet covering the statues. The community walked The Stations of the Cross—another medieval innovation of the Franciscans that became a Church sacramental—and snuffed out candles. The congregation chanted the *Miserere*; then ratchets, rattles, and clackers made a terrifying noise "symbolizing the confusion of nature at the time of Christ's death" (Webb 1982: 271); such was the *Tenebrae* (darkness) service of Good Friday. On Holy Saturday the priest blessed salt, new fire, holy water, and the paschal candle. The choir sang the *Exsultet*, followed by a performance in which an effigy of Judas Iscariot was hung in the mission plaza, to be beaten, shot at, spat upon, and chastised. They sang the *Gloria*, rang bells, freed statues from their purple covers, and revealed the altar once again. On Easter morning the Indians dressed in their cleanest, most colorful garb, to celebrate the Resurrection of Christ. In all these observances they followed the patterns of late medieval Spanish Catholicism.

Every May 3rd the missions enacted the pageant of "The Finding of the True Cross." During the spring and summer, statues of the Virgin Mary were processed about while the participants said the Rosary and hoped for rain. The friars blessed waters and crops and the mission properties. Ritualism was thus combined with the discipline of hard work to educate the Indians in the ways of Christian piety and propriety, hour by hour and throughout the liturgical year.

Some missionaries admitted that the Indians did no more than imitate the gestures and sounds made by their teachers—Father Geronimo Boscana remarked that, "The Indians of California may be compared to a species of monkey; for in naught do they express interest except in imitating the actions of others, and particularly in copying the ways of the 'razon,' or white men, whom they respect as beings much superior to themselves," but unfortunately, he said, they copied the worst habits of the Whites (Boscana 1846: 335). Some twentieth-century scholars have concluded that the recitations of Spanish prayers and doctrines amounted to little more than the repetition of meaningless sounds (Engelhardt 1920: 131). "How little is the faith of these Indians in the teachings of the Catholic truths!" said Father Boscana, relating an episode of firsthand experience:

> A missionary, of the mission of St. Luis Rey, who had baptized several adults, the youngest of whom had reached his fiftieth year, attempted to explain, after the ceremony was concluded, the sort of life which they were to observe for the future; and he told them what they were to do to avoid the influence of Satan. By invoking the sweet names of Jesus and Mary, he said, and by the sign of the holy cross, well performed, we destroy the power of the devil, and drive out all unholy thoughts. A *satrap*, or governor, of one of the rancherias, smilingly observed to the others, "See how this pádre cheats us! Who believes that the devil will leave us, by the sign of the cross? If it were to be done by dancing, as authorized by Chinigchinich, he would depart; but that he will do so, by the means which *he* says, I do not believe!" The others united with him in laughter, and appeared unimpressed with the efficacy of such ceremony. (Boscana 1846: 338)

Although it is said that most neophytes were refused the reception of communion because "comparatively few comprehended the full significance of the Holy Eucharist" (Engelhardt 1912: 253), over time the California Indians adopted Catholic religious forms "and with each generation the new religion sank in more deeply" (Borah 1991: 14). Indian artists put themselves into the paintings they produced— one can find Virgins and saints with Indian faces in some missions— and internalized at least the gestures and words (if not the theological underpinnings) of Christianity. In 1791 Presidente Lasuen provided a portrayal of mission life:

All attend holy Mass every day, and they are already aware that he who absents himself on days of obligation deserves punishment. Most of the adults confess once a year; many receive holy Communion, and there are always some who receive the Sacraments twice and three times a year. They also assist with fair devotions at the other religious functions, at the Rosary on Sundays and other feast-days of the year. In the frequent disagreements, which necessarily happen at all hours among so many people entirely dependent upon the care of us missionaries in spiritual and temporal things, we fail not to instruct them in their Christian duties. We already note that these neophytes gradually appreciate their Faith and baptismal character, and that they are making the progress that could be expected from their capacity and from the time since which they have become Christians. The sick, even when they happen to be very far from the mission, as a rule, show much concern and anxiety to make their confession. At the hour of death, generally, they manifest very good and even admirable sentiments regarding our holy Religion. Thanks be to God! Likewise many pagans, who live far from the mission, when they are sick, are accustomed to send for the missionary in order to be baptized. (In Engelhardt 1912: 449).

At first the Franciscans attempted to suppress all aboriginal expressions of California Indian religiousness. "After a while, however, they realized that the Indians had to be left some outlet for releasing emotion, and so later the missionaries even encouraged dances, but always supervised them" (Borah 1991: 13). In the evening the priests permitted the neophytes to enjoy native amusements, "as long as decency and Christian modesty were not offended" (Engelhardt 1912: 255). Contemporary illustrations of the missions show Indians dancing forms of their traditional ritualism under the watchful eyes (and perhaps direction) of the pastors. The Indians in these illustrations wear their feathers, shells, and paints. California mission Indians persisted in using their sweat lodges (*temescal*) in the missions. The priests tried at first to stop these sweats—which the Indians employed as cure-alls but which served instead to spread the new eruptive, contagious diseases brought by the Europeans—but later condoned their use. The padres also encouraged Indian artists to employ native designs in the decoration of churches and chapels. Lucario Cuevish, an old Luiseño born at San Luis Rey and who remained there until the mission closed at the time of the Mexican-American War, recalled in the early twentieth century that the padres never objected to the Indians' performance of religious dances, and if the Indians did not speak Spanish they were allowed to pray in their Indian languages. The diffusion of native cults such as the one venerating Chinigchinich took place through the missions, and when gentile Indians came to San Luis Rey for Christian instruction, they also received initiation into Chinigchinich by ingesting jimson-weed (*toloache*) (DuBois 1908: 74–76).

A Luiseño Indian in the 1830s remarked that dancing continued as a regular part of the neophytes' life: "the Indians of California dance not only for a feast, but also before starting a war, for grief, because they have lost the victory, and in memory of grandparents, aunts and uncles, parents already dead. Now that we are Christians we dance for ceremony" (Tac 1958: 22). He described several dances and native games permitted by Fray Peyri at San Luis Rey. And a French navigator, Auguste Duhaut-Cilly, observed an Indian dance after nightfall on the feast of St. Anthony on June 13, 1821, at San Luis Rey. Accompanied by Father Peyri, the seaman saw twelve men in breechcloth and feathers, dancing vigorously in the torchlight until they sweated considerably, at which they scraped off their bodies with a wooden ferule. An orchestra of women, boys, and old men accompanied the dancers, and hundreds of spectators looked on. From time to time they all "would simultaneously and very noisily expectorate up into the air. This, I was assured, was done to chase away the evil spirits; for, although they are all Christians, they still observe many old superstitious customs, and the Fathers, out of prudence, pretend not to notice them" (in Engelhardt 1921: 64).

Padre Antonio Ripoll orchestrated Chumash festivals at La Purisima Concepción and Santa Barbara missions and baptized several Chumash *joyas* (male transvestites) without making moral objection to their way of living (Sandos winter 1991:76–82). Many aspects of Chumash aboriginal culture prevailed inside missions such as La Purisima, including the use of jimsonweed and tobacco in order to attain ecstatic, revelatory states; the power of religious leaders who initiated youths; the sexual liaisons among certain in-laws and transvestites; the killing of firstborns in order to assure future births; the ritual license to engage in bawdy and scatological behavior (Sandos 1991: 302–303). These practices were repugnant to the padres, but they were unable to prevent them in many cases. The priests wished the Indians to acquire Christian ways, but they could not snuff out all of the traditional religion. At least some of the Franciscans tried to accommodate native cultural expressions and incorporate at least the trappings of traditional religious expression in art and rite.

In 1812 the Spanish Minister of Foreign Relations in Mexico, Don Ciriaco Gonzales Carvajal, asked thirty-six questions of all civil and ecclesiastical authorities in the Spanish dominions, requiring them to provide written answers for his edification. Between 1813 and 1815 the padres of the California missions responded to the *Interrogatiorio*, providing particulars of the contemporary (partially Christian) and aboriginal Indians in their areas. They wrote accounts of social organization, history, manners, and morals, as well as administrative concerns, and we find in the padres' reports a profile of socioreligious change and persistence among the neophytes, at least from the priests' perspective.

The friars wrote of the Indians from San Juan Capistrano: "Their superstitions are as numerous as they are ridiculous and are difficult to understand" (Geiger and Meighan 1976: 47). At San Gabriel the clerics found "some superstitions or rather vain practices peculiar to recent converts. However, we are successful in having them give up these practices gradually." The same hope that "succeeding generations" would give up "old practices" was expressed at Mission San Francisco, but at San Jose the missionaries found the Indians' reliance on dreams "extremely obstinate." At San Gabriel the padres wished that they could separate the children from their elders so as to cut the chain of Indian tradition among them. Some priests reported no "idolatry," but others noted the offerings of smoke and pollen to the sun and moon and other spiritual beings, even while the neophytes listened to instruction regarding "God, the Creator of heaven and earth and of all things." The friars at Mission San Gabriel suggested gains they had made: "from savage men, the missionaries have succeeded in bringing the Indians to act as rational and decent beings and as good Catholics" (ibid., 47–61), but at the more recent missions, according to Fray José Señan at San Buenaventura:

> The son counts eighteen years as a Christian but the father is an obstinate savage still enamored of his brutal liberty and perpetual idleness. The granddaughter is a Christian but the grandmother is a pagan. Two brothers may be Christians but the sister stays in the mountains. A neophyte twenty years a Christian marries a woman but recently baptized. Such is the situation. (61)

Even so, the priests saw progress. The Indians wore clothes. They recognized God as "sovereign" (ibid.). They grew Spanish crops and raised cattle. They prayed and did the tasks assigned them. They were

at peace with one another, whereas before they had fought regularly.
Fray Juan Amoros at San Carlos said:

> Whereas twenty years ago the fathers and veteran soldiers were com-
> pelled to make them attend Mass and pray nor would they subject
> themselves to the rule of others or show signs of civility, today they as-
> sist at Mass, pray, frequent the sacraments and wish to die as Christians.
> They recognize authority and show marks of civility.

Twenty years ago they "had to be punished continually"; now all they
lack as Christians is "constancy" (63).

The pastors claimed that gentile Indians' marriage customs—
arrangements through family contacts, impermanent alliances, divorces—had been replaced by the rules of the Council of Trent, as
brokered by the missionaries, and were indissoluble. Indian concepts
of time and natural processes were now superseded: "The Christians
regulate their lives by the mission clock. For timing their rest, meals
and work, we sound the bell" (81). The Franciscans found the neophytes still immoral, lazy, dishonest, and lustful. They engaged in
theft, gambling, revenge, fornication, and abortion, said the priests,
and syphilis was destroying the Indian population as a result of sexual
contacts with Whites. The padres agreed that aboriginally the California Indians had some ideas about souls and afterlife, but that only with
Christianity had doctrines of heaven, hell, purgatory, and judgment
come into their consciousness, and these ideas were having an effect,
e.g., at Mission San Diego: "We know that they possess the idea of
eternity, reward and punishment, of the last judgment of purgatory
and hell and heaven. As a result some live temperate lives, others go to
confession. . . and all ask eagerly for the holy sacraments at the hour of
death" (143).

Friars Fernando Martin and José Sanchez provided a lively account
of this, the oldest and southernmost of the Alta California missions.
They commented that the Indians held "a good deal of fondness for
the Europeans and Americans; for they wish to serve them and to live
with them. No hatred or rancor is observed" (in Engelhardt 1920:
179). The missionaries taught them manual arts, although the neophytes were averse to labor; "the male and female neophytes of this
Mission serve the military of the presidio nearby, because they voluntarily desire to serve them," the priests claimed (183). The padres noted
that, "To this mission come every year from paganism those who desire to be Christians, and a large proportion are old people" (180).

These old converts died at the mission, causing the rate of death to exceed the rate of birth; indeed, in 1814 the deaths outnumbered the baptisms in the mission 118 to 75. The major killer was venereal disease. In burying their dead the Indians "in the presence of the missionaries, throw a few seeds of grain into the grave, and then raise a wail which lasts for some days" (182).

At Mission San Diego the neophytes continued in the practice of some traditional religious expressions. The fathers described the medicinal practices of sucking doctors, whom the priests regarded as fakes; and many of the Indians captured hawks, which they believed able to "liberate them from their enemies and grant them whatever they ask" (180). After capturing a hawk, the Indians fed it for a year and then killed and burned it, offering it seeds, beads, and other gifts. The priests tried to "break them of this foolishness" and "all who are caught practicing it are severely punished in public" (ibid.). The missionaries found the neophytes proud and rancorous, prone to "impurity, stealing, and murder. . . , inclined to tell lies, especially in reporting anything incriminating; for they dread chastisement and that is the reason for their lying" (182).

Just to the north, at San Luis Rey, Fathers Antonio Peyri and Francisco Suñer wrote:

> At this mission we have the condensed catechism which contains what a Christian has to know which is in the Indian and Spanish languages. It also contains the acts of Faith, Hope, Charity and Contrition. The Indians are also taught in both languages the Our Father, Hail Mary, the Creed, the *Salve*, the commandments of the law of God and of the Church, the sacraments and the Confiteor. (53)

As at San Diego, the San Luis Rey padres worked hard to change the ways of the Indians, and although the Indians may not have had "any particular fondness" for the Spanish, there was no overt hostility, and they learned their lessons with "mildness, submissiveness, and humility" (Engelhardt 1921: 24). The fathers recounted several religious practices—the taking of jimsonweed, the ritual sacrifices of hawks, the emotional responses to new moons and eclipses—and testified that they were trying to overcome such "superstitions" and "idolatry," as well as the medicinal practices of herbalism and sucking of disease objects; however, one priest conceded that

> in the matter of their superstitions regarding sickness, idolatry, and witchcraft, they are so rare . . . , full of deceit, and reserved, that although I have been among them since the foundation of this mission,

that which I can most readily manifest regarding these matters, is my
ignorance of them. They never confess more than what they cannot
deny. (In Kroeber 1908: 10)

Although the priests could not fathom the traditional religious ideas
of the neophytes, they observed the changes in religious practice, e.g.,
the adoption of Christian burials rather than the aboriginal practice of
cremation. The Indians always believed in souls and afterlife, but the
mission taught them of punishment and reward after death.

In 1835 while attending school in Rome, a Christian Indian named
Pablo Tac produced a document, "Conversión de los San Luiseños de
Alta California," that throws further light on the process of conversion
and the missionary regime at San Luis Rey. Tac was born to Luiseño
parents in 1822, and when Father Antonio Peyri quit California in 1832,
the priest took Tac and another boy with him, first to Mexico City and
then to Spain. Eventually the boys entered the Urban College in Rome
in 1834. The other youth died in 1837, and Tac died of smallpox in 1841,
but not before he had produced (under the supervision of a clerical
linguist) what was probably the earliest literary work by a California
Indian. While preparing his manuscript, the teenage boy was planning
to devote his life to Christian missionary work.

He says of his people's lives before the coming of Peyri, that it was
"very miserable, because there was always strife. The god who was
adored at that time was the sun and the fire. Thus we lived among the
woods until merciful God freed us of these miseries" (Tac 1958: 12)
through the agency of Father Peyri and Spanish soldiers in 1798. "O
merciful God, why didst Thou leave us for many centuries, years,
months and days in utter darkness after Thou camest to the world?
Blessed be Thou from this day through future centuries" (ibid., 13).
Tac told how Peyri, with the support of a local Indian captain, got the
Indians to make a clearing in the woods and to bring stones from the
sea to construct a foundation for the mission church. They made
bricks and roof tiles; they cut beams and reeds. Within a few years
the church was completed. In the meantime Peyri was baptizing some
of the five thousand Indians in the area.

The mission possessed three altars, two chapels, two sacristies, two
choirs, a flower garden, a high tower with five bells, (two small and
three large), and a cemetery with a crucifix in the middle for the neophytes who died at the mission. Before long the population dropped

from five thousand to three thousand due to diseases. Around the church there was a mason's house and a storehouse for wine—used for mass and to sell to English travelers trading cloth from Boston; the wine was "not for the neophytes, which is prohibited them because they easily get drunk" (15). The mission contained rooms for travelers, a refectory, a space for the missionary's servant, houses for the mayordomos of the mission, a large room for the neophyte boys, a soap house, a room for the girls, a corral for stock, a mill, an enclosure for lambs, a shepherd's house, granaries, an infirmary, a stable, kitchens, barracks, a bakery, storehouses, a garden, looms, an oil shop, blacksmith's shop, shoemaker's shop, carpenter's shop, presses, a room for skins of animals to be sold. A sunken garden held pears, apples, peaches, quinces, pomegranates, watermelons, other melons, vegetables, cabbages, lettuces, radishes, mints, and parsley. None but the gardeners was permitted in the garden, although some snuck in for fruits.

The father appointed alcaldes from the people—those who spoke better Spanish "and were better than the others in their customs" (19). These carried rods as symbols of their power of judgment, and they reported each day to the missionary and, after receiving orders from him, made announcements to the people. In addition to the main mission there were several other stations, including San Antonio de Pala. At each site the mission required work, with a Spanish mayordomo in charge "to punish the guilty or lazy one who leaves his plow and quits the field keeping on with his laziness" (20). They ate their meals regularly but worked the whole day, either in the fields or shops, producing numerous goods: "butter, tallow, hides, chamois leather, bear skins, [red] wine, white wine, brandy, oil, maize, wheat, beans and also bull horns which the English take by the thousands to Boston" (21). As for authority:

> In the Mission of San Luis Rey de Francia the Fernandino Father is like a king. He has his pages, alcaldes, majordomos, musicians, soldiers, gardens, ranchos, livestock, horses by the thousand, cows, bulls by the thousand, oxen, mules, asses, 12,000 lambs, 200 goats, etc. (20)

Ten soldiers made their rounds on horseback, reinforcing the authority of the priest and mayordomos. In this way the missions christianized the Indians systematically by degrees, even though aspects of traditional religiousness persisted to the close of the mission period.

INDIAN REJIJTANCE

As a counterpoint to the gradual christianization of the Indians, revolts took place from time to time at many of the California missions, all of them ultimately unsuccessful. From the start neophyte resistance was chronic and frequently violent.

In 1785 under the leadership of a Christian Indian, Nicolas José, and inspired by a sorceress named Toypurina, an organized band of warriors attempted to destroy San Gabriel Mission. The warriors entered the grounds at night, expecting to find the two padres dead of Toypurina's bewitchment. The plot failed because a soldier had overheard the plans, and the Spaniards dressed two soldiers in monks' garb, and laid them out as if dead. When the Indians cautiously approached, the soldiers leaped forward and arrested many of them. A governor's inquiry found that the Indians resented the presence of the mission on their land. In particular, they hated that their pagan rites were not permitted.

Toypurina's testimony proved compelling: she was a fiercely nationalist young woman—twenty-four at the time—who wanted the detested foreigners dead and gone. Whereas twenty conspirators received lashes, and José was imprisoned for six years (and then banished to a distant mission), Toypurina was immediately "sent into perpetual exile" (Engelhardt 1927: 61) with the hope of Governor Pedro Fages that she would become a Christian in due time. Two years later she accepted baptism, taking the Christian name of Regina Josefa Toypurina, and at San Carlos Borromeo she married a soldier in the royal presidio in 1789 with Governor Fages serving as witness. Her children received baptism, and she died with sacraments at Mission San Juan Bautista in 1799. An enterprising scholar (Temple 1991) has tracked down her story and her numerous present-day descendants.

Less dramatic demonstrations of neophytes' dissatisfaction with the mission regimen included refusals to work, petty crime, and complaints. In some missions, personal revolts on the part of women included the aborting of pregnancies. Hugo Reid wrote that when the priests found out that Indian women at San Gabriel were aborting the results of copulation with Whites, the mission authorities punished Indian women whenever an aborted fetus was discovered: "The penalty inflicted was, shaving the head, flogging for fifteen subsequent days, iron on the feet for three months, and having to appear every Sunday in church, on the steps leading up to the altar, with a hideous painted wooden child in her arms!" (Reid 1991: 149).

Reid's account suggested a pattern of cruelty on the part of at least one padre at San Gabriel who shackled together married neophyte couples who fought publicly: "they were fastened together by the leg, until they agreed to live again in harmony." This priest, said Reid, "must assuredly have considered whipping as meat and drink to them, for they had it morning, noon and night" (ibid., 150). As a result, Indians attempted to run away from the mission:

> Indians of course deserted. Who would not have deserted? Still, those who did had hard times of it. If they proceeded to other missions, they were picked up immediately, flogged and put in irons until an opportunity presented of returning them to undergo other flagelations. If they stowed themselves away in any of the rancherias, the soldiers were monthly in the habit of visiting them; and such was the punishment inflicted on those who attempted to conceal them, that it rarely was essayed. (142)

Hence, runaways—*hindras*, they were called—took to the mountains, sometimes returning to their traditional villages, sometimes traveling to the east or even to foreign Indian groups like the Miwoks.

Sometimes the priests sent trusted neophytes to round the fugitives up, but on one occasion at least, in 1795, Indians who had escaped Mission San Francisco killed seven search party neophytes. As a result, neophytes were no longer commissioned as truant officers, and it became the custom for soldiers to bring back the hindras. In 1797, when more fugitives made their escape, Governor Borica ordered troops to capture them. Following a battle, the soldiers remanded over eighty Christians and nine gentiles to Mission San José, and most of the fugitives were returned to San Francisco. The soldiers recorded their reasons for running away:

> Tibúrcio claimed he was flogged five times by Fr. Danti for crying at the death of his wife and child. Magin asserted that he was put into the stocks when ill. Claudio said he was beaten by the alcalde with a stick, and forced to work when ill. José Manuel declared that he was struck with a bludgeon. Liberato ran away to escape dying of hunger like his mother, two brothers and three nephews. Otolón charged that he was flogged for not caring for his wife after she had sinned with the cowboy. Milán complained that he had to work with no food for his family,

and was flogged because he went after clams. Potabo's excuse was that he had lost his family and had no one to take care of him. Orencio's alleged reason was that his niece had died of hunger. Toríbio confessed that he was always hungry. Magno stated that he had departed for not receiving any rations because when he was occupied in tending to his sick son, he could not work. . . . Tarazón . . . maintained that he had visited the country and had felt inclined to stay. (Engelhardt 1912: 507)

The missionaries said that neophytes ran away because of their "ungovernable passion. . . . Those at this mission cannot entirely gratify their lust, because of the vigilance of the missionaries. Hence they run away in order to give full sway to their carnal desires" (in ibid., 508). Presidente Lasuen blamed the fugitivism on deaths at the mission in 1795–1796. Nevertheless, one of the Franciscans, José Maria Fernandez, told the Governor that the two friars at San Francisco worked the Indians too hard, supplied them with too little food, and treated them with physical cruelty. At the same time, Padre Antonio de la Concepcion Horra of Mission San Miguel reported to the viceroy in Mexico that the Franciscans of California were flogging the neophytes, shackling them, and generally mistreating them. Both friars were quickly deported from Alta California and declared insane, although both of them lived on in Spain, Fernandez, at least, "in good health" (Geiger 1969: 85).

As a result of these charges, Governor Borica demanded an investigation of the mission system, and in 1800 Presidente Lasuen issued a lengthy defense that included a general depiction of the mission routine at the turn of the century. Lasuen described the catechetical lessons, morning and afternoon, in Indian and Spanish languages. He insisted that sufficient instruction preceded baptism—there were twenty-seven thousand baptisms to that point in all of Alta California—and except those who were baptized at the verge of death, all neophytes lived at the missions and received leaves of absence each year to visit friends and relatives. Lasuen claimed that Indians were provided three warm meals a day, in generous quantities, and were never punished by withholding food from them. When they ran away, he stated, it was because they were enslaved to their old customs, their old haunts, their old foods and associations. The work of the mission, he wrote, was regular but not too taxing, neither in the fields nor shops, and the products of their labor brought no profits to the friars themselves. The padres gave the Indians ample time for games and other amusements. On holidays the neophytes were given free time to serve as cooks, washers, and water carriers to the white soldiers, and in general were not prohibited from intercourse with the military. The priests tried to keep them away from the presidio but to little avail, and there they earned money, learned to play cards, engaged in sexual activity, and on occasion wedded the soldiers—there had been twenty-four such legal marriages since 1769. According to Lasuen, only when Indians overstayed their leaves did "they receive a few blows with the lash" (in Engelhardt 1912: 568).

Lasuen explained the system of punishments at the missions: the shackles, the lashes, the stocks. He said the padres always warned and chastised before applying the more severe measures:

> The stocks in the apartment of the girls and single women are older than the Fathers who report on the mission. As a rule, the transgressions of the women are punished with one, two or three days in the stocks, according to the gravity of the offense; but if they are obstinate in their evil intercourse, or run away, they are chastised by the hand of another woman in the apartment of the women. Sometimes, though exceedingly seldom, the shackles are put on. Such are the chastisements which we inflict on the Indians in keeping with the judgment with which parents punish their own beloved children. We have begotten the neophytes for Christianity by means of our labors for them, and by means of Baptism in which they received the life of grace. We rear them by means of the Sacraments and by means of the instruction in the maxims of Christian morals. We therefore use the authority which Almighty God concedes to parents for the education of their children. . . . The Indians feel that they are never chastised without being well convinced of their guilt. . . . Hence it is that the neophytes accept with humility the chastisement and afterwards they remain as affectionate towards the Father as before. (In ibid., 573–574)

Some civil authorities recommended that the pastors should baptize Indians but permit them to live in their own villages, according to their own authority. In 1802 Lasuen argued against such an idea:

> There is no doubt that in all pagan rancherias heathen practices prevail. Who will remove the opposition which the Christians encounter, if they continue to live among their tribesmen at the very scene of those heathen customs? and who will prevent them at the same time from joining their tribesmen or even witnessing the orgies? Accustomed to their abominable feasts, and every hour finding their recollections revived, what place will they give to the catechism, and to the obligations contracted in Baptism which they have received? They possess no en-

ergy to apply themselves to what is conducive to a rational, social, and
civilized life. . . . the king wants the Indians to be brought . . . to the
Christian way. How will this royal and Catholic intention be carried
out if the Indians are left to their wild freedom and in their rancherias
after they have been baptized? (In ibid., 586–587)

Over the next decade the Franciscans brought large numbers of gentiles into the mission and continued to chase after runaways, sometimes with violent results. In 1805, for instance, a friar left Mission San
José to lure back some hindras in a gentile rancheria five miles away. A
battle ensued, and a punitive expedition to the rancheria ended in several deaths before the fugitives returned to the mission. The new presidente, Fray Estevan Tapis, asked Governor José Joaquin de Arrillaga
to increase the military presence in the missions in order to quell fugitivism. With so many neophytes at each mission, and with so many
visits from gentiles (interested either in instruction or in raiding), the
Indians now knew how little military power existed at each establishment. In their turn, however, the soldiers increased Indian dissatisfaction because of their violence.

Against persistent charges that the friars were coercing conversions,
Fray Estavan Tapis wrote to the governor in 1805:

I have observed that the pagans who are reduced . . . gladly embrace
baptism and with free choice. During the time they are being catechized which can be called a period of probation, they become ac-
quainted with the maxims, laws and precepts of religion. They see the
physical labors done by the neophytes and witness as well the punishments administered to delinquents when mildness does not serve to
correct them. In a word, from the time of their instruction they know
what they will have to do and practice once they become Christians.
With a knowledge of all this they ask for baptism when they can with
full liberty return to their villages and remain in their pagan state. (In
Guest 1979: 4–5)

At the same time, "Considerable anxiety was felt in Mexico as well
as in California on account of the great mortality among the neophytes
as reported annually by the missionaries" (Engelhardt 1912: 608). In
1804–1805 a Doctor José Benites surveyed the situation, finding the
causes of death to be dysentery, fevers, pleurisy, pneumonia, venereal
diseases, and scrofula. He said that moist climate—most of the missions were along the coast—continuous fogs, bad water, overcrowd-
ing, the wearing of wet wool, as well as "the unreasonable use of the

temescal or sweat-house from which perspiring freely they jump into
cold water," were exacerbating their ill health. Neophytes in a rancheria told the doctor that "the missionaries wanted to kill them" (in
Engelhardt 1912: 609).

At some missions it was the neophytes who tried to kill the friars.
In 1801 Indians reportedly poisoned priests at Missions San Miguel
and San Antonio de Padua. In the same year, when an epidemic destroyed many Indians, a neophyte woman at Santa Barbara exhorted
her fellows to murder the padres at the orders, she alleged, of a deity
who warned gentiles against baptism and insisted that neophytes
renounce Christianity and resume their pagan offerings. Sometimes
the violence against the priests occurred in heated response to chastise-
ments, e.g., at San Diego in 1804, where a neophyte, upon being discovered in a crime, hit the priest with a stone. At other times the
neophytes plotted the deaths of the padres with elaborate plans. In 1811
the San Diego mission cook, Nazario, poisoned the soup of Fray José
Pedro Panto because the priest had given him 200 lashes the previous
day. The poison was not fatal, but the following year he succumbed to
another attempt and died. In that same year, 1812, at Santa Cruz a
group of conspirators murdered Fray Andres Quintana "in a most
revolting and diabolical manner" (Engelhardt 1913: 12) and escaped
discovery for two years.

In 1877—well after the actual events—Lorenzo Asisara, a Costanoan
Indian born in 1820, drew upon family traditions to describe the murder of Quintana after the cleric allegedly flogged one of the men with a
wire whip. A woman aided the conspirators by calling the priest to her
home several times to minister to her husband, feigning a mortal illness. Each time the conspirators were frightened of the padre and
could not bear to seize him. Finally, at her insistence, they grabbed
him, cut off one testicle, and then crushed the other when he revived,
thus murdering him. The military autopsy stated that he died a natural
death, but when the plot was finally discovered, five of them received
sentences of several hundred lashes and work in chains from two to ten
years at the distant San Diego Mission; two died in prison before sentencing. The neophyte Asisara justified the murder by saying, "The
Spanish Padres were very cruel toward the Indians. They abused them
very much, they had bad food, bad clothing, and they made them
work like slaves. I also was subjected to that cruel life. The Padres did
not practice what they preached in the pulpit" (in Castillo 1991: 10; see

Asisara 1892). Nevertheless, the governor at the time found no evidence of the priest's cruelty; to the contrary, he reported that "this good Father went to excess, not in punishing his Indians but in the love with which he ever regarded them" (in Engelhardt 1913: 14). The governor found that in general the friars used lashes of two ropes to whip fornicators and thieves, but applying them in a manner "more adapted to children of six years than to men, most of whom receive it without an exclamation of pain" (in ibid., 14).

The era around the turn of the nineteenth century has sometimes been referred to as the "Golden Age" of the Franciscan missions of Upper California. Nevertheless, the period witnessed its share of strife and discontent at most of the missions. In later decades, as the missions declined amidst political turmoil, full-scale revolts took place—the most famous among the Chumash at Santa Barbara, La Purisima, and Santa Ynez in 1824—but even in the "Golden Age" neophyte resistance was not uncommon.

Although the California missions may have appeared relatively isolated from events and conditions throughout the rest of New Spain and in Europe, when Napoleon invaded Spain in 1808 he set into play a series of circumstances that served to destroy the missions within a generation. In 1810 the twenty-one missions and several asistencias housed nineteen thousand neophytes under the rule of forty fathers; the establishments had reached their "height of spiritual success and temporal prosperity" (Engelhardt 1912: 648). In the chaos that followed the Napoleonic invasion, revolutionary movements began in the New World and continued for over a decade. These forces did not affect California directly, in the sense that there was no fighting there as there was in Mexico. On the other hand, California ceased to receive its steady supplies from the capital and from Spain. The presidios were forced to supply themselves, as the missions had already done, and by 1814 the soldiers were demanding that the missions provide for the support of the soldiers—whose presidios were meant as protection, in part, for the padres and their neophytes. In theory the presidios were to pay back the missions for their support, but by 1820 the presidios owed the missions more than they could ever reimburse.

The practical result of this situation was that the neophytes were required to perform their labor not only for the benefit of the missions but also for the presidios. At San Luis Obispo, e.g., the neophytes worked in order that the soldiers at Monterey should have supplies.

The missionary there wrote: "The Indians go barefooted in order that they may provide shoes for the troops and their families. They eat their food without butter in order that the troops may have it" (in Geary 1934: 58). The soldiers and civil authorities perceived the missions as wealthy, overstocked enterprises holding all the arable lands, hence well able to afford the supplies. In addition the missions could afford to have the Indians work directly at the presidios as servants. Finally, missions made "forced contributions in cash" (Engelhardt 1921: 46) to the soldiery.

Perhaps the coerced support for the military contributed to the Chumash uprisings in 1824. One of the immediate causes of the revolts was the flogging of a neophyte at Santa Ynez, ordered by a corporal at the mission. In revenge the Indians attacked the soldiers, and the revolt then spread to two other missions, Santa Barbara and La Purisima, before troops quelled the riot and executed its leaders. Still, there were other factors. Governor Argüello attributed the rebellion to an attempt to "free the country from the power of whites and to reintroduce pagan liberty" (in Engelhardt 1913: 194). More recent scholars have pointed to the missions' "struggle with Chumash culture" (Sandos 1991: 305) as the underlying cause, pointing out that the neophytes revolted at the point at which they were required to confess their sins in the performance of their Easter duty.

Maria Solares, an Indian, describing (in the early twentieth century) the events that took place before her birth (Blackburn 1991), claimed that a sacristan discovered the Santa Ynez neophytes engaging in drug-induced initiations; he informed the priest that the Indians planned to shoot him, and the padre called in soldiers. Some of the Chumash religious leaders asserted that the soldiers' weapons would not harm those wearing certain amulets—a claim quickly proven untrue, particularly at the major battle at Santa Barbara. At Santa Ynez, "The priest prayed while the soldiers shot" (ibid., 60). Although the Indians took some care not to disturb Christian paraphernalia—e.g., the wines and cruets used for mass—many fled the missions and tried to return to their traditional culture, including sexual practices and gambling, and they ceased to pray as Christians, having run as far as the Miwok region. When soldiers rounded them up, the leaders received the sacraments of penance and Holy Eucharist before their execution. The padres tried to reincorporate the escapees as quickly as they could into the mission routine—after all, their labor was needed to keep the Californians alive—and in the years that followed, Christian culture seemed truly to take hold among the Chumash. Many years after the breakup of the mission the Indians formerly of Santa Ynez gathered piously for Holy Week services (Sando 1991: 316–321). Maria Solares and the other Chumash interviewed by ethnographers in the early twentieth century could still recite their prayers—the Lord's Prayer, Nicene Creed, Hail Mary—as well as the Ten Commandments and the Short Catechism learned as children at the mission many decades earlier.

Nevertheless, many California Indians learned those ritual forms under some duress, if one takes at face value the descriptions of the missions made during the early nineteenth century by English, American, Russian, and French visitors to the territory. A French shipman visiting San Carlos Mission in 1786 compared that establishment to slave plantations in the Caribbean, only in California the routine of labor was undergirded by religious discipline:

> Corporal punishments are inflicted on the Indians of both sexes who neglect their pious exercises, and many faults which in Europe are wholly left to divine justice, are here punished with irons or the log. In short, to complete the parallel with the religious communities, from the moment a neophyte is baptized, he seems to have taken an eternal vow. If he runs away and returns to his relations among the independent villages, he is summoned three times, and should he still refuse to come back, they apply to the authority of the governor, who sends a party of soldiers to tear him from the bosom of his family, and deliver him to the missions, where he is condemned to a certain number of lashes. (Perouse 1892: 55)

Hence, Perouse wrote, the Indians were "so destitute of courage" (ibid., 55) that they submitted to a handful of soldiers and a couple of priests who treated them like children.

One firsthand account of Mission San Francisco in 1816 portrayed the neophytes at a service as cowed and confused participants listening to a sermon in Latin. Captain F. W. Beechey observed the same mission in 1826, suggesting not only a superficiality of conversion but also coercion in the reception of the sacraments. He said that soldiers with fixed bayonets and bailiffs with whips, canes, and goads loomed over the neophytes in prayer. He also told of military expeditions to bring back refugees and alleged that these expeditions sought to gain additional gentiles for conversion (see Costello 1991: 237–269). Alfred

Robinson visited Mission San Luis Rey in 1829 and had this to say of religious services:

> Mass is offered daily and the greater portion of the Indians attend; but it is not unusual to see numbers of them driven along by alcaldes, and under the whip's lash forced to the very doors of the sanctuary. . . . The condition of these Indians is miserable indeed; and it is not to be wondered at that many attempt to escape from the severity of the religious discipline at the Mission. They are pursued, and generally taken; then they are flogged, and an iron clog is fastened to their legs, serving as additional punishment, and a warning to others. (Robinson 1846: 25–26)

As neophytes became more deeply christianized in the nineteenth century, there also occurred a deepening resistance and a coercive edge to the mission administration under political and economic duress.

SECULARIZATION

In 1810, amidst the political upheaval in Europe, a group of Spanish men established themselves as the Cortés of Spain and claimed to be the country's governing body. One of the laws they passed in 1813 stated that all missions in New Spain had to be secularized after ten years of activity. This law was not promulgated in Mexico until 1820, and news of it did not reach California until 1821. At that point in theory the Franciscans should have turned over nineteen of their missions immediately to the neophytes, since the clerics were "merely the legal guardians of their convert Indians and, without compensation, they managed the property accumulated by the thrift of the Indians for the benefit of the whole community" (Engelhardt 1921: 46). The Franciscans offered to do so, but the California authorities were not certain that the secularization law was binding, at least yet. The Cortés, thus, did not effect immediately its anticlerical goal of secularizing the missions, but when Mexico declared its independence in 1821, the combined motives for secularization—anticlericalism, diocesan solidification, liberalism, and above all, greed for mission land and properties—undermined the mission system. After Mexico proclaimed its independence, California's governor Pablo Vicente de Sola attempted immediately to take over the authority of the missions, as demanded by the 1813 Cortés, seeking to gain what he considered to be the unlimited wealth of the missions. Sola required that Indians pay taxes, so by the end of 1821 the missions were paying not only a large portion of their proceeds to the state but also the individual taxes of the neophytes.

In 1825 the Mexican constitution demanded that the Franciscans in California take an oath of allegiance to the new government. Most of the padres were Spanish and not sympathetic to the liberal Mexican revolution; therefore, they declined to make the oath and became, in effect, estranged from the California government of José Maria Echeandia. Although the governor declined to move against the priests (he found them indispensable to his economic livelihood), even when a law was passed to expel all the priests, tensions increased between Church and State throughout California in the 1820s, and by the end of the decade some of the padres were fleeing in the face of imminent banishment. In 1826 Echeandia initiated a circular emancipating "from mission tutelage" (Engelhardt 1921: 73) all the Indians who could become Mexican citizens in the military districts of San Diego, Santa Barbara, and Monterey. In 1828 this plan included the district of San Francisco.

For some neophytes the emancipation began smoothly. For instance, the priests at San Diego told of one Christian Indian:

> Citizen Gil, native of Mission San Diego and carpenter by trade, desires to separate himself from said Mission where he is now, in order to go where he can exercise his trade with adequate profit. In complying with the petition presented by Gil Riela on April 4, 1826, we have to say that he is a Christian from his infancy, having been born at the Mission of parents who are Christians of long standing, that he is of regular conduct, married to Pia who was baptized at Mission San Luis Rey. He is 29 years of age and has three children. His trade is that of carpenter by means of which he maintains himself in some comfort. Therefore, he has our leave to separate himself from the Mission. (In Engelhardt 1920: 213)

It was up to the padres to emancipate those Indians they thought capable of independent life. Concurrently, however, a drunk San Luis Rey Indian in Los Angeles publicly berated all authority, predicting an immediate emancipation of all Indians from the missions. In 1827 the neophytes at San Luis Rey and San Juan Capistrano refused to work in the fields, expressing the revolutionary rhetoric of Mexican independence, and military supervision had to be increased. The immediate effect, therefore, of the 1826 circular was the "demoralization and degradation of the neophytes but it also ended in many cases their contentment with mission life" (Geary 1934: 99). By 1829 missions such as San Diego were impoverished, and their very existence threatened.

In 1830 Governor Echeandia proposed the confiscation of all mission property, a final solution to the question of secularization. In the rapid changes of government in California over the next several years, his decree was debated and forestalled; however, numerous forces existed to destroy the missions. California officials, colonists, and soldiers wanted the mission land and properties. Mexican liberalism wanted the neophytes emancipated.

At this time 1,455 neophytes still lived at Mission San Diego, the result of 6,522 baptisms at the mission since 1769, and the mission held 4,500 head of cattle, 13,250 sheep, 150 goats, 220 horses, and eighty mules. A little secularized pueblo, San Dieguito, was organized in 1835 for emancipated neophytes, housing 113 Indians from the mission. At San Luis Rey there were 2,819 neophytes, along with 26,000 head of cattle, 25,500 sheep, 1,200 goats, 2,150 horses, and 250 mules. In over three decades Father Peyri had performed 5,298 baptisms before he left for Spain in 1832. His administrative successor, Fray Vicente Pasqual Oliva of Mission San Diego, became "melancholy and almost crazed on account of the evils and disorders" (in Engelhardt 1921: 89) in the missions, according to Presidente Narciso Duran in a letter to Governor José Figueroa in 1833. The governor had forbidden corporal punishment at the missions, and Duran called for "regular correction with the rod" in order to end the Indians' "insubordination." The problem at the missions, he said, consisted in the "lack of adequate punishment" (in ibid., 89).

In the same year he wrote another letter to the governor, noting the "threatening" attitude of the Indians at San Luis Rey and San Diego (in ibid., 90). The soldiers were taking concubines from among the Christian Indians, and there was constant gambling and drunkenness in the disorder that prevailed at these establishments in the early 1830s. According to Indians, not only neophytes and soldiers engaged in debauchery—at Mission San Buenaventura the girls used to throw cloth over the walls for the Indian men and soldiers to climb into the nunnery to have sex with them—but at least one priest gained a notorious reputation for womanizing. Fray Blas Ordaz was said to have fathered several children during the 1830s, including a Vicente Ordaz, whom Fray Blas himself baptized at Santa Ynez. Rumors had it that Blas would enter the nunnery at night, order the girls to sing, and then have sex with one or another while the chanting drowned out any amorous noise. One Indian said, although not from firsthand knowledge, "The Priest's will was law. Indians would lie right down if the priest said so" (Librado 1991: 33).

The Mexican National Congress passed a secularization bill in 1833, and in 1834 the California legislature issued the *Reglamento Provisional*, a law that transformed the missions into parishes and pueblos. The edict emancipated those who had been Christians for twelve years or longer, were married, and knew how to farm or operate a trade. The authorities at each mission were to choose the neophytes to be freed, but these Indians were to remain subordinate to the padres, who would continue as parish priests with spiritual powers. The emancipated were to receive seed for the first year; they were also to assist the mission planting. Local commissioners and missionaries would decide where to place a pueblo of such Indians, and each family was to receive its plot. The emancipated Indians became Mexican citizens, subject to municipal and military rule. If they refused to work they could be declared vagabonds and returned to the mission. The territorial government was to take over the administration of the mission temporalities. Lands would be distributed to heads of families, as would be shares of livestock, implements, and the like. The Franciscans were permitted to live in sections of the missions as they chose, and according to the law "the emancipated Indians will be obliged to take part in the indispensable community work. . . . The emancipated Indians will render to the missionary Father the personal service necessary" (in Engelhardt 1913: 526).

Neither the governor nor the Franciscans regarded the Indians ready for complete freedom as citizens, doubting the neophytes' ability to defend themselves or their property. From the north Fray Garcia Diego wrote that,

> none can be secularized. . . . The neophytes must be treated with kindness and vigilance as though they were children. The missionary must care for their clothing, their health, food; he must instruct them, put them to work, in short be everything to them. . . . If entirely independent of the missions, who will induce them to attend Christian instruction, keep away from sinful diversions, accept corrections? I am sure that the missionaries would have to content themselves with celebrating holy Mass, and hearing the confessions of the few who might call. Even now they attend holy Mass but reluctantly. (In ibid., 487)

Fray Duran wrote that at the older missions an experimental and limited secularization scheme might work; however, it would be difficult to get the Indians to work diligently on their own. Among the Indians, he said, there is "no love of work; for this is against their naturally wild disposition and habits, which they inherited from their pagan state" (in ibid., 491). Governor Figueroa wrote to the president of Mexico in 1833, explaining why secularization was doomed from the start:

> I myself have personally ordered more than sixty families at Mission San Diego and more than one hundred at Mission San Luis Rey to be registered with a view to emancipate them from the control of the missionaries, and to found separate pueblos. I allotted land to them with water from the mission supply itself, also live-stock and everything nec-

essary for establishing themselves. I collected them and accompanied them to their new habitations. I explained to them the advantages they were about to acquire and the liberty they were to enjoy; yet I had the grief to hear them refuse everything for the sake of remaining in the servitude in which they had lived, and no arguments were powerful enough to convince them. The result is that of them all only ten families from San Diego Mission and four from San Luis Rey remained emancipated. (In ibid., 497–498)

Nevertheless by the end of 1835 the California missions were secularized. Lands and properties that were supposed to go to the emancipated neophytes were looted and taken. More than fifteen thousand mission Indians (perhaps as many as thirty thousand) were cut loose for exploitation. They were put to work, taken from their religious devotions. Women were raped. The freed Indians refused to work, and many of them escaped the immediate areas of their former missions. The next decade witnessed the "real plunder and destruction of the mission system" (Geary 1934: 169), in a period of revolutionary chaos.

The men who had called for secularization and confiscation of mission properties became the commissioners in charge of the process. Pio Pico and Pablo de la Portilla took over Mission San Luis Rey and Pala. Juan Bandini became manager of Mission San Gabriel. José Joachim Ortega was named administrator over San Diego and Santa Ysabel. Their captains could not get the Indians to work for them. At San Luis Rey the former mission Indians shouted: "We are free! We do not want to obey! We do not want to work" (in Engelhardt 1921: 96), neither for the missionaries nor for their new masters, the secular administrators and the soldiery. Some Indians fled with horses and cattle, and Pico had to send his soldiers out to retake fugitive neophytes so that he could have workers for his new estate, the former Mission San Luis Rey. Some priests tried to protect their former wards from exploitation; for instance Father Oliva in 1839 argued that Asistencia Santa Ysabel should be regarded still as a mission with its church, cemetery, cultivated fields of corn, wheat, barley, beans, horse-beans, peas, vineyards, orchards, and more. The California solicitor attempted to confiscate Santa Ysabel lands, claiming they were uncultivated, and Ortega succeeded in plundering the asistencia.

In 1834–1835 the novice seaman R. H. Dana observed the missions in California. He heard that over the decades the neophytes had been "serfs, in tending their vast herds." But in recent years,

Ever since the independence of Mexico, the missions had been going down; until, at last, a law was passed, stripping them of all their possessions, and confining the priests to their spiritual duties, at the same time declaring all the Indians free and independent *Rancheros*. The change in the condition of the Indians was, as may be supposed, only nominal; they are virtually serfs, as much as they ever were. But in the missions the change was complete. The priests have now no power, except in their religious character, and the great possessions of the missions are given over to be preyed upon by the harpies of the civil power, who are sent there in the capacity of *administratores*, to settle up the concerns; and who usually end, in a few years, by making themselves fortunes, and leaving their stewardships worse than they found them. (Dana 1976: 141)

A Luiseño Indian recalled the years of Pio Pico's administration at San Luis Rey as an era of utmost cruelty: "They did not pay us anything but merely gave us our food and a breech cloth and blanket, the last renewed every year, besides flogging for any fault, however slight. We were at the mercy of the administrator, who ordered us to be flogged whenever and however he took a notion." In contrast, he remembered the priest from those days as "sympathetic and considerate toward the Indians; in fact, he was very loving and good" (in Cesar 1991: 13). Of Father José Maria Zalvidea, the last minister at San Luis Rey after secularization, who died in 1846, he said, "He was a very good man, but was already very ill, and had mental disorders. He struggled constantly with the devil, whom he accused of threatening him. In order to overcome the devil he constantly flogged himself, wore hair-cloth, drove nails into his feet, and, in short, tormented himself in the cruelest manner" (ibid., 14). Only several hundred neophytes remained at San Luis Rey and Pala, and when Zalvidea died, both missions collapsed.

During the 1830s some mission Indians fled to the east, to the hills, and to other lands distant from Mexican control; others to pueblos and cities such as Los Angeles. Scarcely five thousand Indians were identifiable as former neophytes by 1840 (out of eighty-one thousand baptisms performed between 1769 and 1831), and an 1844 report indicated that the neophytes were "scattered for want of ministers." The report found the neophytes "demoralized, . . . in a state of moral impossibility of ever raising their heads" (in Webb 1982: 296). No laws forced the Indians to abandon the collapsing missions; however, hostile circumstances made them leave, despite the supposed promise of the mission land and properties. The Spanish Crown had held title to the general areas controlled by the California missions. The Catholic Church owned only the buildings, cemeteries, orchards, and vine-yards. The Spanish Crown passed its ownership to the Mexicans, but the Church attempted to maintain its ownership of the central build-ings. The Indians who were presumed to inherit the mission lands they had cultivated for several decades received virtually none of it.

Those who migrated to towns such as Los Angeles—in 1844 there were six hundred and fifty ex-neophytes from the southern missions living there among several thousand gente de razon—performed man-ual labor and were often reduced to drunkenness and impoverishment. R. H. Dana found the ex-neophytes who remained about the missions devoid of money and morality: "I have frequently known an Indian to bring his wife, to whom he was lawfully married in the church, down to the beach, and carry her back again, dividing with her the money which he got from the sailors" (Dana 1976: 144). By 1838 there were Indians from San Luis Rey who petitioned the new governor, Juan B. Alvarado, for a return of the missionaries. Alvarado appointed an Englishman, William Hartnell, to assay the situation, and he reported a regime of floggings, stocks, and chains—a system falling apart as the secular overlords sold away the profits and let conditions deteriorate. The Asistencia Pala was especially bad, he offered, with Indians living in rags. As a result, there was an attempt to dismiss Pio Pico as admin-istrator, but he took even more of the mission properties, including those of its outposts. By 1842 Pala and the other stations were in ruins, and Indian bands were raiding their former holdings for horses and cattle, while the California legislature sold off the former mission properties now plundered. Presidente Duran wrote in 1844:

> Whence are the missions? Who raised them? Who are the legitimate masters and proprietors? Is there an infant in the whole territory that does not know that the Indians, and the Indians alone, are the owners? Is there any one that does not know that if only one family, only one individual of the community survived he is the natural heir, and enters into all the rights of the community? With what justice, then, does the Excellent Assembly proceed in decreeing the sale of the missions? (In Engelhardt 1915: 290)

Despite the creation of the Diocese of California in 1840, with Francis-can Garcia Diego y Moreno as bishop, despite attempts to restore the missions in 1842–43, the missions collapsed as institutions, and the In-dians dispersed or died. Father Duran found in 1844 that San Luis Rey "possesses scarcely anything, and the Indians have all run away and are demoralized" (in ibid., 323). Only four hundred Indians lived there, and only one hundred at Mission San Diego. The Mexicans had already taken over the Indian Pueblo of San Dieguito, less than ten years from its founding.

Seeing the utter destruction of the missions, and hearing the calls of ex-neophytes to restore the Franciscans, the new governor, Manuel Micheltorena, tried to restore the missions to the Franciscans in 1844; however, Pio Pico and others active in the confiscation and sale of the missions drove the governor from the country in 1845 and proceeded to auction off the remaining lands, including those of San Luis Rey and Pala. "Here and there one hears of Indians clinging to pitiful scraps of paper which they claimed gave them title to their lands" (Webb 1982: 300). Nevertheless, the Californios did not allow the validity of Indian claims to land and burned their homes and evicted the former neophytes, and then arrested them for vagrancy and required them to serve as peons for their sentences. Pico's *Reglamento* of 1845 arranged for the sale of all additional mission properties and the complete emancipation of the remaining neophytes:

> The Indians are free from their neophyteship, and may establish themselves in their Missions or wherever they choose. They are not obliged to serve the renters, but they may engage themselves to them, on being paid for their labor, and they will be subject to the authorities and to the local police. (In Engelhardt 1915: 448)

Those Indians who wished to stay in the area of the missions were to appoint "a sacristan, a cook, a tortilla-maker, a vaquero, and two washerwomen for the service of the priest," as well as three boy servants. Musicians and singers were to "lend their services in the churches, at the holy Masses and the functions which may occur" (in ibid., 448–449). So disgusted was Presidente Duran with the disaffection of the Christian Indians that he wrote: "The Indians, in my opinion, do not deserve to be directed by a missionary. A Slavedriver is what they ought to have" (452). He complained of those Indians who ran away from him, naming several of them "whose absence I do not mind, except that they are musicians whom it has cost me twelve years of labor to teach" (452).

After almost one hundred thousand baptisms at twenty-one missions between 1769 and 1846, including 7,125 at San Diego and sixty-five hundred at San Luis Rey—the last baptism at Mission San Diego took place in June 1846, a child seventeen days old, the legitimate son of José de la Luz and his wife Teresa, Indians of the presidio; the child's given name was José Antonio (Engelhardt 1920: 225)—the Franciscan mission system of California came to a close, although some Franciscans continued to minister to Indians through the 1850s.

The end came in the American invasion. Amidst the squabbling of the Mexican administrators and generals, Captain John Charles Fremont arrived in 1845 and set up fortifications. United States citizens staged the Bear Flag Revolt in 1846 in hope of setting up an independent republic like that of Texas, and shortly after, the United States declared war against Mexico. By the following year the United States held firm control of California, including its former mission properties, some of which served as barracks and stables for the troops. Some Indians helped the invading regiments, others supported the Mexicans. Still others avoided the conflict or used the opportunity to stage their own battles. The U.S. troops received orders that "no damage or desecration is offered to the church or any other religious fixture" (in Engelhardt 1915: 594). As soldiers entered San Luis Rey, San Diego, and other missions, they found them deserted, or nearly so. They made note of the fraudulent sales of land made by Pico between 1845 and 1846, and in 1847 Governor Richard B. Mason appointed Captain J. D. Hunter the subagent of Indians with responsibility for the mission Indians. Stationed at San Luis Rey, Hunter encouraged Indians to work their former fields, although he found the mission deserted, and an alcalde at an Indian village a mile away held the keys. The Treaty of Guadalupe-Hidalgo in 1848 ceded Mexican sovereignty of Alta California to the United States, and when gold was discovered in that year, the hordes of Americans entered the territory. As the Anglo invaders arrived, the Indians of California were vitiated; they turned to more drink, thievery, murder, and prostitution. Governor Mason issued a circular in 1849, noting that "the Indians of the southern missions of this Territory, freed from the restraint formerly imposed upon them by the military and ecclesiastical authorities of the country, have contracted habits of indolence and vice, and are now reduced to a state of great destitution and want, trusting mainly to charity and theft for the means of subsistence." He encouraged those in authority to help the remaining missionaries in "inducing them to pursue a more honest and industrious course of conduct" (ibid., 645), although he admitted that it was not workable to give the padres the authority they once had over the neophytes. Invading gold prospectors were not likely to provide charity for the Indians; indeed, when the military rule ended, and California became a state in 1850, a period of indiscriminate killing, dispossession, and enslavement began for California's Indian population.

Under the Treaty of Guadalupe-Hidalgo the citizens of Mexico were supposed to become citizens of the United States with all land titles intact. However exploited the mission Indians were, they were technically Mexican citizens; nevertheless, the United States never came to consider them Americans. California treaty negotiators usurped Indian lands in eighteen illegal treaties in 1851 and 1852, leaving reservations for several Indian groups. When Congress refused to ratify the treaties, the Indians were left in the dark. They considered the lands they had ceded as lost, but they mistakenly viewed their reserved lands as secure. At the same time, in 1850, the State of California passed an Act for the Government and Protection of the Indians, which gave local white jurisdictions the right to determine how much land Indians needed. When in 1851 Congress passed an Act to Ascertain and Settle the Private Land Claims in the State of California, Indians were not called to present their claims, and without presenting them they received no grants. Hence, they were dispossessed, even though they continued to use some lands in the mountains and deserts until U.S. citizens entered those lands and seized them legally by purchasing the "free" land from the United States. As increasing numbers of Americans entered the state, Indian land claims were denied as a matter of course. Lacking lawyers and lacking written deeds to their plots, the Indians were left propertyless, subject to arrest and enslavement. Institutionalized kidnappings of Indian children became commonplace. The worst conditions prevailed in the northern half of California, where the Anglo-Americans "went on a genocidal rampage" (Milliken 1995: 10), but in the southern counties the demoralization of the former mission Indians continued as Indians became a minority in their former lands. In the 1840s and 1850s in San Diego, for instance, the mission Indians were reeling from several generations of forced adjustments: "Progressively and simultaneously, the native was acculturated, converted, dominated, educated, employed and ignored by the influx of Spanish and Mexican settlers. Within four or five decades, those whose ancestors had lived in San Diego for hundreds, probably thousands, of years were relegated to the status of squatters and indigent"

(Carrico 1984: 18), some of them violently opposed to the new order. In January 1852 Cahuilla, Luiseño, and other Indians, regarding the Anglos as "infidels and untrustworthy" (Carrico 1980: 168), staged a revolt led by Antoni Garra, attempting in vain to oust the newcomers from their territories.

The first agent for the Indians of San Diego and Los Angeles Counties, D. B. Wilson, described the mission Indians in 1852. He said that there were seven thousand of them, half the number when the clerics lost control over them eighteen years before. They had been trained in the missions as masons, carpenters, plasterers, and the like; they had taught the incoming Americans how to make adobes; they knew how to irrigate, plant, and harvest. The women married foreigners and Mexican Californians "and made exemplary wives and mothers" (in Engelhardt 1921: 164). Yet they lost their tenure under the Mexican and U.S. rule, and now lived in poverty. "Three years ago they were practically slaves. American freedom does not profit them. They soon fall into the bad way of their Christian (?) neighbors" [sic]. He found them "docile and tractable, and accustomed to subjection" (in ibid., 164–165), but the Whites regarded them as thieves and insurrectionists.

In the same year an American described the Indian village at the former Asistencia Santa Ysabel: "A roofless church and a few miserable huts are now all that remain. Nevertheless the inhabitants cultivate the soil, and by means of irrigation, which they well understood, raise wheat, maize, pumpkins, and beans." Some Diegueño Indians dressed in finery; others were filthy, half-clad, gathering roots and seeds. Most Diegueños "call themselves Christians; but they live in a most degraded state of indolence and poverty" (in Engelhardt 1920: 269–271). At Los Angeles another American delineated the mission Indians, also in 1852:

> They are a miserable, squalid-looking set, squatting or lying about the corners of the streets, without occupation. They have now no means of obtaining a living, as their lands are all taken from them; and the missions for which they labored, and which provided after a sort for many thousands of them, are abolished. No care seems to be taken of them by the Americans; on the contrary, the effort seems to be, to exterminate them as soon as possible. One of the most intelligent of them . . . was unacquainted with the name of the tribe to which he belonged, and only knew that it had been attached to certain missions. (In Engelhardt 1915: 648)

During the 1850s U.S. courts attempted to determine the ownership of the former mission acreage, considering the land sales of 1845–1846 fraudulent. The bishop of California, José Sadoc Alemany, O.P., wrote at the time:

> the old Franciscan Missionaries explain to me that the tracts of mission land were, as they believed, the real property of the Indians, who cultivated the same under their direction and more especially under their alcaldes or chief Indian officers elected by the Indians themselves, and acting under the direction of the Fathers, but that the Churches, Church Edifices, Stores, Cemeteries, Orchards, and Vineyards with the Aqueducts should be considered the property of the Church. (In ibid., 683)

Now that the lands of the mission were lost to the Indians, the Church made a successful effort to regain at least the central structures of the evangelical establishments, certainly petty holdings—e.g., the U.S. Land Commission granted the Catholic Church twenty-two acres of Mission San Diego in 1855—but Indians were less successful in regaining lands. Forty thousand Catholics lived in the State of California (out of a population of one hundred and fifty thousand); only several thousand were Indians. The missionary era had come to a close, and the mission Indians found themselves overwhelmed not only on their lands, but also in the Church.

THE NEOPHYTEƒ' DEƒCENDANTƒ

What happened to the California neophytes and their descendants? Thousands died of diseases, not only during the mission period but in the years following secularization. Smallpox and other epidemics ran repeatedly through the populations of ex-neophytes. Genocide devastated the Indian population throughout the state so that by the turn of the twentieth century there were only sixteen to seventeen thousand Indians, and only a small proportion of those were the direct descendants of the mission Indians. Some mission Indians married Mexicans, and even fewer married Anglos; many of their offspring lost their identity as Indians, although other mestizos continued to live within Indian communities, and through them a general hispanicization of the mission Indians took place. Unlike the northern California Indians, those of the south assimilated somewhat to the larger population:

> The Ibero-Americans have always had a facility for assimilating the native which was not possessed by the Anglo-Americans, and this characteristic made it much easier for the mission Indians to merge with the general population, not only politically and economically, but culturally. Another strongly favorable influence has been the Catholic Church, not because of its propagandizing activities but because it brought the Spanish and Indian components of the population together on a common ground of faith and ritual . . . in a definitely friendly rather than indifferent or hostile atmosphere. . . . The merging of the native into the general population has proceeded farther in coastal southern California than anywhere else in the state and perhaps on the west coast. (Cook 1976: 379)

Hence, some mission Indians—it seems impossible to determine the numbers—bore offspring who ceased to identify themselves as Indians. Some of those surely maintained Catholic loyalty, but others probably left the Church, joining Protestant denominations or sharing in the anticlerical attitudes of their Mexican-American relatives.

Of those Indians who came to be known as "Mission Indians" in the second half of the nineteenth century, some were descendants of the neophytes at San Diego, San Luis Rey, San Juan Capistrano, San Gabriel, etc.; however, others were the offspring of Indians, like the Cahuilla, who had remained aloof during the mission period at the fringe of Franciscan influence, living primarily as gentiles. The Indians away from the Pacific Coast were missionized in the sense that the padres visited them periodically for baptisms and other sacraments, but they did not live, for the most part, in missions as neophytes, like the Indians further west—with the two exceptions of the asistencias at Pala and Santa Ysabel. In the twentieth century, "Most reservation members are the descendants of these relatively uncontrolled, undisturbed people of the more interior mountainous regions plus survivors and refugees from the coastal missions" (Shipek 1987: 24). A historian comments: "It is, indeed, one of those ironies of history that the Mission Indians aligned with the Franciscan coastal missions eventually died out, mostly due to the white man's diseases, while the surviving Indians having the least contact with those missions" (Harley n.d.: 1)—Cahuillas, Serranos, some Luiseños—are known today as "Mission Indians," a term many of the Indians resent.

During President Grant's Peace Policy of the 1870s, the United States granted Episcopalians the administrative control over the Mission Indians, much to the outrage of Catholic Church officials, only a few of whom had made any consistent effort to look after the Christian Indians since the missions had been secularized. In the conflict between Episcopalian and Catholic officials there occurred an "intensifying social and religious disorientation" among the Indians (Castillo 1978: 113); however, their Catholic practices persisted. In 1881 Indian agent S. S. Lawson reported:

> The Mission Indians are as much civilized as the population by which they are surrounded. . . . No active missionary labor is at present conducted among them. The greater portion of them, however, especially the older people, have had, in years past, the benefit of Christian instruction by the Catholic fathers, who conducted the famous missions whose ruins are yet objects of veneration and curiosity. They have orthodox views as to morals, God, and the future life, and it is not unusual to see sacred pictures, the crucifix, and the rosary, adorning the walls of their adobes and lodges. The priest still makes his annual rounds and baptizes the children; but aside from this no missionary work is carried on, their nomadic habits and settlements over an extended mountain and desert rendering little else practicable. (In Engelhardt 1921: 174)

Rev. José Mut was one of three priests who served the southern California Indians between the 1850s and the 1880s from his base at San Juan Capistrano. These priests traveled over extensive territory, instructing, blessing marriages, baptizing, and sanctifying graves. They baptized well over one thousand Indian children during this period.

By the twentieth century, except for the "Mission Indian" reservations in the southern part of the state, the christianized Indians were difficult for outsiders to identify. The anthropologist A. L. Kroeber wrote in 1908: "Back of San Diego and San Luis Rey there are still Indians who preserve memory of the past; but in the remainder of the mission region, from San Juan Capistrano to San Francisco, the Indians are gone, nearly gone, or civilized and Christianized into a state of oblivion of ancient customs and beliefs" (Kroeber 1908: 2). Kroeber was not claiming the descendants of the missionized Indians to be extinct; he was suggesting that their remaining numbers were so thoroughly Catholic that they could tell him nothing of their aboriginal culture. Other white observers had difficulty finding the Christian Indians because they did not live in identifiable communities, outside the south. Pala was a rarity, having several hundred Catholic Indians— Luiseños and Cupeños—and at San Luis Rey and San Diego a few scattered families could be found. Mesa Grande had seventy-five; Santa Ysabel, a hundred; San Manuel, forty. But at San Francisco there were no Catholic Indians, per se; neither at San Gabriel; at San Carlos, San Miguel, San Luis Obispo, Santa Barbara, only a few mestizos; forty-five Indians worshipped at Santa Ynez, fifteen at San Diego, ten at San Luis Rey. Thus one mission historian said: "A few scattered remnants are all that remain" (James 1912: 295). During the same decade visitors discovered that Indians continued to leave offerings for their ancestors in the mission cemeteries: china and glassware, shells, calico, stones, flowers; at one cemetery a broken alarm clock, valued for its metal, hung from a cross. At San Juan Bautista the parish priest told of Old Pablo, one of the local Indians, crying at the grave of his mother who died thirty years earlier. A fire had burned the cross above her grave, and he mourned the desecration. This was in 1912 when Pablo was about eighty years old (Saunders and Chase 1915: 321–323). One often hears that the missionized Indians are all gone; yet the Diocese of Fresno lists around twenty-five hundred Catholic Indians in four parishes, and Sacramento counts 270 at one church (Beaver 1979: 155). There are still Chumash and Costanoan Ohlones, as well as the Luiseños and Diegueños of the south. Santa Ynez houses the remaining Chumash, scattered around Santa Barbara in 1887 when their last mission village was destroyed. At Mission San José the Ohlone Galvan family is still very much in evidence. At the mission one can see a photo of Dolores Marine Galvan, who died in 1982 at an advanced age, granddaughter of Chief Tarino. Her grandson, Father Michael Galvan, serves a nearby parish. On Columbus Day 1992 Andrew Galvan, wearing a headdress, greeted Bishop John Cummins in a quincentenary ritual.

California today has close to two hundred and fifty thousand Native Americans, second only to Oklahoma as the states with the largest Indian populations; however, the vast majority of these Indians come from outside the state—from the Southwest, Midwest, and Plains. There are perhaps as many as two hundred thousand Indians in the Los Angeles area alone, members of as many as one hundred and thirty-five tribes, many of whom came to the area during the U.S. program of Relocation that began in 1952, encouraging reservation Indians around the country to move to urban areas in search of employment. Father Paul Ojibway—himself an Indian—ministers to the Catholic Indians within the Los Angeles Archdiocese. Father Ralph Monteiro conducts an Indian ministry in the northern diocese of Santa Rosa. Yet in four of the five upper California dioceses—Sacramento, San Francisco, San Jose, and Oakland—the Catholic hierarchy's view is that there are "no Indians" extant (Monteiro, November 19, 1992), even though thousands of Indians live in these areas. Nevertheless, if one is to find the most salient descendants of the "mission Indians," one needs to consult the thirty-two different reservations of southern California, from Campo at the Mexican border to Santa Ynez in Santa Barbara County. Almost all of them are in San Diego and Riverside counties, the two southernmost in the state.

Santa Ynez
(SANTA BARBARA COUNTY)

San Manuel   SAN BERNARDINO COUNTY

○ San Bernardino   Twenty-nine Palms

                                    Morongo

                    Banning ○

○ Riverside

        San Jacinto ○   Agua Caliente
                    Soboba   Cabazon

        RIVERSIDE COUNTY   Augustine

                    Ramona

    Temecula   Cahuilla   Santa Rosa   Torres-Martinez
        ○ Pechanga

Fallbrook ○
            Pala   Los Coyotes
                Pauma   ○ Warner Springs
        Rincon
                La Jolla   SAN DIEGO COUNTY
        San Pasqual
    Escondido ○   Mesa Grande   Santa Ysabel

                    Inaja   Cosmit

Southern California Indian   Barona
Reservations, 1990s   Capitan Grande

    ○ Cities and towns
        Reservations   Viejas
                                        Cuyapaipe
                            Sycuan   Manzanita
San Diego   La Posta
                            Jamul
                                    Campo

Mission San Antonio de Pala, erected as an asistencia for San Luis Rey in 1816, has the distinction of being the only remaining Indian mission still used for Indians' religious expression. The Indians there include Luiseños—who live also in neighboring reservation villages at Pauma, Rincon, La Jolla, and Pechanga—and Cupeños, formerly of Cupa to the east but removed to Pala in 1903. Along with the Cahuillas to the north and the Diegueños to the south, they comprise the main of mission Indians still extant in their own reservation communities. The Luiseños, Cupeños, and Cahuillas have often intermarried over the years, and they are closely associated with one another. The family names of many Luiseños demonstrate continuity with the nineteenth-century mission population, according to Florence Shipek (1987: 26–28), and many of them have maintained association with Catholic tradition, despite long periods of relative disassociation from the Catholic clergy and numerous sources of friction to this day.

After 1846 missionary priests came only "sporadically" (Carillo 1959: 11) to the Luiseños, and yet one can say that "Pala Mission has the unique distinction of being the only mission in California which has ministered without interruption since 1816 to the needs of the Indians for whom it was originally built" (ibid.). A generation after the last Franciscan left Pala, the superintendent of Indian affairs for California, Charles Maltby, said of the mission:

> The mission buildings here are in a fair state of preservation. The Indians here have recently repaired their Church, and enlarged their burying grounds by the advice and under the direction of Manuel Cota [an Indian headman], and one of the Priests formerly connected with the Missions, recently visited them, consecrated their burying ground, baptized their children, and married all those who were living together unmarried. Most of those Indians understand and speak the Spanish language, and have great respect for the Priests, who have considerable influence and control over them. (In Weber 1988: 40)

In the same year, 1866, Father Anthony Ubach arrived as resident pastor of San Diego and within a few years established himself as the primary spiritual caretaker for the Catholic Indians of southern Cali-

fornia. He established two schools in San Diego for Indian children—
Our Lady of Peace in 1882 and St. Anthony's Industrial School four
years later; these were superseded in time by St. Boniface Indian
School in Banning and the federal government's Sherman Institute in
Riverside. Ubach was often a champion for Indian rights. In 1873 he
composed a "Report of Conditions among the California Indians" for
the newly formed Bureau of Catholic Indian Missions, in which he
counted over a hundred Catholics at Pala and Pauma, as well as several
hundred Catholic Luiseños at La Jolla and Temecula, and over a thousand among the Diegueños. Ubach found them all poor and powerless, and sometimes desperate. He termed the Cahuillas—as many as
two thousand of them—"bold and brave," the instigators of the "trouble we had up in Pala" (in Weber 1965: 145) in which troops were required to suppress an uprising. Ubach tried to visit all the Christian
Indians every month, and he was impressed by their industriousness as
farmers. They hired themselves out as cattlemen but found themselves
mistreated by the Whites, and when they drank alcohol, they were
readily demoralized. Ubach noted sadly that no reservation, no Indian
agent, protected the Indians against white squatters. The Indians were
better at repelling a Methodist minister than they were at keeping land
grabbers at bay.

In the mid-1870s a newspaperman described Pala during the fiesta
of San Luis Rey. He found the mission buildings in decay, with
tourist-vandals stealing everything of value. At the fiesta the Indians
had all manner of food and goods for sale to their Mexican and Indian
visitors, crowding in from far and near. Indians playing guitars and
violins led quadrilles and other dances. At Pauma the Luiseños made
baskets for sale. A priest was on hand to hear semiannual confessions
and to say mass. The journalist commented on horseracing and story-
telling in a raucous atmosphere: "The *fiesta*, though originally a religious ceremony, has degenerated into a mild revelry" (in Weber 1988:
47). In 1876 a church official accompanying Bishop Francis Mora to
Pala for Indian confirmations found two white squatters in the church
buildings. These men had been there for several years. With the
strength and numbers of the Indians, the churchmen evicted the two
intruders, following a bitter dispute. At the time the Church had no
title to the buildings but claimed a hundred years of mission work as
its right to ownership. The Indians had no titles whatsoever.

At the suggestion of Father Ubach, the federal government in 1875

began to withdraw public lands from sale in order to create reservations for the permanent use and occupancy of the "mission Indians" of
southern California. These included Pala and Santa Ysabel, and in the
following years Rincon, Pechanga, La Jolla, and Pauma. The Indian
Homestead Act of 1875 and the Allotment Act of 1887 encouraged individual Indians to press claims for personal allotments and to separate
from their tribes. Often Indians wanted these allotments because they
thought that these arrangements were the best way to maintain their
lands. These allotments did not lead to losses of land nor the dissolution of tribal government among the Luiseños or other Indians of
southern California. In part because of the writings of Helen Hunt
Jackson, the federal government in 1891 passed the Act for the Relief of
the Mission Indians, which provided for an investigation of Indian
land tenure and increased some Indian holdings. Further executive
orders expanded the reservation lands so that by 1917 twenty-eight
reservations existed in the southern part of California, the majority of
which were inhabited, at least in part, by the descendants of the former
neophytes.

A Mr. William Veal—who operated the Pala store—obtained a land
patent from the United States in 1877 for lands and buildings of the
Pala asistencia. This "irritated" the Luiseños. In 1883 his wife per-
suaded him to give the chapel, cemetery, and two rooms of the mission to "the Church" (Carillo 1959: 11). In the early 1880s some
reservation lands were secured, but other regional Indians were being
pushed further from their holdings, and these losses were validated in
the courts, most prominently in the Warner's Ranch case, which resulted in the eviction of Cupeño Indians in 1903, and their removal to
an expanded Pala reservation where ten Luiseño Indian families still
lived. In the 1880s Helen Hunt Jackson found the California mission
Indians in a "pitiable state" (Jackson 1902: 113), living like gypsies on
the outskirts of white settlements and retreating into the mountains.
Of the Temecula Indians—evicted from their homes by land-hungry
Whites and now living in hovels: "Every face, except those of the very
young, was sad beyond description. They were stamped indelibly by
generations of suffering, immovable distrust also underlying the sorrow" (ibid., 122). From the 1850s to the 1880s, said Jackson, the mission Indians had sometimes been taxed, sometimes treated as citizens
with duties toward the state, sometimes refused the right to vote or
own land because they were not citizens. Executive orders sometimes

protected their lands, but as often as not those orders were ignored or remanded to benefit the Whites. In the winter of 1882 she visited San Pasqual Valley, where Whites had pushed the Indian inhabitants into inaccessible canyons. She wrote: "The Catholic priest of San Diego is much beloved by them. He has been their friend for many years. When he goes to hold service, they gather from their various hiding-places and refuges; sometimes, on a special *fête* day, over two hundred come" (129). When she arrived with a priest, several Indians greeted them, "the ragged poverty-stricken creatures, kneeling on the bare ground" (130). The Indians maintained one of the old bells of the San Diego Mission, dated 1770, swinging on a frame in front of the small chapel. An old, blind Indian recalled his days at the San Diego Mission, where he always had plenty of food. In the midst of that fond remembrance, he and his fellows were now poor and hungry.

In the Pala Valley a priest from San Juan Capistrano visited the faithful Indians occasionally to hold services—probably José Mut—but Jackson found that the "dilapidated little church is not half filled, and the numbers are growing smaller each year" (150). On the day she visited, a memorial service was taking place in the chapel. The Indians draped the altar with black and silver lace and burned candles: "a row of kneeling black-shawled women were holding lighted candles in their hands; two old Indians were chanting a Latin Mass from a tattered missal bound in rawhide" (150). The mass was for an old Indian woman, Margarita, sister of Manuelito, a chief of the Luiseños. The poor Indians paid the priest twelve dollars, and they had put out more funds for the lace and candles. Not far from Pala, Jackson found two Indian villages, Rincon and Pauma, where the Indians maintained fences, irrigated fields of barley, wheat, and hay, where horses, cows, and sheep grazed. She found an ancient Luiseño who recited the old mission prayers. Writing in 1883, Jackson found several old Catholic Indians who remembered their youth in the missions with nostalgic fondness. Their original mission lands had been confiscated during secularization, but they preserved their faith and built their local chapels to receive priestly visitations.

Into the late nineteenth century Cahuillas continued to live in isolation with their captains, their lands, and their villages, in the mountain ranges to the north of the Luiseños. Some were descendants of San Gabriel neophytes; others had never been in the mission system. In the 1880s, when Helen Hunt Jackson saw them, Whites from San Bernardino were threatening Cahuilla lands.

To the south, Diegueños associated with Santa Ysabel persisted in their christianized life, in which they had accomplished an "absorption of Catholicism into their traditional ways" (Sorensen 1985: 8). Tribal leaders who had been prayer chiefs during the mission period now became the religious leaders, burying their dead, for example, in the absence of priests. They led their community in songs and prayers, becoming, as it were, priests in their own right. They blessed and gave sermons and preserved a syncretistic faith into the twentieth century. An observer in 1899 remarked that the general of the tribe at Santa Ysabel was its lay religious leader who recited the services on Sundays. Every Saturday night the Indians rang bells left over from the old asistencia, and the cemetery had old crosses marking the Christian burials of former days. At Mesa Grande, not far distant, "religious worship is the most important feature of the day" (Du Bois 1899: 323), and a priest who had served his flock there for thirty years, preaching in Spanish at services, was a "commanding presence" and a "law giver" (ibid., 323–324).

In 1899 an earthquake at Christmas collapsed sections of the Pala mission. In 1901 Charles F. Lummis, president of the Landmarks Club of Los Angeles, began plans to restore the church. In 1902 he purchased those asistencia buildings not already owned by the Church and began restoration of the whole. He received the labor of Indians, Mexicans, and Whites living near Pala, and even from the Cupeños, who were recently arrived from their eviction from Warner Springs. From this time on the Pala Indians had a resident priest and regular services. In 1901 *The Los Angeles Herald Magazine* stated that, "These Indians (now at Pala) are quiet, unobtrusive, law-abiding, honest, clean, thrifty, holding in respect the marriage tie; their women are chaste. They are religious, following the observance of their Church under many difficulties" (in Engelhardt 1921: 219). In the same year an Episcopalian bishop traveling among the mission Indians of San Diego county had this account:

> The captain took us to the church, for these Indians, poor as they are, and having had no visit from a priest for "many, many years," meet on Sunday for prayers, and a young woman leads the people. The captain reverently entered the church and we after him. The little altar was of

adobe, with tin candlesticks and a few poor outer ornaments. It was all clean and orderly. It occurred to me that few Protestants, isolated as these people have been, with no visit from a minister, under hopeless conditions, would have maintained their religious rites. (In ibid., 221)

In the restoration of 1903 the Palatinquas were furious when the interior of the chapel, painted by an Indian with designs reminiscent of the mission days, received a whitewashing. The Cupeños were especially incensed:

Unfortunately, soon after the Palatinquas came here, the resident priest, whom Bishop Conaty appointed to minister to them, did not understand Indians, their childlike devotion to things hallowed by association with the past, and their desire to be consulted about everything that concerned their interests. Therefore, being suspicious, too, on account of their recent eviction, they were outraged to find the chapel interior freshly whitewashed so that all its ancient decorations were covered. This was another white man's affront which caused irritation and bitterness that it required months to assuage. (James 1916: 43)

Another Indian artist, Antonio Lugo, restored the beloved designs. Later, yet another Indian crafted the altar of stone after termites destroyed the original wood altar. The Luiseños also contributed artistically to their church over the years.

The Cupeños had lived to the northeast of the Luiseños and maintained ties with the Cahuillas, Luiseños, and Dieguenos, as well as with the Catholic missions in the early nineteenth century. In 1844 during secularization, a naturalized Mexican citizen from Connecticut, Jonathan Trumbell Warner, obtained a grant to the hot springs at the center of Cupeño territory. The Indians continued to live on the lands and employ the springs, and when the United States took over California the Indians never made an official claim to the land. They charged admission to tourists who came to use the waters at Warner Springs, as the place came to be known. When Warner died, another White purchased the area and tried to evict the Cupeños, who resisted but lost in court. Congress then appropriated $100,000 in 1902 for the Cupeños to have 3,500 acres added to Pala, where "a few discouraged Indian families . . . still living in the valley close to the Mission" (Carillo 1959: 23) were willing to share their home. In 1903 the Cupeños were evicted from their homes, and most came to Pala.

An eyewitness in 1903 saw the sorry eviction taking place. One Cupeño woman threw books and other material into a fire: "She explained that now they hated the white people and their religion and their books" (James 1916: 51). When they reached Pala, the same observer wrote that, "Although devout church members—scarcely a name among them being unwashed by baptism—they refused the first Sunday to hold services in the restored Pala Mission, or anywhere else." They asked the visiting priest, "What kind of God is this you ask us to worship, who deserts us when we need him most?" (ibid.). Although the priest, Father Edmund La Pointe, who had only just arrived to minister to the Indians, was able to secure the old Warner Springs chapel for the Cupeños and then arranged a week-long fiesta to celebrate, it took twenty-four years for the Cupeños to lift a curse they made upon Warner Springs. It may seem as if some of the Cupeños turned their backs momentarily on their faith in the bitter eviction; however, others of them brought a small statue of St. Francis of Assisi with them to Pala. It has stood in the Pala chapel through the years, and on the feast of St. Francis every October 4 they have carried the statue around the mission grounds, a symbol of their continuity with missionary Christianity. They have made Pala their home, creating a Cupeño Cultural Center not far from San Antonio de Pala church. With the population increasing to three hundred and fifty, Pala became an Indian Bureau Agency in 1903, with sewers, a park, a school, clinic, prison, and government buildings.

Although the federal government had arranged to increase Pala's size to accommodate the Cupeños, during the next few years, when tourmaline gem crystals were discovered on Pala lands, the Bureau of Indian Affairs took the mineral regions from the Indians and handed them over to mining companies, thus preventing the Indians from a valuable source of income.

As the Cupeños were being removed to Pala, Bishop Thomas James Conaty was reestablishing a Catholic ministry to the mission Indians of the diocese of Monterey-Los Angeles. He assigned five priests to serve the four thousand Indians of the diocese, including Edmund La Pointe, who built a chapel at Santa Ysabel and restored the Pala chapel, and George Doyle, who served as pastor to the Luiseños. At La Jolla "He raised the peoples' enthusiasm by the conditional promise of a church there." At Pauma "a few devoted people" kept up the little adobe chapel dating from the nineteenth century: "It was almost pathetic in its neglect & the faded decorations put up for Easter, in spite of their isolation" (San Diego. Indians. May 3, 1910). Bishop Conaty wrote that "The building of the little chapels at Rincon and La Jolla has pleased the Indians very much and I am going to promise a new one at Pechang[a] for I understand that they have felt quite hurt because nothing has been done there lately. The Indians are so much like children that one needs to humor them in many ways" (ibid., November 4, 1910). A representative of the Bureau of Catholic Indian Missions, Rev. William H. Ketcham, wrote to the bishop, having visited the Luiseño Catholic communities: "I noted a very marked change for the better at Pala & the mission stations attended from there" (August 17, 1910). He found Father Doyle to be a spiritual leader much appreciated by the Indians. Ketcham recommended that Doyle perfect his Spanish in order to be able to communicate with the old Indians, for whom it was their first language.

In 1909 Fathers William Hughes and William H. Ketcham had journeyed to La Jolla, where they stayed with Pio Amago, a Spanish-speaking Indian, his wife, and their children. They found that "their children were weaned away from Mother Church by the want of the sacraments." The children they found "intensely religious, hungering for the faith of their fathers," but seizing upon anything they could for spiritual edification: Christian Science, Moravian Protestantism, e.g. Their father said to the priests: "I am a Catholic and so is my wife. We have grown old in the faith of the misioneros (priests and Indians). But our children who have attended the Sherman Institute, have left

the way we tread and gone the way of the new. Whose fault is it? . . .
Father dear, I do not wish to say" (in Hughes 1910: 7). A year later,
after Father Doyle had established himself, when Hughes visited La
Jolla, Pio Amago told him, "Our home is blessed again. The children
know their religion. We have holy Mass and Mystica [Amago's daugh-
ter] is teaching Catholic prayers and catechism to the children of the
tribe" (ibid., 7–8). Conaty not only established Father Doyle at Pala
but also supported Saint Boniface School in Banning, earning the title,
"the Indians' Friend" (ibid.).

In 1910 there were three groups of Indian missions in the Diocese
of Los Angeles–Monterey: Pala, with its five outlying missions ministered by Father Doyle; the Diegueño communities at Santa Ysabel,
Mesa Grande, and other sites, ministered by Father La Pointe; and the
San Jacinto Missions of Cahuilla, Soboba, Los Coyotes, etc. Father
J. J. Burri was building a chapel at Cahuilla, and the Santa Rosa Indians wanted one, too. In addition, Father B. Florian Hahn cared for
the reservations of Torrez-Martinez and Cabazon from his base at St.
Boniface School in Banning. But there were still many Indians in the
diocese who were basically without priestly contact: "Scattered sheep
from the folds of the ancient missions are to be found huddled together . . . in the mountains . . . , on the coast . . . , on the desert"
(ibid., 18), and elsewhere. A 1913 report, "Indian Reservations in
Southern California" (San Diego. Indians), estimated four thousand
Indians in forty-two separate communities.

As Bishop Conaty developed the Luiseño mission, each community
asked for a chapel at its own location. As Father Ketcham wrote to the
bishop,

the Indians at Pechanga complained bitterly that nice chapels were being
built for other Indians who, according to them were "very poor
Catholics", while they, the Pechangas, who had been driven from Temecula, which eviction, is so graphically described in "Ramona", and who
had always been very good and faithful Catholics, were left to worship in
the poor old dilapidated chapel which they themselves built at their own
expense with much labor and sacrifice. They cited Soboba, La Jolla and
Rincon. (San Diego. Indians. October 25, 1910)

The complaint at Santa Ysabel was that Father La Pointe was
stretched too thin with his various assignments and could not pay
enough attention to this community. José Juan Piapa wrote from
Santa Ysabel to Bishop Conaty in 1910, saying, "I am going to tell you

a very importan[t] thing that we all the people want a priest here at
Santa Ysabel mission. No priest around here[.] We are very lone-
some[.] The people don[']t like Father La [P]ointe because he never
come and say Mass every Sunday" (ibid., June 21, 1910). The Santa
Ysabel community was worried that Whites were going to evict them
from their lands, and for much of the year the bishop tried to reassure
them that their holdings were safe, and that Father La Pointe would
try to spend as much time as he could among them. Other Santa
Ysabel residents apologized to the bishop about Piapa's complaints,
and it is clear from the correspondence that the Indians desperately
wanted the priest's presence among them.

On the Los Coyotes Reservation the Indians wanted a new chapel
rather than a repair of the old one, and they argued with Father J. J.
Burri during the year of 1911. Burri doubted the wisdom of a new
chapel there, for as he explained to Bishop Conaty, "Among all the
men in all the four Reservation[s] there are not *ten* who have been to
the Sacraments for several years" (ibid., April 6, 1911 [emphasis his]).
The desire for clerical and churchly presence did not necessarily translate into a regular reception of the sacraments.

When it came to funeral services, however, the communities turned
out. In 1911 Anadot Chapuli died, the last captain of a small Indian
group and a good Catholic according to the priests. His people lived
between Warner Springs and Santa Ysabel, Diegueños who hid out in
the mountains when the Cupeños were evicted in 1903. His people
sang old Spanish hymns at his funeral, marking a great passing in their
beleaguered community.

In 1913 a visitor at Pala for an August fiesta was disappointed to find
nothing of wild Indians there. Instead she found Catholics not only
conducting a festival, giving speeches, running the games of chance,
but also attending Sunday mass said by Father Doyle on an outdoor
altar. He said a Latin mass and delivered a sermon in Spanish and English: "The Missions totter, my people . . . but the Faith lives in the
hearts of the Indians" (in Weber 1988: 84). In August 1917 the Pala community marked the centennial of Pala's founding. Fathers La Pointe and
Doyle helped in the celebration of mass, followed by a fiesta with bar-
becue, games of peon, dancing in the old Spanish style, the racing of
horses, and the saluting of the American flag, unfurled above the mission by Chaves Sliperosa, the oldest member of the mission (purportedly 113 years old) and said to have helped build the original mission.

To the north the Cahuillas and their neighbors clung to their pastor, and when he left them after many years, they were distraught. In 1919, Mr. and Mrs. Isidor A. Costo wrote to the Bureau of Catholic Indian Missions, remarking that "It is very pathetic that our people are left without a guide and spiritual advisor and especially now. . . . While on our trips to the different reservations we notice that the Indians are losing all interest in religious matters . . ." (San Bernardino. Missions, Indian. March 8, 1919). Five years later, a priest from San Jacinto with some contacts among the Cahuilla and Soboba Indians—there were over a hundred at each reservation—wrote, "In my opinion these Indians need and are worthy of the ministrations of a priest. But they are Government wards and possess only the mere necessities of life: hence the finances necessary to their spiritual needs cannot come from the Indians" (San Bernardino. Cahuilla Reservation. May 12, 1924). His own parish among Whites was too poor to carry the burden of an indigent Indian ministry. Without their own funds, the mission Indians— numbering about three thousand in the early 1920s—could not always count on regular priestly visits, and their Catholic faith was therefore often precarious.

In the 1920s Franciscans returned to the Pala ministry, serving for a score of years until 1948. They found the Indians very poor, with little money to give to the Church (Father Ignatius Ganster, O.F.M., collected only one dollar and twenty-six cents from Pala and seventy cents from La Jolla one Sunday in 1929). Their religious expression particularly flowered at funerals. In the mid-1920s, Rev. Julian Girardot, O.F.M., described (Weber 1988: 139–142) the death of old Ramon at Pala. The sacristan rang the bell outside the church to announce the death. The community placed the deceased in his home, candles at his side. Relatives provided food for visitors, and they purchased calico and gingham to place upon his grave. People arrived with flowers and stayed by the body all night. A prayer leader recited the rosary and sang songs, including native chants accompanied by gourd and deer hoof rattles. Early the next morning the men dug a grave. No one would dig at night, fearing that evil spirits would enter the open grave in the dark. Before the burial the Indians intoned a requiem high mass, and then deposited the body in the grave, along with the man's clothes. They placed the calico and gingham on the grave, and non-relatives took pieces of it. To end the services, the community shared a meal. Rev. Ganster made similar observations at Pala, concluding, "All in all, our Mission Indians are childlike characters, of amiable disposition and sincerely good in soul" (*The Indian Sentinel* 12, no. 3, summer 1932: 110).

The Indians also celebrated the feast of St. Anthony by holding fiestas on the weekend after the feast day, selling tamales to the visiting Indians who came to Pala to celebrate. Father Girardot asked for dispensations from the laws of fast and abstinence on Friday, Saturday, and ember days, so that the Indians could celebrate, and so that "their business might not be impaired" (San Diego. Pala. May 23, 1935).

At the time that San Diego became a separate diocese in 1926, Girardot and the Luiseños were building a new concrete chapel at La Jolla. The priest wanted a new building there, "especially with Protestantism trying to break in among them." He then built a new chapel at Rincon to replace the old one that was caved in and infested by vermin: "The Indians are already pouring concrete for the foundations of the new structure." The Luiseños at Rincon begged for the new chapel, St. Bartholomew's, and supported the church building with their labor and money, although Girardot wrote in November 1936: "I can get no more money from the Indians. They gave me all they could, and are still giving a little but not enough to help much" (ibid.). Rincon dedicated its new chapel at the feast of Corpus Christi, 1937. That same year Maria de los Angeles—the last of the Mission Indians, according to Father Girardot—died and received burial at the Pala Mission. The priest described her as a "faithful Catholic" (in *The Indian Sentinel* 17, no. 3, March 1937: 46) who remembered the prayers she had learned in the mission and recited them daily before a crucifix in her hut in the mountains.

Girardot served a territory 1,300 square miles in area, counting over six hundred Catholic Indians in 1937, in addition to Mexicans and Whites numbering over a hundred. Pala was the central mission, with over three hundred parishioners, but the priest also traveled to Pechanga (67), Pauma (43), Rincon (63), La Jolla (103), Warner Springs (50), and Los Coyotes (48). He said mass at Pala every Sunday and at the four Luiseño stations of Pechanga, Pauma, Rincon, and La Jolla once a month as a second Sunday mass. Some Cupeños and other Indians still dwelled at Warner Springs, and he visited there only when there was a fifth Sunday in a month. He estimated that at Pala one hundred and seventy-five parishioners attended mass on Sunday, and at the Stations, forty. Approximately half of the Indians fulfilled their

Easter duty by saying confession and receiving the Eucharist, and over a hundred children received catechetical instruction. Girardot informed Bishop Charles F. Buddy in 1937 that the Pala church was on six acres of land owned by the diocese, surrounded by reservation land. Ten miles east of the church the diocese owned 1,300 acres and used to own far more but sold it: "This tract was kept because of positive indications of the presence of gems or semiprecious stones" (San Diego. Pechanga-Temecula. July 27, 1937). The Franciscans in the 1930s leased the land to support the church, earning $100 each year.

The district was poor, and at Pala the Indians could not afford a second collection on Sundays. Despite their poverty, Girardot was impressed with the way in which the descendants of the San Luis Rey and Pala missions had maintained their faith in the second half of the nineteenth century, when they received only occasional visits from priests, and in the late 1930s he thought their Catholicism secure.

Superintendent John W. Dady of the Mission Indian Agency in Riverside, California, congratulated Bishop Buddy for the work that Father Girardot and a second priest, Francis Dillon, were performing among the Luiseño and Diegueño Indians in the diocese of San Diego: "I wish to express my deep appreciation to you for the sp[l]endid way in which you and your Priests in charge of the several parishes located within the mission Indian Agency jurisdiction are cooperating with our constructive efforts to assist our Indian people to live sober, industrious, and morally correct lives toward the end that they may be happy and comfortable." The superintendent was especially gratified at the Church's efforts among the mission Indians to "persuade the Indian people to abstain from the use of intoxicating liquors" (San Diego. Indians. June 29, 1937). Buddy replied to Dady that he had learned from reliable sources that "the officers appointed to protect the Indians are guilty of supplying them with intoxicating liquors" (ibid., July 2, 1937) and asked him to investigate the charges.

Church relations with the U.S. Government during the 1930s were none too good, especially with the changes wrought by Commissioner of Indian Affairs John Collier's "Indian New Deal." Collier insisted upon Indian freedom of religion, not only on reservations but also in government schools, like the Sherman Institute, attended by various Indian children. Diocesan authorities preferred that Catholic Indian children attend St. Boniface School in Banning; however, at the federal boarding schools, religious worship and instruction had been required, and the Church could maintain direction over the youths' faith in a secular setting. R. G. Valentine, commissioner of Indian affairs in 1910, composed "General Regulations for Religious Worship and Instruction of Pupils in Government Schools," which stipulated that "Pupils shall be directed to attend the respective Churches to which they belong or for which their parents or guardians express a preference" (ibid.). But in 1934 Commissioner Collier ordered that boarding school students need not attend Christian worship, instituting changes that the Catholic authorities found "radical," since they "strike at the radices—the roots—of our faith."

> In the old days, Indian boys and girls were kept strictly apart. They marched at stated times to their Catholic or Protestant chapel and, as a result of this physical and spiritual discipline, there existed submission and obedience to authority. Today, because of Mr. Collier's edict that Indian wards of the Government are "not obliged" to attend religious services, there is chaos in the vast majority of Indian boarding schools. Scarcely five per cent of our Catholic children attend Mass and religious instruction at Sherman Institute. There is likewise entirely too much mixing of the sexes, with a resultant breakdown in morality which is truly appalling. Protestant as well as Catholic workers note the pagan tendency of the new regime. (Ibid., November 5, 1937)

In 1938 the bishop passed on the complaint to Collier, and a diocesan commission called for qualified female catechists from the local Indian reservations to be hired at the Sherman Institute. The commission members hoped to lobby the parents of the students to authorize the Church personnel to require religious instruction of their children while at school. Francis Dillon, president of the commission, told Bishop Buddy that "The missionary should have power of acting between the parents and school authorities, and bringing the wishes of the former to the authorities" (ibid., February 17, 1938), since it was not practical to expect the parents to advise the school personnel directly. He suggested that the Indian Bureau's policies supported "the system in Mexico, which tends towards communism and irreligion," and he asserted that "drunkenness is universal among the Indians even among the young." A priest serving the Sherman School said to Buddy that the school officials "encourage" Indian children to attend religious services, but this did no good as long as Collier's "pagan program" left the choice to the students themselves (ibid., March 8, 1938).

While attempting to maintain control over the Catholic Indian children away at school, the Church continued its ministry on the reservations, building new chapels and delivering sacramental services. Sometimes the Indians invited the priests to say mass in their homes, and at other times they agitated for control over building projects. The diocese tried to assert its authority not only in the boarding schools but also in the Indian communities, attempting to purchase the lands on which the chapels lay and seeking the support of reservation leaders. In some Indian communities the Catholic Indians expressed their appreciation enthusiastically, e.g., at Santa Rosa Indian Reservation. When Bishop Buddy visited the community in 1939, the tribal spokesman, Jack Meyers, Captain Alex Tostes, and three committeemen thanked him for his stay, which inspired the people to "remain Catholic." In a letter approved at a tribal meeting they wrote:

> We Mission Indians of the Santa Rosa Band have been taught to conduct ourselves in a Catholic manner and that ideal has been instilled in us from our fathers and grandfathers. They told us that when you first came to California with the Catholic religion it was not forced upon us. And the early Mission Fathers did not try to make us forsake our own beliefs or the manner of expressing our devotion to the deities whom we to this day still hold in reverence and awe. Our people have embraced the Holy Roman Catholic Church as their one Church which we hold in high and holy esteem. But deep in our hearts we have a reverence for the things our fathers taught us. And we still carry on with certain ceremonial for our dead, which do not conflict with our Catholic hearts. Your religion dear Bishop has never denied us this worship or tried to take it away from us.

They promised that in the new chapel the bishop had blessed, "that when we use the sacristy for our Tribal meetings that nothing will be done there that will in any way . . . defame our Church and religion" (ibid., October 16, 1939). The bishop found the letter "very beautiful" (October 20, 1939) and had it published in the diocesan newspaper, *The Southern Cross*.

But at other reservations, e.g., Torres-Martinez, Augustine, and Cabazon, with a population over a hundred baptized Catholics, the hiatus in clerical visitation—they went through the 1930s without a regular priest—led to a decline of Catholic faith: "The result is that many have fallen away, and many others have gone over to Protestantism" (San Bernardino. Torres-Martinez. March 16, 1942).

In the 1940s the Pala community was much like any other Catholic community. They celebrated Holy Week as one would expect: singing *Glorias* and *Exsultets*, expressing devotion to the crucifix, conducting Easter egg hunts. For their church weddings, at which Luiseños and Cupeños married Mexicans, other Indians, and Whites, they dressed in tuxedos and white gowns. Luiseños served in the Second World War, enthroned pictures of the Sacred Heart in their homes under the instigation of Father Girardot, and acted as the priest's helpers. Girardot noted that the Temecula Catholics, despite their history of dispossession, continued to repair their chapel and remained "very faithful to their religious duties. . . . The faith implanted by the early missionaries has survived, we are merely fostering it" (*The Indian Sentinel* 24, no. 4, April 1944: 54). At Pala he praised Esperanza Fidelio, baptized as a child by Father Anthony Ubach at Warner Springs in one of his seasonal visits. The Church sent her to St. Boniface Indian School, where she became a favorite of the sisters. During her stay in school, her Cupeño people were evicted and settled at Pala, and when she graduated she came to Pala "a model Catholic young woman" who married, had six children, sang in the choir, and proved to be a "noble Christian soul," who sang at a requiem mass at a neighboring reservation right before her death in 1945 (ibid. 25, no. 4, May 1945: 57, 58).

Still Rev. Bonaventure Oblasser, O.F.M., found the Indians of the diocese of San Diego in need of continuing instruction in Christian faith. In 1945 he wrote to Bishop Buddy from the Campo Indian Reservation:

> There is but a small minority made up of the descendants of the neophytes, formerly enrolled at Mission San Diego who have kept up continual contact with Catholic priests and sisters, viz. the inhabitants of . . . Jamul and Barona Indian Reservations near San Diego and the members of the Osuna and Banegas families in the Santa Ysabel district. To these we could add the few Indians who have married good Catholic whites. The greater part of the native population is still addicted to paganism in varying degrees. Some adhere entirely to its tenets, as most of the Quechan near Yuma. Others, although professing Catholicism, are guided more by heathen principles, as the Dieguenos of Campo. The

remaining majority hold to ancient beliefs as an important factor in forming their life habits. This protracted clinging to paganism must be attributed to a lack of instruction.

He contended that the Church needed trained missionaries who knew how to "eradicate what is harmful in the old system" (San Diego. Indians. San Diego and San Bernardino Dioceses. March 12, 1945). The following year the Franciscan wrote again to the bishop, asserting that "There is still such a vast untilled field among the Indians, that it will be to the great advantage of the Indian work to separate it from that of the old time Christians.—These Indians, the greater part of them, are still neophytes, and must still receive the basic training of Our Holy Religion." The friar asked the bishop to turn over the diocesan Indian missions to his Franciscans in order to follow the "time honored methods of Our Order . . . to try to make good Catholics of these Indians, most of whom have never gone through a period of Mission training" (San Diego. Indians. San Diego and San Bernardino Dioceses. February 19, 1946). A year later Rev. Oblasser told Buddy: "*It is too early in the Christian training of our Indians in the Sierras to expect such a strength of Faith.* Even the descendants of the Old Mission Indians, of whom there are less than 200 *in the Indian country* of Southern California, have, through two generations of public school training, lost very much of the lively Faith of their grandparents" (ibid., October 23, 1947 [emphases his]).

For several years Oblasser lobbied with the bishop to secure the Indian missions of the diocese of San Diego for the Franciscans on a permanent basis, arguing that the Indians needed the friars to make real Christians of them, as the padres had done in the eighteenth and nineteenth centuries. He found the "anti-racial attitude" of at least one member of the secular clergy to be harmful to the Indians' spiritual growth, claiming that the Indians' poverty did not endear them to those clergy more interested in bringing in revenues for their ministry (San Diego. Santa Ysabel. February 28, 1948). Bishop Buddy resisted Oblasser's overtures, not out of disrespect for the early Franciscan missionizing, but because he could not abide their independence as an order within his diocesan jurisdiction. In 1948 he informed Oblasser that the diocese did not want the Franciscans to continue in the diocesan Indian missions, thanking Oblasser for his help during the Second World War but sending him on his way, back to Arizona where he had served in previous years. Buddy turned, instead, to a mission order, the Sons of the Sacred Heart Missionary Society, to take over the Indian missions in the diocese. Oblasser replied:

> It was a great consolation to receive your letter, which assured me that these poor missions were not to be divided among the neighboring parishes, as stepchildren, but were to be entrusted to one association and to be treated as missions. Except the *few* descendants of the Old Mission Indians, (at Barona, & Santa Ysabel from San Diego) (at Soboba from San Juan Capistrano) who will not total 200, the rest of the two thousand Indians are still neophytes, and stand very much in need of thorough Catholic instructions. . . . The Indians themselves, on account of the unfortunate policy of California in the past, will *never* have the means to support these missions. (Ibid., October 7, 1948 [emphases his])

In December 1948 Buddy signed an agreement with the provincial of the Sons of the Sacred Heart for the "spiritual care" of "Indian Missions" at Santa Ysabel, Mesa Grande, Inaja, Barona, Viejas, Campo, La Posta, Manzanita, Warner Springs, Los Coyotes, Santa Rosa, Cahuilla, Soboba, Pala, Temecula, Pechanga, Pauma, Rincon, La Jolla, Sycuan, Jamul, and elsewhere as needed. Four priests and one lay brother arrived to care for these Indian communities, and at Pala they hoped to establish a parochial school, "the most urgent need for our Indian population" (San Diego. Pala. September 20, 1949). This order—known at various times as the Verona, or Comboni, Fathers—continued its ministry to the mission Indians of Pala and its environs until 1991 when the priests moved on to other fields.

The Verona Fathers tried to curtail the Indian wakes, with their singing and traditional ritualism, but the Luiseños and Diegueños refused to stop: "Nobody could understand why they wanted to stop us. We fought them" (Hyde and Hyde, November 8, 1992). At Santa Ysabel the Indian women were so angry with Father Januarius M. Carillo that they pushed him down into a creek in an attempt to rid themselves of his presence.

Some parishioners complained that the Italian priests of the new order spoke accented English, making it difficult to understand their sermons and instruction. Mrs. Marcus Galsh, married to a Rincon Indian, complained of the priests' slang and wondered to Bishop Buddy if Indians were not considered worthy of a proper American priest. She said that the Indians were "well capable of having a priest that speaks English and not Italian jestures—we have been brow beaten for generations, and if its to be I guess we can hold up under this—but it seems so unnecessary—we do love our church and respect our priests. But may God see fit to send us a leader that we can understand, for we have so few privileges out here we need a good priest" (San Diego. Pala. May 27, 1953). The secretary to Bishop Buddy, Rev. Donald Kulleck, responded to Mrs. and Mr. Galsh:

> In offering complaint you probably have not taken into consideration the fact that our good Indian people are getting more than twice the amount of service from the priests than they did a few years ago before the advent of the Missionary Sons of the Sacred Heart. Evidently you have forgotten the special care now given to your children, the number of new churches and catechetical halls built to provide for you and the general progress that has been made by these devoted priests. Pulpit oratory is a minor thing. (Ibid., May 28, 1953)

In addition, the secretary wrote, the bishop "must go East and beg funds" for you poor people, who pay less than "one-thirteenth of the overhead costs." The Sacred Heart fathers claimed that the complaints derived from a "[P]rotestant inspired" (ibid., June 3, 1953) movement that called the Italian priests Communists and spies. Some Indians longed for their beloved Franciscans once again and resented these new priests in their first few years of service. By the middle of the 1950s, however, the Italian priests had made themselves at home among their Indian parishioners.

In March 1949 Rev. Angel Barbisotti, F.S.C.J., was able to collect seventy-seven dollars from five Indian communities—Pala, Temecula, Rincon, Cahuilla, and Soboba—for the Bishops' War Relief Fund; however, the following March, Juliana Calac wrote to Bishop Buddy, soliciting money for the Pala Mission. Signing her missive "a humble worker," the woman asked for the bishop's blessing and prayer "for all of us poor Indians of the Pala Mission. I know the Lord loves us that is the reason He made us poor. We are thankful we have Mission so near" (ibid., March 2, 1950 [sic]). Father Carillo told the Bureau of Catholic Indian Missions in 1950 that the Santa Ysabel Indians were too poor to care for their orphans (San Diego. Santa Ysabel. March 25, 1950).

The Sacred Heart Fathers tried to encourage and control Indian Catholic devotions, as did Bishop Buddy. Barbisotti planned a Forty Hours Devotion in Pala in February 1951 and asked permission from the bishop for an outdoor procession with the Blessed Sacrament through the village streets. Buddy responded that the procession must have "a sufficient number of adorers" who would "pray while they march along. . . . Where there is no devotion, there is nothing to warrant having such a procession." He recalled that the Mexicans in San Diego used to have a procession but it was "all show and noise and no devotion" (San Diego. Pala. January 10, 1951). In the early 1950s the Church officials attempted to tone down the Indians' Spanish-based devotionalism, with its processions and fiestas, in favor of the sacramentals popular with Anglo-Americans throughout the United States. As a result, there were complaints that the Church "has influenced the Fiesta time to be cut from a week to one day. . . . The Indians are discouraged by the priest from participating in the games" (ibid., c. May 29, 1952) associated with the Corpus Christi celebration.

A pattern of friction occurred at various reservations as priests moved on and new ones arrived. Each priest seemed, at first, to have difficulty in having the Indian community accept him, and yet when he left, the same community mourned his passing and complained of the new priest. Indians argued with the clergy over the ownership of the chapels, the names to be given them—often the "titulus" for the chapels was determined by donors, frequently through the Marquette League or the Extension Society, and Indians who had become devoted to a particular saint would have to get used to a new personage as patron of their chapel—and the Indians argued with the bishop over the Church personnel in their midst.

As Bishop Buddy ousted the Franciscans from the diocese in 1952–53, over the issue of ecclesiastical authority within the diocese, some Indians raised a cry about their beloved friars, now departing. Mrs. Mariano Saubel of the Morongo Reservation went so far as to protest directly to Pope Pius XII in 1952:

> I am appealing to you in behalf of the Catholic, Indian people concerning the withdrawal of the Franciscan Order from St. Boniface Indian School and our own little chapel on the Morongo Indian Reservation, near Banning California Diocese of San Diego. Why the Franciscan priest are being ordered out of this part of the country I don't know. History shows and every one knows that the Franciscans belong in California. They were the first my people knew. They are humble and so are my people. They understand us and help us, not only spiritually but every way possible for our welfare. So again I plead please leave our own Franciscans with their children. (San Bernardino. Morongo. May 23, 1952 [*sic*])

Fifteen fellow Morongo Indians affixed their signatures to Mrs. Saubel's letter. When the Vatican forwarded the letter to the diocesan headquarters, someone in Buddy's office inquired about the signatories: "Please inform me 1) How many of these signers have made their Easter Duty? 2) How many assist at Mass & support the Church?" The local priest reported to Buddy that only Mrs. Saubel and perhaps one or two others had made their Easter duty; indeed, only three ever attended mass, and only Mrs. Saubel "more or less regularly" (ibid., September 19, 1952). He pointed out to the bishop that when the Franciscans had mass at Morongo, only eight to ten Indians attended twice a month. Collections were three to four dollars per Sunday, but he did not know, of course, who gave how much. In the several months since the Franciscans left, virtually none of the Morongo Indians made the effort to attend mass in Banning, where a priest was stationed at St. Boniface School, even though they had cars and often came to shop in Banning during the week. He reported that there were fifty or more Indians on the reservation, and Protestants had made serious inroads to the community: "In short the faith of these Indians has already suffered sever[e]ly, and where it is not entirely dead it is weak and wavering" (ibid.). He himself could not afford to travel to the reservation, except for funerals and baptisms.

For all the complaints about the Verona Fathers, when one of them left, called back by the order to their headquarters in Cincinnati, the Barona Indian Reservation sent a petition asking for his return: "We have learned to love him as one of [our] own people. We believe he is the only Priest we have loved so much since the late Rev. Fr. LaPointe" (San Diego. Santa Ysabel. n.d.). The Indians appreciated his frequent visits, his catechetical instruction, and his initiative in starting an Altar Society. La Pointe's twenty-nine years at Santa Ysabel had earned him a community hall named after him, despite criticism of him in his early years. Now the Verona Fathers were establishing themselves as parts of the Indian communities in which they served.

During the 1950s the priests among the mission Indians prided themselves on the progress they made in furthering Catholic Indian faith. Father Barbisotti baptized the Diegueño centenarian from the Inaja Reserve, Joaquim Paipa, just before his death in 1951. Father Carillo praised "Good Chief" Ramon Ames of Barona for inspiring a project to build a rectory on the reservation, to draw more regular visits from the priests. The Cahuilla Catholics came out in force in 1952 for the funeral of the "faithful Catholic," Juan Costo, over one hundred at his death and a longtime advocate for his people in Washington, D.C. In the years when priests visited his people only rarely, he led them in rosaries and hymns to the Virgin. When priests came to visit, Costo housed them. In the years before his death he received the sacraments at home and said the rosary (*The Indian Sentinel* 32, no. 9, November 1952: 136–137). Even as Protestants gained members from disaffected Catholics at several reservations, Catholic devotions were prominent at many locations. The Diegueños at Santa Ysabel attended the Way of the Cross and Holy Week services in 1953 and enacted a pageant honoring Our Lady of Fatima. Adults renewed their baptismal vows and sang in choir. Even fifty years after the theft of their precious mission bells in 1926, Santa Ysabel Catholics were said to revere the "venerable relics" of their mission years (ibid. 34, no. 6, June 1954: 83).

The priests relied on the help of prayer leaders such as John Felisho ("Juan Angel") and his wife Margaret at Santa Ysabel, who in the years before regular mass led Sunday prayers and singing and conducted funeral services for the Indians in their community. Even with Father Seraphin Meneghello, F.S.C.J., serving the southern reservations, Juan Angel, a "staunch Catholic," but independent in his authority, continued as funeral master of ceremonies for eight different Diegueño reservations. Father Meneghello reported that the Indians of Santa Ysabel regarded Holy Souls as a major religious day of the year, spending hours in the cemetery, placing candles and paper flowers on the graves. The priest led them in evening prayers before a cross: then they sang hymns until the candles burned out. John Felisho often replaced the priest in leading the prayers. The Indians said of him: "When Juan Angel prays, . . . we feel the presence of our beloved dead. It is just like he was conversing with them and God." The priest added that, "In fact, some Indians did not think it made much difference whether the priest or John conducted burial services" (ibid. 38, no. 2, March-April 1958: 20–21). One day Father Meneghello found Felisho and other Indians at Barona Cemetery, fixing the earth and praying over a grave that had sunk. Felisho explained to the priest that it was their belief that such a grave must be tended or there would be a death among the relatives. Felisho said that he himself did not believe such things, but tending the grave fostered respect for the dead, and that was good. The priest got him to see that such customs were better dropped, and he encouraged his people to cease the practice. Prayer leaders like Felisho and Steve Ponchetti may have acquiesced in some matters; however, they have more recently been depicted as traditionalists who fostered their aboriginal culture, "sometimes disguised within Catholicism" (Sorensen 1985: 8). In 1947, when Ponchetti was appointed to the Board of Trustees of the Warner Union School, the first Indian to be named to that board, Father Oblasser was pleased. He wrote Bishop Buddy that it was an opportunity to get out the *"Indian vote"* in future school board elections: "since the *Indians* are *Catholic*, we hope to get a decent Catholic representation on the board" (San Diego. Santa Ysabel. April 24, 1947). The priests thought of Ponchetti, partly Swiss but mostly Diegueño, as a devout Catholic who sang hymns after supper every night. He helped build the Santa Ysabel chapel for Father La Pointe. At the same time, however, he preserved the Ipai language at services for the dead on several reservations, and it was the Indian community at Santa Ysabel that commissioned him and his wife Florence to be prayer leaders. They represented the community as well as the priest, and part of their representation consisted of learning about the old ways—knowledge of spirits, knowledge of nature—and passing them down to the next generation. The Ponchettis raised twenty-two orphans, in addition to their own son (now an engineer for General Dynamics), and traveled throughout southern California, and even Mexico, promoting a mixture of native and Catholic spirituality.

Particularly at Santa Ysabel the Diegueños exhibited their "talent for synthesis" (Luomala 1978: 595) of native and Catholic religious elements, as in their Fiesta de las Cruces, held annually on November 14, in which the Indians hosted a harvest festival with barbecues, games, sports, processions, prayers for rain, firecrackers, guns, noise, and general celebration (Quinn 1964: 24–25). At their "year-after" memorials for their dead, e.g., a year after Ponchetti's 1984 death, they continued the ancient custom of burning clothes in order to free the soul to leave the earth. White onlookers might notice the Catholic form of the hundreds of Indians who went to attend a memorial mass; however, they would miss the aboriginal content of the service:

> At first glance, everything about the memorial ceremony might have appeared to be Roman Catholic: the hymns, the prayers, the white cross over the grave. Yet everyone there, except perhaps the Catholic priests, knew that the very purpose of the ceremony, as well as the man it was held for, were purely Indian. How that is possible, how one culture can survive within the shell of another, taking the new form

but keeping the old substance, is the 300-year story of the Diegueño Indians. (Sorensen 1985: 8)

Many of the catholicized Indians of southern California have maintained "philosophical assumptions" (Bean and Shipek 1978: 562) and ritual practices of their pre-Christian lifeways.

Among the Luiseños certain aspects of traditional religious culture persisted amidst, and even through, Catholic life. Father Carillo wrote in 1959 that,

> On the whole, it can be said that there was little opposition between Christianity and the native religion. Some older Catholic Indians have stated to the writer: "We believed the same thing before, only we called God by a different name." This may be the reason for the success of the work of the early Franciscan missionaries among them. In embracing the faith, the Indians found the sacraments of Baptism and Confirmation akin to their initiation rites, and the funeral rites of the Church an even more spiritual expression of their mourning rites. (Carillo 1959: 26)

He said of the Luiseños that "Their clan and group ceremonies and ancient traditions have survived to the present although they are rapidly fading. . . . The Indians still show respect and awe for the rites and teaching of their primitive, non-Christian religion, passed down to them from their pre-Mission society" (ibid.). He mentioned specifically initiation rites for boys and girls, sweat house ceremonies, mourning for the dead, moralistic sermons at initiations, and ideas regarding the afterlife and future reward and punishment. As far as he could see, only mourning and remembrance of the dead continued into the modern day as a regular practice of the Luiseños. Earlier in the century various observers found the persistence of initiations, dances to foster vegetal growth, eagle dances, and various expressions of the Chinigchinich religion. But for many Luiseños these practices and beliefs became things of the past by the middle of this century, although for many whatever aspects of the traditional religion remained took on increased importance. Writing in the 1950s, one outsider said, "Even though all the Luiseños are nominally Christian, the old native religion along with its cosmogony and origin myths is crucial to all that remains of the culture core" (White 1991: 543). At the same time, they identified themselves through their Catholic worship, as well as through their remembrance of their native religiousness. The Luiseños remembered their old religion, but they also revered their Catholicism. Father Carillo said that in the 1950s Luiseños spoke of their mission experiences as formative influences on their contemporary community. For example, he claimed that "relatives of Pablo Tac are still living in Pala and speak of him—the faithful Luiseño Indian boy who accompanied Fr. Peyri to Spain and Rome over a century ago" (Carillo 1959: 15), and their remembrance fostered their Catholic identity.

In the late 1800s the Luiseños celebrated saint day fiestas as a means of promoting social solidarity not only within each community but among the various Indian communities in southern California. The Corpus Christi fiesta continued as the most prominent, "celebrated in Pala every year since the founding of the Mission in 1816" (ibid., 29). Taking place at the Thursday following Trinity Sunday, sixty days after Easter each year, it has usually been combined with the feast of St. Anthony, the patron of Pala's mission, and the fiesta has drawn upon the Spanish pattern of celebration. The Indians cleaned and decorated the village for several days before, erecting shines for the procession route, building ramadas for the preparation and sale of cooked goods to visiting Indians. After solemn high mass, representatives from other reservations on horseback would arrive with banners of their patron saints. The Indians conducted a procession of the Blessed Sacrament, followed by benediction, accompanied by gunshots and bells. Then several days ensued of barbecues, dances, gambling games, and other amusements. So many Indians came to Pala that mass had to be said outdoors. The federal government tried to curtail the festivities in the 1920s, and in 1940 an Act of Congress impinged on the gambling that took place at the fiesta; however, the festival has continued to the modern day, although "outsiders" (Magee 1992) have taken over its operation, particularly Mexican Americans in the area.

At Rincon the Indians celebrated the feast of San Luis on August 25. They constructed a ramada and brushed the area clear. On the morning of the 25th, everyone gathered at the church for "mass." The Indians called it mass, but it consisted of rosary, prayers, and songs, led by a native prayer leader. Invitations to the surrounding reservations brought contingents of Indians by horse and wagon, led by their hosts to the fiesta site near the church. The kitchen area was full of food, with beef hanging for the guests. The Rincon Store, run by Whites, was stocked with goods for sale. After mass everyone celebrated. "It really had nothing to do with San Luis," but emphasized joyous celebration: peon and roulette, horse races, firecrackers. The Indians danced for the fun of it. Guests played guitars, violins, and drums, and sang: "It was exiting." People drank alcohol, but "we didn't know what it was like to be drunk," because everyone was so happy (Hyde and Hyde, November 8, 1992). What has been the religious content of these fiestas? Purportedly they celebrate Catholic saints or honor the body of Christ. Nevertheless, these fiestas seem to celebrate the communities themselves. They have served as an occasion to gather, eat, gamble, dance, and raise funds. They have served as expressions of Indian solidarity as much as Catholic spirituality.

The same has been true for the most salient of Luiseño rituals, those surrounding death in the communities. The Luiseños, like other Indians of southern California, used to cremate their dead, but since becoming Christians they have buried their dead in the Catholic cemeteries. Funerals and wakes have been very important to the community, as All Souls Day remembrances have been, when Indians have lit candles on the graves of their deceased. The cemetery at Pala has continued to be a special place, reserved only for the descendants of the original Pala Indians; other Palatinguas are buried in a second gravesite east of the mission buildings. Whereas Sunday masses might go unattended, the funeral service seems to have been the continuing center of public Luiseño religious practice, serving the function (like the fiestas) of solidifying the Indian community. In both cases—the fiestas' affirmation of the living Indian community and funeral services' affirmation of the continuing bonds between the living and the dead—the Luiseños have adapted Catholic forms to their own community ends. To the present day "The whole community comes out from under the bushes" (Cribbin, November 7, 1992) at funerals, at which the Indian community coalesces. A small group of Luiseños attends mass regularly, but almost everyone attends funerals. Into this religious culture the Verona Fathers attempted to instill a more purely Catholic practice. Yet over the years "Native religious ceremonies persisted alongside Catholicism, often tolerated by the priests under the guise of 'secular' events, but sometimes carried out secretly. . . . To a greater degree than is generally realized, native religious systems persisted, some of them to the present" (Bean and Vane 1978: 670).

In 1955 Father Januarius Carillo recalled that Father Peyri had once built San Antonio mission at Pala with "Indian labor freely and piously performed." Now, "the descendants of his converts were repeating" (*The Indian Sentinel* 35, no. 4, April 1955: 51–52) their act of generous service by rebuilding the new Pala rectory. At the dedication of the new building, mission Indians from Pauma, Rincon, Pechanga, La Jolla, Temecula, Santa Rosa, Cahuilla, and of course Pala, celebrated by singing the hymn, *Dios te Salve, Maria,* handed down to the present day "from an earlier generation" (ibid., 64). In the same year the Pala Indians created a float for the Pioneer Days Parade in Fallbrook, presenting the early history of the mission in a pageant. They depicted an Indian chief conducting Father Peyri to Pala in 1816 and also the bell tower of San Antonio de Pala, which for the modern Indians "is still the center of spiritual life" (ibid. 35, no. 7, September 1955: 110). A white observer said of the prize-winning float that the performers really looked like Indians!

Rev. Januarius Carillo and his fellow Verona Fathers moved toward their goal of building a Catholic school on the Pala reservation for the nearly six hundred Catholic Indians on the five small reservations adjoining each other in the San Diego County hills. Although "scarcely any other Indians have been dealt with so harshly," he wrote, in the 1950s these "contented" Indians appeared happy and were offering their labor to construct the parochial school (ibid. 37, no. 2, March-April 1957: 20), which one Indian referred to as "our school" (ibid. 37, no. 5, September-October 1957: 70). In 1959 the Indians had completed the reconstruction of the mission as a replica of the old edifice, making the adobe bricks and cutting down cedar trees for beams. The Mother Katherine Drexel Foundation funded the completion of the Pala Mission School in 1959, and in 1960 the Sisters of the Blessed Sacrament came to Pala to operate the facility, the only Catholic school for Indians in southern California.

Juliana Calac thanked the priests for reopening the small mission that had begun to crumble from disuse over the century. From Mrs. Calac and her husband Macario the missionaries received $150 each year, and she worked constantly for the Church, as vice-president of the Deanery Council of Catholic Women and in other capacities. Father Carillo told Bishop Buddy, "There are other Indians that deserve the same recognition, but Mrs. Calac has been more outstanding than others. . . . A recognition given to her would help a lot in our work for and with the Indians, and it would show how the Church loves her Indian children" (San Diego. Pala. April 13, 1959). When Mrs. Calac died, she left her land to the Missionary Fathers, much to the anger of some Pala Indians, who accused the priests of caring more about the Indians' land than about their souls (ibid., June 16, 1968). Other Pala residents had no objection to her gift; after all, it was her personal allotment to do with as she willed (Magee, November 6, 1992).

Through the 1960s and 1970s Pala continued to grow, becoming one of the largest Indian villages in California, with a population of over six hundred and fifty. Tourists came to visit the quaint church, set on a reservation that had grown to almost twelve thousand acres. The Cupa Cultural Center drew visitors, and tourists purchased Christmas cards made by Indian children at the Pala Mission School.

In 1944 the diocese reported 1,630 Catholic Indians within its territory; in 1953 the figure had risen to 3,480; by 1963 the numbers had grown to 4,644, with forty adult and 277 infant baptisms in the previous years. By the 1980s there were 1,375 Luiseño and Cupeño residents, and 1,651 additional tribal members from Pala, Pechanga, La Jolla, Pauma, and Rincon (Shipek 1987: 186–191), and the Church continued to support their local congregations, as well as those on the various Indian reservations throughout the diocese.

The relations between the Church and Indian people over the last several decades have not always been easy. In 1965 six women from Soboba Indian Reservation, parishioners of St. Joseph's Church, wrote to the bishop of San Diego to complain about the behavior and attitude of Father Michael Greco, their parish priest, who—they claimed—slammed the door on a group of Indian mothers trying to discuss catechism classes with him. This and other incidents led to people avoiding mass and refusing to send their children to catechism classes (San Bernardino. Soboba. February 21, 1965). Rev. Greco acknowledged his difficulties in preparing the Indian children for confirmation: "This is not a normal, usual and up-to-date parish—the Indians move slowly—obey after long persuasion—and the faith is not well understood. The children have not been attending their Catechism classes as well as they should. . . . The conditions here are difficult and primitive, as you well know, dear Monsignor" (ibid., January 7, 1966). When Mission Indians have received spiritual care from parish priests with duties to non-Indian communities, or when Catholic Indians have been told to integrate themselves into the white Catholic communities of worship, the results have not always been conducive to active participation and Church loyalty. Father Greco found the Indians' poverty an obstacle to their Church involvement: "The Indians are old and sickly—their government pension permits them to donate only a few dimes or quarters to the Church. The youths are away from the reservation—there's no way to raise money on an abandoned desert. No business house, no stores, no firms—no one to help or donate a penny" (ibid., November 25, 1967). Priests have found it hard to support themselves among Indians and thus only those priests with a special calling to Indian ministry have wanted Indian parishes or missions. The number of such dedicated priests has dwindled in the post-Vatican II era, at least in California. When Rev. Norman F. Lord, C.S.Sp., took over St. Joseph's at Soboba in 1968, he discovered that "Getting the Indians to church is a big job and so many haven't received the Sacraments in ages—the invalid marriages are the main obstacle" (ibid., n.d.). After five years of service, however, he was able to report: "In general they are not regular in church attendance or support. But there is a good attitude toward the Faith and we no longer have baptisms delayed or omitted as in the past." He said that four young couples had been married in the church in 1972: "This is equivalent to the Padres winning the pennant! The rapport with the people couldn't be better." At Santa Rosa, nearby to Soboba, he blocked the inroads of the Jehovah's Witnesses, but the Indians' participation in Church affairs was minimal: "The Indian is not a devout Catholic. To have any success we must go to them—they will not attend church in the town usually. And while they are not that good at attending Mass here, they are not anti-clerical" (ibid., January 2, 1973).

The following year another priest, Rev. Francis X. O'Reilly, C.S.Sp., reported to Bishop Leo T. Maher that he was responding to a call by Morongo Indians to hold a regular mass there. A sister had organized them to request such services, and he had a meeting with the community, letting them know in advance "that if only women were present, I would turn around and go home immediately." Thirty adults attended a meeting with him: "Most spoke from simple ignorance but a few were making demands. . . . I quieted them down by telling them . . . that they should not dare to play games with God," or He might strike them dead. Father O'Reilly consented to go to their reservation on Sundays, or perhaps acquire a bus to bring them to town each week for services (ibid., October 26, 1974).

Priests were sensitive to criticisms not only from Catholic Indians, but also from non-Indian commentators. In 1973 a curator from the Southwest Museum in Los Angeles wrote to the San Diego chancery, asking about a Manzanita Reservation church she and a photojournalist had seen, "obviously held in great reverence by the older people. . . . It seems to be well-tended by the Indians, but there is no evidence of a priest living nearby" (San Diego. Santa Ysabel Mission. n.d.). She wanted to know how often a priest came to Manzanita, and how often the Indians received sacraments and catechism. Rev. Frank DiFrancesco, F.S.C.J., replied with what he called a "not . . . very polite" letter, responding angrily to a newspaper article written by the photojournalist about the ninety Manzanita Indians "being abandoned and the priest going there only for funerals." Father DiFrancesco told her that he was "more interested than some photojournalist looking for news about the poor abandoned Indians" (ibid., October 29, 1973); that almost all of the ninety Manzanita Indians lived off the reservation, and only three Catholics lived permanently on the territory. He explained that he traveled once a month to nearby Campo from his station at Santa Ysabel, and that he wrote letters in advance to those Catholics at Manzanita, telling them when they could find him. The Manzanita Indians knew that they could call him anytime at Santa Ysabel, and he would come to them. In short, with Catholic Indians living in small numbers in isolated areas, priests have found it difficult to deliver spiritual services with the regularity that some Indians and others might wish. Indian communities sought control over church buildings on their reservations and argued with priests over autonomy; however, when the priests did not make regular visits to the reservations, the Indians complained.

In August 1977 a group of Indians from the San Diego diocese, including representatives from Barona, Viejas, and Sycuan, made it clear that they wanted priests in their communities, not just once a month, and not just bringing in programs designed for white communities. They wanted mass in their own chapels. They wanted catechism designed especially for their children, with insight into traditional Indian ways. If there was a funeral, a priest must come, since the Indians found it particularly distressing when priests ignored their mourning process (San Diego. Indians. August 23, 1977). Bishop Maher understood that the Indians desired mass in their local chapels:

> They are very sensitive people and need special attention. To ask them to mingle and to join in with the large congregation is depriving them of participation in their own liturgies. Over a period of time, perhaps they can be brought into the community life, but this can only happen through proper education. . . . It is my desire that we have Mass for them as often as possible in their little Chapels. (Ibid., December 13, 1977)

Even though Indians of southern California have not regarded mass attendance as a crucial part of their Catholic spirituality, the Church has attempted through the 1980s to provide a presence on reservations, to foster Indian self-esteem and to provide counseling to treat alcoholism, unemployment, and other social dysfunctions. Whenever possible, the Church has repaired the Indian chapels, e.g., in 1984 at Santa Rosa, in order to deepen the faith of Indian Catholics who "have been struggling for many years to practice it in unfavorable circumstances" and to win back the "fallen-aways" (San Bernardino. Santa Rosa. December 27, 1984). The diocesan Native American Commission conducted educational seminars and intensified its evangelization at San Manuel Reservation in order to soften the "hostility" of the Indians there to the Church, even employing native catechists (Marquette. DCRAA. 1983, 1986). Sister Eileen Cotter, who served the Indian Catholics in what is now San Bernardino Diocese (which was carved out of the diocese of San Diego in 1978) for many years, encouraged her Church to support Indian ministry: "It is important that they (the Indians) can still express their Indianess in being a Catholic" (in Watson 1985: 6. [sic]). Toward that end the diocese of San Diego has created a "national Parish" of Blessed Kateri Tekakwitha on the Barona Reservation which anyone can join, irrespective of location. It is "national" in that it draws on a nationality—in this case Indians—rather than being geographical like most Catholic parishes. Some have approved of this policy to treat Indian Catholics as separate peoples; others have criticized methods that have left Indians segregated from the modern Church, living—as it were—in the backwaters of the Catholic past. When Sister Mariella Lewis came to Pala in 1981 to serve as principal, she found that "Many Indians had little knowledge of their faith. They had been neglected by the church that baptized them" (San Diego. Pala. October 16, 1987), she said. She claimed that one family did not know how to use a Bible; most had never heard of the Second Vatican Council.

Rev. Xavier Colleoni, pastor at Pala, admitted that the priests had kept the Bible from the Indians there, "not sure the people would understand it. We were afraid to put the Bible in their hands whereas the Protestants have lived in the Bible" (in Gorman 1985: 14). In the 1980s he and the other Verona Fathers began offering Bible study classes; however, more sweeping changes waited until the 1990s.

CONTEMPORARY INDIAN CATHOLICS AND THE CHURCH

In San Diego and San Bernardino dioceses none of the thirty-one reservations has more than 600 residents (Morongo and Pala are more populous than the rest), and several (e.g., Ramona, Capitan Grande, Cuyapaipe, Inaja, and Cosmit) have no year-round residents. The Diocese of San Diego serves nineteen reservations staffed through seven parishes, and the Diocese of San Bernardino reaches twelve reservations in eight parishes. There are at least 4,346 Catholic Indians in San Diego diocese out of the 14,000 Native Americans there, as reported by the Office of Multicultural Affairs, but the figure could be as high as 5,000. Of these, 1,750 are Luiseños and Cupeños primarily on and near the reservations of Pala, Rincon, La Jolla, and Pauma; and Santa Ysabel has 1,250 Diegueño Catholics on the reservation and in its vicinity. In San Bernardino the figures for Catholic Indians are about 3,500 out of the 8,000 or so Indians in the area.

Figures from the diocesan offices in the 1980s and 1990s report that there are probably about 22,000 Indians in the two dioceses, out of which perhaps 8,000 identify themselves, or are identified by the Church hierarchy, as Catholic. That is, more than one-third of the Indians are Catholic in some sense, and these tend to be the Indians indigenous to the area. On the other hand, over 10,000 additional Indians living in the dioceses reside away from reservations and their vicinities. Living in various non-Indian parishes, they may be participating in Catholic life but not necessarily identified by the Church as Indians. Many of these Native Americans come from other locales. In 1983 the San Diego diocese reported that 90 percent of the reservation Indians were Catholic (San Diego. Indians. November 18, 1983); in San Bernardino the percentage of Catholic Indians on reservations is closer to 60 percent.

These figures are difficult to speak of definitively. For example, 90 percent of the Indians at Pala consider themselves Catholic, including the Cupeños, who constitute the main population there. A recent pastor at Pala estimated that 98 percent of his parish was Catholic (Bahr 1993: 127), but only 30 percent practice their faith in a way that the parish priest recognizes, i.e., attending mass regularly (Lawson,

November 7, 1992). A Chancery office employee says that the Indians in San Diego are baptized but are "not very good Catholics," in that they are "not practicing" (Stonehouse, November 11, 1992).

Many of these Indians are said to be "practicing Roman Catholics but retained an attenuated form of their pre-contact religion" (Bean and Shipek 1978: 561). Thus we read of Cahuilla Catholics who think of Jesus and Moses as "powerful Medicine men" and who practice forms of folk healing which the Church regards as "devilish" (Modesto and Mount 1989: 27). The layers of traditional religion keep surfacing in ways that are surprising to Catholic authorities. So, e.g., when the Salesian Society that conducts the Pala Rey Youth Camp agreed in 1987 to allow a mining company to develop 110 acres of Salesian property along the San Luis Rey River, the Pala Indians were incensed. These Indians have continued to use this land to gather herbs and to travel to The Indian Head, a site sacred to the Pala community, although it is off the reservation. The Salesians were never aware that the Indians used this land, and yet Palatinguas like Mona Sespe made highly emotional and successful appeals to the County Planning Department to prohibit the sand and gravel operation. "I'm not afraid to beg because this is a very sacred place. . . . I'm begging you to vote no on this one," she testified (San Diego. Pala. June 11, 1987). Pala Indian Don Magee fought against a landfill project in 1990 because the enterprise would desecrate the Indians' sacred mountain—a place where it is said that a fireball deity once visited and where puberty rituals were once held and herbs were gathered. Although the puberty rituals no longer take place, the site is still revered by the Pala people. Said Magee: "I'm a Catholic and I don't go to the Vatican, but it's still a very sacred place to me" (ibid., August 24, 1990).

At the same time, a parish priest at Pala attests that there are probably only three of four "full blooded" Indians in the whole community. He describes the population as "diluted, watered down," one that lacks a "traditional religious culture" (Cribbin, November 7, 1992) upon which to inculturate Catholic worship. The priests serving the Luiseños say that they have tried to increase Pala Indian Catholic participation by encouraging a native expression, but there isn't any to build upon. The old people tell them that the old culture is completely gone. A spokesperson for the Office of Multicultural Affairs for the Diocese of San Diego says of the aboriginal kinship with nature, the use of jimsonweed, the role of medicine men, the puberty rituals for boys and girls, singing and dancing, mourning wakes, burning of clothes and cremation of bodies, the myths of creation, the first people, migrations, the Sun, Earth Mother, Wiyot, etc.: "These things are virtually gone now" (Stonehouse, November 11, 1992).

When Robert H. Brom became ordinary of San Diego in 1990, he instituted a new policy regarding Catholic Indians within the diocese. No longer would there be the "paternalism" of the missionary past. The emphasis would now be upon "lay participation and responsibility" (ibid.) of the parish communities. No longer would special ministries treat Indians directly, apart from the regular diocesan and parish structure. If Indians wanted to experiment with liturgical inculturation, they would have to do so through the centralized liturgy committee and through the local parish pastor. This policy was due partially to personnel shortage; there weren't enough priests to have special ministries to Indians throughout the diocese. In part, however, it came from a contemporary viewpoint that Indians had been treated as objects of missionization far too long, and the time had come for them to be fully supporting members of the Catholic community. In short, the secularization that was to have taken place in the 1830s was now to be carried to its conclusion. Once again Catholic Indians would need to adjust to a change of policy conceived and put into effect from the non-Indian Catholic hierarchy. The Office of Multicultural Affairs for the diocese works today with twenty different cultural groups, and Indians are just one of them, with no special claim on diocesan services or wherewithal. Ines Stonehouse, the director, says that the Indians have grown accustomed to missionary status, even though diocesan priests have served many of them for years, since the diocese was formed. Many of those diocesan appointments were "not the best" (ibid.) because the priests did not want to serve Indians. The Verona Fathers acted like missionaries, treating their charges like adult children, making all decisions for them and giving them no churchly responsibility. Now there are diocesan priests at Pala and elsewhere to treat the Indians as members of the diocese, using all the regular machinery of the diocese rather than special Indian commissions, ministries, and liturgies. The new diocesan policies are still in the process of formation, and they have a long way to go in Indian communities, where the people have resisted them. The Diocese of San Diego has no permanent diaconate program for Indians—a program found in many other dioceses around the country with sizable

Indian populations. The bishop is still new, and people are looking into models of Indian diaconates employed by the National Tekakwitha Conference. Such a program for Catholic Indian leadership has "not yet begun." Ms. Stonehouse acknowledges that the relationship between Indians and the Church structures has not always been "the best" (ibid.), and there is still much to accomplish. She hopes that the diocese will win Indians' trust for the future.

One can see the changes taking place at Pala. In 1991 the Pala Catholic School lost its principal, Sister Mary Yarger, a graduate of the school nearly thirty years ago. The loss of this Indian sister has made the Pala Indians nervous that their traditions would be neglected in the school curriculum. The school had one hundred and fifty students, 80 percent of whom were Indians. Tuition was $750, but Indian parents bartered their services in return for free tuition. Sister Mary Yarger regarded the school as an important part of community cohesion because it integrated Native American and Catholic traditions; with her departure questions arose about the place of native culture in the curriculum and the tuition bartering system.

In 1991 the Verona Fathers left their Indian mission, and the diocese replaced them with two diocesan priests, Father William Lawson—a former Episcopalian priest—and an Irish priest, James Cribbin. Neither had pastoral experience with Indians, although Cribbin had served briefly in an Indian community in New Mexico.

The new pastor, Father Lawson, lets it be known that "this is a parish, not a mission," even though it has the word, "mission" in its title. He is not sure when it became a parish, but he is sure that it is. A parish is "self-supporting" (Lawson, November 7, 1992), and Pala—with its outlying chapels—is "supposed to be so." It has a parish council and a financial council, both created by Lawson, that meet twice a month. The Verona Fathers never could get the Indians to form a council, and the members of the parish never had a part in the budgetary processes. The Pala Indians have resisted the changes wrought by Lawson and directed from the chancery. Lawson says that the Indians do not understand the necessity of change; they do not understand that change can be positive. They have yet to experience the modernism of Vatican II, which he plans to bring about there at long last.

In November 1991 a worker almost fell through the roof of the Pala church. Termites had eaten its beams. Lawson saw immediately that the church needed to be thoroughly reconstructed and began the pro-

ject, now completed. The Indians feared that the repairs were an excuse to close the mission. These "deeply traditional" (Montali 1992: 13)
people distrusted the changes they saw: first the diocesan priests, now
a newly furbished church over which they feel they hold longstanding
proprietary interests. In the course of conversations with Lawson and
the diocesan offices, the Indians learned that they belonged not to an
Indian mission, but rather to a "tri-cultural parish—Anglo, Hispanic,
and Native American" (ibid.). Lawson says that the whole episode of
the roof shows how resistant the Indians are to change. They were
against the project, even though it was absolutely necessary from his
viewpoint, because it might change what they consider mistakenly to
be "their" church. In the same way, they fear all the other changes he
is bringing to them because the changes threaten "their" practice of
Catholicism.

The Indians, in his view, have a "great belief in externals, but no
internals," leading to a religious practice that is not grounded in
understanding. He says that their Catholic spirituality is "largely
superstitious," rather than an "informed expression of faith" (Lawson,
November 7, 1992).

The Indians do not understand the preparation necessary to receive
sacraments like baptism and matrimony. They need to be "informed,"
he declares, before they can partake of the mysteries of the Church.
Though they still have a "receptive mode" to the Church; they will not
"take ownership." The Verona Fathers practiced a "trickle down, very
hierarchical model" of Church, treating the Pala Indians with "patron-
izing" control. Now the Indians resist anything that will make them
responsible for their Catholic lives. Lawson attributes this reluctance
to "own" the Church to "Indian mentality and psychology." For these
people the community is supreme, and no one likes to stand out from
the group. It is difficult to elicit leadership from them because each
person will say, "I don't know enough; I'm unworthy," and so forth.
No one will volunteer to perform parish tasks, even though they think
of the Church building as their own, and so Lawson is required to appoint individuals to positions of responsibility and service.

Lawson sees very little Catholic spirituality among his Indian
parishioners, remarking that people are more interested in "things of
the flesh." He sees alcoholism and drug addiction as serious obstacles
to Indian spiritual development, causing them to drop away from the
Church because they feel unworthy; they despair at their ability to re-

cover. Their families feud with one another, so that one group will avoid services if its members know another faction will be present. He regards much of the community as "dysfunctional," with a "gossip mill, a rumor mill" construing every change negatively and with resentment. The Indian families, he contends, engage in "bad parenting" and physical abuse; incest is "kept hush hush." "Parents don't have the skills they need," he asserts, to raise their children as bona fide Catholics in a Catholic culture.

He does not have firsthand experience of the Indian home life, and he admits that his observations come from secondhand information; however, he knows from his own experience that there is vandalism directed at the church edifice. He himself is not threatened, nor is the rectory, but the signs of alienation from the Church are real. Though some Indians who have conversion experiences can become intensely faithful—there are model Catholic Indians, "very fine" ones throughout the parish—nevertheless in general, he thinks that the Catholic Indians in his parish have much to achieve in the practice of their faith.

He speaks of the Pala School, referring to it not as the Pala "Indian" School. He says that the diocese never envisioned it as an Indian school when it was built in the late 1950s, but rather as a "parochial school, favoring Indians." Whites attended from the beginning and paid tuition, which made it possible for the Indians to attend gratis. The Verona Fathers promised the Indians that they would never have to pay tuition; the Indians remember that today. In the 1970s a fresh group of Sisters of the Blessed Sacrament came to the school and brought with them a "doctrinaire" view that the school was for Indians; that its role was to support Indian culture. About one hundred white families felt unwanted and stopped sending their children. The Veronas and the sisters were in conflict, and in the late 1980s those particular sisters left. Sister Mary Yarger then took over as principal. Though a splendid teacher, she was not a skilled administrator. Wanting to return to the classroom, she resigned in 1991 with the school in deep financial difficulty. She tried to get tuition from Indian parents but never collected much. Tuition today is $1200, almost double that of the year before, but many of the Indian families can afford this, Lawson avows. They are not as poor as one might think, he states, and the school will not turn them away for lack of money. Today there is a lay principal, Robert J. Clark, and sisters no longer serve the school as teachers. Thirty to forty Indian families continue to send their children to the school, but only several families are white. In 1990–91 there were 180 students; today there are only 110.

While other priests in California and around the United States are emphasizing a special ministry to American Indians, Lawson and the San Diego diocese are attempting to treat Indians without undue regard for their Indianness. Ralph Monteiro, with a pastorship among the Hoopa and other Indians in the northern Santa Rosa diocese, comments, "We've done so much damage that we have to provide a special ministry so they can see that the Church has something to offer" (Monteiro, November 19, 1992). The Diocese of San Diego thinks that special ministry has done harm to Indians, and it is time they were treated like everyone else.

The Luiseños have greeted these changes with resentment and resignation. A Catholic Indian from Rincon calls the last two years an "interesting time of turmoil" (Arviso, October 12, 1992). In Pala an Indian man says, "Just accept it. It's just a fact" (Freeman, November 7, 1992) that the Pala Mission Church does not belong to the Indians, but rather to the diocese. It has been hard for the Catholic Indians to accept this over the last years, but he says that he has, finally, after being involved in the rebuilding of the church. The Indians understand that the Franciscans and Verona Fathers had treated the Indians as a special ministry, but that will no longer be the case. Of a recent parish council meeting it was said: "Bad news coming. Pala Mission is going to cease to be Indian. To the diocese we're just a parish" (Arviso et al., November 5, 1992).

A parish council meeting reveals that fact. Of the two dozen members, half are Indians, half are Whites, with the Whites comprising the budget committee, and the council served primarily by Indians. The discussion (Pala, November 9, 1992) focusses on finances. How will the parish pay the $200,000 spent on the church repairs? How will Father Cribbin's new quarters—which cost $25,000—be paid for? Some accuse Father Lawson of going ahead on the roof project without consulting the committees. Father Lawson replies that these committees were not really in existence at the time. The parishioners retort that the committees came into existence while the project was underway, yet they still do not know how the money was spent. Lawson has brought his personal friend, an Episcopalian who keeps the parish books, to report on parish finances, but it is the pastor who makes the reports and retorts. The weekly money coming into the parish has been dropping steadily over the past year, from $1,400 when Lawson arrived, to $700 in the most recent week. Does this reflect a lowered commitment to the church? Is it the recession? No one can say. Lawson warrants that the diocese has "already given us a lot," and that the parishioners need to begin in 1993 a campaign of "sacrificial giving." The diocese wants to know if our parishioners are willing to give to support their local Catholic church. He says of the parish debt: "Don't expect a blank forgiveness." He asks the question repeatedly, how much commitment is there among the parishioners to support the church? The support must be local, he confirms. Even with such commitment, it is clear that Father Cribbin will be moving on, perhaps in a year, and he will not be replaced by a full-time priest. Consequently, one priest will serve the Luiseño and Cupeño communities, and funds will be saved in the retrenchment. One white member of the parish council notes that the money saved will be spent "on hospital bills when Father Bill has a nervous breakdown" (ibid.); however, spiritual services will be cut anyway. There will be fewer masses in fewer chapels. Religious outreach will shrink in the immediate future. At La Jolla, Rincon, and Pauma, the Luiseños will no longer be able to expect masses every Sunday, as they do now. Perhaps they will be expected to travel to Pala if they wish to attend mass. The question is, will they make the trip, or will they be disaffected?

At the parish council meeting it is noticeable how quiet most of the Indians are. For many of these Indians—King Freeman, Peanuts Magee, Milonny Arviso, and others—the hierarchy of the Church, its bureaucratic institutions, seem strange and unnecessary. In private conversation they ask why one needs to have these chancery offices, these accounts, these bureaucratic procedures, committees, and hierarchies? Why are these necessary to promote human morality and spirituality? Do these things bring people closer to God? The Indians gripe that the priests of the present day treat religion as a business. The Indians say that parish council meetings make it more difficult for them to think of the Church as a sacrament, a means to holiness, rather than a White Man's obfuscation, an obstacle to faith. One senses at such a meeting that the Church gets in the way of their spiritual development.

The bureaucracy of the Church confuses them: "the diocese," "the order," "the parish"; who owns the church buildings? There are all these rules, instituted beyond their purview, and they fear that what underlies many Church decisions is "the Almighty Dollar" (Arviso et al., November 5, 1992). Some find that Church structures set up for Indians—for instance, the Commission for Native American Catholics, established several years ago in the diocese—are "going nowhere," because power lies where the money is, and the money is not in the Indian communities.

George Arviso of Rincon serves as chairperson of the commission because no other Indian would take the job. He does it to give Indians a voice in the Church, although he thinks that Indians are basically powerless because they are poor. Before the commission, he served on a diocesan pastoral council. He was chosen for that, he says, because of "tokenism": the chancery wanted an Indian so the hierarchy could say that there was one in diocesan decision making. In such a setting his voice, he says, wasn't heard. "Well, yes, they always *listen* to you. But what comes of it?" he queries. So in 1990 he took the position as chairperson of the commission, but already in 1992 the chancery officials are regarding that body as "inactive" (Stonehouse, November 11, 1992). Ines Stonehouse suggests that the diocese will move to another model, using the pastors of each Indian parish as the liaisons to the diocesan office, rather than relying on Indian representatives, who were unable to get together on a regular basis, coming as they do from many different communities. Such commissions and committees are a way in which the Church tries to yoke Indian communities to the central decision making bodies; however, for the Indians, each community is central to its concern, not the Church. The Indians see decision making as something that arises out of each community. George Arviso says, e.g., that he regards himself only as a "mouthpiece" for the Indians, not from seventeen different communities, but from Rincon. He is not even an official representative from Rincon and can have no authority for his neighbors. He hopes that there could be a voice for each of the seventeen different groups, but the diocese will not allow such diversity of voices. The churchmen emphasize centralism; the Indians emphasize localism.

This localism is clear among the Luiseños. There is some jealousy amongst the different communities—Pala, Pauma, La Jolla, Rincon, etc.—in vying for the Church's attention within the Diocese of San Diego. People from each community are critical of Luiseños from elsewhere. At Pala the main cemetery is the domain of the Luiseños, and with space running out, they are jealous of every plot. Even the Cupeños, who came here in 1903, have their own cemetery set apart. Their Catholic faith may be the same, and it is a potential force to join them into a single community; however, localism keeps them apart, even in such a tight place as Pala. The attempt by the diocese and the parish to centralize and routinize their religious life faces great difficulties, because it goes directly against their local sense of autonomy, as well as their general disaffection from the Church as an institution of outsiders.

The Catholic Indians of the Pala parish resent the intrusion of foreigners in their communities. They resent the Whites; they resent the Mexicans; they resent the Church itself. "We used to know everybody," says an Indian man at Pala; "now we lock everything." There are a lot of new faces, and there has been a "lot of change. We sure do feel overrun by outsiders" (Magee, November 6, 1992). Whites have been attending San Antonio de Pala for decades, at first because of the "romance of the mission" (Lawson, November 7, 1992), but in increasing numbers since the Second Vatican Council because they were dissatisfied by the liberal changes in liturgy in their home parishes. They came to Pala because the Verona Fathers conducted a conservative liturgy. The church became a "haven" for unhappy, conservative Whites. They have given money; indeed, they are the "primary financial support" (ibid.) of the parish. Nevertheless, they have no long-term commitment to the community. They attend mass and depart. By attending, they have pushed out the Indians, who have been drifting away for several decades. The Pala Indians say that Whites have "hijacked their chapel" (Cribbin, November 7, 1992). Fascinated by the old church, Whites today constitute 90 percent of the congregation. Some come from within the parish geography; others come from further afield, and some are tourists, passing through. At Pauma the Indians make it clear that they do not want outsiders at their services. At Rincon tourists and other Whites are made to feel welcome, because the people of Rincon say that they are Catholics, and so they welcome any Catholics at a mass. On the other hand, they acknowledge that Indians have a long history of being run out by Whites and other intruders, and the Indians want to protect their privacy, space, and property. They are tugged by two identities: as Catholics they want to be good hosts; as Indians they would like to keep outlanders at a distance (Arviso, November 8, 1992).

In the nineteenth century the Mexicans overran these Indians, as the Anglos did later. Marriages took place among all three ethnic groups, and the contemporary Luiseños and Cupeños reflect that ethnic biological diversity. Nevertheless, they see Mexicans, as well as Anglos, as a threat to their community. They resent the Mexican farm workers who come to the area to pick oranges. These migrants have rented trailers on the reservations and thus live within the boundaries of the Pala parish. In order to meet their spiritual needs, the diocese has organized a Spanish-speaking chapel, Centro Guadalupano, set between Pala, Pauma, and Rincon, with a weekly mass in Spanish. A page of the parish bulletin is in Spanish. Some Luiseños express sympathy for the Mexicans—largely illegals—who live all around them, both on and off the reservation. Some live in great poverty, dwelling in storm culverts or in pits they have dug in the hills. Some Indians offer their Christian charity to impoverished people who need physical and spiritual help; however, it is hard to accept them. The Mexicans argue that they, too, are Indians, and as one Indian woman said, "You know, they're right, they probably have more Indian blood than most of us" (Arviso et al., November 5, 1992). Nevertheless it is hard to feel their kinship when they are moving into Indian land. Georgiana O. Viveros suggests that the Luiseños and Mexicans share a common spirituality through devotion to Our Lady of Guadalupe: "We are more like Mexicans than we admit" (ibid.), and the priests try to instill this attitude of acceptance. On the other hand, virtually none of the Luiseños speaks Spanish, and in school there is little Indian sympathy for the Mexicans' speaking Spanish ("Make them learn English. We did"). The Luiseños regard the Mexicans as their enemies; they resent their presence in their churches and their votes on parish councils. They believe that the diocese is favoring the Mexicans and other ethnic groups over the eldest inhabitants of the area, themselves.

A Pauma Indian calls the Church a "brokerhouse" (Dixon et al., November 11, 1992), in which the hierarchy goes where the money and the population are. So, if Whites and Mexicans outnumber and outspend the Indians in their own parish, then it ceases to be "their" parish. And if that alienates the Indians into withdrawing—which it has—so be it. There are Luiseño Indians who believe that the Church is that cynical, that heartless, toward the Indian communities. Other Luiseños say that they no longer mind the presence of Whites and Mexicans, having become inured to them.

In communities where Indians still decry the fact that scientists put the Mt. Palomar telescope "in the center of our universe" (ibid.); where many are tired of the prying questions of scholars and "do-gooders"; where many characterize the cultural life of Whites as "pay rent and taxes and die" (ibid.); where most know their history well enough to realize that neither Mexicans nor Anglos have proved often to be their benefactors, to say the least; the fact that the diocese has decided that Pala is a multiethnic community with no special obligations to the Indians causes sustained sullenness. The pastors in Pala recognize that the Indians take umbrage at the Church partially because they resent Whites, who have usurped their lands and now are in the process of taking over their churches. The Indians even say that outsiders have taken over their fiestas and are driving them away from the Catholic Church they regard as their own.

The Irish priest, Father Cribbin, comments that in Ireland the practice of Catholicism is a means by which the Irish of the Republic (and of the North) proclaim their Irish identity. Catholic worship is a form of protest against the secular state, akin to the political dimension of Polish Catholic practice during the years of Communist rule. He wonders why the Indians don't have the same political dimension to their Church life, but he admits that they do not. Their Catholic identity exists, but it is ambivalent because they regard the Church as a white institution. They want to receive baptism; they wish their marriages and funerals to take place in the church, but otherwise they stay away. Theirs is a "love-hate relationship" with the Church (Cribbin, November 7, 1992).

The Luiseños recognize their ambivalence toward the Church. They ask themselves why it is that their people fall away from the Church. In part, they recognize that "it is hard to be a Catholic Christian" (Arviso et al., November 5, 1992), because the Church demands that you aim for perfection in your "faith walk," even knowing that you will fall short constantly of the ideals. There are high moral standards, demands of conscience, ritual expectations. These make Catholic life a burden. But there are more mundane reasons for disaffection. On reservations throughout southern California there are many "inactive" Catholics who smart under their pastors, or feel alienated by the bureaucracy, or are unmoved by the rituals, or who have no easy access to a chapel.

A goodly number of the fallen-away Catholic Indians of southern California have joined Protestant denominations. Although only 10 percent are officially Protestant, and almost all the rest are said to be "nominally Catholic," many have "become fundamentalist" (Monteiro, September 1, 1992) in recent years. Anita Castillo, an ex-Catholic from Pala, raised her first four children as Catholics, but not the younger four:

"How many of us have gone to church without knowing why we were going?" she asks. "My mother was a great Catholic and she brought me up strictly, but she's no longer Catholic—she's a Jehovah's Witness—and now I'm going to other churches, too. I'm beginning to understand the Bible for the first time. I didn't know what the darn thing was when I was going to the Catholic church." . . . Why are Indians leaving the Roman Catholic Church? "Because we're not brainwashed anymore to stay Catholic." (Gorman 1985: 14)

Various Protestant bodies have existed among the Luiseños throughout the century; indeed, on several reservations Moravians and other denominations have preceded the Catholics in erecting local churches. Today the Assemblies of God and other pentecostal churches are attractive to the Luiseños, providing spontaneity, community, and emotional release. They offer fellowship and appeal to Indian localism. They teach Bible stories more thoroughly than the Church did in the past. Hence, even for Catholic Indians who "wouldn't dare look at their church; we'd look the other way" (Arviso et al., November 5, 1992), the Protestants have proved popular alternatives to the distant, hierarchical Roman Catholic Church. They evangelize aggressively, and when the Catholic Indians are feeling their displeasure with the Church, they are apt to state ruefully that "As an Indian Catholic community we aren't going to survive. . . . We'll become pentecostal, or revive our Indian religion" (ibid.). Sr. Patricia Dixon, a Luiseño from Pauma, notes, however, that even when Catholic Indians have converted to Protestantism, their Catholicism has remained their frame of reference (Dixon et al., November 11, 1992).

Their Catholicism, however, is a complex of spiritual yearning and bitterness. The faith of Catholic Luiseños incorporates a discontent towards the Church. One Luiseño man says, "I'm bitter a little. I admit it" (Arviso et al., November 5, 1992). He and his fellows are indignant that the Church destroyed their traditional Indian culture and that they know so little of their ancestors' ways. A Luiseño woman depicts her entire life as a struggle against her own hard feelings. Indians inherit this attitude; they learn it from their parents, from their community. It is part of being an Indian.

If religious life is an attempt to overcome the acrimony within one's soul, it must also be said that one's religiousness also expresses that bitterness. Luiseño Catholicism is partially an attempt to overcome resentment toward Catholicism itself, and it is partially an expression of that animosity. Ideally the Mystical Body of Christ should offer a person the spiritual wherewithal, the sacramentalism, the grace, to neutralize personal hatreds; however, for Indian Catholics, there is such ambivalence toward the visible Church that Catholicism constitutes an obstacle to its own sacramental goal.

One of the greatest sources of rankling among Catholic Luiseños is the loss of aboriginal culture brought about through Church evangelism. The Indians of the Diocese of San Diego had their religions "suppressed," according to one Indian; "we were very well evangelized." As a result, one will not find many "local Indian customs" (ibid.). Another Luiseño reports that "90 percent of the traditions are gone" (Freeman, November 7, 1992). In the late nineteenth century the reservations at Pala and its environs kept much of what was left of the culture in the wake of the Franciscan missions, arranging the old and new aspects into new patterns. But the boarding schools did the job of killing the language and uprooting the youth; and in the twentieth century the diocese placed priests in each community, which forced traditional practices underground, and in time most of them disappeared. At the more remote communities, like Pauma, the old religion of the Luiseños was still functioning side by side with Catholicism into the 1940s. Elderly women today recall their puberty rituals; they claim to have traditional values. They say that in their youth their religion was kept separate from Catholic practice; the two faiths were "lived differently" (Dixon et al., November 11, 1992), because their practitioners did not want Indian and Catholic ways joined. . . . What can you mix?" These elders have passed down features of the old religion to this day, not intact but still vital. Their children say, "We're lucky we were raised with the little that was left" (ibid.). Sr. Patricia Dixon recalls that when she had her first menstruation, her grandfather announced it to the Catholic congregation as they left the church in Pauma. He declared, "She is now a woman," and gave a speech saying what the community could now expect of her. This was a traditional pattern of announcement placed into a Christian context (ibid.). Her relatives report that in the present day Luiseños at Pauma still take sweat baths after Sunday mass; they "break out the rattle and sing" (ibid.) on many occasions when the extended family gathers. They threaten to go back to these ways if the Church "gets too strict on us."

On the other hand, Indians from Rincon like George Arviso state that for them "traditionalism. . . . is the Roman Rite. It's what we were born into" (Arviso, October 12, 1992). When he attended the Pala Mission School, "The most I learned about Indian culture there was painting tipis on Christmas cards" (ibid.), which the school used to sell to support the institution. Some of those Indians raised completely in Catholic culture want nothing to do with expressions of Indianness in their Catholic religion, but for others there is resentment that they can not turn to their Indian traditions these days because there is so little left. Edna Mamake, an elderly Pauma woman, says that a college teacher came around to learn something of the old Luiseño culture, and after a short conversation, said to her, "You live the same as we do." She retorted in exasperation: "What do you expect?" (Mamake, August 8, 1992). Mark Macarro, a Pechanga Luiseño who teaches Luiseño language in Rincon, is committed to preserving what is left of Indian culture and wishes to promote Indian community solidarity. His hope in the modern day is that one can be Catholic without ceasing to be Indian, but given the history of the relationship, he is not certain (Arviso et al., November 5, 1992).

Since the Second Vatican Council the Church has been encouraging Indians to express their national culture through their Catholic faith. This process of inculturation requires that Indians have a native culture that is at least partially viable. Many Luiseños are uncertain that theirs is. George Arviso states that when he attends multicultural assemblies in the diocese, the committee members ask him, "Why don't you share your Indian spirituality?" (ibid.). The non-Indian Catholics want him to smoke a pipe, or beat a drum, but these are not his people's rituals as he knows them, and he is piqued that the Church destroyed his people's religious culture; now it wants enrichment from him, and he cannot deliver it. He says that Church authorities today emphasize "local faith community." They say, "Teach yourselves," but the Luiseños did not learn enough about their Catholic faith and were not permitted to pass on enough about their Luiseño faith. Now, with a shortage of priests in the Church, the Indians are being thrown back upon themselves. Mr. Arviso finds it ironic, because aboriginally the Luiseños were "faith communities" par excellence, each local group with its own chief, healer, calendar keeper, spokesperson, and local lore. Localism was their strength. The Church stepped into these local circles and took over all authority, emphasizing the "Catholic," the universal. Today the old Luiseño ways are being held up as a model, and many Luiseños are not able to reinvigorate them. They are not sure that there is enough Indian culture left for them to express. Sr. Patricia Dixon says that since the Luiseños have lost so much of the structure of their old religion, which provided them with meaning and direction in life—since they had this old religious culture "knocked out of us " (Dixon et al., November 11, 1992)—the Catholic Church has provided the "missing holes" in the structure: the ritual, the explanatory system. She finds the Church's teachings "profound," but there are painful feelings over the losses incurred.

In order to experience Indian spirituality in the present day, some Luiseño Catholics attend regional and national meetings of the National Tekakwitha Conference, an agency sponsored by the Bureau of Catholic Indian Missions which supports the inculturation of Catholic faith into Indian modes of worship. The message of this organization is that a person can be Indian and Catholic simultaneously; however, some of the California Indians find that the conference tries to establish a pan-Indian Catholic ritualism that is basically Plains Indian in form, one that flattens all other modes of expression. The conference is trying to establish ritual norms that can win Vatican approval; hence, it is understandable that the variety of Indian cultural forms cannot be expressed; however, these Indians find that their own culture gets left out.

Nevertheless, they are attracted to the rituals of Father John Hascall, an Ojibway priest and medicine man from Michigan. One Pala man calls Father Hascall "a great man" (Magee, November 6, 1992) who has had a profound influence on some Luiseños and other Indians of southern California when he has come to visit. At Tekakwitha Conferences Father Hascall leads sweat lodge rituals and combines his Ojibway spiritualism with Catholic rituals, even in the saying of the mass. Lorena Dixon does not approve usually of the mixing of Indian and Catholic religion, but she says of Hascall's mass at a Tucson Tekakwitha Conference in 1990: "It was a nice mass. . . . It was different. . . . At least it seemed authentic" (Dixon et al., November 11, 1992), unlike the attempt by Father Lawson to use sage at a local mass, which she found "phony." She argues that Father Lawson does not even believe in the purifying power of sage, so how can he appropriate the religion of Indians to make it appear that he values their spirituality? When Hascall performed an Indian mass in Tucson, the "pink hats" (ibid.)— the bishops—got upset because the mass was "too Indian." According to some Luiseños, the Tekakwitha board wants only to include some Indian peripherals in an essentially Roman rite, whereas the Indians need more authentic, local, Indian expression.

In recent years the Tekakwitha Conference has witnessed internal rancor over the degree of Indianness that is appropriate in Catholic worship. At several national conferences there have been public arguments, and it would appear that the Luiseños are on the side of those who want fuller Indian expression in Catholic ritual. It may seem ironic that mission Indians, who admit that their culture has been almost thoroughly transformed over the past two centuries, are the ones calling for the greatest expression of traditional culture in Catholicism. On the other hand, their critical stance may reflect their overall dissatisfaction with the Church as an institution. The leadership of the Tekakwitha board tends to include Indians who are relatively comfortable with white culture, or who were brought up almost totally in white cultural forms—e.g., the two Indian bishops in the United States, Donald Pelotte and Charles Chaput. The Luiseños regard themselves as more authentically "Indian" than these men and others on the Tekakwitha board. They say that the choice of Pelotte and Chaput as bishops took place because they were only peripherally, vestigially Indian, unfamiliar with Indian religious life. How can they (the bishops) help incorporate valid Indian spirituality into the Church if they do not know Indian religious forms from firsthand experience? Edna Mamake says that "the leadership is terrible" (Mamake, August 8, 1992) because it does not listen more to the desires of grassroot Indian communities like her own—even though she acknowledges that she lives her life wholly like a white person. Still, despite their complaints, these Indians are prepared to attend future Tekakwitha national meetings, even though they have found the past meetings too "political," without enough "spiritual" content (Magee, November 6, 1992).

Sister Patricia Dixon thinks that Indian spirituality has much to offer the Church beyond the Indian community, although in San Diego the hierarchy in her view is unreceptive to Indian spirituality even for Indians. In San Bernardino diocese Father Rafael Partida is the Vicar for Indian Affairs, and he encourages inculturation in both his own diocese and San Diego. Although he was not raised in an Indian community, his mother is Tohono O'odham (Papago), and he avows that he inherited an Indian spirituality. Over the past several years he has organized sweat lodge ceremonies and fasts for Indians of southern California, following the patterns he learned from Father John Hascall. He says that he is not trying to blend Indian and Catholic spirituality, but to have them "walk hand in hand" (*Tekakwitha Conference Newsletter* 11, no. 1, March-April 1992: 10). Since 1992 he has been joined by Father Tony Garduño, a Mexican American with Indian ancestry. Partida tells how "clean" (Partida, August 7, 1992) he felt in leading sweats at Pala, a cleanliness that the Creator intended for life on earth. He tells the Indians that Catholic and Indian spirituality are two ways we have to express our souls, as types of art. They are not in competition with each other, just as one art form does not compete with another. Indians should use both forms of art: Indian and Catholic.

Within the two diocese, Partida has taken criticism for his Indian liturgies, he says, but not from the people who really know liturgy, what is permitted and what is not. He himself was trained in liturgy, and he wishes to lead the mission Indians in liturgical forms that will help them embrace not only their Catholic faith, but also their Indian faith (Partida, August 8, 1992). This does not convince all members of the Catholic hierarchy in southern California. He reports that someone in the San Bernardino diocese said to him, "There weren't any Indians here until you showed up" (ibid.), and he has experienced some malice from other priests in the area. George Arviso reports an incident in the San Diego diocesan office in which Partida's name came up. A priest termed Partida a "phony" who claims today to be an Indian, but when he was in the seminary he "went along" with mainline Catholic liturgy without ever mentioning his Indianness (Arviso et al., November 5, 1992). Nevertheless, Partida continues to offer Indians of southern California, like the Luiseños, a chance to emphasize cultural forms that they can claim as their own as part of their Catholic expression, even though his superiors in San Bernardino diocese have ordered him to "cut out" (Lenz, November 19, 1993) his liturgical experimentation.

Under Partida's, and Hascall's influence, Luiseños and other Indians are now conducting their own sweat lodges. King Freeman, a Luiseño who operates the Pala Store across the street from the church, and who served as tribal chairman at Pala for twenty years, runs regular sweats and has even invited Father Lawson to participate. Having spent all but six of his years on the reservation, he has also traveled to most of the Indian communities in southern California, and from these contacts he has grown interested in shared cultural forms among the different tribes of the area. In the 1970s he learned to play peon, a gambling game using sticks and accompanied by songs. The Luiseños used to play it, for example, at the yearly fiestas, but the practice had been lost in the 1950s. Freeman says that the Indians who taught him peon took sweat baths to purify themselves before playing—because games are also rituals to these people. From this contact came a revival in the sweat lodge, encouraged by Hascall and Partida and also by Freeman. Sweats had never completely disappeared from Luiseño life, not in the mission days, not up to World War II. When many Indians left the reservation in the 1950s under the Relocation Program of the Bureau of Indian Affairs, the sweats almost ceased. In the late 1970s, however, as part of "a phase people go through" of heightened cultural awareness (Freeman, November 7, 1992)—as Blacks, Mexicans, and Hawaiians have recently experienced—the Luiseños revived the practice. Freeman regrets that his grandparents did not pass down their language to him. He wanted to learn it as a youth but they said that he did not need it, not to waste his time. Now very few Luiseños speak it fluently. When he and other Pala Indians sing in their sweats, they are voicing songs taught them by other Indians, and they are still learning more songs from others. For Freeman, Indian religion takes hard work to hold together and pass down because it is not a matter of written texts. The religious complex comes apart easily under pressure from outsiders. His hope is to pass on as much of it as he can. At the same time, he is a practicing Catholic, a member of the parish council. He says of himself, "I'm not devoted but I try to go to church every Sunday" (ibid.), and on a Saturday morning in November one can find him with the choir, rehearsing Christmas hymns in the chapel of San Antonio de Pala. Like other Luiseños, he regards *religion* very highly, more highly than any particular religious *form*, such as a Catholic mass. He says, "Although mass isn't necessary, religion is. Every kid needs a religious background, whatever it is, in order to be a good person, if not a holy person" (ibid.). Sister Patricia Dixon notes that the Luiseños may not always know the jargon of Catholicism, but their theology is "lived." They are profoundly religious people: "They know things deeply, whether it's Catholic or not" (Dixon et al., November 11, 1992).

In so saying, the Indians may be expressing the contemporary ethos of American spirituality—and there are those who say that the Catholic Indians in southern California are very much influenced by "new age spirituality"; that their religious culture today is a "hodge-podge" of influences without a solid tribal grounding (Steltenkamp, August 9, 1992)—but they may also be expressing the view of a people who have adopted Catholic forms without giving up their attachment to native forms. Hence, they come to value *religiousness* over any one form, as a way of mediating potential conflict between the two.

Freeman acknowledges that most Indians at Pala—both Luiseños and Cupeños—neglect church, except for baptisms, marriages, and (especially) funerals. As the Indians see it, "Church is not necessary to be good. . . . It helps them along, I guess" (Freeman, November 7, 1992), to build morals, but there are good Luiseños who attended mass very rarely as children. Freeman does not believe that parents or priests should force children to attend mass; they may go to mass when they get older. Mass simply is not a high priority for most Pala Indians.

Peanuts Magee says that when he was young, it seemed that every-one went to Sunday mass, but now only a handful attends, certainly "not as many as there should be" (Magee, November 6, 1992). He sug-gests that the "outsiders" at mass discourage the Pala Indians from at-tending. Other elderly Luiseños say that the changes in liturgy gained during Vatican II—changes initiated not in their community but by Catholic leaders from around the world—left them feeling alienated. Before her death in 1994 Villiana Hyde stated that she did not want to attend mass anymore, because of the changes: "I expected people to get up and dance in church" (Hyde and Hyde, November 8, 1992). Since a bout of pneumonia, since her eyes went bad, since her hearing could not bear the noise of air conditioning in church, she ceased to attend with any regularity. And yet other Luiseños speak of their local masses with a jealous control regarding the liturgy. At Pauma the late Lee Dixon described his weekly attendance at mass—and except for funerals and weddings, he would attend no other church but his own in Pauma—as a means of community ownership of the ritual, in oppo-sition to the parish priest's attempts to take over all liturgical forms.

In Rincon the Luiseños are fiercely possessive of their chapel—so much so that they still are irked that in the 1930s the diocese changed its name to St. Bartholomew without consultation with the commu-nity. They are proud that their ancestors built the concrete block build-

ing and that they themselves have kept it up. It is located at the center
of the reservation, next to the Assemblies of God church and the Rincon Store. At Sunday mass the church is full with sixty people, about
half of them Indians. George Arviso serves as lector; a Luiseño youth
is the altar boy, but there are also Mexicans, Filipinos, and Whites,
including visitors and tourists. An observer listens to the reading from
Maccabbees in which a king is threatening the Jews to give up the
sacred customs of their ancestors—explicitly their prohibitions against
pork. The Jews refuse, and the visitor wonders if the Indians see themselves, or their ancestors, as analogues to the Jews and the Christian
missionaries as more recent versions of the king; however, there is no
indication of such a connection in the Indians' minds.

Father Lawson's sermon draws from the gospel, in which the Sad-
ducees ask Jesus a trick question about a woman who marries seven
brothers, as each one dies: to whom will she be married in heaven?
Jesus answers that there is no marriage after death. The life to come is
radically different from this one. Lawson says that the life after death is
grounded in God's will, not in our wishful thinking. We cannot know
the afterlife in advance except through our poetic images: harps, and
so forth. But what we *do* know is that our place in it, whether we go
there with fear or joy, depends on how we live our lives today. We
were given choice, and we choose our eternity by choosing how we
live. Lawson thereby replicates the thematic focus of the Franciscan
doctrinas of the mission days, with their emphasis on reward and punishment in the hereafter. The congregation listens attentively, and
many receive the Eucharist. Afterwards the Indians serve coffee and
desserts in an adjoining room. It is a service one might find in any
rural Catholic church in the United States, with no particular reference
to Indian culture or the particular history of these Indian people. It is
normative, to a fault.

Although in Pala the congregation consists mostly of Whites and
Mexicans, the Indians from the community prepare the church:
sweeping the floors and dusting the statues of St. Anthony, Jesus,
Mary, and Kateri Tekakwitha, while tourists amble through with their
cameras, enjoying the refurbished building, its new steel infrastructure
hidden behind the massive wood beams and newly painted Indian designs on the plaster walls. The cemetery continues to serve as a vivid
record of the Indian community, and many of the graves have numerous marks from melted candles, many as recent as All Souls Day.

Peanuts Magee rings the bell in the tower at the western end of the cemetery to announce mass and funerals. He also sells tourmaline jewelry across the street in front of the Pala Store, while the church vends its devotional items in its own store behind the chapel.

Magee grew up in Pala and has lived there almost all his life. His mother, he recalls, was "quite a religious woman" (Magee, November 6, 1992) who attended daily mass. When he was a child, she required him to attend mass on Sundays, and so he was brought up a Catholic. When he entered military service during the Korean War he started drinking; he "ran around" and "forgot about religion," yet he did confess his sins to a military chaplain. Then, when he came home and was drinking heavily, he turned to Church personnel and ritual "only if I needed something." He married, divorced, drank, traveled, and finally moved back to Pala, suffering from cirrhosis of the liver. He had earned a living as a barber off the reservation, but "you're always drawn back to the reservation. It's a nice life," he opines.

At this low point he turned back to Catholic practice: "You gotta put God up there someplace." He gave up drinking and has never gone back to it in nearly a quarter century, since 1970. In the early 1980s he became involved in a "Renew Program," and he has become even more active in Church activities over the last decade. He serves on the parish council; he works for the church and its school. Most of the Indians will not volunteer for church assignments. Magee wonders, "Why always me?" and feels trapped in his tasks, but he performs them anyway. He attends mass frequently, almost daily. He tries to get others to attend mass and to quit their drinking. In turn, "the boys" try to get him to have a drink with them. He says that he derives spiritual enrichment from attending mass: "It's always deeper than you think." But for the past few years he has been taking part in sweats with King Freeman, especially since these rituals are aimed at sobering up young men and boys. Magee says that in the sweat "we all respect each other, Catholics and non-Catholics. We pray to Our Father, Grandfather, Earth." He used to belong to a Bible study program at Pala, but he wondered, "Was I doing too much religious stuff? Always praying. Was it for me or for God?"

Magee resents outsiders who have intruded on the Indians' life at Pala. Yet he is married to a white woman who used to be a Catholic sister, a teacher at the Pala School. He makes it clear, jokingly, that he did not seduce her from the sisterhood. They married in the 1970s, after he received an annulment from his first marriage. Both of them serve on the parish council, and they have traveled to National Tekakwitha Conferences, but for the most part they do not associate with one another publicly on the reservation because his friends deride him for marrying a White. They suggest that she wants to be an Indian and appropriate their culture; hence, Magee does not take her to peon games or other events of Indian cultural expression: "It's been rough on her, pretty rough," he comments. Their Catholic activity is one area in which their lives are brought together.

In Rincon, George and Milonny Arviso also share in their community's Catholic life. Milonny conducts the catechetical program at Rincon for some thirty children. She organizes Confraternity of Christian Doctrine classes through the public school system of Valley Center, where most Rincon students are enrolled, and she watches sadly as many of her students "fall away" from the Church as teens. Milonny is also secretary of the Pala Parish Council, a position she did not want. Father Lawson insisted that she accept the assignment, and so she takes her minutes of the council meetings quietly.

Her husband attends the council meetings, and although he is not a member, he asks many questions and involves himself in many aspects of parish life. The parish priests praise Arviso as an "intelligent, articulate, strong Catholic," but when the Indian man starts talking about Luiseño sovereignty, the Irish Cribbin ribs him: "Where is your flag, your army, your passport?" (Cribbin, November 7, 1992). The Arvisos love their Rincon home and the surrounding hills; they serve their Indian community, where they have lived for almost their whole lives (he was in the army for a while). They are also devoted, though critical, members of the Catholic Church.

George Arviso says that "fifteen years ago I didn't commit myself to God or Church" (Arviso et al., November 5, 1992); however, for the last decade he has studied his Catholic faith "on an adult level," and he has also learned that politics play a role in hierarchical Church decision making. He speaks of the "two-facedness" of the Church ("because it's human"), but he attests, "I am an idealist when it comes to the values of Jesus." He expects of Church officials what he expects of himself, a daily life according to those values; he often finds himself disappointed. People think him naive—and it is true that Luiseños from other villages wish that he would treat the Church with more public ire and accusation—but he says that his goal is to call the structure of the Church, quietly but persistently, to the ideals of Jesus: "I still have hope" (Arviso, November 7, 1992). After several years of attending diocesan committee meetings and hearing the conversations that take place "downtown," he makes a conscious effort not to relate all those conversations to his Luiseño friends, fearing that the politics would scandalize them and push them away from the Church. He is disillusioned but faithful.

Besides serving as president of the Diocesan Commission for Native American Catholics, Arviso is a lector at masses in Rincon. No one in the hierarchy has ever asked him to become a deacon, but he and Milonny looked into the process several years ago, finding that the costs are prohibitive and that it requires regular trips into San Diego, which might interfere with his job with the county and with his family life. If the diocese were to cover the costs, he might consider becoming a permanent deacon; however, he finds that the diocese does not support Indian Catholic leadership in such tangible ways. Still, he persists in what he calls his "faith walk," along a path established by the gospels and the Church, in a manner prescribed by them. He says that one is to conduct one's walk properly and with concentration upon the end toward which the path leads. His faith walk, he says, is a way of life, particularly a Catholic way of living a life, that eventually "comes around to the source, the Creator" (Arviso et al., November 5, 1992). He tells of airplane pilots he has read about whose last words before crashing (as recorded in their planes' "black boxes") were "cusswords, rather than prayers of praise, or prayers for forgiveness." He hopes that his last words and thoughts will be directed to God; indeed, his faith walk is a preparation for those words, which will indicate where his eternal life lies. He tries to form a lifetime habit of praising God; he and his fellow Catholic Luiseños think that "You can't praise God enough or too much" (ibid.).

On his twenty-third wedding anniversary, a Sunday, he has attended two masses, read from the Old and New Testaments with authority and conviction, and spoken over coffee with visitors about his faith. The sermon was about life after death, and he wonders about the supposed after-death experiences reported in the media over the last twenty years. With his accustomed skepticism, he doubts that the people who had those experiences were really dead. It was different with Lazarus, depicted in the gospels, who was dead for four days. That story showed Jesus' mastery over the natural processes, his miraculous power over the irreversible nature of death. But even that story: is it to be taken literally? he asks himself. George Arviso spends a goodly portion of his waking hours pondering such religious questions.

After mass he greets two "former Catholics, real nice women" (Arviso, November 8, 1992), coming out of the Assemblies of God Church. He comments that the evangelical Protestants deride the Catholic devotion to ritual. They say that Catholics are worshipping statues, a charge Arviso sets aside but then tries to make sense of it. He says that to understand Catholic ritual, its attention to externals like statues, a person must understand the Bible. The rituals Catholics perform are the means by which we act out our religious attitudes, placing us in relation to the Bible. The rituals direct us toward God. He comments that the pentecostals have their rituals, too, their program of services. You can't have a religious tradition, he says, without established patterns of behavior because that is what a religious tradition is. Arviso attended one of the Assemblies of God prayer meetings recently because a Rincon acquaintance asked him to, as a favor: "I prayed to go with an open heart," without prejudice against his Protestant brethren. He was impressed with the amount of "fun" they had, but he was not interested in attending again. Shortly after, he received two telephone calls. He recounts that one asked him, "Have you left the Church, George?" and the other said, "Praise God, George, you've seen the light" (Arviso et al., November 5, 1992). He chuckled at both and continued on his Catholic path.

On a weekday evening George Arviso and a half dozen Catholic Luiseños meet in the tribal hall on the Rincon Reservation, north of the deserted bingo hall, in a room serving as library and cultural repository. Pausing only for a supper of beans, rice, fry bread, salad, soup, soda, and donuts, they discuss their faith with one another. This is a supportive group, listening intently to one another, praising each other's virtues: one's talent at playing the organ is a musical gift to the Church; another is a "helpmeet" to her husband; George Arviso is, to one woman, "God in our midst" (ibid.). Arviso declares, only partially in jest, "We're orthodox Catholic here!"

Georgiana O. Viveros is the organist at various churches and likes to shake up the Catholic liturgy a bit (she played "When the Saints Go Marching In" on All Saints Day this year). She loves attending mass — usually three times each Sunday, regarding it as a "privilege" to participate in Catholic services. She says in her characteristic spirit of affirmation, "I'm a cradle Catholic and I'll die a Catholic. I can't speak for my children, but I'll die Catholic" (ibid.). She and others speak about the central point of the gospel, Jesus' main theme, the goal and promise of Christianity: God's forgiveness of us and our forgiveness of others. They say that for themselves, as Indians, forgiveness is profoundly difficult because of the resentments they have toward others, but also because of their ingrained self-hatred. They must forgive themselves in order to bring themselves to forgive others. They must love themselves in order to love others, according to Patty Duro.

She says, "I think there are very few evil people, *really*," and she chides George Arviso for holding himself to impossibly high standards of moral behavior. Another woman says to him, "Your faith walk is teaching. You don't have to judge yourself harshly. Live well" (ibid.). Patty Duro has heard that "highly educated people don't believe in God. They intrigue me." For this group of Catholic Luiseños, the possibility of atheism is an alien concept, at best.

These Luiseño Catholics know their Bible, although they claim not to have received biblical training in their youth. They refer often to biblical phrases which they use as guides to their faith walk. They declare, "Romans 5 . . . this is how we ought to live." They comment that if we really look at the daily missal, it is filled with the Bible. Some Catholics say that the Church does not use the Bible enough, but in fact Catholic ritual guides like the missal—Amelia Calac is devoted to hers—lead Catholics through the Bible. These Indians are not literalists in regard to the Bible: they agree that the Bible is filled with poetry that employs a metaphorical language. The biblical texts themselves have been filtered through centuries of translations, and one needs care and guidance in understanding it. The Bible, to them, is no talisman to be opened for instant inspiration, but a guidebook to their faith that takes intense study to fathom. The same is true for Christian prayers, e.g., the Apostles' Creed, which Patty Duro refers to as the "nutshell of faith," filled with "the most profound staff of life." (One cannot help but remember that for these California Indians acorns were the traditional staff of life; they are on display in the cultural center in Rincon, and many Luiseños still gather them to make traditional cuisine.) When George Arviso tries to explain his Catholic faith to Protestants, he turns to the Apostles' Creed, explicating each phrase.

In the 1980s newcomers to the Pala Mission were shocked by what they saw as the low level of biblical and theological awareness among the Luiseños. The Verona Fathers had not catechized sufficiently, according to their critics. The Catholic Luiseños today say that the Veronas' motto was, "Don't rock the boat." The priests felt that "we couldn't understand things. . . . Keep it simple, sure, but you have to know the foundations" (ibid.). Amelia Calac attended Sherman Indian School but ceased to attend Catholic services there when the Bureau of Indian Affairs abolished them as requirements in 1932. Later she went to pentecostal services, and through them came back to Catholicism, reading Catholic devotional literature. She says the Verona Fathers starved her for spiritual knowledge. For several years she has attended a Benedictine retreat house in Oceanside, asking the monks there to "feed me spiritually!" She and Georgiana O. Viveros delight in asking the Benedictines questions about theology and the Church, trying to make up for the lack of intellectual religious life they have experienced on the reservation, where they have been treated "only as Indians." The Catholic Luiseños assert that in the parish one never asked the priests a question; rather, one gave "blind obedience." George Arviso adds that the "greatest gift" from God to humans is "choice." He and his fellows say that they need information in order to make their moral choices in life. Arviso recalls that he once asked a priest what he thought the greatest gift was, and the priest said, "Jesus." Arviso told him that he thought choice was as important. To inform their faith walk choices, these Indian Catholics are attending Eucharistic meetings off the reservation so they might converse with non-Catholics, non-Indians, and especially with converts to Catholicism, whose enthusiasm and wide-eyed appreciation for the Church they find contagious.

They also are familiar with the Twelve-Step programs of Alcoholics Anonymous, and they draw upon it as a means of expressing their Catholic faith. Amelia Calac says that the twelve steps come from Christianity: the introspection, the overcoming of denial, the path, the placing of trust in a Higher Power. But she also says that the twelve steps have brought out in the contemporary Church its original healing purposes. Jesus healed the body and soul, the psyche, the whole person. He treated people's traumas. We are now understanding the psychological functions of religion, and this is very important and useful. "Twelve Steps," she testifies, "I believe in this."

The Indians regret what they regard as a second-rate Catholic education from the Pala Mission, and they aim to improve it now on their own initiative. Mark Macarro from Pechanga, director of the Rincon cultural center, says that in his youth the Church authorities set up the sacraments like school hurdles; they were things you needed to get to the next stage, tests to be passed to get a grade rather than profound instruments to receive God's grace. Now, he thinks the Luiseños should be learning not only how to speak their own language (he teaches such a language course), but how to speak the language of Catholicism with informed intelligence (ibid.)

In residential Escondido before her death, Villiana Hyde and her daughter Lorraine sat in their living room; a crucifix hung over the couch. The elder Hyde wrote a book about Luiseño language (Hyde and Elliott 1994). Anthropologists and linguists came to her for their data. She was teaching Mark Macarro the details of Luiseño grammar so that he could pass on her knowledge to the children of Rincon, where she lived for many years. When she was a little girl, "as long as I knew myself" (Hyde and Hyde, November 8, 1992), she learned the Catholic religion from her uncle, Juan Sotelo Calac, who was "like a priest" to her people. He taught the children how to kneel and pray the Hail Mary and other prayers. He listened to each one pray and made certain that the children learned their prayers correctly. He taught in Spanish, but the language gave Villiana nightmares of the Devil so she gave it up. She was more fluent in Luiseño and English than in Spanish, although Spanish was necessary for her parents, who worked for the Mexican-American ranches in the area. She attended school in Rincon, and then the Sherman Indian School, where she went to confession, received a Catholic training, and took confirmation. Her mother became ill, however, so she came back from school and never returned to complete her studies. But from her religious training she learned about God the Father, who sees everyone and everything we do. She learned that we must do what is right because no one lives forever, and we shall be judged according to how we live—the sermon message delivered by Father Lawson on the morning of our conversation. She learned that the Angel and Devil watch us. Each has a scale and a book. When we do bad, the Devil dances for joy, weighs our evil, records it in the book. The Angel records our good. There are two trails. It is our duty to choose the right trail. We choose where we shall walk. She learned as a youth that to understand these matters was to enter the Catholic life.

When she married, she lived in the hills near Santa Ysabel. In the early part of the century, people did not travel much from reservation to reservation except for visits at the various fiestas, yet she married a man who was part Cupeño, Cahuilla, and Diegueño. Her husband was a member of the band of Indians who escaped into the hills when the Cupeños were evicted from Warner Springs. His family took church bells, saints' pictures, images of Jesus, altar cloths, and placed these ecclesiastical objects of devotion in their home in the hills as a repository and shrine. When she married, she and her husband's family built a chapel and priest's quarters in order to continue their Catholic life. Mrs. Hyde laments that in 1985 thieves stole the items saved in the 1903 eviction: "It was terrible," she said. She taught in Warner Springs, and for eighteen years she raised foster children, Father Carillo serving as her reference. She taught them to pray and obey, as she had as a child. She kept the rosary she received as a child and recalls as a youth that she and her fellow Luiseños were afraid of hell: "We were shaking with fear." She passed on that faith to her foster children and found that they were "angels." She taught them to trust God as a protector, telling a story about her own grandmother, who in the 1860s was alone in her home with her baby daughter (Villiana's mother) when "some bad Spaniards"—armed outlaws who raided the Indian villages—came on horseback to her house, just as she was about to eat. She prayed, then took her baby into the hills and hid until the men had gone, having eaten her supper. She felt that God had answered her prayers by saving her life. Mrs. Hyde tried to instill that faith in God to her foster children, and although in her old age she did not attend mass regularly, she maintained some of that faith to her death.

At Pauma the members of the Dixon family voice a different kind of Catholic faith. If a visitor comes to Lorena Dixon's doublewide trailer looking for the "devotional set," he has come to the wrong house. Lee Dixon explained, "We're the radicals" (Dixon et al., November 11, 1992). They are Majel clan members who have continued to practice their aboriginal religion to some extent, and they continue to teach their children to perform dances and other rituals. They perform for other Luiseños who have not kept up their traditions, e.g., in Pala and Rincon ("You can't refuse, if someone asks you to sing for valid reasons. When we sing, we know who we are") at clan gatherings, funerals, and healings. They say that their Luiseño religion is embedded in their natal identity as members of a clan, whereas Catholicism is part of the superstructure of their lives. "We're insurance Catholics," said Lee Dixon. They have their children baptized. They attend mass twice a month when the priest comes to Pauma to their chapel. These are practices of "insurance" against the possibility that the claims of the Church might be true, that to attain heaven one must engage in Christian ritual life. When they were young they may have had "blind faith," but not anymore. Some of them believe in their Luiseño medicines more, their sweats more, but they still take "insurance," without paying attention to what they call the "dogma" of the Church.

Sr. Patricia Dixon teaches Native American studies at Palomar Junior College in Escondido. She is a Sister of the Precious Blood; however, she lets it be known that she is more involved in her academic work than she is in liturgical reform, Eucharistic ministry, or the Tekakwitha Conference. Amelia Calac calls her "a real Indian," and George Arviso states that the sister will not "take guff" (Arviso et al., November 5, 1992) from Church officials. Sr. Patricia says that if the Church hierarchy were to forbid Indian spirituality for Catholic Indians, and she were forced to choose between Catholic and Indian religious orientations, she would opt for the Indian mode. It is "not as condemning," and it is where her identity lies. On the other hand, she thinks that Luiseños should attend mass regularly if they are to consider themselves Catholic. Her people have gotten too lax in their Catholic practice, she suggests, baptizing their children without intending to raise them as Catholics. She says that if her people do not go to church on Sundays, they should not baptize their children. She has respect for her mother, Lorena Dixon, whom she describes as a Catholic "conservative" who would "flip at women priests." Her Aunt Flossie is scandalized by the contemporary Church willingness to grant annulments to married couples, and Sr. Patricia herself has a conservative strain to her radical Dixon spirit. She says that "We can't blame the Church for everything. If we see problems with our Church, we can do something about them."

The Luiseños express their ambivalence toward the Church through their attitudes about the priests and religious who have served among the Indians. The elders remember the days before priests were plentiful in the area. Perhaps once a month a priest might come to Rincon to say mass in the days before Father George Doyle arrived. In the olden days a local man or woman led prayers, baptized children, and officiated at marriages. These were chiefs who had their own Indian songs—like Villiana Hyde's uncle, Juan Sotelo Calac, who led songs at burials, fiestas, and other liturgical events. These community servants responded immediately when their people called them. They were *of* the community and *for* the community, deriving their authority and responsibility from their kinfolk. They kept track of the liturgical year, marked Sundays, holy days, fiestas. In short, the Indians "mostly" (Hyde and Hyde, November 8, 1992) conducted their own religious lives.

When the diocese assigned priests—secular clergy, Franciscans, then the Verona Fathers—the local prayer leaders continued to serve, but their authority was eclipsed, and there is still some rueful memory of the days when the Indian people had more control over their spirituality. There is a difference of opinion among the Indians about the Verona Fathers. Some remember them with fondness. King Freeman, for instance, recalls that the Italian priests were available to the community. Once their English could be deciphered, they came to be rather popular. One priest, who had served as a missionary in Africa, showed the children slides of that wild continent (as it seemed then, to the Indians) and called the Luiseño youths "my little savages" (in Freeman, November 7, 1992). So well accepted did the priests become that Indians kidded them about being missionaries, threatening in jest to cook them in a big pot. That is, some Luiseños were willing to play the parody of the "natives" in relation to the missionary "fathers." The Veronas may have been paternalistic, but they had a "sense of community" (Dixon et al., November 11, 1992), and they were willing to "let us be Indians." Despite being called "little savages," the Indians felt respected. The priests did not join the Indians in the sweat lodge (some Catholic sisters did), but they were always available to have a cup of coffee in their "pastoral" duties. One Indian calls Father Januarius Carillo—now retired—"the best father, who did so much for our people" (Hyde and Hyde, November 8, 1992), and another remarks that the Veronas "made God very personal" (Dixon et al., November 11, 1992). The Luiseños at Pala have even given permission to these priests to be buried in their crowded church cemetery, a sign of appreciation and affection.

On the other hand, some Luiseños rue, "We didn't learn anything from the Veronas but a nice attitude. We were treated like little children. Now we're paying the price. . . . On our faith walk we're only taking baby steps. We're infants. . . . We're not even kindergarten level" in understanding Church theology and ecclesiology, after decades of Verona "condescension," according to Patty Duro (Arviso et al., No-

vember 5, 1992). The Catholic Luiseños did not question these priests,
but deferred to them. As youths, the Indians thought of the fathers as
"wearing a halo." It was a shock to find them smoking cigarettes or
wearing shorts. For all their accessibility, they ruled over spiritual matters without any discussion to explain their viewpoints. In addition
they obtained gifts of land and sold the properties to maintain their
order, even selling off antiques from the Pala church. But whatever
complaint the Indians have about the Verona order, they know that
most white priests have not wanted to serve Indian communities.
Missionaries like the Verona Fathers have been the "donkeys of the
Church" (ibid.), carrying the heavy burden of ministering to suspicious Indian congregations in remote locales.

The Luiseños also appreciate the Indian ministry of Catholic sisters, such as Sr. Josepha Mauss, O.P., a Dominican who put in many
years on fourteen different reservations in the San Diego diocese, living in a trailer and traveling constantly to visit the sick, the elderly, and
the impoverished. She had a stroke several years ago and has now retired, pushed aside by the new diocesan policy of eschewing special Indian ministry in favor of control by the parish priests. When Sr.
Eucharista Mitchell left Pala in 1992, after serving the school and the
community for many years, the Indians sang Luiseño songs in her
honor. Yet, several months after her departure some of the Indians she
worked with could not recall her name. One always has a strong feeling in Indian communities like these that the non-Indian Catholic personnel are transitory presences, perhaps appreciated, often resented,
but forgotten before long. The Luiseños sometimes express this
plainly: "The clergy come and go. They institute new policies, make
changes, and then they go. They cause havoc, destruction, and
pain. . . . We adjust. . . . We survive" (Dixon et al., November 11, 1992).

The Luiseños are faced with a shortage of priests in the future, and
some of them hesitate to criticize the present pastor: "If you disagree
with him, he'll pull out" (Arviso et al., November 5, 1992). They recognize that the Church will assign priests where a community can support them; the clergy go where the money is, in effect. Sr. Patricia
Dixon says, "People with money run this Church. It's rather shocking"
(Dixon et al., November 11, 1992). Many of them, however, do not
worry about religious leadership in their own communities. One
woman suggests "married priests, women priests" (Arviso et al., November 5, 1992) as solutions to sacerdotal shortage. Others say that

their community can always call upon their own people—prayer leaders like George Arviso, traditional song leaders like the Majel clan—to inspire spiritual life. These people can do everything a priest can, say some Luiseños; furthermore, they are local, and they know everyone.

Contemporary Luiseños save their greatest clerical invective for their present pastor and their most distant pastors, the Franciscans of the eighteenth and nineteenth centuries. They recall their native prayer leaders with nostalgic love; the priests from the 1900s to the early 1990s they regard with ambivalent appreciation. However, the most recent and the most remote are objects of sustained bitterness.

Neither Father Lawson nor Father Cribbin wanted to come to Pala in 1992. George Arviso says, "I was there at the meeting" in the diocesan offices, and the two priests "freely admitted that they knew nothing about Indians" (Arviso and Arviso, November 7, 1992) and were not prepared to take up an Indian ministry. Other Luiseños assert that Father Lawson left the Episcopal Church because he was against the ordination of women, and his theological conservatism can be seen in his opposition to expressions of native spirituality in Church settings. They charge that his goal is to rid his new parish of its Indianness, so that it will be "all Catholic, no Indian" (Dixon et al., November 11, 1992). He claims to be bringing Vatican II reforms to the parish, but there is "nothing substantive" to that claim in that he overrides all community power, controls all decisions, and has no interest in the inculturation of Catholicism to Luiseño and Cupeño people.

Part of the problem, in the Indians' view, is that the priests are new, and they need to "do some visiting" around the reservations "to get to know us" (Magee, November 6, 1992). In communities where religion is largely a matter of personal contact, the priests have yet to make that contact, to make the Church personally palpable to the parishioners. Some of the Indians note that Father Lawson served an "upper class" community before coming to Pala, and so he does not understand the people's poverty. "The man wants money" (Dixon et al., November 11, 1992) to pay for structural improvements in the church and the rectory. Lawson is reputed to have complained that the rectory was at "subhuman standards" when he moved in, even though several Verona Fathers were living there until his arrival. He put in a satellite dish and paid a lot of money for improvements. He drives a Volvo; his personal accountant drives a BMW; Lawson insisted on a modern church with a fancy altar, a big confessional, air conditioning, and a new room for

the priests, all of this in a "very simple community" (ibid.). At the
parish council meeting there is some anger expressed over Father
Cribbin's new, expensive quarters. The Indians refer to his refurbished
digs as "Father Jim's Penthouse," but the priests say, "We deserve that.
We need that for our comfort" (Arviso and Arviso et al., November 5,
1992). The parish council does not want to pay for such improvements, which they regard as luxuries. Father Cribbin replies, "That
was the bishop's personal gift to me" (Pala, November 9, 1992). If that
is so, the Indians and the white parishioners, too, want the bishop to
foot the bill. The tribe agreed to give $50,000 for the repairs to the
church when the roof needed replacement, but now they resent being
asked to carry the whole cost for improvements they did not want.
As a result, people are peeved: "Father Lawson is asking for money,
money, money. I thought the gospel was free of charge" (Magee, November 6, 1992). Instead, the Indians, who were accustomed to paying
"a dollar at a time" for baptisms are outraged at the prices charged by
the present pastor, who does not take a vow of poverty, who does not
live communally like the Verona Fathers. Father Lawson is said to "put
a price on everything" (Dixon et al., November 11, 1992), including
$100 for funerals. Accusations such as these find echos among Cupeño
Indians living in Los Angeles, who refer to Catholicism as a "money-
hungry religion" (in Bahr 1993: 116).

   Even worse, the priests do not participate in the community rituals
they consider outside the Catholic sacramental system. The pattern at
wakes was for an Indian ritual to take place with songs in Luiseño. The
priest came and led Catholic prayers: sisters kept company with the
mourners, eating, drinking coffee, and paying respects to the community. The Indians claim that the present priests and sisters will not come
to the wakes—which are the most important religious rituals of the
Indian community, more important than mass—or only as their schedules dictate. The whole community attends the mourning services: "If
the priest doesn't show up, it's bad" (Magee, November 6, 1992).

   The Indian Catholics complain that the priests today are too busy
to perform pastoral duties. They have answering machines, days off,
office hours: "Nobody ever sees them" (ibid.). They perform their
priesthood as if it were a job, a profession, a business. George Arviso
asks Father Lawson about his impersonal answering machine: What if
an urgent call comes? "What if it's important?" Father Lawson replies,

"If it's important, they'll leave a message" (as quoted by Arviso et al., November 5, 1992).

For some of the Luiseños, the animosity toward their present pastor is intense and has led to a 60–70 percent dropoff in Indian church attendance in his first year on the job. "It's hard to find a nice thing to say" about him, according to one Indian. "He didn't want to come here and is still angry about it," says another. They claim that "he sucks up to rich white people" and insists that everything in the parish will be run "his way." They say that he snubs Indians in the parish and is more interested in the books than in the people. They are irate that he has insisted upon parental instruction before he will baptize anyone, issuing a moratorium on baptisms in the community until he is satisfied with the catechetical prowess of the parishioners. He will not distribute the Eucharist to people who arrive late for mass. In short, his pastorate is guided by what the Indians call his "by-the-book stuff" (Magee, November 6, 1992). One anonymous parishioner brands him an "anal retentive, chauvinistic homosexual" who can deliver a good sermon but makes all the Indians despise him, and by extension, the Church.

Chancery personnel defend both clerics, calling them "very capable priests who want to serve" (Stonehouse, November 11, 1992), even without an expertise in Indian cultures. Luiseños respond to such praise by saying of the diocesan officials that they are part of the package of policy instituted by Bishop Brom to terminate any special Indian status within the Church. Of the Mexican-American director of the Office of Multicultural Affairs, they contend, "She won't tell you the truth." As for those Indians who have left the Church in the past year, Sister Patricia Dixon says, "I don't think he'll ever get them back" (Dixon et al, November 11, 1992). Perhaps the Indian Catholics would return if Father Lawson left, and some Luiseños acknowledge that they would like to find a priest who suited them better. Another priest in California Indian ministry says that the Luiseños tried to "kidnap" him (Monteiro, November 19, 1992), because they are so dissatisfied with their present pastor. They desire a priest who wants a special Indian ministry. Sr. Patricia Dixon says that her community wants to "take the Church back." A Catholic community exists among the Luiseños: "We'll survive him" (Dixon et al., November 11, 1992), she asserts.

Postscript: Both Fathers Cribbin and Lawson have left the Luiseños since the writing of this book, replaced by a new priest, Rev. Stephen Gross. With no experience in Native American ministry, he is trying to make adjustments. The Luiseños, too, must adjust. With only one priest, Sunday services are now limited to Pala and Rincon. The Pala School has also closed. "They've cut back a lot," says Milonny Arviso (October 12, 1995). "It's really sad."

☀ IV ☀

Detractors and Defenders

PATTERNS OF CRITICISM AND REBUTTAL

The Luiseños' criticisms say as much about their anger toward the Church's long-term relationship with their people as it does about the realities of the pastor and his assistant. These "Mission Indians" harbor longstanding grudges against the early Franciscans, asking why the missionaries thought they had the right to impose themselves upon the California Indians: what did they think they were accomplishing in rounding us up, destroying our culture, and forcing changes upon us. They say that they have trouble understanding or appreciating the worldview and motivation of the padres. Did they really think that they were introducing us to religion, to faith, to marriage? Did they not realize that "we believed before they came" (Arviso et al., November 5, 1992)? In the Luiseños' view, their Indian ancestors "baptized" one another before the arrival of the Spaniards and sought God in their own cultural formulas. Without ever hearing of Jesus or Christianity, the gentile Indians already constituted a "Church" that taught morals and organized a ritual life for the reception of God's grace. The community acted as witness to marriages and established the "Community of Saints" for the deceased at mourning ceremonials.

Luiseño criticism of the Franciscans follows a long tradition, in which detractors have condemned the missionary enterprise and Church personnel have defended it. A review of the patterns of criticism and rebuttal can help us take stock of the Spanish Catholic missionary enterprise across these hundreds of years, not only in California but throughout northern Mexico and the American Southwest. It will also help us appreciate the complex relations between Catholic Indians and the Church.

From the beginning of the Franciscan enterprise in Alta California, the padres defended their goals against the judgments of civil administrators, soldiers, and Indians alike. In their letters and reports, the friars justified and even praised their own work. The writings of Presidente Serra (Tibesar 1955–1966) established a pattern followed by his successors, like Lasuen. Immediately following Serra's death in 1784, Fray Francisco Palóu gathered together the materials of the founder's life for a biography, and since its completion in 1787 "Palóu's biography has been the basic text employed by writers in producing the books, articles, brochures, pageants and orations about Serra that in almost endless succession have appeared down to our day" (Geiger 1955: ix). In this way a particularly *Franciscan* perspective on the Franciscan missions has gained ascendancy, although other chroniclers and scholars have differed in their evaluation of the padres. Palóu concluded his study of Serra by recounting the man's virtues: his humility ("the foundation of the spiritual life," ibid., 267); prudence; justice, especially in regard to the Indians; fortitude ("Never did the fear of losing his life at the hands of the savages make him turn back," ibid., 276); temperance. In addition to these cardinal virtues, he also possessed the theological virtues of faith, "explaining in his doctrinal sermons these sovereign mysteries of the Faith to the rudest and most unlettered people" (ibid., 281); hope; charity; and religion. No Franciscan has ever opined that every one of the padres in California held these virtues as did Serra, but the continuing perspective of these men—who announced the word of God through Jesus Christ and the Roman Catholic Church, by building Christian communities under their authority in the northern domain of New Spain (and later Mexico)—was that their edifice was noble and proper, even saintly.

When John Gilmary Shea wrote his history of Catholic missions of North America, he addressed some of the criticisms made of the California evangelization, concluding:

> The discipline was indeed severe, and the whole establishment conducted like some large factory. This has excited, in modern times, great outcry; but the missions have been abolished, and the Indians left to the "enlightened" men of our day. Under their care the Indians have perished like smoke before the wind, and men now sigh for the missions. (Shea 1855: 105)

As a Church historian, Shea did not doubt the necessity of evangelization, and he praised the Franciscans of California along with the other Catholic missionaries in other times and climes.

Not all the civil authorities agreed wholly with this judgment. Some of them charged that the Franciscans held too much power and wealth; they exerted too strenuous a discipline over the Indians and worked them too hard; the mission environment proved destructive to the neophytes' health; the effects of christianization appeared attenuated and superficial. Visiting traders, shipmen, and other travelers sometimes corroborated these criticisms, while Indians themselves continually resisted the missionary program and revolted against it. Each of these groups may have had ulterior motives for seeing the worst in the mission system: civil administrators who wished to seize power and wealth for themselves; Protestant foreigners whose prejudices against Catholicism prevented fair assessment; criminals within Indian communities who resented Franciscan assertions of authority. Nevertheless, not every negative evaluation owed its origin to ulterior motives, and when the secular historians such as Hittell (1885–1897) and Bancroft (1886–1890) wrote their histories of California, they found some cause to criticize the priests, employing the same allegations made during the mission period. That these historians held no special love for the Church, and they did not regard it above secular criticism, made their verdicts galling to Franciscans and other Church apologists who believed the missions to be fundamentally embedded in the salvific structure and purpose of God's history on earth.

While Hittell and Bancroft were composing their unloving histories, Helen Hunt Jackson and other liberal American reformers were attempting to protect the remnants of the mission Indians against the continuing onslaught of American citizens. When these liberal reformers of American and Californian policies compared the contemporary condition of Indians (in the 1880s) to that of their ancestors under the Franciscan rule, they found the earlier regime to have been far more protective and caring in its treatment of the native Californians. In her report on the mission Indians of California (1902: 3–101) and in her famous novel, *Ramona* (1886), both published first in the 1880s, Jackson painted a favorable portrayal of the missionaries and their effect upon the Indian peoples. The Franciscans' austerity, their zeal, their courage in the face of greedy administrators, their religious faith; all these qualities impressed her, and she fostered her picture of these virtues among her many readers, helping to create a romance regarding the missions that has persisted to the present day. Her mission Indians sang their hymns, processed on feast days, confessed their sins to attentive priests whom they held in pious devotion and affection. Land developers in California in the late nineteenth and early twentieth century—ironically, most were Protestant, and tragically, much of the land they wished to sell was taken from Indians—helped attract buyers by imbuing their acreage with a romantic history of the missions, whose structures lay in ruins. As Californians tried to preserve the heritage of those early years by rebuilding all twenty-one of the original missions, critical evaluations of the padres were turned aside.

In the early twentieth century several writers and photographers made their living and reputation documenting the historic ruins of the old missions. While enthusing over the architectural details, they commented upon the evangelical enterprise. One wrote:

> The system of the padres was patriarchal, paternal. Certain it is that the Indians were largely treated as if they were children. No one questions or denies this statement. Few question that the Indians were happy under this system, and all will concede that they made wonderful progress in the so-called arts of civilization. From crude savagery they were lifted by the training of the fathers into usefulness and productiveness. They retained their health, vigor, and virility. (James 1912: 295)

Others noted that the "antagonists of the Padres" made much of the whipping of neophytes: however, this was the mode back then, for children as well as adults. Now and then the padres may have gone too far, whipping the cook when the friar got indigestion, for instance. Sometimes the Indians resented the discipline and wanted no more of the Christian system; "but in a general way one should not think hardly of the missionaries for resorting to the practice with their misbehaving red children (who, indeed, never grew up), for it was meant as a corrective" (Saunders and Chase 1915: 363). The mission Indians may have disappeared, they wrote, and when one of their ancestors was baptized and his name placed in the record books of the mission, "Did he but know it, that writing is his death-warrant" (ibid., 334)? They concluded:

> Those children of the Missions, doomed to pass away at the coming of the new religion that seemed to promise them better life—were not they in their way, innocent victims for Christ? And do not they, too, somewhere triumph, happy that they should have provided the needful sacrifice? (Ibid., 335–336)

While non-Catholics of the early twentieth century romanticized the missions and sighed over the disappearing mission Indians, the German-born, American-reared Franciscan, Zephyrin Engelhardt, was composing his monumental *apologia* for the California missions. Following stints as a missionary himself in the Great Lakes region of the American Midwest and at St. Boniface School, Banning, California, Engelhardt produced a brief volume on the Franciscans in Arizona (1899); then, between 1908 and his death in 1934, he penned over a dozen books on the California Franciscans, including a four-volume study of the entire system (1908–1915) in Lower and Upper California and individual monographs tracing the history of each mission. He dedicated his four grand volumes to "Mary Immaculate, The patroness of California," St. Joseph, "patron of the California conquest," St. Michael the Archangel and St. Francis of Assisi, and he regarded his works as productions of devotion to God and Church and Order.

Fray Engelhardt proved a vituperative combatant as well as a prodigious scholar. Anyone who undervalued the California Franciscans—including their Spanish and Mexican contemporaries, foreign visitors, Indians, and secular historians—received the priest's epithets as "bigots," "irreligious" (Engelhardt 1912: 265, 266), and so forth. He lay aside all criticisms from Mexican officials as "propaganda" (Engelhardt 1921: 70) created by greedy *paisanos* preparing to reduce the Indians to serfdom after the missions could be secularized, confiscated, and destroyed. He discredited the business practices of traders who found fault with the friars, and he chided the secular historians Hittell and Bancroft as perpetuators of anti-Church diatribes. He wrote: "Numerous other works on the subject have been published, but they generally reveal the mind of the writers rather than historical facts. . . . The reader may confidently rely on the statements made in this work, since they are based on official documents and other trustworthy authorities" (Engelhardt 1920: v).

As for the Indians, he had this to say: "All accounts agree in representing the natives of California as among the most stupid, brutish, filthy, lazy, and improvident of the aborigines of America" (Engelhardt 1912: 224). Drawing upon the testimony of the Franciscan missionaries, he found the Indians' culture devoid of the essentials of civilized existence, including religious life itself:

> It may be said that, before the advent of the missionaries, the California savages had no Religion whatever. Religion is the bond between the Creator and creature, the reverent acceptance of whatever the creator has revealed directly or indirectly, and the eager endeavor of the creature to praise, thank, propitiate, and petition the Creator for the purpose of being united with Him in everlasting bliss. (Ibid., 237)

The California natives had none of this. And since they had no religion aboriginally, they also had no morals. They were liars, thieves, and ingrates. They barely practiced marriage, holding unmarried girls as public property. Some of their men lived as women, "kept for unnatural purposes" (420), and both men and women were perpetually dirty, even though they bathed all the time. As Father Boscana once wrote, "They passed a wretched life, ever idle, and more like the brutes than rational beings" (225). Hence, for Engelhardt, to observe the missions was to observe the process by which the Franciscans raised the Indians above their horrid state before contact. Engelhardt reminded his readers that the padres came to California to convert to Christianity—as Jesus Christ had commanded and both Church and State made possible—"an entirely naked, brutish people who had no conception of human dignity. . . . the habits of the Californians were scarcely above those of the lowest wild beasts" (244).

In addressing criticisms of the missions, Engelhardt never lost sight of his basic principles (which were the principles of the early Franciscans in California): that the Indians were in desperate need of uplifting from their native condition; that christianizing and civilizing were part of God's plan and the Church's purpose. If Indian parents complained of their girls being taken from them at age nine and placed at night in the *monjerio* (nunnery), and if white authors voiced those complaints, the padre retorted: "owing to the brutish character of the Californians, it was so necessary and reasonable that it is amazing to meet with writers who can find fault with it" (ibid.: 249). To those who criticized the practice of segregating the neophytes from their pagan kinsmen: "If the Lord found it necessary to separate the Israelites from the other nations in order to preserve them in the true Faith" (250), so, too, did the Franciscans exercise discrimination.

Engelhardt insisted, against persistent charges, that "No one . . . was compelled to join the mission" (263). The friars lured the gentiles with gifts, kindness, and food, and only after instruction did baptism take place. Nevertheless, once an Indian accepted baptism, it was an indelible decision, similar to that of a soldier enlisting in an army. Once baptized, Indians could not become traitors and leave the mission, "because they bore the indelible mark of a Christian upon the soul which it was not allowed to desecrate" (264). Now they had "taken an oath" (264), and they could not "desert" the mission. Furthermore, if neophytes left, they became a "menace" to the mission: "If he was a traitor to his Religion and the missionaries, he would not hesitate to turn against the Spaniards. . . . The runaway was, therefore, followed by the mission guards and brought back" (264).

The padres were the fathers at the missions and "the neophytes were regarded and treated as children. . . . In spite of all missionary efforts, they remained children" (265–266). As paternal authorities, the missionaries drew up "police regulations" (275) for their neophytes, drawing upon the authority invested in them by the Spanish Crown, which gained its authority through its Christian discovery and conquest of the New World. Instruction, warning, admonishment, and punishment: these were within the authoritative purview of the padres. Their appointed officials—the mayordomos and alcaldes, as well as the soldiers—saw to the task of incarceration, segregation from gentile kinsmen, stocks, pillory, shackles, extra work, the lash, and other punishments. In a chapter entitled "Mission System Vindicated," Engelhardt argued that the system of flogging—(Jesuits instituted it in Lower California; "Fr. Serra retained it for the Indians under his charge," 276)—was necessitated by the Indians' indolence. They did not object to imprisonment because it freed them from work; hence, they required more vigorous measures in punishment (Engelhardt 1908: 128). For Engelhardt, as for the missionaries of the eighteenth and nineteenth centuries, the neophytes "had to be treated like unruly boys if other remedies failed. . . . The Indian was an overgrown child. As such he was treated" (1912: 276–277).

To gullible or misinformed writers who asserted that the friars forced the Indians to attend services or work in the shops and fields, Engelhardt replied that one might find an alcalde with a whip accompanying the neophytes to mass as we might find a school teacher today with "unruly boys" (Engelhardt 1920: 187); however, this did not constitute coercion. Whipping was the only means to induce "the lazy Californian savages to earn their living by means of labor; . . . make them dress decently and refrain from moral disorders" (Engelhardt 1913: 456). Physical punishments were necessary in populous establishments with "half-savage Indians" (Engelhardt 1921: 69, fn. 9), where they engaged in all manner of subterfuge for the "gratification of their animal propensities" (ibid., 70). Engelhardt stated, "It must be remembered that, if the neophytes were to produce anything, the poor Fathers had to labor with them at every kind of work. Like boys, the Indians needed the master around; else little work would be done. Even at the present day, those who hire Indians know this very well" (1920: 216).

If neophytes rebelled; if they conducted work slowdowns; if they tried to escape; or if they attacked the priests; Engelhardt found their "excuses" groundless: "Thus complaints were made by some of the neophytes at all the missions because they hated work, or chafed under the restraint put upon their animal propensities" (1912: 507-508). When Nazario, the San Diego mission cook, attempted to poison Fray José Pedro Panto in 1811 in retaliation for 200 lashes he claimed the priest had given him, Engelhardt found the charge "too absurd to need disproval" (1920: 164), despite Panto's reputation for severity. In short, Fray Engelhardt's role as Franciscan apologist prevented him from taking a critical stance in regard to any issue of controversy concerning the missionaries.

As Father Engelhardt was completing his histories of the Franciscan missions, two processes were taking place that have collided with each other over the past several decades. First, in 1934 proceedings began within the offices of the Roman Catholic Church to consider the missions' founder, Junipero Serra, for canonization, 150 years after his death. For fifteen years a historical commission appointed by the Bishop of Monterey-Fresno gathered all the information its members could find regarding Serra's life and work, in order that his virtues might be evaluated, according to the process established by Church authorities when a person is considered for sainthood. Father Maynard Geiger, O.F.M., archivist and historian of Mission Santa Barbara, served as the resident scholar, and in the process he wrote a biography of Serra (1959) and sketches of all the other California Franciscans (1969). The historian, Herbert Eugene Bolton, author of numerous books and articles regarding Catholic evangelization in New Spain (e.g., 1927, 1960), served with Geiger on the commission, and together they planned their testimony before the Sacred Congregation of Rites in 1949, where a devil's advocate questioned the cause for sainthood. The *transumptum*—the collected record of the Serra case, including the complete transcripts of answers provided by Geiger and Bolton about Serra—is still held in secret by Father Noel F. Moholy, O.F.M., at the Mission Santa Barbara (Sando 1988: 1260); nevertheless, over the past half century an enormous literature of devotion has accumulated within Church circles, acclaiming Serra's virtues, as well as those of his fellow Franciscans. Father Geiger has proved himself far more critical of some Franciscans than Engelhardt and far more even tempered in adjudicating between critics and defenders of the mission system. At the same time, he has held to the basic worldview of the missionaries, characterizing the Indians of Baja and Alta California as "primitive" people. For instance, he described the foods, clothing, trading habits, character, marriage customs, and housing of the San Diego natives: "Upon this primitive culture the missionaries had to build a civilized Christian community" (Geiger 1959: 231).

As the canonization movement commenced, ethnographers were

beginning to take unfriendly aim at the padres. John P. Harrington in 1930 was one of the first modern anthropologists to write of the Indians in the California missions as unwilling participants and encouraged scholars like Bolton to incorporate the Indian points of view into the history of the missions. Harrington's former wife, Carobeth Laird, wrote of her interview with the Inezeño Indian, Maria Solares, who portrayed her neophyte grandmother as a "slave of the mission" who "had run away many, many times and had been recaptured and whipped til her buttocks crawled with maggots. Yet she had survived to hand down her memories of the golden age before the white men came. Now her descendants were all very good Catholics" (in Sandos 1988: 1262–1263).

Following upon Harrington's challenge, and as a response to Nazi policies against ethnic minorities, Sherburne Cook wrote the first full-scale analysis of the mission system, focussing upon its effects on the Indians themselves. Cook was a scientist who was interested in the physical effects of deprivation on Indians. He was comparing Indian mission to concentration camps. His stance was secular; his method was statistical; and his tone was judgmental of the Franciscans. He was interested not in their motives or spirituality nor their controversies with civil authorities, but rather in the physical environment the missions presented to the neophytes.

Cook traced the population decline among native Californians from 1770—he estimated 133,500 at that time, to 100,000 at the close of the mission period in 1849, and down to 20,500 by 1880. He estimated that 54,000 gentiles received baptism (in addition to those born at the missions of neophyte parents), and in 1834, before secularization wrecked the missions and dispersed the neophytes, approximately 15,000 Indians lived in the missions (down from a peak of 21,000 in 1820). He made it clear that the great decline in population took place after 1849, with the discovery of gold and the American invasion. In the "literal extermination" (1976: 255) that took place under U.S. jurisdiction, "the old mission population utterly disappeared, except for a few scattered individuals in the north and the desert peoples of the south" (ibid., 6).

Cook emphasized the cultural change the mission Indians underwent as neophytes; their task of adaptation to the new surroundings was monumental, because the missions were designed for the purpose of uprooting them from their cultural environment: "In the course of conversion it was considered essential to remove the native from his normal ecological niche and to transport him to a completely new environment. Indeed, an organized effort was made to eradicate in his mind many of the distinctive cultural traits which had been an integral part of himself and his ancestors for generations" (ibid., 9).

Cook made it clear that diseases killed many of the neophytes. Father Palóu wrote in the vicinity of Santa Clara in 1777—and Cook quoted him—that, "By the month of May . . . the first baptisms took place, for as there had come upon the people a great epidemic, the Fathers were able to perform a great many baptisms by simply going through the villages. In this way they succeeded in sending a great many children (which died almost as soon as they were baptized) to Heaven" (18). There were "remarkably few" (17) of these major epidemics in Alta California; 1777, 1802, and 1806 marked the three major epidemics; the latter two were pneumonia/diphtheria and measles; the former was unknown. The major disease in the mission history, however, was syphilis: "venereal disease constituted one of the prime factors not only in the actual decline, but also in the moral and social disintegration of the population" (23). The disease entered the California Indian population about a decade after the first mission of 1769. Sexual relations between soldiers and Indian women, including prostitution, were "notorious" (24), and the clergy tried to control it and to instill Catholic values regarding marriage, to little avail—especially in the areas of the presidios. Cook writes that by 1791 one mission reported that, "Most Indian deaths are due to syphilis" (26). Indians also spread the disease among themselves, since "promiscuity was extensive" (30) both within each mission and between the mission population and their gentile relatives back in their villages. Orgies often attended festivals. Adultery was common, and even among the baptized, divorces and remarriages took place regularly.

Cook documented the chronic apostasy that the friars reported from at least the year 1781. He calculated 3,464 desertions to 1831, and during the tumult leading up to secularization the figure rose to 5,428. Of the eighty thousand baptisms to 1831, one out of every twenty-four "resorted actively and successfully to flight" (59). He noted the difficulties of running away, the punishments meted out to fugitives, and the armed expeditions to bring them back in the later decades. He also noted the several failed attempts of neophytes to revolt against the mission system, particularly those of 1775 and 1824. "That the neophytes were not all completely happy and contented in their new environment was entirely obvious to those who lived with them and watched over them" (67), Cook concluded. When the Spaniards questioned the neophytes regarding their desire to leave the missions, the most common reasons they gave were that they had been flogged, or were suffering from hunger, or they were simply homesick.

In the face of Indian disaffection and fugitivism, Cook claimed, the friars turned to stringent measure to hold the neophytes and recruit gentiles. Cook wrote:

> neither the plans of the Franciscan hierarchy nor those of the political government of New Spain contemplated conversion of the heathen on any other than a voluntary basis. . . . The method of kindliness and persuasion sufficed to bring in large numbers of heathen during the first twenty years of the missions. . . . They emphasized the externals of their religion—the ceremony, the music, the processions. They also sought to make mission life as attractive as possible by holding out the inducements of clothing, shelter, and food. (Ibid.: 73)

Between 1790 and 1800, however, the Franciscan policy shifted, and expeditions went out to peaceful villages to gather new neophytes, perhaps persuading a chieftain to undergo baptism and bring in his people. When Indian villages resisted, military threat and action served to recruit gentiles, while at the same time bringing back the *hindras* (runaways). "By 1810 extensive expeditions in search of fugitives were established policy. At the same time many prisoners were taken and brought back to the missions. . . . toward the end of the mission period all pretense of voluntary conversion was discarded and expeditions to the interior were frankly for the purpose of military subjugation and forced conversion" (76). Prisoners became converts, according to Cook.

The California missions aggregated larger and larger numbers of neophytes, despite diseases, and the padres did not want to leave baptized Indians in remote areas. Neither did they wish the neophytes to abandon the missions after several generations. The missionaries argued that the Indians would revert to their original barbarism; if the Indians left the missions, there would be "tremendous religious and economic loss" (87). Cook thereby reminded his readers that the missions were concentrated populations that performed work. He did not say that the work was heavy; indeed, he calculated seven to eight hours a day, five to six days a week, referring to it as "light labor" (94); nevertheless, it was—in his opinion—"forced labor" (95).

According to Cook, the priests asserted their authority through punishment: flogging, imprisonment, hard labor, even death. They punished the neophytes for crimes: theft, armed robbery, arson, murder, rape; but also for moral offenses: fornication, adultery, incest, sodomy; and political actions: fugitivism, apostasy, conspiracy to revolt, destruction of mission property, refusal to work, conducting medicine dances. The defenders of the padres said that the maximum number of lashes was twenty-five; however, Cook found records of fifty and even a hundred lashes. Cook reported on the controversy regarding corporal punishments from the earliest days of the missions, and he noted the Franciscans' defense of their authoritarian practices.

Despite the thoroughness of mission discipline, Cook found that "the mission Indians never assimilated the full significance of Christian ethics in so far as they pertain to social conduct" (141). He stated that the shift from their autonomous village culture to the acculturative missions did not create assimilated Spanish Catholics of the Indians:

> Based entirely upon the premise of total conversion to orthodox Christianity, it was vitally necessary to extirpate those individual beliefs and tribal customs which in any way whatever conflicted with the Christian religion. . . . The missionaries needed to erase, not only pagan or idolatrous tenets of belief, but also external manifestations like ceremonial rites. . . . all persons had to be eliminated who, under the gentile system, had exercised the slightest spiritual authority. (145–146)

Cook concluded: "the process, actually, was too swift, too sudden, to be complete. The Indian mentality was too fixed and rigid to give ground, to make the shift and adapt itself within one or even two generations. Consequently, in many instances, the effect was one of absolute restriction rather than an easy redirection" (147). Cook observed various forms of traditional religious life that persisted among the neophytes: They continued to regard their catechists as medicine men; to believe in witchcraft; to use jimsonweed in initiations and other ceremonies. He related that in the later years the priests themselves encouraged the Indians to put on their native dances for the amusement of the civilian population. Nevertheless, he acknowledged that many converted to Christianity in the mission process: "Most members of any church would be inclined to concede as a bona fide convert the man who faithfully observes the prescribed forms of the faith and who, in so far as his mental equipment allows him, subscribes to its cardinal tenets. Judged on this basis, there can be no question whatever that many thousands of Indians became genuine Christians," although one might question the "depth of the conversion" (154).

One might say that the mission Indians practiced their traditional religion and the adopted religion alternatively, moving from one to the other depending on circumstance. Hugo Reid had argued that case in the 1850s. But Cook suggested that, "No individual can easily retain two independent sets of beliefs. They imperceptibly but inevitably merge with each other until the result is a single philosophy compounded out of elements drawn from both. . . . We cannot pretend, naturally, that the average mission Indian or his descendant ever achieved a perfect philosophical union of Christianity and paganism" (155); nevertheless, Cook favored this model of "fusion" as a means of understanding the way in which the minds of the neophytes adapted to the missions: "Despite the most intensive moral suasion and pressure, the Indians retained the basic pattern of their culture intrinsically unaltered. Indeed, they went so far as to adopt and modify Christianity and to incorporate it in such a way as to conform to their own manner of thought" (157).

Without rancor toward the missionaries, Cook focussed scholarly attention on the effects the mission system had on the Indians: their population, their culture, their religiousness. Anthropologists who have drawn and elaborated upon his findings, and have acted as advocates on behalf of native Californians, have shown less kindness to the Franciscans. Robert F. Heizer, e.g., writes of the missions: "The Native Californian victims of this religious enterprise learned nothing useful to them. It is not wrong to characterize the mission period (1769–1834) as an unmitigated disaster for the coastal tribes" (1976: 2). Without doubting the sincerity of the padres in bringing what they regarded as civilization and salvation to people who were to them "animals in human form who had to be made truly human by conversion to the Faith" (Heizer 1978: 124), he makes it clear that his sympathies lie not with the priests in their frontier outposts: "It is small wonder that the strain was too much for a few of them, and they went mad, or that the pressures were so great that some forgot their vows of celibacy and contracted syphilis, or took their duties so seriously that they became cruel in inflicting punishment" (125). He declares that "The neophyte in the mission was, in fact, a slave. By agreeing to conversion he gave up his freedom and became completely subject for the rest of his life to the rule of the mission priests" (135), performing tedious labor according to a foreign rule of work and receiving punishments for political and religious activities as well as crimes: "flogging was very common, and . . . the priests believed that this was the only way in which their control could be maintained" (129–130). Heizer claims that the missions disrupted the sexual lives of the neophytes, leading to greater licentiousness, sodomy, homosexuality, abortion, and infanticide. Indian women may have protested their condition by preventing births; consequently, birthrates plummeted over time. With the low rate of birth, high death rate, and increased fugitivism after 1790, the Spanish were unable even to use military power to provide "fresh Indians" (126) for the missions, because the military power was insufficient and the resistance so great. In sum, for Heizer, "the Franciscan missions in California were ill-equipped, badly managed places where Indians came to be subject to unaccustomed labor, unsanitary living conditions, disease, poor food, and a disruption of family ties and accustomed social relationships. And through these experiences their lives were very often the cost" (126).

Some scholars have taken a less condemnatory tone regarding the priests, recounting the importance of the training in trades and farming that the friars passed on to the neophytes—teaching skills that helped the natives survive the Mexican and American regimes as well as they did. In their organization of economic life the missions proved successful, but because of the diseases they spread they "tended to destroy the Indians they had been sent to save. The missionaries would have preferred to have dead Christians rather than live pagans" (Archibald 1978: 184).

Florence Shipek has tried to imagine what might have attracted Indians to the missions in the first place—suggesting, for example, that Kumeyaay and Luiseño Indians thought the priests and their soldiers were powerful sorcerers possessing magical guns and horses; hence, the natives felt compelled to oblige them (Shipek 1991: 174–180). She accuses the padres of ignoring the cultural realities of the Indian communities they were attempting to overturn (Shipek 1987: 20), and she castigates the padres for making the neophytes labor for the sustenance of soldiers, their families, visitors, and the priests themselves, "in effect imposing a labor tax upon their neophytes" (1987: 25). Another writer emphasizes the missions' purpose "to support the colonial regime" (Jackson 1991: 197; cf. Jackson and Castillo 1995) of New Spain. Still others observe how rapidly the neophytes abandoned the missions under secularization, evidencing their desire to free themselves of institutions they had detested for decades beforehand (Phillips 1991: 384–394). One popularizer of mission history refers to the Franciscan institutions as "Holy Concentration Camps" (Terrell 1979: 151).

A recent study of the missionized Indians around San Francisco concedes that many of the Native Americans "despised the missions" (Milliken 1995: 1) for the "paternalistic controls on their work schedules, on their sexual practices, their eating habits, their religious expression, . . . threats of punishment in this life and an eternal afterlife. And the missions were breeding grounds for disease." At the same time, he notes, the Indians continued to join the missions in sizable numbers, and "they were not marched to the baptismal font by soldiers with guns and lances." The first converts came voluntarily for baptism because of the superior technology of the Spaniards—including the soldiers who possessed terrific, dangerous weapons. Some native elders sent in the first converts in order to ally themselves with the Spanish newcomers. Other Indians were excited by the novelty of mission life, and they were attracted by the ample stores of food—especially when overgrazing by Spaniards' livestock led to a depletion of natural resources.

Over time the neophytes may have come to hate as well as admire their missionary overseers; however, their subjection to the mission regimen led to "psychological disintegration" (ibid., 136) among the neophytes. "The missionaries sought to make the native people feel ashamed of their traditional way of life and envious of Spanish culture," the author writes. "The missionary campaign of denigration, presumably motivated by good will, turned out to be a campaign involving psychological violence" and producing "deep emotional trauma" (223, 219). As a result of their experience in the missions, California Indians lost their faith in their old way of life. The missionary campaign was successful. Baptized Indians came to be ashamed of their native identity. Those who listened to the Christian creed became convinced that they deserved punishment because they were sinners of a lesser social order. The Indians "internalized" (223) the lessons they were taught, at least while they remained in the mission settings. The longterm effect, Randall Milliken suggests, was devastating: "To accept a foreign culture as inherently superior to one's own is, in a sense, to deprecate one's self. Such self-deprecation can cut away at an individual's psychological foundations and internally injure that person" (224).

Edward D. Castillo, a Cahuilla-Luiseño anthropologist, character- izes the Spaniards as "members of an authoritarian empire whose soci- ety was populous, complex, and . . . steeped in a legacy of religious intolerance and conformity featuring a messianic fanaticism accentuat- ing both Spanish culture in general and Catholicism in particular." He adds that the Spaniards in California possessed "a political philosophy that condoned large-scale duplicity . . . with a history of almost con- stant warfare stressing conquest" (Castillo 1978: 99). With this salvo he counterattacks centuries of derogatory perspectives regarding Indians. Concerned that the Columbian quincentennial and the efforts to can- onize Fray Serra—the combination of what he characterizes as "His- panic boosterism and religious conviction"—will serve to "mask the not so flattering realities of the Spanish Colonial empire" (Castillo 1989: 377), he has conducted a preemptive attack upon the Franciscans. He sums up the condemnations of the mission system that have accu- mulated since the late eighteenth century but have coalesced since Cook's scholarship. For Castillo, the missions were part of Spain's im- perial rivalry with other European colonial powers. The priests and military were partners in this enterprise; they stole Indian lands and established "feudal domination" (Castillo 1989: 378) over the Indians, who became serfs, and later through secularization, would become peons. The missionaries used "clever inducements" (378) to bring In- dians into the system and then attempted to hold them captive. The soldiers protecting the priests—their partners in crime—raped Indian women and girls, spread venereal disease, and provided intimidation against cultural expression, escape, and revolt. Nevertheless, the Indi- ans resisted. The women practiced abortions and infanticide to ex- punge the offspring of soldiers. Indians continued to practice their traditional religions in the missions insofar as they could, resisting christianization and maintaining traditional worldviews; they escaped in large numbers, risking whip, stock, and armed expeditions to bring them back. The Indians assassinated the friars who were especially brutal and in some cases engaged in armed riots and revolts. Even those priests whom the neophytes referred to as "good" were part of an evil regime. Taking into account the Franciscans' role in New Mexico as well as California, he concludes:

> The long history of colonial Franciscan Christianization efforts in New Spain is riddled with confrontations between traditional native cultures and the demands of colonial religious authorities. . . . While Franciscan-authored histories have attempted to minimize the coercive and military aspects of their participation in the conquest of New Spain, their assistance to the Crown in this matter was crucial to the success of that empire-building enterprise. (Castillo 1991: xix)

The recent critique of Christian missions penned by a Native American Lutheran (Tinker 1993: 42–68) comes to similar conclusions aimed directly at Junipero Serra.

THE CONTEMPORARY APOLOGIA

While the judgments of contemporary social scientists regarding the Franciscans and other Catholic missionaries in the New World has grown increasingly condemnatory (e.g., Gutiérrez 1991), some mission apologists have dug in against the attack. Many clerical scholars have eschewed an institutional stance—Charles Polzer, S.J., is but one example—but others have placed themselves in line with the viewpoints of the missionaries whose lives they are evaluating and, therefore, against the "modern secularist or neo-pagan" (Dunne 1968: viii) scholars who raise accusatory questions. One Jesuit student of Baja California missions, for instance, has ridiculed anthropologists who decry missions for supposedly destroying the Indians' "religion (if he had any), his culture (if any existed)" (ibid., viii).

For the past generation, the most persistent scholarly defender of the Franciscans has been Father Francis F. Guest, O.F.M., Professor of Church History at the Franciscan Theological Seminary in Berkeley, past director of the Academy of American Franciscan History, and more recently archivist for Mission Santa Barbara Archive-Library. He has responded to the criticism of the California missions voiced by some scholars and Indians in several lengthy articles, and he has authored a biography of Presidente Lasuen (1973). He perceives six accusations made against the padres: (1) they were guilty of paternalism; (2) they forced conversions; (3) they coerced neophytes to work as their serfs without freedom to leave; (4) they engaged in punitive brutality and cruelty; (5) their missions caused widespread death, particularly due to diseases; and (6) they destroyed native cultures. These charges have been made against the whole of the Franciscan enterprise and specifically against Presidente Serra for having founded the mission system.

Guest's work has attempted to refute Sherburne Cook's conclusions, which Guest refers to as "newsreel history," as opposed to his own "scientific history" (Guest 1983: 1). He finds Cook's discussion of Indian mortality, whippings, and fugitivism in the California missions to be "thorough, comprehensive, and exact but not adequately intelligible in itself; plain enough and clear enough but, at bottom, unexplainable" (ibid., 1). Guest's method of explanation has been to place the missions in the cultural context of the Franciscans: how did the padres understand themselves, their work, their world, their Indians, and their God. In short, Guest tries to have his modern readers understand the Franciscans as the Franciscans understood themselves, explicitly and implicitly.

Academics and Indian critics claim that the neophytes were badly mistreated by the mission system, held in "virtual slavery," or "slavery" pure and simple. Guest blames the critics' lack of theological understanding for making such rash judgments: "It is difficult to escape the feeling that if earlier researchers, like Father Zephyrin Engelhardt, for example, had devoted more attention to the theology of the missionaries" (1985: 238), twentieth-century inferences would have been drawn differently. Just as Engelhardt attempted to correct the nineteenth-century histories of Hittell and Bancroft, Guest has presented a more sophisticated defense for the contemporary age.

Father Guest has defended Serra and his fellow friars against the charges of "paternalism" by saying that in the context of late eighteenth- and early nineteenth-century Spain, paternalism was the norm. Priests like Serra judged intelligence by class and culture; Indians were of the forest and were so judged. The missionaries did indeed regard the Indians as children; they seemed that way, not knowing Spanish ways. Guest reminds his readers that the Franciscans thought of themselves with *españolismo*, a "complacent self-satisfaction with everything Spanish, accompanied with a disdain for everything foreign" (ibid., 239). Like every other people, the Spanish friars thought of their cultural and religious ways as *the* norm for all people. Their cultural (and religious) ideas and practices limited their views of other people, causing them to regard and treat the Indians as children. In addition, the Spanish Crown gave the Franciscans the duty to treat the Indians as fathers treat their children. The padres were paternalistic because they were legally and spiritually *fathers* to the Indians, whose autonomy had been superseded by Christian Spanish sovereignty. Spanish law made the friars legal guardians of the natives, who were excused for certain moral lapses, even when they were baptized, because of their "inculpable ignorance" (ibid., 229) in regard to ethics. Yet in the long run, "the ultimate purpose of the Spanish government and of the Catholic Church in the Spanish empire was to embody the missionized Indians into Spanish society" (Guest 1989: 6). In order to do this, the converted Indians had to change three basic areas of their lives. They had to accept Spanish legal authority, courts, judges, etc. They had to accept Catholic marriage customs and sexual mores. And they had to acquire Spanish notions of property rights. Guest contends that the Spanish policy in California was peaceful. Spanish governmental instructions stated that the Indians were to be treated with "kindness, gentleness, good treatment, and gifts" (Guest 1966: 195). This was the policy in which the missionaries functioned, serving the Spanish government in California: "The conversion, education, government and correction of the converted Indians was to be left entirely in the hands of the missionaries, who were to stand to their charges in the relationship of fathers to children" (ibid., 195). The military served to protect the padres and further the goals of the missions.

> At the same time, the civil authorities needed to protect the Indians from the soldiers: It was forbidden for any soldier to enter an Indian village on any pretext whatsoever, except only when he served as the guard for a missionary. Violation of this rule was to be punished with eight days of sentry duty in which the guilty soldier was to take the watches at night and at dawn, the most difficult. . . . If a soldier had entered a village in search of a female Indian to seduce, or if he had solicited a female Indian in or outside of a village, his punishment was to be doubled. . . . The soldiers had a strict obligation to instill into the Indians love for the Christian religion and Spanish customs. For the conquest of the Indians must be spiritual as well as political. (Ibid., 197)

Spanish rules did not alter the soldiers' behavior appreciably. "Notwithstanding the good intentions of the viceroys and governors, Spanish soldiers sometimes got themselves into trouble with Indian women, both pagan and Christian" (ibid., 198). More specifically, between 1769 and 1773 the soldiers who accompanied the Franciscans had raped so many Indian women in California, with such violence, that Serra sought the status of wards for the neophytes in order to provide protection to the Indians from the soldiers themselves—who were present to enforce the padres' authority. In 1772 the Crown declared the neophytes wards of priests, making them legal minors. States Guest, "The status of neophyte girls as minors gave them protection against licentious soldiers who might wish to live with them in a state of concubinage" (1989: 28). In this way, Serra and his fellow friars came to regard the Alta California aborigines as "adult children" (ibid., 29).

In examining Sherburne Cook's contention that gentile Indians were "forced into the missions" or "coerced into accepting conversion and baptism," Guest replies that, "Neither of these two questions can be answered accurately or completely with a simple yes or a simple no." In principle, the Spanish empire "consistently required the voluntariness of baptism for all Indians who had reached the age of reason" (1979: 2). In such a context, conversions could not be forced. Guest notes that in 1775 and 1787 the padres made explicit statements against forced conversion, although in the later years—after Serra's time—there was "limited employment of force" which Guest says "can be explained pretty well" (n.d.: 2). More pointedly, "In the history of Alta California there is no valid or reliable documentation which proves that a governor, presidio commander, or missionary sent an armed party of soldiers or missionized Indians into the wilderness to force non-Christian Indians to be reduced in a mission in violation of this law." On the other hand, "some Indians were forced into certain missions but not specifically for purposes of reduction," rather, for example, into "private service" (Guest 1979: 2–3). At Mission Santa Clara in 1794, however,

> Father Manuel Fernández was accused of employing both threats and force to compel certain non-Christian Indians to enter his mission community. The Indians were under the impression that if they did not become Christians he would burn down their villages. According to another story, he cudgeled an Indian either for not coming to the mission himself or for dissuading his relatives from coming. (Ibid., 3)

Although these claims were not specifically proven, says Guest, the local military commander ordered that the Indians be told that their conversions were, in fact, voluntary, and the friar's spiritual superiors told him to "moderate his zeal" (1979: 4).

The padres may have attracted the gentiles with music, art, liturgy, the novelty of mission life, its tools and utensils, and the kindness of missionaries. Indians may have been drawn by the "wrong reasons" (1983: 35): to secure abundant food in certain years and locations when there was scant rainfall; to escape enemies; or "after suffering a military defeat" (1983: 35) by the Spaniards.

Once the friars had baptized the Indians, it was necessary, writes Guest, to keep the neophytes from their pagan relatives "against the proximate occasion of grave sin," including "casual cohabitation" (n.d.: 3), homosexuality, divorce, and violence in gentile communities.

The padres did allow visits home for periods of several weeks each year, but neophytes had to return to the missions after these home stays, as required by a Spanish law dating to 1604. The whole point of the missions was to change the Indians' way of life by having them live a hispanicized, or more to the point, a sanctified, christianized way of life. They had to live at the mission for the system to work. The priests needed to give the baptized Indians an orderly routine so they would be available for catechism twice a day. Moreover, and more to the point, "For the friars, the missionized Indians who had become fugitives in the forest were like adult children who had run away from home and had become involved in serious spiritual danger" (Guest 1985: 233). Their own theological principles compelled the Franciscans to bring back neophyte fugitives. Naturally the Indians wanted to backslide, go home, see their relatives; however, the friars were their spiritual guardians. If the Indians went home and sinned, the friars "would incur the same guilt the offenders had in falling into such defects" (234). Bearing such responsibility, the friars had to obey their dicta, and they were justified in using even force to bring back the hindras and punish them.

Why did Indians run away from the mission? Because, according to Lasuen, and also to Guest, life in their home villages was "free" and "lazy." Guest writes: "The truth was that anyone who embraces a civilized life must, of necessity, relinquish some measure of the freedom he knew in the uncivilized world whence he came. This was the point, a subtle point, impossible to explain to the Indians" (1966: 208). When Indians wished to quit the missions and return to their homes, it was because they could not live up to the standards of mission life: "Not a few of the California Indians who tried Christianity found themselves wanting," particularly those who succeeded in returning to what Guest refers to as the "wilderness" (ibid., 209), i.e., their village homes.

Sometimes Indians ran away from the missions because they were not accustomed to the disciplines the friars meted out "to an Indian, who most probably had never been punished by his parents, any punishment at all was too much" (215). Soldiers who investigated the large number of runaways at Mission San Francisco in the 1790s elicited from the fugitives the "three *muchos*: too much work, too much punishment, and too much hunger" (212). Guest adds that the neophytes were trained poorly, or too quickly, and they felt alienated in the missions where more than one Indian culture group dwelled. Squabbles made them want to leave, as did the presence of the soldiers, whom they regarded as their enemies. He concludes, however, that the most important reason for fugitivism was "the great contrast that existed between their native aboriginal way of life and the civilized style of living at the missions" (1983: 40).

Spanish law forbade armed expeditions from forcing conversions; however, it empowered authorities "to send armed parties to punish or imprison Indians who had harmed Spaniards or peaceful Indians either in their persons or in their property" (Guest 1979: 8). The padres were able to use this law to justify armed expeditions against neophytes who escaped the missions to return to their families, communities, and countries, because such occurrences constituted "rebellion against Spanish authority," which was firmly established by the rights of discovery and conquest. Guest notes that "Not infrequently, both Christian fugitives and non-Christian Indians were involved in . . . small insurrections" (9), and for these acts they received whippings and imprisonments due them in trying to escape to freedom from Spanish Christian authority. Those gentiles who aided them were also criminals: An

> offense for which Indians might be punished and imprisoned was protecting and sheltering fugitives from the missions. . . . Spanish law forbade converted Indians to live outside the reductions to which they belonged. One must remember that the missions were a creation of the state as well as of the Church. They were governed by state laws just as other branches and institutions of the Church were in the Spanish empire. This law regarding the residence of Indians at their mission was observed by both military and clergy, just as other laws were. The king ruled by divine right, one must remember. His laws were sacred. (Ibid., 10)

Yet, the neophytes persisted in their escapes: "The trouble was that the Indians loved their little home in the wilderness and always had a strong yearning to go back to it." They missed their lands; they feared mission diseases that were killing so many of their fellows; they wanted to be buried at home; they rebelled against the work they were required to perform; and they resented the punishments "for faults committed" (11–12). Another reason for fugitivism was

> the love of the Indians to be loved. When the missionaries first approached the Indians, it was with charity, with gifts, with kindness and

affection. After the Indians had been won over to conversion, instructed and baptized, they could not be left on their own responsibility and expected to persevere by themselves. The missionary had to keep on winning them with more kindness, more affection, more love. If he should become too much involved in mission temporalities, the management of mission estates, the hide and tallow trade, and the purchase and sale of commodities, and if, in consequence, he should neglect to bestow upon the neophytes an adequate measure of personal and individual attention, they would feel unappreciated, unloved, unblessed, (ibid., 12)

even though the padre's labor was all "for their own benefit."

Guest shows that the missionaries employed a chronological progression of techniques for returning neophytes to their missions. In the earlier years the padres went with a few soldiers or Christian Indians to "induce the fugitives to return." When, in 1795, the hindras offered armed resistance to being retaken, a new policy was necessary. Hence, after 1800 the priests sent soldiers to Indian villages, claiming that they were scouting out a new mission site. They were to act kindly, cultivate friendships among the gentiles, and along the way let it be known that sheltering fugitives was against the law. Despite their disingenuous denials, "one of the purposes of these ventures was to recover Christian fugitives" (ibid., 13). If peaceful methods did not work, "eventually force had to be employed to return fugitive Indians to their missions" (13–14) to comply with Spanish law. By 1810 force had replaced peaceful means. From thence until the close of the missions, the "presidial companies depended very heavily on the missions for food and clothing. . . . Hence the missionized Indians, whose workload was usually light, had to apply themselves to their tasks much more strenuously—a condition that, in all likelihood, contributed all the more both to fugitivism and to horse stealing." Governor Pablo Vicente de Sola "cracked down rather sharply on fugitivism" during his term between 1815 and 1822; his soldiers needed the mission Indians for their support, even if it took violence to keep them at work (15). The next governor, Luis Antonio Argüello, gave an eight-day ultimatum in 1823 to fugitive Indians: return, or be considered rebels subject to military attack. The padres responded that the neophytes were, in Guest's words, "addicted to their pre-Christian way of life," and "had it not been for the restraining hand of the military guard. . . . most of the Indian converts would return to their brethren in the forest" (16). The governors sent out punitive expeditions, and those captured were taken to presidios to serve prison sentences set by the governor, e.g., one year for apostates and six months for their gentile protectors. Guest states that in the course of these punitive expeditions, the "frightened, confused, grief-stricken" gentiles "asked for baptism" when their villages were ransacked, their relatives arrested or killed. In Guest's view, these Indians were not necessarily "compelled to accept conversion," but rather they acted freely to "appease the victorious Spanish" (27–28). When faced with these non-Christian Indians asking for baptism, who had been brought in by military sorties, the friars had to consult their deeply ingrained theology of baptism that insisted on faith, adequate knowledge of Christian doctrine, and voluntary, sincere intent for any adult to be baptized by a priest. Guest asks, "But what does voluntariness mean?" (30). Perhaps these Indians were motivated by terror, but could the priest refuse them? Terror could lead, through instruction, to faith and free choice. The friars could not turn the captive gentiles away. It was only their job to make sure that voluntariness was present in the gentiles by the time baptism took place.

For Guest, the most vexing "anomaly" about the Franciscans is how to "reconcile the cross the missionaries carried in one hand with the whip they bore in the other." He concedes that "there is incontrovertible testimony that delinquent Indians were whipped, sometimes excessively, by the padres" (1983: 7); however, his goal is to "weaken the charge, heard so often in recent years, that the missionaries in the treatment of the neophytes, were brutal and cruel" (1989: 85).

For centuries before the beginning of the California missions, Spanish missionaries in the New World practiced corporal punishment, and the custom of imposing punishments on neophytes for objectionable behavior was continued by Junipero Serra and his successors" (ibid., 31). Serra instituted and defended corporal punishment, and because of him it became part of the missions' daily routine. Were the missionaries brutal or cruel? Guest finds the history of the missions "unintelligible" (n.d.: 7) if this were so, since missionaries were supposed to attract gentiles with kindness, and because the priests traveled alone among Indians without coming to harm. "Mission discipline" constitutes the touchiest topic to modern sensibilities, he avers: "It would certainly have been better if the missionaries, in their well meant efforts to maintain good order at the missions, had

chosen milder and more progressive methods" (ibid., 15). Nevertheless, in light of their era, their situation on the frontier, their cultural
baggage, and the role of whipping in European child rearing, they
could not have acted differently. "Abuses sometimes occurred" (16)—
the most obvious cases concerning Father José Pedro Panto at Mission
San Diego—and Mission Indian families have passed down tales of remembered cruelty; however, Guest says that the missionaries' authoritarianism was justified.

　　Governor José Joachin de Arrillaga (1800–1814) once said that "if a
stranger should travel through Lower and Upper California and observe the manner in which the Indians were treated, he would consider
it cruel and tyrannical. But if he would probe beneath the surface of
things and study the subject more thoroughly, he would change his
mind" (Guest 1985: 252). Father Guest guides moderns through the
historical context of the colonial Franciscans to make sense of their
practice according to their own contexts: "Without the aid of the cultural perspective . . . an American reader might easily be led to describe
the Franciscan missionaries as callous and brutal in the way they punished delinquent Indians" (1983: 21). According to Guest, whipping as
a policy was "an error in judgment," but "not . . . necessarily an exercise in brutality" (ibid., 22).

　　Within the missions, Guest says, Indians engaged in criminal behavior—he points to an adulterous lover killing a man's spouse as an
example—and their punishments were lenient because the Indians
were not considered fully rational, fully capable of understanding
Spanish Christian law and justice. Despite the leniency, and although
"nothing was to be done to provoke the Indians to hostility or insurrection" (Guest 1966: 203), punishments were necessary not only for
cases of criminality, but also for attempts to escape and for rebellions:
"Records of small insurrections of this kind are relatively numerous"
(ibid., 202). The punishments included flogging and shackling, as well
as increased work. These were also the kinds of punishments meted
out to the lower classes in Spain at the time.

　　European ideas regarding whipping, education, and human freedom were changing in the late eighteenth and early nineteenth century. Presidente Serra was a traditionalist, and although he called for
leniency for Indians, he defended whipping and other forms of corporal punishment in his days in California. His successor Lasuen
wrote rules for disciplining the neophytes, stating, "And now as to

punishments: it is obvious that a barbarous, fierce, and ignorant country needs punishments and penalties that are different from one that is cultured and enlightened, and where the way of doing things is restrained and mild" (in ibid., 207); Guest declares Lasuen's point to be that the Indians deserved leniency because they didn't know any better. The padres were to treat them gently, exhausting all mild reproaches and punishments as correctives. Though there were exceptions like Fray Matias Noriega at San Carlos, who had a reputation for cruelty, most friars treated the neophytes as a teacher would a pupil in Spain: or a father would a son: with admonishments, whippings, and shackles.

In the California missions, Presidente Lasuen limited the lashes to twenty-one. Guest estimates such a scourging to have taken less than two minutes, assuming five seconds per lash. Moreover, it was noted that the strokes were "more adapted to children six years of age than to men, most of whom receive it without an exclamation of pain" (Governor Pablo Vicente de Sola's conclusions regarding Father Andres Quintana, in the investigation of his murder, Guest 1983: 16). Comparing this evidence to the fact that during the same period British seamen often received as many as a thousand lashes with a cat-o'-nine-tails—the Franciscans used only knotted cords, chains (cf. photos, ibid., 19, 38), reeds, or canes—Guest determines the disciplines to have been relatively benign. Indeed, Guest goes so far as to say that "they were not real whippings," resembling "a spanking" (1989: 33–34) more than a flogging. For the padres, the lashes represented but a remedial flagellation, a "salutary humiliation" (ibid., 44) for intellectually, morally, and spiritually immature wards. By 1833 Fray Francisco Garcia Diego y Moreno ruled that the time for such discipline had passed—arguing that those who were whipped became the most incorrigible—and he forbade his friars from employing the practice any longer. In the meantime, however, the missionaries applied the whip without qualms—except for two late eighteenth-century friars who raised an alarm about the punishments; Guest refers to one as "the demented missionary" (1966: 208) and to the other as "not a well man . . . probably an epileptic" (ibid., 217–218).

To understand the whippings, he states, we must first grasp "the penitential spirit" (1989: 9) of the Franciscans in the eighteenth century. He points to the long history of penitential whipping in the Church, dating as far back as St. Pachomius (d. 348), who employed the whip for delinquent monks. In the Middle Ages whipping became a way of imitating Christ's suffering, and in the eleventh century St. Peter Damian (d. 1072) popularized self-flagellation. Although scourging oneself or one's fellows may be "indefensible" (Guest 1983: 14) by today's standards of Catholic theology, "whipping played a significant role in Spanish culture in the eighteenth and early nineteenth centuries. It was part of the domestic, social, and religious life of the people" (14), but especially the friars'. They possessed a "profound consciousness of sin" (Guest 1989: 9) in themselves and others, and they attempted in their mission to inculcate such feelings of personal sinfulness among the Indians. Whipping played a role in that training. If we look at the catechisms current since the Council of Trent, and particularly those we find in the mission libraries in California, we find a consistent emphasis on the need of humans to provide "satisfaction" for their sins. Jesus Christ's death was not enough. We humans must endure our afflictions, accept pain with humility and docility. This is what the priests were trying to teach the Indians by whipping them, and they tried to get the Indians to accept the whipping in a spirit of mortifying submission. The crucifixes in the missions portrayed Jesus' bodily sufferings; the friars themselves whipped themselves in public; hence, the Indians were to accept for themselves what the Franciscans applied to themselves. These men of the rule were taking in Indian neophytes as if they were junior members of the religious order, having them observe the practices of the Franciscans themselves. They were introducing the Indians not just to Christianity, but to monastic spirituality.

Gerónimo de Mendieta, a sixteenth-century Franciscan, wrote that whipping was beneficial to the Indians: "Punishment was as necessary for them as bread" (ibid., 24). Of course the priest should make the Indians understand that the punishment derived from love, from a sincere desire for improvement and christianization. Clerics should administer it with moderation and without anger. If these conditions were followed, the Indians "would thank the missionary" (ibid., 25) for defending the Indians from their own sinfulness.

Guest assumes that California Indians were accustomed to avenging injuries with death. How could the friars have whipped the Indians—as they did from the beginning in California—without risking their own deaths from vengeance? He does bear witness to the attempts on the missionaries' lives, but these, he says, were aberrations from the usual pattern in which the priests could walk among Indians without any harm. He concludes that the Indians accepted the whipping, that it was not offensive to them. He also suggests that to answer the question: "Why did the missionized Indians submit to these whippings so patiently?" (1983: 17), one can ask a further question: "Was it not because they knew that he [the padre] whipped himself much harder and more often than he did them?"(ibid., 20).

Guest suggests what the neophytes "would" (1989: 11) have felt as they were whipped, based upon the contemporary catechism teaching about what a Christian ought to have felt. He writes that receiving the lashes administered by the mission authorities "could very appropriately have been, for the neophyte, a means of participating in the passion of Christ" and "would have provided him with . . . religious motivation" (ibid., 52) to persevere as a Christian. Elsewhere he notes that a military guard at each mission, consisting of five soldiers and a corporal in most places, was "unquestionably an encouragement to the Indians to accept their punishment with patience" (ibid., 8).

In regard to the death rate among the neophytes, Guest apologizes for the friars' "inculpable ignorance" (n.d.: 9). Neither they nor anyone else in their day knew about bacteria, and the missionaries were befuddled when so many neophytes died in the concentrated populations of the missions. Even knowing that these deaths would occur—judging from the earlier Baja missions—the Franciscans still felt compelled to gather them into the reductions as Jesus commanded, the Crown required, and their Franciscan order trained them. The population loss had nothing to do with the spiritual goals of the missions but occurred wherever Indians met Europeans throughout the Americas.

How could the Franciscans continue to bring Indians into their missions when they observed that more Indians were dying there each year than were being baptized? Guest's answer is that the Franciscan Spanish, coming from a country with a high death rate, were inured to death. "One does not wish to present all this evidence as an apologia for the Spanish missionaries, excusing them of all blame for the high rate of mortality among the neophytes," states Guest; indeed, "the missions themselves, as institutions, were an important cause of death among the converted Indians" (1983: 6). Guest concludes that the high death rate resulted not from malnutrition, or even from epidemics, per se, but from the condition neophyte Indians experienced having been "depressed by separation from their aboriginal way of life" (ibid., 52). Their cataclysmic culture change sapped their collective and individual will to live, and they died of cultural anomie.

That the mission system destroyed the Indians' culture—and populations—Guest finds regrettable: "The Church today, when so many missionary bishops and priests are anthropologists, insists that, in the delicate, prolonged, and complex process of Christianizing aboriginal people, their culture be left as undisturbed as possible" (n.d.: 14). He warrants that the Franciscans employed a technique among the California Indians in which "one should not be hasty about detaching them from the religious rites and ceremonies to which their tribal tradition had long accustomed them. If these religious practices did not involve a clear and open violation of the divine law, they should be tolerated until, little by little, the Indians were weaned away from their ancient form of worship" (1989: 3). But he grants that, in general, Serra and his followers rarely paid attention to the details of aboriginal culture, nor cared for its continuance.

If it was right for monks in the Middle Ages to introduce Roman Catholic culture to Teutons, Slavs, and Celts, why was it wrong in California? The fact that the losses of Indian culture and population are fresh makes the history painful in the short run, but in the long haul the christianization has been, and will continue to be, a benefit to the Indians.

Guest contends that before the missionaries arrived in California the various tribes were constantly at war with one another. By joining diverse tribes in single mission units where they served, side by side, in Spanish regiments ready to fight the French, the friars brought "peace" to the Indian cultures.

Finally, he asks: "If one assumes that the missionaries were habitually guilty of grave mistreatment of the neophytes, how does one explain the enduring attachment of so many of the descendants of the missionized Indians to Catholicism?" (ibid., 6). One proof of the beneficial consequences of the missions is "the extraordinary fidelity of the California mission Indians, over a period of one hundred and fifty years, to the Catholicism handed down to them from the past" (ibid., 5). Hence, the Franciscans could not have acted so ignobly as their critics claim.

Guest writes that "Some Indian family traditions keep alive memories of Franciscan harsh treatment. It would be surprising if these departures from the virtues of justice and charity had not occurred. On the other hand, however, the same kind of traditions recorded as sworn deposition in the 1940s reveal that, among Indian as well as non-Indian families, Junipero Serra's reputation for holiness of life was firmly upheld" (in Costo and Costo 1987: 232).

THE ƒERRA CONTROVERƒY

The Church's continuing evaluation of Fray Serra to determine if he is a bona fide saint—"The purpose in identifying these holy men and women is to set them before the faithful for their emulation. . . . to 'canonize' means to declare that a person is worthy of universal public cult" (Woodward 1990: 17)—has kept the issue of the Franciscans, and by extension the issue of Catholic evangelization among Native Americans, in the public consciousness. The archive of the Diocese of San Diego contains a filing cabinet drawer filled with articles from the Catholic press of California, correspondence regarding the bicentennial of Serra's death in 1984, educational materials, and the like—over a thousand items that indicate the importance of this Franciscan to the Catholic authorities and faithful since the move for canonization began in the 1930s. Three glossy booklets for children (Sullivan 1984a, b, c) idealize him as a paradigm of Catholic virtues and values, suggesting that we follow in his footsteps, calling him a "national hero" (1984b: 25) whose life was rooted in the visions of Abraham, Moses, David, Mary, Jesus, and St. Francis of Assisi. One of these books says of the Indians:

> *Soon the native people*
> *Lived the Christian way.*
> *They liked to work together,*
> *To plant, to sing, to pray.*
> *Soon the place was buzzing*
> *With so much there to do,*
> *Many to be baptized,*
> *To be taught and married, too.* (1984c: 20)

Sometimes, however, the natives grew angry "And threatened then to raid" (1984c: 20). As a guide to teachers using these books, the author states, "With adult prompting children will sense: how much Father Serra loved God . . . how good Father tried to be to the natives." His life was hard but peaceful, providing messages of joy, forgiveness, unselfish love, and an "acceptance of the differences of others" (1984c: n.p.).

The archives indicate, however, that not all has been peace and joy in regard to Serra's pending canonization, in particular, and the relations between Indians and friars, in general. In March 1972, for instance, a group of about twenty Indians, led by a Sioux, encamped at Mission San Antonio de Padua northeast of Monterey and claimed it, and by extension the other twenty missions as well, basing their claims on the 1773 Secularization Act of Spain, which stipulated that the missions would become the property of the Indians when they were civilized. When the United States took over California, supposedly the Spanish laws (continued by Mexico) were to prevail; however, under Abraham Lincoln the United States granted the missions legally to the Catholic Church, and its authorities have held them since. The band of Indians making these charges received an offer from the Franciscans at Padua to stay indefinitely as guests—an invitation refused. Within two weeks, however, the encampment ended with the issues unresolved (San Diego. Indian Seizure of Missions. 1972).

As part of a year-long retrospective of Fray Serra at the bicentennial observation of his death, and as a goad toward his beatification, a scholar of Catholic missionary theory published a defense of Serra's achievements from the perspective of contemporary evangelical ideals. In consultation with Father Guest, Father Louis J. Luzbetak wrote that Christian missionaries, including the California Franciscans, have received too much criticism. They may have shared the "ignorance, paternalism, racism, and imperialism" of their epochs, but an examination of Serra discovers in him "one of the greatest frontiersmen the Americas have ever seen, one of the greatest friends the American Indians have ever known, and one of the greatest missionary saints the Church has ever produced. . . . Of one thing we can be absolutely certain: if Junipero Serra were alive, this great frontiersman, missionary, and ascetic would not be behind the times but well ahead of them" (Luzbetak 1985: 512).

Luzbetak reviews the three models—ethnocentrism, accommodationalism, and contextualization—which have served Christian missionaries over the centuries. Ethnocentrism is "the tendency to regard one's own culture as the norm for all societies." Imperialism, racism, genocide, triumphalism, and paternalism may all share an ethnocentric basis, but they are different by degrees of both intensity and form. The padres' ethnocentric failing was that of "rank *paternalism*. Indians were but 'adult children,' . . . never to be trusted, never to be left alone even for a moment lest they get into some mischief. Paternalism is basically false compassion which makes the so-called 'beneficiary' ever more dependent on the would-be 'benefactor'" (ibid., 513). The padres kept the neophytes from their fellows, and when the neophytes tried to escape, the padres sent out their soldiers "as the padre's truant officer." Serra and his padres were guilty of a "misguided sense of parental responsibility," sentencing Indians to the whip and the stocks "as if the adult were indeed a child that had misbehaved" (514).

Accommodationalism is an attempt by missionaries to use in pagan culture whatever is compatible with the gospel message as building blocks of a Christian culture. As Luzbetak has said, the task is "to make the beautiful in a so-called 'pagan' heart even more beautiful, to seek out the naturally good in order to make it supernaturally perfect, to present Christianity not as an enemy of the existing way of life but as a friend possessing the secret that will enable the non-Christian culture [to] reach its God-intended perfection" (514). The Church Fathers spoke of paganism carrying the seed of Christianity, the *logoi spermatikoi*. Gregory the Great gave the orders to missionaries to respect pagan shrines and ways and by baptizing them, to make them into Christian shrines and ways. Luzbetak says that although Serra was an ethnocentrist, he was also an accommodationalist who found the Indians to be "gentle, peaceful, cordial, courteous, charming, interesting, gifted, mild, affectionate, submissive, amenable, tractable" (515).

Today the Church's missionary method emphasizes contextualization, or inculturation. The Church is now pan-cultural, truly Catholic. Each culture is recognized as a context necessary for any person to understand the text of the gospel. The contemporary Church sees accommodationalism as an attempt by the missionary to place a superficial veneer on the gospel. Today each community must understand the gospel in its own cultural terms, its own context: "What would Jesus teach the Indians if he himself had been an Indian?" (517). Serra was certainly not a contextualist, nor could one expect him to have been, in his day and age. Nevertheless, it was Serra's intent, and the intent of his Franciscan followers, to christianize the Indians and at the same time to protect them from colonialist destruction. These were worthy goals, noble intent, says Luzbetak.

In 1985 the Vatican's Sacred Congregation of Rites recommended that Serra be declared venerable, a possible step toward canonization, leaving the rest of the process to miracles that might prove Serra's sanctification. When the Church declared Serra venerable in 1985, after fifty years of lobbying by Franciscans—with the help of business executives, political leaders, and the Catholic hierarchy of California— some California Indians raised a protest. A woman of Chumash descent, CheqWeesh Auh-Ho-Oh, made an uninvited speech at the Mission Carmel in the presence of twenty-four bishops and others at a mass concluding a year-long bicentennial of Serra's death. She asked that her people, who built the church and are buried beneath it, be remembered. After mass she condemned Serra and argued against his canonization: he imprisoned Indians, punished them for running away, and flogged them. Though he may not have done these things personally, she said, he instituted the system that did. Like Hitler, she claimed, "Serra was an architect of a genocidal system" (in Wintz 1987: 30). She termed Serra's Carmel mission "Auschwitz with roses." Angry Church officials termed her "that witch" (San Diego. Serra and Indians Controversy. 1985–1990). Other Indian activists joined in the chorus of accusation against Serra and the Franciscans. There was fear and loathing on the Padres' Trail.

In reply, Bishop Thaddeus Shubsda of Monterey released the "Serra Report" in 1986. The Bishop hired a public relations specialist to compile a series of statements by scholarly advocates for Serra's canonization, arranged in the form of interviews meant to refute the long-standing, but immediate, accusations.

In the report Dr. Iris Engstrand, professor of history, University of San Diego, concedes that the mission practice of preventing neophytes from returning to their families was wrong; however, "As far as beating the Indian, I assume there were floggings and there were other punishments, and I think most everybody's pointed out that flogging is the typical 18th century punishment for kids in school, sailors, soldiers, whatever. . . . As far as I know, I don't think anybody could come up with examples of Father Serra's beating Indians" (in Costo and Costo 1987: 192-193). Dr. Michael Mathes, professor of history, University of San Francisco, declares, "Considering colonial systems as inevitable, the Spanish system, for all of its faults, was the best available at the time" (in ibid., 210). He notes that Serra tried to protect the Indians from the Spanish soldiers, who tried "getting at the girls" of the mission, making the neophytes drunk, and introducing gambling. Serra "didn't want these people to be tainted with any possible immoral activities that the soldiers might be involved with," so he clamped down on the neophytes' freedom somewhat. Nevertheless, Serra was good to the Indians; there is no proof of his cruelty: "Let's see proof. . . . You have to have some proof" (211).

Several of the scholars in the Serra Report proclaim that the Indians' aboriginal culture was destined to end. Dr. David Hornbeck, professor of historical geography, California State University, Northridge, says, "The Indians were doomed as a culture. . . . The mission system was a real attempt to ensure that Indians, the aboriginal society, was moved into Spanish society in some sort of transition. That they were able to move from their wild heathen state into a civilized state. Of course, Spain dictated what civilization was. The Indians had no chance to define what they thought was civilization. Now, you say, all right, there was a problem there, but you can't condemn Spain for what it was doing" (196); other European nations were doing the same thing at the same time. Dr. Harry Kelsey, Chief Curator of History, Los Angeles County Museum of Natural History, observes that, "The Indians were delighted to come into the missions. They had been living on the bare edge of existence. . . . And there was constant warfare. . . . This idea that they lived in a sort of pastoral Eden, in perfect peace with one another, is just the greatest malarkey. There's absolutely no truth to it at all" (207). Dr. Gloria E. Miranda, professor of history and Chicano studies, Los Angeles Valley College, adds: "The tribes practiced polygamy, which was degrading to women. Abortion and incest were common practices among Native Americans" (213); therefore, the missionaries did a good thing to change and improve the Indians' ways of living. Dr. Norman Neuerburg, retired professor of art history, California State University, Dominguez Hill, concedes that the missions utterly destroyed the Indian culture, "but it was inevitable . . . their civilization was doomed in any case. . . . All things considered, the Spanish Franciscans did a relatively good job" (215–216). What did Catholicism do for the Indians? Dr. Doyce Nunis, Jr., professor of history, University of Southern California, avows:

> For the first time it dignified the individual. Up until that time, the Indians had no sense of fidelity to each other, there was no spirit of loyalty. There was no spirit of commitment. You stayed together out of necessity rather than out of appreciation. In other words, they had no idea of a social compact. . . . They had no sense of morality. They participated in free love. . . . They had no sense of place. Only a sense of area. . . . Life was very hard. Very hard. They simply had to really grub

for a living. And that living meant just eating and staying alive. (In ibid., 220–222)

John Johnson, curator of the Santa Barbara Museum of Natural History, states that the Chumash joined the missions because they were fascinated with the "magical" technologies of the Spanish, although some came in for religious reasons, too, "true conversion. . . . So, there are all kinds of advantages, social, and economic, to join a Mission" (203). And Professor Nunis imagines the exhilaration of the conversion process for the California Indians:

> Has it ever dawned on anybody that many of these California mission Indians may have truly accepted with joy, and great happiness and great fulfillment the new religion? The priest down at San Luis Rey had 3,000 Indians under his control, never any problems. Those Indians went back out to Pala and built their own little chapel and decorated that chapel. That was an act of fealty . . . of love. You mean to tell me that there were no true Christians among the mission Indians? I've seen people on television being converted through one sermon, if you can believe it. So, why wouldn't it be true that the Franciscans could do the same thing? I think there was a core of Christian Indians who were truly converted. Maybe they didn't understand everything. . . . (In ibid., 219)

The response to the Serra Report within the Indian community was immediate and rancorous. Members of the National Tekakwitha Conference, an agency supported by the Bureau of Catholic Indian Missions, with grassroots membership in Indian parishes throughout the United States, aired the issue at its board meetings and in its *Newsletter*. The Tekakwitha Conference draws several thousand Indians and religious in Indian ministries to its annual conference, with the goal of elevating the seventeenth-century Mohawk, Kateri Tekakwitha to sainthood through prayers and other forms of devotion. The conference supports the process of inculturation, encouraging Indian Catholics to express their tribal and pan-Indian religiousness in coordination with their Catholic worship. Catholic Indians and non-Indians in the conference have rallied around the cause of the Indian convert and decidedly *not* around Junipero Serra, the missionary. Because Kateri Tekakwitha was a Mohawk Indian, the Vatican has treated her cause with special urgency in an attempt to please and appease Indians. In the same way, the Vatican regards Serra's cause as a response to the lobbying of another special interest group within the Church, the

Franciscan order, and to some extent to the white Catholic faithful of California.

With Pope John Paul II scheduled to meet the annual conference in Phoenix in 1987, Tekakwitha members began to lobby against Serra's elevation to sainthood because of the accusations made against him and his fellow Franciscans. Indian Catholics from around the country, eager to celebrate their Catholicism in coordination with the pope's visit, expressed ambivalence and even animosity toward the missionaries—including the California Franciscans—who introduced them to their Catholic faith. Members of the conference signed a statement supporting the "right" of California Native Americans "to defend their own history" against the Serra Report, which (they contended) "is grossly inaccurate and totally misrepresents the native understanding of its own history and culture" (Twohy et al. 1987: 17). The executive director of the conference at the time, a non-Indian priest, Gilbert Hemauer, O.F.M. Cap., went on record publicly and argued privately in high Catholic circles that there are "rumblings within the Native community" against the glorification of a man whose California mission system included beatings and other systematic brutality against Indians. In particular, he hoped that the pope and Church would "avoid the embarrassment" of promoting Serra at the 1987 meeting in Phoenix (Hemauer, August 9, 1986).

When the pope addressed several thousand Indian Catholics in September 1987, he elevated neither Tekakwitha nor Serra. He spoke of the "harsh and painful reality" of White contact for Indians. On the other hand, he said, there were also "positive aspects" of this contact, especially with respect to those missionaries who supported Indian rights. They learned Indian languages in order to bring them the gospel and sought Indians' benefit. They taught universal love—love for all peoples—and today this gospel is the highest possession Indian Catholics have. In sharp contrast to the criticisms by Tekakwitha Conference personnel, the pontiff praised Junipero Serra's work specifically, professing that the missions he founded were designed to protect Indians from exploitation, carrying out the objectives of Pope Paul III, who in 1537 proclaimed the peoples of the Americas to be fully human and therefore worthy of protection and conversion. Not all members of this Church, said the pope, have lived up to the ideals of the Church; however, we must be "grateful" to those who brought the gospel: "people with good minds and hearts" (Phoenix, September 14, 1987).

By the time the pope spoke in Phoenix, a chorus of critics was intoning the refrain of accusations against Serra and the friars:

> Father Serra did lay the groundwork for the entire chain of missions; he determined the system to be used in their operation. He is credited with all the good things about the California missions, so called. He can't be given the responsibility for the positive alone, if indeed there were positive things. In the end, he must bear responsibility for the totality, the total adverse, brutal, unconscionable, inhuman impact of missionization upon the California Indians. To canonize Serra, the zealots who are promoting this honor must prove that he was a man who has accomplished good works. (Lewis 1987: 96)

The most salient of the voices belonged to two Native American scholars, Rupert Costo (Cahuilla) and his wife Jeannette Henry Costo (Cherokee), then editors of The Indian Historian Press in San Francisco. They gave public speeches—one of them published in the *Tekakwitha Conference Newsletter*—in which they refer to the Franciscan missions as "coercive, authoritarian institutions" in which "flogging with a barbed lash, solitary confinement, mutilation, use of stocks and hobbles, branding, and even execution for both men and women characterized the 'gentle yoke of Catholicism' introduced by the Franciscans to the neophytes" (Costo and Costo 1986–1987: 8). They emphasize the political and economic aspects of the missions, quoting Governor Felipe de Neve, who wrote during Serra's tenure as presidente in 1780: "The unhappy treatment which the Franciscans give the Indians renders the Indian condition worse than slaves. The fathers aim to be independent and sovereign over the Indians and their wealth" (in ibid., 132). Father Hemauer was "taken with" (Lenz, November 19, 1993) the Costos, and brought them to Phoenix for the papal visit.

The Costos included in their 1987 book, *The Missions of California. A Legacy of Genocide*, the text of the 1986 Serra Report, which came under heavy criticism. Edward D. Castillo characterized the statements of Professor Nunis, in particular, as "cultural chauvinism and racial bigotry" (Castillo 1987: 77), but all of the Serra proponents were accused, in effect, of the same charges.

Rupert Costo conducted interviews with various Indians said to be descendants of mission neophytes, claiming their oral testimony to be our most valid record about the missions—even though the interviews were conducted in 1987, over two hundred years after Serra's death, and 150 years after the secularization of the missions. These Indians support Costo's contention that the missions were places of brutality. Maurice Magante, a Luiseño Indian from Pauma, tells Costo: "The Pala Mission still has the 'prison cell,' with iron flat bars, where our people were punished if they did something considered to be wrong or didn't do what they were told to do. Our people were taken from their villages to the mission compound as slaves. Many of our young were taken from their families and put into slavery" (in Costo and Costo 1987: 134). Tony Pinto, a Kumayaay Indian, tribal chairman of the Cuyapaipe Reservation in southern California, says that his people were forced to become Catholics and remain so today, as a result of the coercion two centuries ago:

> As to making a saint of Father Junipero Serra, I am against it. Why should he be called a saint, so all Catholics would have to worship and respect him, when he was the one who founded the horrible mission system. He probably did not beat the Indians with his own hands. But he sure ordered such things, and he sure approved of it. . . . That such a man could be made a saint is ridiculous. (In ibid., 139)

Contemporary Indians provided Costo with details of mission mistreatment. For example, Marvin Amago, a Luiseño Indian from La Jolla Reservation, asserts:

> Families were separated, forced to work with not enough food, actually starved. They were whipped, beaten, and forced to become Catholics. Runaways were hunted down and forced to return to the mission, or killed. . . . Those who did not want to become Catholics were jailed, and were then forced, through starvation and other means, to become Catholics. (In ibid., 140)

And a fellow Luiseño from La Jolla, Eva Kolb, adds that "in this business of breaking up the families and the tribe, they broke down the whole race" (143). Two Luiseño women from Pauma claim that the missionaries "had to browbeat their religion into us. . . . Many of us find it very hard not to be against the missions, against Christianity. They were cruel to us" (Lorena Dixon and Hazel Maldonado, ibid., 149). The tribal chairman at Rincon Reservation, Max Mazzetti, writes, "I don't know a single Indian in all the southern counties who hasn't got some kind of a horror story or more about the missions and what they did to our people" (155). The Costos solicited and received statements from various tribal governments in southern California—the

Southern California Tribal Chairman's Association, the Los Coyotes Indian Reservation, the Manzanita Band of Mission Indians, the Viejas Tribe, the Chemehuevi Indian Tribe, and others—protesting the potential canonization of Fray Serra. Many of these Indian communities identify themselves as Catholic, yet they oppose Serra's sainthood and decry the treatment of their ancestors in the missions. Catherine Siva Saubel, one of the founders of the Malki Museum, writes to her fellow Cahuilla, Rupert Costo, stating:

> Today I am a Catholic because of the subjection and horrors my people received at the hands of a greed-ridden, murderous reptile, Junipero Serra. I am a Catholic but I still use my religion in conjunction with our ancient God Amnah, our ceremonial house and the commandments our people grew up with before the time of the missions. (In ibid., 144)

A Diegueño woman says that her people used to assert that "the priests were all bad because they made them work. I don't know what the old Indians or the priests used to do or say about God. Nobody ever told me anything about God that I can remember" (Shipek 1991: 53). A Santa Ysabel Indian adds that the whipping post, rather than the cross, should serve as the symbol of the missions (San Diego. Serra and Indians Controversy. 1985–1990).

Many contemporary Indians in California care little about Serra; others are content to aver that his motives, at least, were spiritual. Other mission Indian descendants moderate their condemnations of the padres. Kathleen Hoy, a descendant of the Salinan Indians evangelized by Serra at Mission San Antonio de Padua, regards her people's treatment as enslavement by the Spanish, but she blames the abuses on the military. Serra himself, she states, was beloved and brought her people to Catholic faith, for which she loves and appreciates him (Wintz 1987: 34). Philip Galvan, secretary of the Ohlone Indian tribe near San José Mission, proclaims proudly that his great grandfather burned down the mission in the 1800s, responding to the Spanish friars' and soldiers' cultural genocide. He himself doesn't "give a damn" (in ibid., 33) about Serra's canonization, but he continues to be an active Catholic, attending mass at the nearby mission every Sunday. He keeps a statue of St. Francis in his garden, calls St. Joseph his favorite saint, and maintains the convent of his neighbors, the Holy Family Sisters.

Galvan's son, Father Michael Galvan, a parish priest at St. Monica

Catholic Church, director of the Office of Clergy Formation for the Diocese of Oakland, a theologian and spokesperson for the Tekakwitha Conference, challenges those in favor of Serra's canonization:

> They should ask whether or not the understanding of those priests of the eighteenth century would be one which we would wish to proclaim today. . . . This writer does not believe that a model of eighteenth century Spanish Missionary thought would be one that should be emulated in the present Church. (Galvan 1987: 169)

Galvan's Ohlone grandmother used to say that when she went to church she ceased to be an Indian, and when she came home she regained her Indian identity. She asked him when he entered the seminary at age fourteen: "Are you going to stop being who you are? . . . Will you be uncomfortable at home?" (Bozeman, August 7, 1986). Galvan has spent more than a decade trying to make Indians comfortable in the Catholic Church, inspired by the inculturative message of the Second Vatican Council. For Galvan the elevation of Serra sends the wrong message to Indian Catholics. If the contemporary Church exalts the Franciscan missions with all their purported abuses—and he believes those accusations to be correct in the main—then the Church aligns itself with colonialism and violence. If we say that the padres were men of their time, we may excuse them for their cultural sins. But do we canonize them for all time, for *our* time, in the presence of those sins, indeed, partially *for* those sins? The eighteenth-century Franciscan missions, in his view, were not ideals of Christian practice—just the opposite. The padres beat Indians with sticks, patronized them, as did other missionaries in other Indian communities. Today, no group of American Indians feels "at home" with the Church; they resent mistreatment of the past, and they do not want that mistreatment glorified by the Church hierarchy. There are bigger issues in the world of Catholic Indians today—e.g., through the process of inculturation we ask ourselves, "How does one be Native and Catholic at the same time? How does one become transformed into Christ?" (Galvan, May 1987: 1); "If we stop being who we are, we cannot be Catholic" (Bozeman, August 7, 1986)—but the canonization issue challenges the institutional Church to define its values and images, publicly. That definition will have an influence on Catholic Indians' loyalty to the Church in the years to come (Galvan, August 5, 1992; see San Diego. Serra and Indians Controversy. 1985–1990).

A scholar echoes this view in a 1988 article, asking what it is about Serra in the modern day that sets him apart as a saint? Was it his religious zeal? Such zeal can be demonic as well as saintly. Was it his concern for the immortal souls of the Indians?

> Are we to believe that Serra's concern, though expressed in a manner physically damaging to Native Americans, is nevertheless to be universally exemplary because his intention was to save souls? Cannot the Indian interpretation also be applied, namely, that sainthood for Serra is yet another example of white over red, of European dominance over aboriginal culture, but this time not only justified but glorified in the name of religion? (Sandos 1988: 1269)

The criticisms from the Indian community, and the Tekakwitha Conference in particular, did not change the judgment of the pope, nor that of the Congregation for the Causes of Saints judging Serra for canonization; however, the threat of protests did force Pope John Paul II to cancel his plan to beatify Serra during his pilgrimage to California immediately following his visit to Phoenix in 1987, much to the dismay of the California Catholic hierarchy. Instead, the beatification ceremony took place in the Vatican a year later, in 1988, after the pope approved the attribution of a miracle to the intercession of the Franciscan. Jeannette Henry Costo responded to the beatification: "It's not surprising. The Pope doesn't care about what's been done to us. We thought we could expect something better—that he would hold up beatification until we could make our case" (in Bishop, May 5, 1988). Rev. Noel Francis Moholy, O.F.M., presently the official advocate for the Serra cause, replied that Serra had spent his life protecting Indians against exploitation by Spanish soldiers; he was their defender, not their oppressor. A spokesperson for the congregation said that the Costos' book had received consideration, but that it had provided no concrete evidence of Serra's wrongdoing. Contemporary Indians had made accusations based on centuries of hearsay, but "none of the charges were substantiated" (in Suro, September 26, 1988). Msgr. Paul Lenz, head of the Bureau of Catholic Indian Missions, felt that the Vatican had investigated the charges levelled at Serra and found him blameless; hence, the volatile issue was over. He and Indian bishops Pelotte and Chaput attended the beatification ceremony in Rome in 1988.

Following the beatification, vandals defaced a statue of Serra in Presidio Park, San Diego, leaving a spray-painted slogan, "Genocidal

maniac" (San Diego. Serra and Indians Controversy. 1985–1990).
Three artists—including the Luiseño James Luna from La Jolla—and a
historian created an exhibit, "California's Missionary Daze," that raised
accusatory questions about Serra's Franciscan institutions. Concurrently, Church officials, columnists, and archivists in California circled
their wagons against the Indian onslaught: preparing argumentative
notes drawn from the writings of Father Guest, to be used in public
and private debate; attacking the statistical calculations of Sherburne
Cook; and compiling lists of the "anti's," those against the Serra sainthood, headed by those "dreadful" Costos (San Diego. Serra and Indians Controversy. 1985–1990).

To the present day emotions beat in strong counterpoint over the
issue of Serra's canonization in particular, and the Franciscan missions
in general. On the bicentennial of Fray Luis Jayme's murder at the
hands of San Diego Indians, Msgr. I. Brent Eagen celebrates mass in
the mission basilica of the rebuilt Mission San Diego, established by
Serra in 1769 and moved to this location in 1774. In sharp contrast,
Father Ralph Monteiro, O.S.A., another priest engaged in California
Indian ministry, derides those bishops who have "bought into that
Franciscan bullshit" (Monteiro, November 19, 1992). In Mission San
Diego hundreds of Catholic school children from grades three through
eight, dressed in blue uniforms, and transported by their teachers to
the mass, listen to Msgr. Eagen's homily on the "protomartyr" Jayme:
his birthplace in Majorca, not far from Serra's home, his evangelical
zeal, and his death in an attack by "the Native Americans." The monsignor tells his young audience that we are all grateful for the missionary efforts of the Franciscans, and reminds them twice of Jayme's last
words to his murderers: "Love God, my children" (San Diego de
Alcala, November 6, 1992). For the monsignor—and it is his hope, for
the children, as they grow in Catholic faith—the Franciscans are the
heroes of Catholic culture. Their bones lie beneath the sanctuary of
the church, reminders of their exemplary presence. Following mass the
children process to Jayme's place of death outside the mission walls
and then to a little chapel for adoration of the Blessed Sacrament, on
this First Friday of November 1992. In the small church on the Hoopa
Indian Reservation in northern California, Father Monteiro will not
place a picture of Serra on display. For him, and for many Indians, the
Serra cult is a continuous part of colonialism, a refusal to understand

that there is another side—an Indian side—to history beyond that of the missionaries.

Today in San Francisco, Native Americans are protesting a monument in front of City Hall, dedicated a century ago, which features a padre and a cowboy gesturing in triumph over a supine Indian. The Indians insist that the statue receive a plaque reading, "With their efforts over in 1834, the missionaries left behind about 56,000 converts—and 150,000 dead. Half the original Native American population had perished during this time from disease, armed attacks and mistreatment." Local representatives of the Church and state call the wording "a horrible and hateful distortion of the truth" (in Ybarra, May 7, 1996: A14).

The contemporary Luiseños resent the propaganda disseminated by San Diego and the other California dioceses on behalf of Fray Serra's sainthood. Indeed, one family at Pauma avows that the drive for Serra's canonization woke them up to the faults of the Church: "What kind of Church can it be that wants to glorify the man who put into motion the system that made our ancestors slaves" (Dixon et al., November 11, 1992) and destroyed the traditional religious culture? "The Church is in denial" about Junipero Serra, says George Arviso: "They say it was 'back then,' but the missionaries stamped us out in the name of Christ" (Arviso et al., November 5, 1992). The Indians state that their bitterness about present conditions is embedded in the historical circumstances brought about by Serra and the Franciscans. They were the initial and potent source of Luiseño devastation.

When Patty Duro and Mark Macarro visited the archives of the Diocese of San Diego, the archivist showed them Fray Serra's notebooks, and invited them to touch them. The archivist perceived correctly the Indians' alienation from the Church offices and wished to win them over. Ms. Duro said later to her fellow Luiseños that she was very excited to have touched these archival treasures. It reminded them of touching Pope John Paul II's robe when he visited Phoenix in 1987. Their devotion to God carries a powerful attachment to the instruments of Catholic authority, sacrality, and history. At the same time, the Luiseños regret the Pope's praise for Fray Serra, and they wish that they had enjoyed a greater opportunity to disagree with him.

George Arviso once asked a clerical friend of his what is it exactly that the Church finds so wonderful about Serra that we Catholics are supposed to emulate? What stands out about him that makes him more than a man of his time, sharing in the mission era's prejudices and strivings? What makes him a saint for *all* time, for *our* time? The priest was taken aback, but replied, "perseverance" (Arviso et al., November 5, 1992). But what, asked Arviso, did Serra persevere at, that was so wonderful, or rather *is now* so wonderful? Arviso's reply to his own question is that the Franciscan padres' system accomplished the destruction of the Indians who were his ancestors, and even though Serra might have been a good man according to his own judgment and values, there is little that makes him a saint for Catholic Indians in California (or throughout North America) today. Indeed, his canonization might serve to destroy the edifice of Indian Catholic faith first fashioned in the Spanish colonial era and built upon for generations.

BIBLIOGRAPHY

ARCHIVAL SOURCES

All citations of archival sources in the text list place name, file name, and date with a period after the place and file names (e.g., San Diego. Santa Ysabel. April 24, 1947).

Marquette University Memorial Library, Department of Special Collections, Milwaukee, Wisconsin. Files include: BCIM (Bureau of Catholic Indian Missions); DCRAA (Diocesan Correspondence, Reports, and Applications for Aid); JINNAM (Jesuits in Native North American Ministry).

Phoenix, Arizona, Diocese of, Archives.

San Bernardino, California, Diocese of, Archives: San Bernardino. Files include Cahuilla; Missions, Indian; Morongo; Santa Rosa; Soboba; Torres–Martinez.

San Diego, California, Diocese of, Archives: San Diego. Files include Indian Seizure of Missions; Indians; Multicultural Affairs; Pala; Pechanga-Temecula; Rincon; San Diego and San Bernardino Dioceses; Santa Ysabel; Serra; Serra and Indians Controversy; St. Anthony's Indian School; Verona Fathers.

Santa Fe, New Mexico, Archdiocese of, Archives/Records Center: Santa Fe. Files include Albuquerque Indian School; Bernalillo; Bureau of Catholic Indian Missions; Catholic Missions among the Colored People and the Indians; Confirmations; Crownpoint; Cuba; Farmington; Historical: Santa Fe Fiesta; Indian Affairs; Indo-Hispano Affairs; Isleta; Jemez; Laguna; Microfilms; Missions; Missions, Indian (General); Nambe; Peña Blanca; Penasco; San Juan; Santa Cruz; Shiprock-Naschiti; St. Francis Cathedral; Taos; Tohatchi; Zuni.

REFERENCES

Acoma Reservation, New Mexico. January 24, 1987. Author's fieldnotes.

———. January 26, 1988. Author's fieldnotes.

Adams, Eleanor B., ed. and trans. 1954. *Bishop Tamarón's Visitation of New Mexico, 1760*. Albuquerque: University of New Mexico Press.

Adams, Eleanor B., and (Rev.) Angélico Chávez, trans. 1956. *The Missions of New Mexico, 1776. A Description by Fray Francisco Atanasio Dominguez with Other Contemporary Documents*. Albuquerque: University of New Mexico Press.

Agogino, George, and Bobbie Ferguson. Winter 1978. "The Easter Ceremony of the Mayo Indians." *The Indian Historian* 2: 17–20.

Ahlborn, Richard Eigme. 1974. *The Sculpted Saints of a Borderland Mission: Los Bultos de San Xavier del Bac.* Tucson: Southwestern Mission Research Center.
——. 1986. *The Penitente Moradas of Abiquiú.* Washington: Smithsonian Institution Press.

Ak-Chin Reservation, Arizona. January 13, 1988. Author's fieldnotes.

Aldana, E. Guillermo. 1971. "Mesa del Nayar's Strange Holy Week." *National Geographic* 139: 780–795.

Antone, Alfretta. January 8, 1988. Interview with author, Salt River Reservation, Arizona.

Archibald, Robert. 1978. *The Economic Aspects of the California Missions.* Washington, D.C.: Academy of American Franciscan History.

Arviso, George. October 12, 1992. Telephone interview with author.
——. November 8, 1992. Interview with author, Rincon Reservation, California.

Arviso, George, and Milonny Arviso. November 7, 1992. Interview with author, Rincon Reservation, California.

Arviso, George, Georgiana O. Viveros, Verna Ann Arviso, Patty Duro, Amelia S. Calac, and Mark Macarro (Arviso et al.). November 5, 1992. Interview with author, Rincon Reservation, California.

Arviso, Milonny. October 12, 1995. Telephone interview with author.

Asisara, Lorenzo. 1892. "Narrative of a Mission Indian." Trans. E. L. Williams. In Edward Sanford Harrison, *History of Santa Cruz County California,* 45–48. San Francisco: Pacific Press.

Baegert, (Rev.) Johann Jakob, S.J. 1979. *Observations in Lower California.* Trans. M. M. Brandenburg and Carl L. Baumann. Berkeley: University of California Press.

Bahr, Diana Meyers. 1993. *From Mission to Metropolis: Cupeño Women in Los Angeles.* Norman: University of Oklahoma Press.

Bahr, Donald M. 1988. "Pima-Papago Christianity." *Journal of the Southwest* 30: 133–167.

Bancroft, H. H. 1886–1890. *The History of California.* 7 vols. San Francisco: The History Company.

Bannon, (Rev.) John Francis, S.J. 1955. *The Mission Frontier in Sonora, 1620–1687.* New York: United States Catholic Historical Society.

Barker, George C. 1957a. "Some Aspects of Penitential Processions in Spain and the American Southwest." *Journal of American Folklore* 70: 137–142.
——. 1957b. "The Yaqui Easter Ceremony at Hermosillo." *Western Folklore* 16: 256–262.
——. 1958. "Some Functions of Catholic Processions in Pueblo and Yaqui Culture Change." *American Anthropologist* 60: 449–455.

Beals, Ralph L. 1945. *The Contemporary Culture of the Cahita Indians. Bureau of American Ethnology Bulletin* 142.

Bean, Lowell John. 1978. "Cahuilla." In *Handbook of North American Indians,* vol. 8: *California,* ed. Robert F. Heizer, 575–587. Washington, D.C.: Smithsonian Institution.

Bean, Lowell John, and Florence C. Shipek. 1978. "Luiseño." In *Handbook of*

North American Indians, vol. 8: *California,* ed. Robert F. Heizer, 550–563. Washington, D.C.: Smithsonian Institution.

Bean, Lowell John, and Sylvia Brakke Vane. 1978. "Cults and Their Transformations." In *Handbook of North American Indians,* vol. 8: *California,* ed. Robert F. Heizer, 662–672. Washington, D.C.: Smithsonian Institution.

Beaver, R. Pierce, ed. 1979. *The Native American Christian Community: A Directory of Indian, Aleut, and Eskimo Churches.* Monrovia, Calif.: Missions Advanced Research and Communication Center.

Beckett, Patrick H., and Terry L. Corbett. 1994. "Tortugas." In *Native America in the Twentieth Century: An Encyclopedia,* ed. Mary B. Davis, 641–642. New York: Garland Publishing.

Bird, Allison. 1992. *Heart of the Dragonfly: Historical Development of the Cross Necklaces of the Pueblo and Navajo Peoples.* Albuquerque: Avanju Publishing.

Bishop, Katherine. May 5, 1988. "Father Serra, Founder of California Missions, to Be Beatified." *New York Times,* p. A24.

Blackburn, Thomas. 1991. "The Chumash Revolt of 1824: A Native Account." In *Native American Perspectives on the Hispanic Colonization of Alta California,* ed. Edward D. Castillo, 59–63. Spanish Borderland Sourcebooks, no. 26. New York: Garland Publishing.

Bodine, John J. 1979. "Taos Pueblo." In *Handbook of North American Indians,* vol. 9: *Southwest,* ed. Alfonso Ortiz, 255–267. Washington, D.C.: Smithsonian Institution.

Bolton, Herbert E. 1917. "The Mission as a Frontier Institution in the Spanish-American Colonies." *American Historical Review* 23: 42–61.

——. 1927. *Fray Juan Crespi: Missionary Explorer on the Pacific Coast, 1769–1774.* Berkeley: University of California Press.

——. 1960. *Rim of Christendom: A Biography of Eusebio Francisco Kino, Pacific Coast Pioneer.* New York: Russell & Russell.

——. 1986. *The Padre on Horseback.* Chicago: Loyola University Press.

Borah, Woodrow W. 1991. "The California Mission." In *Ethnology of the Alta California Indians,* vol. 2: *Postcontact,* ed. Lowell John Bean and Sylvia Brakke Vane, 5–24. Spanish Borderlands Sourcebooks, no. 4. New York: Garland Publishing.

Boscana, (Rev.) Geronimo. 1846. *Chinigchinich.* New York: Wiley & Putnam.

Bowden, Henry Warner. 1975. "Spanish Missions, Cultural Conflict and the Pueblo Revolt of 1680." *Church History* 44: 217–228.

——. 1981. *American Indians and Christian Missions: Studies in Cultural Conflict.* Chicago: University of Chicago Press.

Bowman, J. N. 1991. "The Resident Neophytes (*Existentes*) of the California Missions, 1769–1834." In *Native American Perspectives on the Hispanic Colonization of Alta California,* ed. Edward D. Castillo, 70–79. Spanish Borderlands Sourcebooks, no. 26. New York: Garland Publishing.

Bozeman, Montana. August 6–10, 1986. Author's fieldnotes, Tekakwitha Conference.

Braden, Charles S. 1930. *Religious Aspects of the Conquest of Mexico.* Durham, N.C.: Duke University Press.

Brandt, Elizabeth A. 1979. "Sandia Pueblo." In *Handbook of North American Indians,* vol. 9: *Southwest,* ed. Alfonso Ortiz, 343–350. Washington, D.C.: Smithsonian Institution.

Brew, J. O. 1979. "Hopi Prehistory and History to 1850." In *Handbook of North American Indians,* vol. 9: *Southwest,* ed. Alfonso Ortiz, 514–523. Washington, D.C.: Smithsonian Institution.

Bricker, Victoria Reifler. 1981. *The Indian Christ, the Indian King: The Historical Substrate of Maya Myth and Ritual.* Austin: University of Texas Press.

Brown, Donald N. 1979. "Picuris Pueblo." In *Handbook of North American Indians,* vol. 9: *Southwest,* ed. Alfonso Ortiz, 268–277. Washington, D.C.: Smithsonian Institution.

Brown, Janet. January 8, 1988. Interview with author, Salt River Reservation, Arizona.

Brugge, David M. 1985. *Navajos in the Catholic Church Records of New Mexico, 1694–1875.* Tsaile, Ariz.: Navajo Community College Press.

Bureau of Catholic Indian Missions Newsletter. 1981–1996.

Burkhart, Louise M. 1989. *The Slippery Earth: Nahua-Christian Moral Dialogue in Sixteenth-Century Mexico.* Tucson: University of Arizona Press.

——. 1993. "The Cult of the Virgin of Guadalupe in Mexico." In *South and Meso-American Native Spirituality,* ed. Gary H. Gossen, 198–227. New York: Crossroad.

Burrus, (Rev.) Ernest J., S.J. 1954. *Kino Reports to Headquarters.* Rome: Jesuit Historical Institute.

——. 1965. *Kino Writes to the Duchess.* Rome: Jesuit Historical Institute.

——. 1971. *Kino's Biography of Francisco Javier Saeta, S.J.* Trans. Charles W. Polzer, S.J. Rome: Jesuit Historical Institute.

Byrne, Janet. December 11, 1994. "In Taos, Dances of Mystery." *New York Times,* pp. 1, 22.

Carillo, (Rev.) Januarius M., M.C.C.J. 1959. *The Story of Mission San Antonio de Pala.* Oceanside, Calif.: J. M. Carillo.

Carrasco, David. 1990. *Religions of Mesoamerica: Cosmovision and Ceremonial Centers.* San Francisco: Harper & Row.

Carrico, Richard L. 1980. "San Diego Indians and the Federal Government: Years of Neglect, 1850–1865." *Journal of San Diego History* 26: 165–184.

Carrico, Susan Hunter. 1984. "Urban Indians in San Diego: 1850–1900." M.A. thesis, University of San Diego.

Castillo, Edward D. 1978. "The Impact of Euro-American Exploration and Settlement." In *Handbook of North American Indians,* vol. 8: *California,* ed. Robert F. Heizer, 99–127. Washington, D.C.: Smithsonian Institution.

——. 1987. "Cultural Chauvinism Offered to Justify Serra Canonization." In *The Missions of California: A Legacy of Genocide,* ed. Rupert Costo and Jeannette Henry Costo, 67–80. San Francisco: Indian Historian Press.

——. 1989. "The Native Response to the Colonization of Alta California." In *Columbian Consequences,* vol. 1: *Archaeological and Historical Perspectives on the Spanish Borderlands West,* ed. David Hurst Thomas, 377–394. Washington, D.C.: Smithsonian Institution Press.

——. May-July 1991. "Mission Studies and the Columbian Quincentennial." *News from Native California* 5: 12–13.

——. 1991. *Native American Perspectives on the Hispanic Colonization of Alta California*. Spanish Borderlands Sourcebooks, no. 26. New York: Garland Publishing.

Cather, Willa. 1926. *Death Comes for the Archbishop*. New York: The Modern Library.

Cavagnaro, (Rev.) Camillus, O.F.M. August 3–6, 1988. Interviews with author, Pine Ridge, South Dakota.

Cervantes, Fernando. 1994. *The Devil in the New World: The Impact of Diabolism in New Spain*. New Haven: Yale University Press.

Cesar, Julio. 1991. "Recollections of My Youth at San Luis Rey Mission." In *Native American Perspectives on the Hispanic Colonization of Alta California*, ed. Edward D. Castillo. Spanish Borderlands Sourcebooks, no. 26. New York: Garland Publishing.

Chamberlain, Eugene K. 1987. "Santa Ysabel Asistencia (1818–1987)." Unpublished ms., San Diego.

Champe, Flavia Waters. 1983. *The Matachines Dance of the Upper Rio Grande: History, Music, and Choreography*. Lincoln: University of Nebraska Press.

Chávez, (Rev.) Angélico, O.F.M. 1948. *Our Lady of the Conquest*. Santa Fe: Historical Society of New Mexico.

——. 1957. *Archives of the Archdiocese of Santa Fe, 1678–1900*. Washington, D.C.: Academy of American Franciscan History.

——. 1967. "Pohe-Yemo's Representative and the Pueblo Revolt of 1680." *New Mexico Historical Review* 42: 85–126.

Cole, D. C. March 23, 1987. Interview with author, Hamilton, New York.

Columbus, Christopher. 1960. *The Journal of Christopher Columbus*. Trans. Cecil Jane. New York: Bramhall House.

Cook, Sherburne F. 1976. *The Conflict between the California Indian and White Civilization*. Berkeley: University of California Press.

Costello, Julia G., ed. 1991. *Documentary Evidence for the Spanish Missions of Alta California*. Spanish Borderlands Sourcebooks, no. 14. New York: Garland Publishing.

Costo, Jeannette Henry, and Rupert Costo. Winter 1986–1987. "Missions and Missionaries in Southern California." *Tekakwitha Conference Newsletter* 6: 7–8, 26.

Costo, Rupert, and Jeannette Henry Costo, eds. 1987. *The Missions of California: A Legacy of Genocide*. San Francisco: Indian Historian Press.

Cowell, Alan. October 17, 1991. "Pope Asks Amends of Brazil's Indians." *New York Times*, p. A3.

——. August 12, 1993. "Pope Celebrates Indigenous People." *New York Times*, p. B10.

Cribbin, (Rev.) James. November 7, 1992. Interview with author, Pala, California.

Crosby, Harry W. 1994. *Antigua Califórnia: Mission and Colony on the Peninsular Frontier, 1697–1768*. Albuquerque: University of New Mexico Press.

Crumrine, Lynne S., and N. Ross Crumrine. 1970. "Ritual Service and Blood Sacrifice as Mediating Binary Oppositions." *Journal of American Folklore* 83: 69–76.

Crumrine, N. Ross. 1968–1969. "Mayo Ritual Impersonation: The Mask, Arousal, and Enculturation." *Anthropos* 63–64: 976–977.

———. 1969. "Capakoba, the Mayo Easter Ceremonial Impersonator: Explanations of Ritual Clowning." *Journal for the Scientific Study of Religion* 8: 1–22.

———. 1970. "Ritual Drama and Culture Change." *Comparative Studies in Society and History* 12: 361–372.

———. 1974a. "Anomalous Figures and Liminal Roles: A Reconsideration of the Mayo Indian *Capakoba*, Northwest Mexico." *Anthropos* 69: 858–873.

———. 1974b. "God's Daughter-in-Law, the Old Man, and the Olla: An Archaeological Challenge." *The Kiva* 39: 277–281.

Crumrine, N. Ross, and M. Louise Crumrine. 1977. "Ritual Symbolism in Folk and Ritual Drama." *Journal of American Folklore* 90: 8–28.

Cypess, Sandra Messinger. 1991. *La Malinche in Mexican Literature from History to Myth*. Austin: University of Texas Press.

Dale, Peggy. June 1990. "Passion of Christ Depicted in Pre-Columbian Indian Dance." *Tekakwitha Conference Newsletter* 9: 15.

Dana, Richard Henry. 1976. *Two Years before the Mast*. [1840.] New York: Dutton.

Davis, (Sister) Gloria. July 7, 1992. Telephone interview with author.

———. August 7, 1992. Interview with author, Orono, Maine.

De Grazia, Ted. 1968. *De Grazia Paints the Yaqui Easter*. Tucson: University of Arizona Press.

Dionne, E. J., Jr. July 5, 1986. "Pope, Backing Indians, Wins Colombia Cheers." *New York Times,* p. 3.

Dixon, (Rev.) James M., S.J. August 7, 1992. Interview with author, Orono, Maine.

Dixon, (Sister) Patricia, Lorena Dixon, Lee Dixon, Joann Dixon, Chris Devers, and Florence Loftin. November 11, 1992. Interview with author, Pauma, California.

Dobyns, Henry F. October-November 1950. "Papago Pilgrims on the Town." *The Kiva* 16: 27–32.

Doerger, (Rev.) Berard, O.F.M. February 15, 1987. "The 'Brown Robes' of the Southwest." *Our Sunday Visitor,* pp. 6–7.

Dolan, Jay P. 1985. *The American Catholic Experience: A History from Colonial Times to the Present*. Garden City, N.Y.: Doubleday. Rpt. 1992. Notre Dame, Ind.: University of Notre Dame Press.

Donohue, (Rev.) John Augustine, S.J. 1960. "The Unlucky Jesuit Mission of Bac, 1732–1767." *Arizona and the West* 2: 127–139.

———. 1969. *After Kino: Jesuit Missions in Northwestern New Spain, 1711–1767*. Sources and Studies for the History of the Americas, no. 6. St. Louis: Jesuit Historical Institute.

Dozier, Edward P. 1958. "Spanish Catholic Influences on Rio Grande Pueblo Religion." *American Anthropologist* 60: 441–448.

Du Bois, Constance Goddard. November 1899. "Some Unknown Missions of California." *Land of Sunshine* 11: 317–324.

———. 1908. "The Religion of the Luiseño Indians of Southern California." *University of California Publications in American Archaeology and Ethnology* 8: 69–186.

Dunne, (Rev.) Peter Masten, S.J. 1944. *Pioneer Jesuits in Northern Mexico.* Berkeley: University of California Press.

———. 1968. *Black Robes in Lower California.* Berkeley: University of California Press.

Duro, Patricia, and Mark Macarro. November 4, 1992. Interview with author, San Diego, California.

"Easter in the Desert: Signs of Hope." Summer 1992. *Trinity Missions* 65: 5–8, 13–16.

Edelman, Sandra A. 1979. "San Ildefonso Pueblo." In *Handbook of North American Indians,* vol. 9: *Southwest*, ed. Alfonso Ortiz, 308–316. Washington, D.C.: Smithsonian Institution.

Edelman, Sandra A., and Alfonso Ortiz. 1979. "Tesuque Pueblo." In *Handbook of North American Indians,* vol. 9: *Southwest,* ed. Alfonso Ortiz, 330–335. Washington, D.C.: Smithsonian Institution.

Edwards, Nancy. January 8, 1990. Personal communication.

Eggan, Fred. 1979. "Pueblos: Introduction." In *Handbook of North American Indians,* vol. 9: *Southwest,* ed. Alfonso Ortiz, 224–235. Washington, D.C.: Smithsonian Institution.

Eggan, Fred, and T. N. Pandey. 1979. "Zuni History, 1850–1970." In *Handbook of North American Indians,* vol. 9: *Southwest,* ed. Alfonso Ortiz, 474–481. Washington, D.C.: Smithsonian Institution.

Ellis, Florence Hawley. 1979. "Laguna Pueblo." In *Handbook of North American Indians,* vol. 9: *Southwest,* ed. Alfonso Ortiz, 438–449. Washington, D.C.: Smithsonian Institution.

Ellis, John Tracy. 1963. *Catholics in Colonial America.* Baltimore: Helicon Press.

Ellis, John Tracy, and Robert Trisco. 1982. *A Guide to American Catholic History.* Santa Barbara: ABC-Clio.

Engelhardt, (Rev.) Zephyrin, O.F.M. 1899. *The Franciscans in Arizona.* Harbor Springs, Mich.: Holy Childhood Indian School.

———. 1908–1915. *The Missions and Missionaries of California.* 4 vols. San Francisco: James H. Barry Company.

———. 1920. *San Diego Mission.* San Francisco: James H. Barry Company.

———. 1921. *San Luis Rey Mission.* San Francisco: James H. Barry Company.

———. 1922. *San Juan Capistrano Mission.* Los Angeles: Zephyrin Engelhardt.

———. 1927. *San Gabriel Mission and the Beginning of Los Angeles.* San Gabriel, Calif.: Mission San Gabriel.

Espinosa, Aurelio M. 1918. "All-Souls Day at Zuni, Acoma, and Laguna." *Journal of American Folklore* 31: 550–552.

Espinosa, J. Manuel, trans. and ed. 1988. *The Pueblo Indian Revolt of 1696 and the Franciscan Missions in New Mexico: Letters of the Missionaries and Related Documents.* Norman: University of Oklahoma Press.

Espinosa, José E. 1967. *Saints in the Valley: Christian Sacred Images in the History, Life and Folk Art of Spanish New Mexico.* Albuquerque: University of New Mexico Press.

Ewing, Russell C. 1938. "The Pima Outbreak in November, 1751." *New Mexico Historical Review* 13: 337–346.

———. 1941. "Investigations into the Causes of the Pima Uprising of 1751." *Mid-America* 23: 138–151.

Fargo, North Dakota. August 2–6, 1989. Author's fieldnotes, Tekakwitha Conference.

Farrell, Timothy W. September 3, 1989. "People Reflect on Faith in Jubilee Essay Contest." *Voice of the Southwest,* pp. 1–2. Publication of the Diocese of Gallup, N.Mex.

Feist, Joe Michael. September 7, 1989. "Texas Missions and Beyond." *Our Northland Diocese,* n.p. Publication of the Diocese of Crookston, Minn.

Fontana, Bernard L. 1989. *Of Earth and Little Rain: The Papago Indians.* Tucson: University of Arizona Press.

Forrest, Earle R. 1929. *Missions and Pueblos of the Old Southwest.* Cleveland: Arthur H. Clark Company.

Freeman, King. November 7, 1992. Interview with author, Pala, California.

Freese, Alison. 1991. "Send in the Clowns." In *The Spanish Missions of New Mexico,* vol 2: *After 1680,* ed. John L. Kessell and Rick Hendricks, 497–504. Spanish Borderlands Sourcebooks, no. 18. New York: Garland Publishing.

French, Howard W. October 12, 1992. "Pope's Mass at Dominican Monument to Columbus." *New York Times,* p. B7.

———. October 14, 1992. "Dissent Shadows Pope on His Visit." *New York Times,* p. A15.

Frost, Elsa Cecilia. 1993. "Indians and Theologians: Sixteenth-Century Spanish Theologians and Their Concept of the Indigenous Soul." In *South and Meso-American Native Spirituality,* ed. Gary H. Gossen, 119–139. New York: Crossroad.

Frost, Richard. 1992. "The Impact of Christianity on Pueblo Religion and Culture." Unpublished ms. in author's possession.

Galvan, (Rev.) P. Michael. May 1987. "Native Catechesis and the Ministry of the Word." *Tekakwitha Conference Newsletter* 6: 1–3.

———. 1987. "No Veneration for Serra." In *The Missions of California: A Legacy of Genocide,* ed. Rupert Costo and Jeannette Henry Costo, 168–170. San Francisco: Indian Historian Press.

———. August 5, 1992. Interview with author, Orono, Maine.

Gannon, Michael V. 1965. *The Cross in the Sand: The Early Catholic Church in Florida, 1513–1870.* Gainesville: University of Florida Press.

Geary, (Rev.) Gerald, A.M. 1934. *The Secularization of the California Missions, 1810–1846.* Washington, D.C.: Catholic University of America.

Geiger, (Rev.) Maynard J., O.F.M. 1955. *Palóu's Life of Fray Junípero Serra.* Washington, D.C.: Academy of American Franciscan History.

——. 1959. *The Life and Times of Fray Junípero Serra, O.F.M.* 2 vols. Washington, D.C.: Academy of American Franciscan History.

——. 1969. *Franciscan Missionaries in Hispanic California, 1769–1848: A Biographical Dictionary.* San Marino, Calif.: Huntington Library.

——. 1970. "Fray Antonio Ripoll's Description of the Chumash Revolt at Santa Barbara in 1824." *Southern California Quarterly* 52: 345–364.

Geiger, (Rev.) Maynard J., O.F.M., and Clement W. Meighan, eds. 1976. *As the Padres Saw Them: California Indian Life and Customs as Reported by the Franciscan Missionaries, 1813–1815.* Santa Barbara: Santa Barbara Mission Archive Library.

Giddings, Ruth Warner. 1959. *Yaqui Myths and Legends.* Tucson: University of Arizona.

Gila River Pima Reservation, Arizona. January 13, 1988. Author's fieldnotes.

Glenmary Research Center. 1978. *Parishes of the Diocese of Gallup: Accomplishments and Challenges.* Washington, D.C.: Glenmary Home Missioners.

Gómez, Arthur R., ed. 1991. *Documentary Evidence for the Spanish Missions of Texas.* Spanish Borderlands Sourcebooks, no. 22. New York: Garland Publishing.

Gorman, Tom. November 3, 1985. "Missions Must Adapt to Modern-Day Indians." *Los Angeles Times,* pp. 4, 14, 15.

Gossen, Gary H., ed. 1993. *South and Meso-American Native Spirituality.* New York: Crossroad.

Gradie, Charlotte M. April 1988. "Spanish Jesuits in Virginia: The Mission That Failed." *Virginia Magazine of History and Biography* 96: 131–156.

Grant, John Webster. 1985. *Moon of Wintertime: Missionaries and the Indians of Canada in Encounter since 1534.* Toronto: University of Toronto Press.

Grayson, Wendy L. December 25, 1975. "Christmas at Taos Pueblo." *New York Times,* p. 21.

Green, L. C., and Olive P. Dickason. 1989. *The Law of Nations and the New World.* Edmonton: University of Alberta Press.

Griffith, James S. 1974. "Franciscan Chapels on the Papagueria, 1912–1973." *The Smoke Signal* 30: 234–255.

——. 1975. "The Folk-Catholic Chapels of the Papagueria." *Pioneer America* 7: 21–36.

——. 1992. *Beliefs and Holy Places: A Spiritual Geography of the Pimería Alta.* Tucson: University of Arizona Press.

Grim, John A. August 27, 1991. Telephone interview with author.

——. 1991a. "From Conversion to Inculturation: 'New Evangelization' in the Dialogue of Native American and Catholic Spiritualities." Unpublished ms. in author's possession.

——. 1991b. "Relations between Native American Religions and Roman Catholicism." Unpublished ms. in author's possession.

Grimes, Ronald L. 1976. *Symbol and Conquest: Public Ritual and Drama in Santa Fe, New Mexico.* Ithaca: Cornell University Press.

Guadalupe, Arizona. April 3–11, 1993. Author's fieldnotes.

Guerra, Francisco. 1971. *The Pre-Columbian Mind.* New York: Seminar Press.

Guest, (Rev.) Francis F., O.F.M. 1966. "The Indian Policy under Fermín Francisco de Lasuén, California's Second Father President." *California Historical Society Quarterly* 45: 195–224.

———. 1973. *Fermin Francisco de Lasuen (1736–1803): A Biography.* Washington, D.C. : Academy of American Franciscan History.

———. 1978. "Mission Colonization and Political Control in Spanish California." *Journal of San Diego History* 24: 97–120.

———. Spring 1979. "An Examination of the Thesis of S. F. Cook on the Forced Conversion of Indians in the California Missions." *Southern California Quarterly* 61: 1–78.

———. Spring 1983. "Cultural Perspectives on California Mission Life." *Southern California Quarterly* 65: 1–65.

———. Fall 1985. "Junípero Serra and His Approach to the Indians." *Southern California Quarterly* 67: 223–261.

———. Spring 1989. "An Inquiry into the Role of the Discipline in California Mission Life." *Southern California Quarterly* 71: 1–68.

———. N.d. "The Cause of Junipero Serra." Unpublished ms., San Diego.

Gutiérrez, Ramón A. 1991. *When Jesus Came, the Corn Mothers Went Away: Marriage, Sexuality, and Power in New Mexico, 1500–1846.* Stanford: Stanford University Press.

Habig, (Rev.) Marion A., O.F.M. 1958. *Heralds of the King: The Franciscans of the St. Louis–Chicago Province, 1858–1958.* Chicago: Franciscan Herald Press.

Hackett, Charles W., and Charmion Clair Shelby. 1942. *Revolt of the Pueblo Indians of New Mexico and Otermín's Attempted Reconquest, 1680–1682.* 2 vols. Albuquerque: University of New Mexico Press.

Haederle, Michael. December 25, 1991. "Indian Artist Blends Catholic and Zuni Traditions in Murals." *Los Angeles Times,* p. F24.

Haile, (Rev.) Berard, O.F.M. 1937. *A Catechism and Guide: Navajo-English.* Saint Michaels, Ariz.: St. Michaels Press.

Hanke, Lewis. 1935. *The First Social Experiments in America.* Cambridge: Harvard University Press.

———. 1974. *All Mankind Is One: A Study of the Disputation between Bartolomé de las Casas and Juan Ginés de Sepúlveda in 1550 on the Intellectual and Religious Capacity of the American Indians.* Dekalb: Northern Illinois University Press.

———. 1975. *Aristotle and the American Indian: A Study of Race Prejudice in the Modern World.* Bloomington: Indiana University Press.

Hann, John H., ed. and trans. 1991. *Missions to the Calusa.* Gainesville: University of Florida Press.

Harley, R. Bruce. N.d. "Indian Mission Chapels of Riverside County." Unpublished ms., San Diego.

Harris, Max. 1990. "*Indigenismo y Catolicidad*: Folk Dramatizations of Evangelism and Conquest in Central Mexico." *Journal of the American Academy of Religion* 58: 55–68.

Hastrich, (Most Rev.) Jerome. September 3, 1989. "Priests in Hopi Land." *Voice of the Southwest,* n.p. Publication of the Diocese of Gallup, N.Mex.

Hawley, Florence. 1946. "The Role of Pueblo Social Organization in the Dissemination of Catholicism." *American Anthropologist* 48: 407–415.

Heizer, Robert F. 1976. *The Indians of California: A Critical Bibliography.* Bloomington: Indiana University Press.

———. Winter 1978. "Impact of Colonization on the Native California Societies." *Journal of San Diego History* 24: 121–139.

Hemauer, (Rev.) Gilbert F., O.F.M. Cap. August 9, 1986. Interview with author, Bozeman, Montana.

Hennesey, (Rev.) James, S.J. 1981. *American Catholics: A History of the Roman Catholic Community in the United States.* Oxford: Oxford University Press.

Hittell, Theodore H. 1885–1897. *History of California.* 4 vols. San Francisco: Pacific Press Publishing.

Hocker, Tom. June 21, 1987. "Mission San Xavier del Bac: Outpost of a Spiritual Kingdom." *Our Sunday Visitor,* pp. 6–8.

Hodge, Frederick Webb, George P. Hammond, and Agapito Rey, eds. and trans. 1945. *Fray Alonso de Benavides' Revised Memorial of 1634.* Albuquerque: University of New Mexico Press.

Hoebel, E. Adamson. 1979. "Zia Pueblo." In *Handbook of North American Indians,* vol. 9: *Southwest,* ed. Alfonso Ortiz, 407–417. Washington, D.C.: Smithsonian Institution.

Horgan, Paul. 1975. *Lamy of Santa Fe: His Life and Times.* New York: Farrar, Straus and Giroux.

Hostler, Hilton. November 19, 1992. Interview with author, Arcata, California.

Hu-DeHart, Evelyn. 1981. *Missionaries, Miners and Indians: Spanish Contact with the Yaqui Nation of Northwestern New Spain, 1533–1820.* Tucson: University of Arizona Press.

Hughes, (Rev.) William. 1910. "Bishop Conaty and the Missions." Unpublished ms., San Diego.

Hultkrantz, Åke. 1981. *Belief and Worship in Native North America.* Ed. Christopher Vecsey. Syracuse, N.Y.: Syracuse University Press.

———. 1983. *The Study of American Indian Religions.* Ed. Christopher Vecsey. New York: Crossroad Publishing.

———. 1985. "Panindianism och Ekumenik bland Nordamerikas Indianer." *Svensk Religionshistorisk Arsskrift* 1: 128–132.

———. 1990. "A Decade of Progress: Works on North American Indian Religions in the 1980s." In *Religion in Native North America.,* ed. Christopher Vecsey, 167–201. Moscow: University of Idaho Press.

Hyde, Villiana, and Eric Elliott. 1994. *Yumayk Yumayk = Long Ago.* Berkeley: University of California Press.

Hyde, Villiana Calac, and Lorraine Hyde. November 8, 1992. Interview with author, Escondido, California.

Indian Sentinel, The. 1902–1962.

"Investiture Controversy." July 24, 1965. *America* 113: 88–89.

Jackson, Helen Hunt. 1886. *Ramona: A Story.* Boston: Roberts Brothers.

———. 1902. *Glimpses of California and the Missions.* Boston: Little, Brown, and Company.

Jackson, Robert H. 1991a. "Gentile Recruitment and Population Movements in the San Francisco Bay Area Missions." In *Native American Perspectives on the Hispanic Colonization of Alta California,* ed. Edward D. Castillo, 187–201. Spanish Borderlands Sourcebooks, no. 26. New York: Garland Publishing.

——. 1991b. *The Spanish Missions of Baja California.* Spanish Borderlands Sourcebooks, no. 16. New York: Garland Publishing.

Jackson, Robert H., and Edward Castillo. 1995. *Indians, Franciscans, and Spanish Colonization: The Impact of the Mission System on California Indians.* Albuquerque: University of New Mexico Press.

James, George Wharton. 1912. *In and Out of the Old Missions of California.* Boston: Little, Brown, and Company.

——. 1913. *Through Ramona's Country.* Boston: Little, Brown, and Company.

——. 1916. *Picturesque Pala.* Pasadena, Calif: Radiant Life Press.

Johnson, George. June 24, 1995. "In New Mexico, an Ancient Rite or a Blood Sport?" *New York Times,* p. 6.

Johnston, Bernice Eastman. 1962. *California's Gabrielino Indians.* Los Angeles: Southwest Museum.

Joseph, Alice, Rosamond B. Spicer, and Jane Chesky. 1949. *The Desert People: A Study of the Papago Indians.* Chicago: University of Chicago Press.

Juan, Vivian. August 8, 1986. Interview with author, Bozeman, Montana.

Kelly, Henry W. 1940–1941. "Franciscan Missions of New Mexico, 1740–1760." *New Mexico Historical Review* 15: 345–368; 16: 41–69, 148–183.

Kelsey, Harry. 1979. *The Doctrina and Confesionario of Juan Cortés.* Altadena, Calif.: Howling Coyote Press.

Kessell, John L. 1970. *Mission of Sorrows: Jesuit Guevavi and the Pimas, 1691–1767.* Tucson: University of Arizona Press.

——. 1976. *Friars, Soldiers, and Reformers: Hispanic Arizona and the Sonora Mission Frontier, 1767–1856.* Tucson: University of Arizona Press.

——. 1979. *Kiva, Cross, and Crown: The Pecos Indians and New Mexico, 1540–1840.* Washington, D.C.: National Park Service, U.S. Department of the Interior.

——. 1980. *The Missions of New Mexico since 1776.* Albuquerque: University of New Mexico Press.

Kessell, John L., and Rick Hendricks, eds. 1991a. *The Spanish Missions of New Mexico,* vol 1: *Before 1680.* Spanish Borderlands Sourcebooks, no. 17. New York: Garland Publishing.

——. 1991b. *The Spanish Missions of New Mexico,* vol. 2: *After 1680.* Spanish Borderlands Sourcebooks, no. 18. New York: Garland Publishing.

Kino, (Rev) Eusebio Francisco. 1919. *Kino's Historical Memoir of Pimería Alta.* 2 vols. Trans. Herbert Eugene Bolton. Cleveland: Arthur H. Clark.

Klor de Alva, Jorge. 1982. "Spiritual Conflict and Accommodation in New Spain: Toward a Typology of Aztec Responses to Christianity." In *The Inca and Aztec States, 1400–1800,* eds. George A. Collier, Renato I. Rosaldo, and John D. Wirth, 345–366. New York: Academic Press.

——. 1993. "Aztec Spirituality and Nahuatized Christianity." In *South and*

Meso-American Native Spirituality, ed. Gary H. Gossen, 173–197. New York: Crossroad.

Knaut, Andrew L. 1995. *The Pueblo Revolt of 1680: Conquest and Resistance in Seventeenth-Century New Mexico.* Norman: University of Oklahoma Press.

Kozak, David. 1991. "Ecumenical Indianism: Kateri and the Invented Tradition." Unpublished ms. in author's possession.

Kozak, David, and Camillus Lopez. 1991. "The Tohono O'odham Shrine Complex: Memorializing the Locations of Violent Death." *New York Folklore* 17: 1–20.

Kroeber, A. L. 1908. "A Mission Record of the California Indians." *University of California Publications in American Archaeology and Ethnology* 8: 1–27.

LaCoste, (Sister) Catherine Louise, C.S.J. November 4–12, 1992. Interviews with author, San Diego, California.

Laguna Pueblo, New Mexico. January 24, 1987. Author's fieldnotes.

Lange, Charles H. 1952. "The Feast Day Dance at Zia Pueblo, New Mexico, August 15, 1951." *Texas Journal of Science* 4: 19–26.

———. 1979a. "Cochiti Pueblo." In *Handbook of North American Indians,* vol. 9: *Southwest,* ed. Alfonso Ortiz, 366–378. Washington, D.C.: Smithsonian Institution.

———. 1979b. "Santo Domingo Pueblo." In *Handbook of North American Indians,* vol. 9: *Southwest,* ed. Alfonso Ortiz, 379–389. Washington, D.C.: Smithsonian Institution.

———. March 30, 1992. Interview with author, Santa Fe, New Mexico.

Langer, Erick, and Robert H. Jackson, eds. 1995. *The New Latin American Mission History.* Lincoln: University of Nebraska Press.

Las Casas, (Rev.) Bartolomé de. 1974. *In Defense of the Indians.* Trans. and ed. Stafford Poole. DeKalb: Northern Illinois University Press.

Laton, Francis M. N.d. *Old Zuni Mission.* Zuni, N.Mex.: St. Anthony's Indian Mission.

Lawson, (Rev.) William T. November 7, 1992. Interview with author, Pala, California.

Lenz, (Msgr.) Paul A. November 19, 1993. Interview with author, Washington, D.C.

Lewis, James. 1987. "The Natives as Seen by the Missionaries: Preconception and Reality." In *The Missions of California: A Legacy of Genocide,* ed. Rupert Costo and Jeannette Henry Costo, 81–98. San Francisco: Indian Historian Press.

Librado, Fernando. 1991. "Breath of the Sun: Life in Early California as told by a Chumash Indian, Fernando Librado to John P. Harrington." Ed. Travis Hudson. In *Native American Perspectives on the Hispanic Colonization of Alta California,* ed. Edward D. Castillo, 17–34. Spanish Borderlands Sourcebooks, no. 26. New York: Garland Publishing.

Lindsey, Robert. November 30, 1986. "Serra Sainthood Is Facing Criticism." *New York Times,* p. 39.

———. September 23, 1987. "Debate Lingers on a Missionary of 18th Century." *New York Times,* p. A18.

Linn, Alan. October 12, 1975. "Chichi: Rites and Revelry." *New York Times,* Travel Section, pp. 1, 16.

Linton, Ralph, ed. 1940. *Acculturation in Seven American Indian Tribes.* New York: D. Appleton-Century.

Loyacono, Susan. February 23, 1990. "Native American Ministry Revived." *The Leaven,* p. 9. Publication of the Archdiocese of Kansas City, Kans.

Luomala, Katharine. 1978. "Tipai-Ipai." In *Handbook of North American Indians,* vol. 8: *California,* ed. Robert F. Heizer, 592–609. Washington, D.C.: Smithsonian Institution.

Luzbetak, (Rev.) Louis J. 1961. "Toward an Applied Missionary Anthropology." *Anthropological Quarterly* 34:165–176.

———. 1967. "Adaptation, Missionary." *New Catholic Encyclopedia* 1: 120–122.

———. 1979. "Missiology." *New Catholic Encyclopedia* 17: 416–419.

———. April 1985. "If Junípero Serra Were Alive: Missiological-Anthropological Theory Today." *The Americas* 42: 512–519.

Macklin, Barbara June, and N. Ross Crumrine. 1973. "Three North Mexican Folk Saint Movements." *Comparative Studies in Society and History* 15: 89–105.

Madsen, William. 1957. *Christo-Paganism: A Study of Mexican Religious Syncretism.* New Orleans: Tulane University, Middle American Research Institute.

Magee, Eugene. November 6, 1992. Interview with author, Pala, California.

Mamake, Edna. August 8, 1992. Interview with author, Orono, Maine.

Marriott, Alice. 1948. *María: The Potter of San Ildefonso.* Norman: University of Oklahoma Press.

Marzal, Manuel M. 1993. "Transplanted Spanish Catholicism." In *South and Meso-American Native Spirituality,* ed. Gary H. Gossen, 140–169. New York: Crossroad.

Masters, (Sister) Lorraine, O.L.V.M. August 6, 1992. Interview with author, Orono, Maine.

Matson, Daniel S., and Bernard L. Fontana, trans. and eds. 1977. *Friar Bringas Reports to the King: Methods of Indoctrination on the Frontier of New Spain, 1796–97.* Tucson: University of Arizona Press.

McDowell, John Holmes. 1987. "Sayings of the Ancestors: The Spiritual Life of the Sibundoy Indians." Unpublished ms. in author's possession.

McLaughlin, (Rev.) Daniel P., S.T. July 8, 1992. Telephone interview with author.

McNeil, Teresa Baksh. Summer 1988. "St. Anthony's Indian School in San Diego, 1886–1907." *Journal of San Diego History* 34: 187–200.

Menchú, Rigoberta. 1993. *I, Rigoberto Menchú: An Indian Woman in Guatemala.* Ed. Elizabeth Burgos-Debray. Trans. Ann Wright. London: Verso.

Merton, Thomas. 1976. *Ishi Means Man.* Greensboro, N.C.: Unicorn Press.

Milanich, Jerald T., and William C. Sturtevant, eds. 1972. *Francisco Pareja's 1613 Confesionario: A Documentary Source for Timucuan Ethnography.* Tallahassee: Division of Archives, History, and Records Managemenet, Florida Department of State.

Milliken, Randall. 1995. *A Time of Little Choice: The Disintegration of Tribal Culture in the San Francisco Bay Area*. Menlo Park, Calif.: Ballena Press.

Mittelstadt, (Rev.) John, O.F.M. January 18, 1987. Interview with author, St. Michael's Mission, Arizona.

Modesto, Ruby, and Guy Mount. 1989. *Not for Innocent Ears: Spiritual Traditions of a Desert Cahuilla Medicine Woman*. Arcata, Calif.: Sweetlight Books.

Moisés, Rosalio, Jane Holden Kelley, and William Curry Holden. 1977. *A Yaqui Life: The Personal Chronicle of a Yaqui Indian*. Lincoln: University of Nebraska Press.

Montali, Larry. November 5, 1992. "Cement, Beams, Steel and Mutual Understanding." *The Southern Cross* 81: 12–13. Publication of the Diocese of San Diego.

Monteiro, (Rev.) Ralph John, O.S.A. September 1, 1991. Telephone interview with author.

———. November 18–20, 1992. Interviews with author, Hoopa, California.

Montgomery, Ross Gordon, Watson Smith, and John Otis Brew. 1949. *Franciscan Awatovi*. Cambridge, Mass.: Peabody Museum of American Archaeology and Ethnology, Harvard University.

Monthan, Guy, and Doris Monthan. 1990. *Nacimientos: Nativity Scenes by Southwest Indian Artisans*. Albuquerque: Avanyu Publishing.

Montoya, Joe L. 1982. *Isleta Pueblo and the Church of St. Augustine*. Isleta Pueblo, N.Mex.: St. Augustine Church.

Morales, (Rev.) Francisco, O.F.M. 1973. *Ethnic and Social Background of the Franciscan Friars in Seventeenth Century Mexico*. Washington, D.C.: Academy of American Franciscan History.

Murphy, Jacquelyn. July 27, 1986. "The Faith Journey of the Zuni Indians." *Our Sunday Visitor*, pp. 6–7.

Myers, (Rev.) David A., S.J. April 12, 1993. Telephone interview with author.

Nash, June. 1968. "The Passion Play in Maya Indian Communities." *Comparative Studies in Society and History* 10: 318–327.

———. March 1994. "Judas Transformed." *Natural History* 103, 3: 47–52.

Native American Catholics: People of the Spirit. 1986. TeleKETICS, Franciscan Communications. Videocassette.

Nativism and Syncretism. 1960. New Orleans: Tulane University Printing Office, Middle American Research Institute.

Nutini, Hugh G. 1976. "Syncretism and Acculturation: The Historical Development of the Cult of the Patron Saint in Tlaxcala, Mexico (1519–1670)." *Ethnology* 15: 301–321.

———. 1988. *Todos Santos in Rural Tlaxcala: A Syncretic, Expressive, and Symbolic Analysis of the Cult of the Dead*. Princeton: Princeton University Press.

Oakes, Maud. 1951. *The Two Crosses of Todos Santos: Survivals of Mayan Religious Ritual*. New York: Bollingen Foundation.

O'Brien, (Rev.) James F., S.J. 1977. "Pastoral Ministry Program for American Indian Peoples Living in the Diocese of Phoenix." Unpublished ms., Phoenix.

———. 1982. [Pastoral Ministry Program for American Indian Peoples Living in the Diocese of Phoenix]. Unpublished ms., Phoenix.

———. August 8, 1992. Interview with author, Orono, Maine.

O'Daniel, (Rev.) V. F., O.P., S.T.M. 1930. *Dominicans in Early Florida*. New York: The United States Catholic Historical Society.

Ojibway, (Rev.) Paul, S.A. November 23, 1992. Interview with author, San Francisco, California.

———. August 6, 1993. Interview with author, Seattle, Washington.

Orono, Maine. August 5–9, 1992. Author's fieldnotes, Tekakwitha Conference.

Ortiz, Alfonso, ed. 1979. *Handbook of North American Indians,* vol. 9: *Southwest*. Washington, D.C.: Smithsonian Institution.

———. January 23, 1987. Interview with author, San Ildefonso Pueblo, New Mexico.

Our Negro and Indian Missions. 1926–1976.

Painter, Muriel Thayer. 1986. *With Good Heart: Yaqui Beliefs and Ceremonies in Pascua Village*. Tucson: University of Arizona Press.

Painter, Muriel Thayer, Refugio Savala, and Ignacio Alvarez. 1955. *A Yaqui Easter Sermon*. Tucson: University of Arizona Press.

Pala, California. November 7–9, 1992. Author's fieldnotes.

Pandey, Triloki Nath. 1977. "Images of Power in a Southwestern Pueblo." In *The Anthropology of Power*, ed. Raymond D. Fogelson and Richard N. Adams, 195–215. New York: Academic Press.

Parmentier, Richard J. 1979. "The Mythological Triangle: Poseyemu, Montezuma, and Jesus in the Pueblos." In *Handbook of North American Indians,* vol. 9: *Southwest*, ed. Alfonso Ortiz, 609–622. Washington, D.C.: Smithsonian Institution.

Parry, John H., and Robert G. Keith, eds. 1984. *New Iberian World: A Documentary History of the Discovery and Settlement of Latin America to the Early 17th Century.* 5 vols. New York: Times Books.

Parsons, Elsie Clews. 1918. "Nativity Myth at Laguna and Zuni." *Journal of American Folklore* 31:256–263.

———. 1939. *Pueblo Indian Religion.* 2 vols. Chicago: University of Chicago Press.

Partida, (Rev.) Raphael. August 7, 1992. "Appreciating Our Native American Spirituality." Lecture. Orono, Maine.

———. August 8, 1992. Interview with author, Orono, Maine.

Pelotte, (Most Rev.) Donald E., S.S.S. August 6, 1993. Interview with the author, Seattle, Washington.

Perouse, John Francis Galoup de la. 1892. "Extract." In *History of Santa Cruz County California,* 48–58. San Francisco: Pacific Press Publishing Company.

Perry, Edmund. 1958. *The Gospel in Dispute: The Relation of Christian Faith to Other Missionary Religions*. Garden City, N.Y.: Doubleday.

Pfefferkorn, Ignaz. 1989. *Sonora: A Description of the Province*. Trans. Theodore E. Treutlein. Tucson: University of Arizona Press.

Phelan, John Leddy. 1970. *The Millenial Kingdom of the Franciscans in the New World*. Berkeley: University of California Press.

Phillips, George Harwood. 1974. "Indians and the Breakdown of the Spanish Mission System in California." *Ethnohistory* 21: 281–302.

———. 1975. *Chiefs and Challengers: Indian Resistance and Cooperation in Southern California.* Berkeley: University of California Press.

———. 1991. "Indians in Los Angeles, 1781–1875: Economic Integration, Social Disintegration." In *Native American Perspectives on the Hispanic Colonization of Alta California,* ed. Edward D. Castillo, 395–419. Spanish Borderlands Sourcebooks, no. 26. New York: Garland Publishing.

Phoenix, Arizona. September 12–14, 1987. Author's fieldnotes, Tekakwitha Conference.

"Politicization of the Dead: The Case of Hammonds Meadow." 1992. Unpublished ms. in author's possession.

Polzer, Charles W. 1976. *Rules and Precepts of the Jesuit Missions of Northwestern New Spain.* Tucson: University of Arizona Press.

Polzer, Charles W., Thomas H. Naylor, Thomas E. Sheridan, and Diana Hadley, eds. 1991. *The Jesuit Missions of Northern Mexico.* Spanish Borderlands Sourcebooks, no. 19. New York: Garland Publishing.

Poole, (Rev.) Stafford, C.M. 1989. "The Declining Image of the Indian among Churchmen in Sixteenth-Century New Spain." In *Indian-Religious Relations in Colonial Spanish America,* ed. Susan E. Ramirez, 11–19. Syracuse, N.Y.: Maxwell School of Citizenship and Public Affairs, Syracuse University.

———. 1996. *Our Lady of Guadalupe: The Origins and Sources of a Mexican National Symbol, 1531–1797.* Tucson: University of Arizona Press.

Potsdam, New York. August 2–6, 1995. Author's fieldnotes, Tekakwitha Conference.

Prucha, (Rev.) Francis Paul, S.J. 1977. *A Bibliographical Guide to the History of Indian-White Relations in the United States.* Chicago: University of Chicago Press.

———. 1979. *The Churches and the Indian Schools, 1888–1912.* Lincoln: University of Nebraska Press.

Quinn, Charles Russell. 1964. *The Story of Mission Santa Ysabel.* Downey, Calif.: Elena Quinn.

Reff, Daniel T. 1991. *Disease, Depopulation, and Culture Change in Northwestern New Spain, 1518–1764.* Salt Lake City: University of Utah Press.

Reid, Hugo. 1991. "The Indians of Los Angeles County." Ed. Robert F. Heizer. In *Native American Perspectives on the Hispanic Colonization of Alta California,* ed. Edward D. Castillo, 129–154. Spanish Borderlands Sourcebooks, no. 26. New York: Garland Publishing.

"Report Seeks to Clear Sainthood Candidate." November 28, 1986. *New York Times,* p. A26.

Resendes, Daniel F. March 2, 1993. Telephone interview with author.

Ricard, Robert. 1966. *The Spiritual Conquest of Mexico.* Berkeley: University of California Press.

Riding, Alan. October 12, 1976. "Mexico Dedicating $24 Million Shrine to the 'Indian' Virgin." *New York Times,* p. 10.

————. January 30, 1979. "Pope Tells Mexico's Indians He'll Speak for the Oppressed." *New York Times,* p. A3.

Rincon, California. November 8, 1992. Author's fieldnotes.

Roberts, Don L. 1980. "A Calendar of Eastern Pueblo Indian Ritual Dramas." In *Southwestern Indian Ritual Drama,* ed. Charlotte J. Frisbie, 103–124. Albuquerque: University of New Mexico Press.

Robinson, Alfred. 1846. *Life in California.* New York: Wiley & Putnam.

Ronda, James P., and James Axtell. 1978. *Indian Missions: A Critical Bibliography.* Bloomington: Indiana University Press.

Rosaldo, Renato. 1989. *Culture and Truth.* Boston: Beacon Press.

Rousseau, Dolores. August 6, 1992. Interview with author, Orono, Maine.

Sacaton, Arizona. April 10, 1993. Author's fieldnotes.

Sacred Circle, The. 1990–1992. Publication of the San Bernardino Indian Commission.

Sale, Kirkpatrick. 1990. *The Conquest of Paradise: Christopher Columbus and the Columbian Legacy.* New York: Alfred A. Knopf.

Salt River Reservation, Arizona. January 7, 1987. Author's fieldnotes.

————. January 8, 1988. Author's fieldnotes.

Sanderson, Lucille. November 19, 1992. Interview with author, Hoopa, California.

San Diego de Alcala, California. November 6, 1992. Author's fieldnotes.

San Diego-Sonoma, California. November 6–20, 1992. Author's fieldnotes.

Sando, Joe S. 1979. "Jemez Pueblo." In *Handbook of North American Indians,* vol. 9: *Southwest,* ed. Alfonso Ortiz, 418–429. Washington, D.C.: Smithsonian Institution.

Sandos, James A. 1988. "Junípero Serra's Canonization and the Historical Record." *American Historical Review* 93: 1253–1269.

————. 1991. "Levantamiento!: The 1824 Chumash Uprising Reconsidered." In *Native American Perspectives on the Hispanic Colonization of Alta California,* ed. Edward D. Castillo, 301–325. Spanish Borderlands Sourcebooks, no. 26. New York: Garland Publishing.

————. Winter 1991. "Christianization among the Chumash: An Ethnohistoric Perspective." *American Indian Quarterly* 15: 65–89.

San Ildefonso Pueblo, New Mexico. January 22–23, 1987. Author's fieldnotes.

————. January 22–23, 1988. Author's fieldnotes.

Santa Clara Pueblo, New Mexico. January 24, 1988. Author's fieldnotes.

San Xavier del Bac, Arizona. March 16, 1980. Author's fieldnotes.

————. January 10, 1987. Author's fieldnotes.

Saunders, Charles Francis, and J. Smeaton Chase. 1915. *The California Padres and Their Missions.* Boston: Houghton Mifflin.

Savilla, Joseph. July 7, 1992. Telephone interview with author.

————. August 6, 7, 1993. Interviews with author, Seattle, Washington.

Savilla, Joseph, and Peggy (Cornelius) Savilla. August 5, 1992. Interview with author, Orono, Maine.

Schechner, Richard. 1993. *The Future of Ritual: Writings on Culture and Performance.* London: Routledge.

Scholes, Frances V. 1937. *Church and State in New Mexico, 1610–1650.* Albuquerque: University of New Mexico Press.

Schweitzer, John, and Robert K. Thomas. September-October 1952. "Fiesta of St. Francis at San Francisquito, Sonora." *The Kiva* 18:1–7.

Seattle, Swinomish, and Lummi, Washington. August 4–8, 1993. Author's fieldnotes, Tekakwitha Conference.

Senne, Edgar P. March 1986. "An Indian Easter Liturgy: The Creative Syncretism of the Arizona Yaquis." *The Cresset* 49: 6–14.

Seowtewa, Alex. October 14, 1994. Lecture. Clinton, New York.

Seowtewa, Alex and Adele. February 10, 11, 1991. Interviews with author, Clinton, New York.

Seowtewa, Ken. Winter 1992. "Adding a Breath to Zuni Life." *Native Peoples* 5: 10–16.

Servín, Manuel P. 1991. "The Secularization of the California Missions: A Reappraisal." In *Ethnology of the Alta California Indians,* vol. 2: *Postcontact,* ed. Lowell John Bean and Sylvia Brakke Vane, 119–135. Spanish Borderlands Sourcebooks, no. 4. New York: Garland Publishing.

Shea, John Gilmary. 1855. *History of the Catholic Missions among the Indian Tribes of the United States, 1529–1854.* New York: Edward Dunigan & Brother.

Sheridan, Thomas E., Charles W. Polzer, Thomas H. Naylor, and Diana W. Hadley, eds. 1991. *The Franciscan Missions of Northern Mexico.* Spanish Borderlands Sourcebooks, no. 20. New York: Garland Publishing.

Sherry, Gerard E. June 4, 1989. "St. Catherine's Indian School of Santa Fe." *Our Sunday Visitor,* pp. 8–10.

Sheyka, Arlen. January 18, 1987. Interview with author, Zuni, New Mexico.

Shipek, Florence Connolly. 1978. "History of Southern California Mission Indians." In *Handbook of North American Indians,* vol. 8: *California,* ed. Robert F. Heizer, 610–618. Washington, D.C.: Smithsonian Institution.

———. 1987. *Pushed into the Rocks: Southern California Indian Land Tenure, 1769–1986.* Lincoln: University of Nebraska Press.

———. 1991a. "California Indian Reactions to the Franciscans." In *Native American Perspectives on the Hispanic Colonization of Alta California,* ed. Edward D. Castillo, 174–186. Spanish Borderlands Sourcebooks, no. 26. New York: Garland Publishing.

———. 1991b. *Delfina Cuero: Her Autobiography.* Menlo Park, Calif.: Ballena Press.

Simmons, Marc. 1979. "History of the Pueblos since 1821." In *Handbook of North American Indians,* vol. 9: *Southwest,* ed. Alfonso Ortiz, 206–233. Washington, D.C.: Smithsonian Institution.

Simmons, Marc, Donna Pierce, and Joan Myers. 1991. *Santiago: Saint of Two Worlds.* Albuquerque: University of New Mexico Press.

Sitts, Richard. January 18, 1987. "Navajo Translation of the Mass Approved by the Vatican." *Voice of the Southwest,* n.p. Publication of the Diocese of Gallup, N.Mex.

Sorensen, Steve. November 7, 1985. "The Spirit of Steve Ponchetti." *Reader* 14: 1, 8, 10, 12–14, 16–19. San Diego.

Sparkman, Philip Stedman. 1908. "The Culture of the Luiseño Indians." In *University of California Publications in American Archaeology and Ethnology* 8: 187–234.

Speirs, Randall H. 1979. "Nambe Pueblo." In *Handbook of North American Indians,* vol. 9: *Southwest,* ed. Alfonso Ortiz, 317–323. Washington, D.C.: Smithsonian Institution.

Spicer, Edward H. 1940. *Pascua: A Yaqui Village in Arizona.* Chicago: University of Chicago Press.

———. 1954a. *Potam: A Yaqui Village in Sonora.* Menasha, Wis: Memoirs of the American Anthropological Association.

———. 1954b. "Spanish-Indian Acculturation in the Southwest." With comments by Florence Hawley Ellis and Edward P. Dozier. *American Anthropologist* 56: 663–684.

———. 1961. *Perspectives in American Indian Culture Change.* Chicago: University of Chicago Press.

———. 1972. *Cycles of Conquest.* Tucson: University of Arizona Press.

———. 1980. *The Yaquis: A Cultural History.* Tucson: University of Arizona Press.

———. 1988. *People of Pascua.* Ed. Kathleen M. Sands and Rosamond B. Spicer. Tucson: University of Arizona Press.

Steltenkamp, (Rev.) Michael F., S.J. August 7–9, 1992. Interviews with author, Orono, Maine.

Stockton, William. December 25, 1985. "Morality Play Becomes a Joyous Mexican Rite." *New York Times,* p. 26.

Stogre, (Rev.) Michael, S.J. October 13, 1990. Interview with author, Anderson Lake, Espanola, Ontario.

Stonehouse, W. Ines. November 11, 1992. Interview with author, San Diego, California.

Strong, William Duncan. 1929. *Aboriginal Society in Southern California.* Berkeley: University of California Press.

Sullivan, (Sister) Gertrude Ann, B.V.M. 1984a. *In His Footsteps: The Life Journey of Junipero Serra.* Sacramento: California Catholic Conference.

———. 1984b. *Rooted in Vision: The Life Journey of Junipero Serra.* Sacramento: California Catholic Conference.

———. 1984c. *Small and Mighty: The Story of Junipero Serra.* Sacramento: California Catholic Conference.

Suro, Roberto. September 26, 1988. "An Assailed Missionary to America Is Beatified." *New York Times,* p. A12.

Swanson, Tod Dillon. 1988. "A Crown of *Yage:* Mission Christs and Indigenous Christs in South America." Unpublished Ph.D. dissertation, University of Chicago Divinity School.

Tac, Pablo. 1958. *Indian Life and Customs at Mission San Luis Rey.* Ed. and trans. Minna Hewes, and Gordon Hewes. San Luis Rey, Calif.: Old Mission.

Taos Pueblo, New Mexico. January 21, 1987. Author's fieldnotes.

Taylor, William B. 1987. "The Virgin of Guadalupe in New Spain: An Inquiry into the Social History of Marian Devotion." *American Ethnologist* 14: 9–33.

Tekakwitha Conference Newsletter. 1981–1996.

Temple, Thomas Workman, II. 1991. "Toypurina the Witch and the Indian Uprising at San Gabriel." In *Native American Perspectives on the Hispanic Colonization of Alta California,* ed. Edward D. Castillo, 326–342. Spanish Borderlands Sourcebooks, no. 26. New York: Garland Publishing.

Terrell, John Upton. 1979. *The Arrow and the Cross: A History of the American Indian and the Missionaries.* Santa Barbara, Calif.: Capra Press.

Thiel, Mark G. July 21, 1986. Interview with author, Milwaukee, Wisconsin.

——. June 4, 1987. Personal communication.

——. June 14, 1988. Interview with author, Milwaukee, Wisconsin.

——. July 26, 1989–August 1, 1989. Interviews with author, Milwaukee, Wisconsin.

——. July 9, 1991. Interview with author, Milwaukee, Wisconsin.

——. December 3, 1991. Telephone interview with author.

——. January 22, 1992. Telephone interview with author.

——. July 22, 1992. Interview with author, Milwaukee, Wisconsin.

——. May 17, 1994. Personal communication.

Thomas, David Hurst, ed. 1991. *The Missions of Spanish Florida.* Spanish Borderlands Sourcebooks, no. 20. New York: Garland Publishing.

Thomas, Hugh. 1993. *Conquest: Montezuma, Cortés, and the Fall of Old Mexico.* New York: Simon & Schuster.

Thomas, Robert K. 1967. "The Role of the Church in Indian Adjustment." *Kansas Journal of Sociology* 3: 20–28.

——. N.d. "Encouraging Indians to Relate Realistically to the Total Cultural Enterprise in the Present World." Unpublished ms., Marquette.

Tibesar, (Rev.) Antonine, O.F.M., ed. 1955–1966. *Writings of Junípero Serra.* 4 vols. Washington, D.C.: Academy of American Franciscan History.

Tinker, George. 1993. *Missionary Conquest: The Gospel and Native American Cultural Genocide.* Minneapolis: Fortress Press.

Todorov, Tzvetan. 1984. *The Conquest of America: The Question of the Other.* Trans. Richard Howard. New York: Harper & Row.

Tooker, Elisabeth. 1950. "The Pilgrims in Church." *The Kiva* 16: 9–13.

Turner, Harold W. 1973. "Old and New Religions among North American Indians: Missiological Impressions and Reflections." *Missiology* 1: 47–66.

——. 1978. *Bibliography of New Religious Movements in Primal Societies,* vol. 2: *North America.* Boston: G. K. Hall & Co.

Twohy, (Rev.) Patrick J., S.J. et al. May 1987. "Statement in Support of the Native People from California." *Tekakwitha Conference Newsletter* 6: 17.

Underhill, Ruth. 1979. *Papago Woman.* New York: Holt, Rinehart and Winston.

Van Well, (Sister) Mary Stanislavs, O.S.B. 1942. *The Educational Aspects of the Missions in the Southwest.* Milwaukee: Marquette University Press.

Voght, Martha. 1967. "Shamans and Padres: The Religion of the Southern California Mission Indians." *Pacific Historical Review* 36: 363–373.

Vogt, Evon Z. 1955. "A Study of the Southwestern Fiesta System as Exemplified by the Laguna Fiesta." *American Anthropologist* 57: 820–839.

Walsh, Catherine. December 1987. "Donald Pelotte: First Native American Bishop." *St. Anthony Messenger* 95: 16–23.

Watson, Gordon. July 25, 1985. "Sister Ministers to Native Americans for 18 Years." *Inland Catholic*, p. 6. Publication of the Diocese of San Bernadino, Calif.

Webb, Edith Buckland. 1982. *Indian Life at the Old Missions.* Lincoln: University of Nebraska Press.

Weber, David J. 1992. *The Spanish Frontier in North America.* New Haven: Yale University Press.

Weber, (Rev.) Francis J. 1965. *Documents of California Catholic History, 1784–1963.* Los Angeles: Dawson's Book Shop.

———. 1988. *El Camino Real: A Documentary History of California's Asistencias.* Hong Kong: Yee Tin Tong Printing Press.

Weigle, Marta. 1976. *Brothers of Light, Brothers of Blood: The Penitentes of the Southwest.* Santa Fe: Ancient City Press.

"White Father Is Heap Bad Medicine," July 16, 1965. *Life* 59: 40B.

White, Leslie. 1935. *The Pueblo of Santo Domingo, New Mexico.* Menasha, Wis.: American Anthropological Association.

White, Raymond C. 1991. "Two Surviving Luiseño Indian Ceremonies." In *Ethnology of the Alta California Indians,* vol. 2: *Postcontact,* ed. Lowell John Bean and Sylvia Brakke Vane, 543–552. Spanish Borderlands Sourcebooks, no. 4. New York: Garland Publishing.

Whiting, Alfred F. Spring 1954. "The Tumacacori Census of 1796." *The Kiva* 19: 1–12.

Wiechec, Nancy. June 8, 1989. "St. Paschal Baylon Feast Builds Community." *The Catholic Sun,* pp. 1, 11. Publication of the Diocese of Phoenix.

Wilken, Robert L. 1955. *Anselm Weber, O.F.M.: Missionary to the Navaho, 1898–1921.* Milwaukee: Bruce Publishing.

Williamson, George H. October-November 1950. "Why the Pilgrims Come." *The Kiva* 16: 2–8.

Wintz, (Rev.) Jack, O.F.M. July 1975. "Respect Our Values." *St. Anthony Messenger,* pp. 34–40.

———. August 1987. "Should Junipero Serra Be Declared a Saint?" *St. Anthony Messenger* 95: 29–37.

Wolcott, John. July 1, 1990. "Appreciating the Gifts of Native Americans." *Our Sunday Visitor,* p. 10.

Wolf, Eric. 1958. "The Virgin of Guadalupe: A Mexican National Symbol." *Journal of American Folklore* 71: 34–38.

Woodward, Kenneth L. 1990. *Making Saints.* New York: Simon and Schuster.

Wynne, (Rev.) John J., S.J. September 22, 1929. "Indian Missions Past and Present." *The Catholic Mind* 27: 341–347.

Yaqui Lent and Easter Ceremonies, 1992. 1992. Guadalupe, Ariz.: Our Lady of Guadalupe Church.

Ybarra, Michael J. May 7, 1996. "Monument Feels the Clash of History." *New York Times*, p. A14.

——. June 9, 1996. "Limitations of Statues in the Light of Today." *New York Times*, p. E4.

Zavala, Silvio. 1943. *New Viewpoints on the Spanish Colonization of America.* Philadelphia: University of Pennsylvania Press.

Zeilinger, Ron. 1984. *Lakota Life.* Chamberlain, S. Dak.: St. Joseph's Indian School.

Zuni, New Mexico. January 18, 25, 1987. Author's fieldnotes.

——. January 27, 1988. Author's fieldnotes.

INDEX

Abeita, Andy, 185–192
Abeita, Bernie C., 187
Abeita, Isidore, 190
Abeita, Pablo, 192
Albeita v. Zuni, 190
Abiquiu, N. Mex., 144, 146, 151
abortion, 44, 237, 246, 250, 361, 383
Academy of American Franciscan History, 365
Accalla, Robert, 171
Acoma, N. Mex., 124, 126–127, 136, 138, 146, 160, 171, 194, 198, 203, 209, 213–214
Act for the Government and Protection of the Indians (1851), 269
Act for the Relief of the Mission Indians (1891), 279
Act of Contrition, 71, 235
adultery, 14, 231, 236, 357, 359, 373
Advent, 8, 40, 183, 240, 295, 351
afterlife, 132, 246, 248, 300, 329, 332, 362. *See also* heaven, hell, limbo, purgatory
Aguilar, Augustine, 166
Aguilar, Martin, 199
Ajo, Ariz., 110–111
Ak–Chin Reservation, Ariz., 115–116
alabado, alabanza, 60, 64, 71, 73, 94, 224, 239
Albuquerque, N. Mex., 144, 172, 188, 191–193
Alcaldes, 19, 53, 231–232, 249, 259, 271, 353
alcohol use, 6, 44, 66, 89, 91, 103, 112, 115, 197, 213–214, 249, 251, 261–262, 268, 278, 289–290, 302, 307, 312, 330, 382
Alcoholics Anonymous, 335
Alexander VI (pope), 4, 9
All Indian Pueblo Council, 194, 202

All Saints' Day, 30, 44, 64, 66, 333
All Souls' Day, 64, 66, 69, 108, 110, 113–114, 155, 175, 177, 179, 181, 302, 329
Allotment Act (1887), 279
altars, 11, 44, 59–61, 64–66, 71, 74, 78, 99, 102, 110, 130, 137, 139, 156, 168, 195, 198, 211, 241, 251, 280–282, 286, 297, 329, 337, 341
Alvarado, Juan B., 266
Amago, Marvin, 387
Amago, Mystica, 285
Amago, Pio, 284–285
Ames, Ramon, 297
Amoros, Juan, 246
ancestors, xv–xvi, 21, 30, 66, 75, 96, 100–101, 108, 110, 113, 136, 155, 185, 198, 205, 207, 269, 274, 321, 328–329, 347, 349–350, 357, 388, 392–393. *See also* the dead
angels, 20–21, 68–69, 74, 174, 240–241, 336–337
Anglo–Americans, 47, 57, 76, 106, 213, 268, 270, 272, 296, 312, 318–319
animal symbolism, 30, 63, 67, 72, 80, 86, 103, 107, 109, 115, 132, 160, 174, 178, 199–200, 203. *See also* deer dancers.
Anne, St., 30
annulment, 331, 338
anthropologists, 77, 157, 159, 178, 180, 258, 274, 336, 355–356, 360, 363, 365, 377
Anthony, St., 164, 244, 288, 301
Antone, Alfretta, xvii, 116
Antone, Lucia, 117
Antram, Cormac, 212
Aora, Juan de, 16
Apache Indians, 87, 91, 93–94, 96–97, 100–101, 112, 114,

Congregation for the Causes of
Saints, 390
Congress, U.S., 153, 189, 262, 269,
282, 301
conquest, xiii, xvi, 3, 7, 9, 11–12,
15–17, 19, 25, 27, 33–34, 36,
38–39, 41, 46, 54, 62, 100,
123–126, 135, 139, 149, 179,
194, 198, 203, 220, 229, 231,
351, 353, 363–364, 367, 370
conversion, xii, xvi, 3, 5–6, 9, 11–12,
17, 19–20, 25–26, 29, 32, 39,
41–42, 44, 46, 48, 52, 54, 61–62,
71, 82, 85, 89–90, 94–96, 106,
109, 124–126, 128, 142–143,
153–154, 159, 172, 205, 207,
209–210, 212–213, 222–223,
225–226, 231, 238–239, 245,
247–248, 254, 258, 260, 269,
302, 313, 321, 335, 352, 357–
360, 362, 365, 367–368, 370–
372, 376, 384–385
Cook, Sherburne, 356, 365, 368, 391
Cordero, Helen, 195
Corn Mothers, 131, 141
Coronado, Francisco Vázquez de, 42,
123–124
corporal punishment, 19, 22, 26, 28,
47, 53, 72–73, 82–83, 86, 89,
129–131, 133, 142, 145, 157,
209, 226, 231, 237, 243, 247,
250–253, 255–256, 259, 262,
265, 353–354, 359–363, 365,
367, 369–370, 372–376,
381–383, 386–387
Corpus Christi, 64, 129, 240, 288,
296, 301
Corpus Christi Parish, Carson City,
214
Cortés, Hernan, 7, 9, 11–12, 15–17,
54, 62, 123, 125, 231
Cortés, Juan, 235–236
Cortés of Spain, 260
Cortez, Colo., 214
Cosmit, Calif., 308
Costanoan Indians, 220, 255, 274
Costo, Jeanette Henry, 386, 390
Costo, Juan, 297
Costo, Rupert, xvii, 386, 388
Cota, Manuel, 277

Cotter, Eileen, 307
Council of Trent, xiii, 7, 235, 246,
375
County Planning Department, San
Diego, 309
creation, 7, 41–42, 62, 66, 266, 310,
370
creation theology, 214
Credo, 4–5, 8, 11, 20, 60, 80, 86,
117, 235, 247, 258, 334, 362
Creek Indians, 43
Crespi, Juan de 222, 224
Crespo, Benito, 143
Cribbin, James, xvii, 311, 315–316,
320, 331, 341–343
crosses, crucifixes, 8, 11–12, 15, 20,
25, 29, 32, 38, 41, 52, 60, 62–66,
68, 70–71, 73, 75, 78, 83, 85–86,
90, 99, 101, 103–104, 107–108,
114, 123–124, 129, 131–137,
139, 141, 147–149, 151, 171,
179, 196, 222, 224, 233–235,
240–242, 248, 273–274, 281,
288, 291–292, 298–299, 336,
372, 375, 388
Crown, Spanish, 9, 19, 21, 27, 42,
46, 50, 95, 124–125, 129, 138–
139, 220, 222, 229–230, 232,
265–266, 353, 364, 366–367,
376
crucifixion, 61, 73
Cuauhtemoc, Mex., 12
Cuba, 42–43
Cuevish, Lucario, 243
Cummins, John, 275
Cupa, Calif., 277, 304
Cupa Cultural Center, 283, 304
Cupan Indians, 220
Cupeño Indians, 220, 274, 277, 279,
281–284, 286, 288, 292, 304,
308, 316–318, 328, 337, 341–
342
Cursillo, 116, 197, 204, 208, 213
Cuyapaipe, Calif., 308, 387

dance, 24–25, 32–33, 46, 52, 54, 58,
62–63, 66–67, 70, 74–75, 77,
79–80, 82, 94, 98–99, 102–103,
108, 110, 112, 125, 129, 132,
134–135, 142, 147–149, 152,